ONE LORD, ONE FAITH, ONE BAPTISM

J. Robert Wright

ONE LORD, ONE FAITH, ONE BAPTISM

*Studies in Christian Ecclesiality and Ecumenism
in Honor of J. Robert Wright*

Edited by

Marsha L. Dutton *&* Patrick Terrell Gray

WILLIAM B. EERDMANS PUBLISHING COMPANY
GRAND RAPIDS, MICHIGAN / CAMBRIDGE, U.K.

Wm. B. Eerdmans Publishing Co.
255 Jefferson Ave. S.E., Grand Rapids, Michigan 49503 /
P.O. Box 163, Cambridge CB3 9PU U.K.

Printed in the United States of America

11 10 09 08 07 06   7 6 5 4 3 2 1

Library of Congress Cataloging-in-Publication Data

One Lord, one faith, one baptism: studies in Christian ecclesiality
    and ecumenism in honor of J. Robert Wright /
    edited by Marsha L. Dutton & Patrick Terrell Gray.
        p.   cm.
    Includes bibliographical references and index.
    ISBN-10: 0-8028-2940-6 / ISBN-13: 978-0-8028-2940-5 (cloth: alk. paper)
    1. Church history. 2. Christian Union.   I. Wright, J. Robert (John Robert), 1936-
    II. Dutton, Marsha L.   III. Gray, Patrick Terrell.

BR138.054   2006
270 — dc22

                                                          2006003738

www.eerdmans.com

Contents

Foreword   viii
The Most Reverend Frank T. Griswold

Abbreviations   x

Introduction   xv

Curriculum Vitae: The Reverend Canon J. Robert Wright   xxv

CHRISTIAN ECCLESIALITY

Catholic Ministry and the Ordination of Women   3
Walter R. Bouman

Confessional and Catechetical Formulas in First- and
Early-Second-Century Christian Literature   14
Richard A. Norris, Jr.

Constructing Christian Communal Identity
in Early Patristic Writers   29
Petra Heldt

Contents

A Meaning Worthy of God: Origen and Scripture
in a Pre-Constantinian Age   42
    Patrick Terrell Gray

Augustine at Ephesus?   56
    Joanne McWilliam

The Flight of Geryon   68
    John V. Fleming

Julian of Norwich, Medieval Anglican   99
    Marsha L. Dutton

American, Anglican, and Catholic   120
    R. William Franklin

Finding a Voice, Defining a Space: John Henry Hobart
and the Americanization of Anglicanism   129
    Robert Bruce Mullin

The Breadth of Orthodoxy: On Phillips Brooks   144
    Joseph Britton

Rearranging the Hierarchy of the Episcopal Church
in the Second Decade of the Twentieth Century   163
    Robert W. Prichard

Christ and Church in the Social Encyclicals of John Paul II   182
    Victor Lee Austin

FROM ECCLESIALITY TO ECUMENISM

Odi et Amo: Loving and Hating Anglicanism   193
    S. W. Sykes

The New Ecumenism of the Possible   208
    C. Christopher Epting

We Ordain Them, They Don't: Must Differences
on Gender and Sexuality Prevent Full Communion?   219
    Ellen K. Wondra

A Ministry of a Universal Primate: An Ecumenical Question   241
    Mary Tanner

Anglican-Orthodox Relations: A Long-Term Overview   262
    E. Rozanne Elder

Lutheranism and Orthodoxy: An Exploration of Complementarity   284
    William G. Rusch

Consistency and Difference in Anglican-Lutheran Relations:
Porvoo, Waterloo, and *Called to Common Mission*   296
    Michael Root

The Gift of Authority: Mountain or Milestone?   316
    Jon Nilson

Sisters and Strangers   325
    George Tavard

Contributors   338

Index   340

Foreword

The Most Reverend Frank T. Griswold

The Rev. Canon J. Robert Wright is the consummate Anglican. His capacity to draw together many strands from varying traditions and to weave them into a coherent fabric is a gift that I and countless others have appreciated over the years. I know of no other person I might call in haste to answer questions concerning arcane matters such as the proper form of ecclesiastical address according to various traditions, or the sometimes complex and nuanced history of the relationship between the Episcopal Church and other ecclesial communities.

Father Wright has been a companion of mine on several official international visits, during which his broad knowledge and capacity for instantaneous recall of salient historical detail have saved me and others from any number of inadvertent gaffes. I remember with particular clarity a visit to a Russian monastery. Our guide was a young monk who upon meeting us asked our translator: "Why are these infidels here?" In spite of his misgivings about us he guided us with a great deal of politeness. Our tour ended before the tomb of the monastery's most recent saint. Having been carefully schooled by Father Wright, I stepped forward with confidence and performed the prescribed threefold veneration. Apparently the young monk was duly impressed, and as we left he informed our translator that it had been a privilege to welcome such devout Christians and their primate.

Over the years the Rev. Dr. J. Robert Wright has been a much valued contributor to the life of the Anglican Communion and the Episcopal Church, particularly in matters historical and ecumenical. With his well-recognized scholarship and close knowledge of ecclesiastical history, ancient and modern, in mind, I felt it was particularly appropriate to appoint him to serve as Historiographer of the Episcopal Church, USA.

This collection of essays by distinguished scholars represents something of the breadth and depth of the scholarship and interests of Father Wright himself. I can think of no better means than this festschrift by which to recognize and thank him for his incalculable contributions in the service of the church catholic as she seeks to bear witness to the immeasurable riches of Christ.

THE MOST REV. FRANK T. GRISWOLD
Presiding Bishop and Primate
The Episcopal Church, USA

Abbreviations

General Abbreviations

A.D.	Anno Domini
B.A.	Bachelor of Arts degree
B.C.	Before Christ
BCP	Book of Common Prayer (1979)
c.	*circa*
d.	died
D.Cn.L.	Doctor of Canon Law
D.D.	Doctor of Divinity
D.Phil.	Doctor of Philosophy
ed.	edited by, editor
EIR	Ecumenical and Interfaith Relations
esp.	especially
Gk	Greek
GTS	The General Theological Seminary
M.Div.	Master of Divinity
n. (nn.)	note (notes)
n.d.	no date
OED	*Oxford English Dictionary*
p. (pp.)	page (pages)
repr.	reprint, reprinted
rev.	revised
supp.	supplementary
s.v.	*sub verbum,* "under the entry"
Th.D.	Doctor of Theology

trans.   translated by; translator
UK   United Kingdom

Biblical Translations

AV   Authorized Version
Douay   Douay Version
NRSV   New Revised Standard Version
RSV   Revised Standard Version

Christian Churches and Bodies

ACC   Anglican Consultative Council
ECUSA   Episcopal Church of the U.S.A.
EDEO   Episcopal Diocesan Ecumenical Officers
EKD   Evangelische Kirche in Deutschland (Evangelical Church in Germany)
ELCA   Evangelical Lutheran Church of America
LWF   Lutheran World Federation
NCCB   National Conference of Catholic Bishops
PCPCU   Pontifical Council for the Promotion of Christian Unity
SCER   Standing Commission on Ecumenical Relations
USCC   United States Catholic Conference

Ecumenical Dialogues and Bodies

ARCIC   Anglican–Roman Catholic International Commission
ARCUSA   Anglican–Roman Catholic Consultation in the U.S.A.
COCU   Consultation on Church Union
CUIC   Churches Uniting in Christ
IARCCUM   International Anglican–Roman Catholic Commission on Unity and Mission
NCCC   National Council of Churches of Christ
ORC   Orthodox–Roman Catholic Dialogue
WCC   World Council of Churches

Ecumenical Documents and Collections

ARC DOC   *Documents on Anglican/Roman Catholic Relations I.* Washington, DC: USCC, 1972.

Abbreviations

BEM   *Baptism, Eucharist and Ministry.* The Lima Text, Faith and Or-
              der Paper 111. Geneva: WCC Publications, 1982.
CCM   *Called to Common Mission.* Cincinnati: Forward Movement
              Publications, 2000.
Communion   *A Communion of Communions: One Eucharistic Fellowship. The
              Detroit Report and Papers of the Triennial Ecumenical Study of
              the Episcopal Church, 1976-1979.* Ed. J. Robert Wright. New York:
              Seabury Press, 1979.
Concordat   *Concordat of Agreement*
Final Report ARCIC. *The Final Report, Windsor, September 1981.* London:
              CTS/SPCK, 1982.
Gift   *The Gift of Authority: Authority in the Church III: An Agreed
              Statement by the Anglican–Roman Catholic International Com-
              mission.* London: Catholic Truth Society; Toronto: Anglican
              Book Centre; New York: Church Publishing, 1999.
Growth I   *Growth in Agreement: Reports and Agreed Statements of Ecumen-
              ical Conversations on a World Level.* Ed. Harding Meyer and
              Lukas Vischer. Faith and Order Paper 108. Geneva: WCC Publi-
              cations; New York: Paulist Press, 1984.
Growth II   *Growth in Agreement II: Reports and Agreed Statements of Ecu-
              menical Conversations on a World Level, 1982-1998.* Ed. Jeffrey
              Gros, Harding Meyer, and William G. Rusch. Faith and Order
              Paper 187. Geneva: WCC Publications; Grand Rapids: William B.
              Eerdmans Publishing Company, 2000.
Niagara   *Niagara Report*
Porvoo   *The Porvoo Common Statement*
Quadrilateral *Quadrilateral at One Hundred: Essays on the Centenary of the
              Chicago-Lambeth Quadrilateral 1886/88-1986/88.* Cincinnati: For-
              ward Movement Publications; London and Oxford: Mowbray,
              1988. (Also ATR supplementary series no. 10, March 1988.)
Virginia   *The Virginia Report: The Report of the Inter-Anglican Theological
  Report   and Doctrinal Commission.* London: ACC, 1997.
Windsor   The Lambeth Commission on Communion. *The Windsor Re-
  Report   port.* London: The Anglican Communion Office, 2004.

Papal Documents

CA   *Centesimus Annus*
EV   *Evangelium Vitae*
GS   *Gaudium et Spes*
LE   *Laborem Exercens*
LG   *Lumen Gentium*
OS   *Ordinatio Sacerdotalis*
RH   *Redemptor Hominis*

SRS	*Sollicitudo Rei Socialis*
Unum	*Ut Unum Sint* (*Encyclical Letter "Ut Unum Sint" of the Holy Father John Paul II: On Commitment to Ecumenism.* Boston: St. Paul's Books and Media, 1995.)
UR	*Unitatis Redintegratio*

Journals, Series, and Encyclopedias

AAS	*Acta Apostolicae Sedis.* Rome, 1909-.
ACO	*Acta Conciliorum Oecumenicorum*
ATR	*The Anglican Theological Review*
CF	Cistercian Fathers
CSCO	Corpus Scriptorum Christianorum Orientalium
FOC	Fathers of the Church. New York: Cima Publishing Company, 1947.
GCS	Die Griechischen christlichen Schriftsteller der ersten Jahrhunderte
NPNF	The Nicene and Post-Nicene Fathers. Grand Rapids: William B. Eerdmans Publishing Company.
PL	Patrologiae cursus completus, series latina. Ed. J.-P. Migne. 221 vols. Paris, 1844–64.
RTAM	*Recherches de Théologie Ancienne et Médiévale*
SC	Sources chrétiennes
Works Aug	The Works of Augustine. A Translation for the 21st Century. Brooklyn, NY: New City Press, 1990-.
ZNW	*Zeitschrift für die neutestamentliche Wissenschaft und die Kunde der älteren Kirche*

Works of Augustine

C duas ep	*Contra duas epistulas pelagianorum*
C Faust	*Contra Faustum manicheum*
C Iul	*Contra Iulianum opus imperfectum*
De agone	*De agone christiano*
De corr et gratia	*De correptione et gratia*
De fide et symb	*De fide et symbolo*
De gest	*De gestis Pelagii*
De quant animae	*De quantitate animae*
De trin	*De trinitate*
Ench	*Enchiridion (De fide et spe et caritate)*

En in Ps	*Enarrationes in Psalmos*
Ep (Epp)	Epistula (Epistulae)
In Ev Ioann	*Tractatus in Evangelium Ioannis*
Lib arb	*De libero arbitrio*
Nat et grat	*De natura et gratia*
S (Ss)	Sermo (Sermones)

Biblical Abbreviations

Col.	Colossians
1 Cor.	First Corinthians
2 Cor.	Second Corinthians
Deut.	Deuteronomy
Ecclus.	Ecclesiasticus
Eph.	Ephesians
Gal.	Galatians
Gen.	Genesis
Heb.	Hebrews
Isa.	Isaiah
Jer.	Jeremiah
1 Macc.	1 Maccabees
2 Macc.	2 Maccabees
Matt.	Matthew
1 Pet.	1 Peter
Phil.	Philippians
Philem.	Philemon
Ps(s).	Psalm(s)
Rev.	Revelation
Rom.	Romans
Song	Song of Songs/Song of Solomon
1 Thess.	1 Thessalonians
2 Thess.	2 Thessalonians
1 Tim.	1 Timothy
2 Tim.	2 Timothy
Tit.	Titus

Introduction

The Reverend Canon J. Robert Wright is, to put it simply, a polymath. He is an Episcopal priest in the diocese of New York, Canon Theologian to the Episcopal Bishop of New York in the Cathedral of Saint John the Divine, the recipient of an earned doctorate of philosophy from Oxford, St. Mark's Professor of Ecclesiastical History at The General Theological Seminary of the Episcopal Church, a noted ecumenist and an Honorary Vartabed, an expert collector of icons, and a basketball coach. He deserves and has indeed received wide official recognition. This book also honors him, with essays by a few of his many friends, colleagues, and former students in acknowledgement and gratitude for all he has done and meant to so many.

As a medieval and ecclesiastical historian Doctor Wright has received four honorary doctorates — two in theology, one in divinity, and one in canon law. He has written two monographs and about three hundred scholarly articles and book reviews, as well as alone or with a collaborator editing fourteen books. His scholarship, however, represents not a desire for professional advancement but responsibility to others, for he has devoted his career to making the wealth of Christian faith and learning accessible to his students, his colleagues, and other scholars. It is thus entirely appropriate that in 2000 he was named Historiographer of the Episcopal Church, nominated by the Presiding Bishop and formally confirmed by the General Convention. He is also the chaplain of the Guild of Scholars of the Episcopal Church (with tenure in perpetuity) and a life fellow of both the Royal Historical Society and the Society of Antiquaries.

The Reverend Doctor Wright is a noted ecumenist and lecturer on ecumenism. The *New York Times* has interviewed or cited him eleven times since

1972, most often on ecumenical questions. He has for many years represented the Episcopal Church ecumenically, serving for example as a member of or consultant to both the Standing Commission on Ecumenical Relations and the Anglican–Roman Catholic Consultation in the U.S.A., and he has been a member of the Anglican-Orthodox Consultation in the U.S.A. He was the principal Episcopalian drafter for the full communion agreements between the Episcopal Church and the Evangelical Lutheran Church of America, and he was the principal drafter of the Ministry document for Churches Uniting in Christ. For his ecumenical work he has been honored with five pectoral crosses and named Honorary Vartabed or "Teacher for the Armenian Orthodox Church" by the Armenian Patriarch of Jerusalem.

Doctor Wright has thus for many years been a face and voice for the Episcopal Church at home and abroad, bringing his faith, his erudition, and his remarkable intellect to bear in many contexts. Through a combination of faith, quick insight, tenacity, and brusque candor, he has made a career of making rough places smooth, breaking through impasses to construct new highways for the church. The Episcopal Church could not have a better representative.

Much of this catalogue of achievements and attributes (and a great deal more) appears on his *curriculum vitae.* But while that reveals a great deal about his life, work, and goals, it is radically incomplete. For above all J. Robert Wright has won admiration, gratitude, and affection for who he is as priest and friend, patron and guide, teacher and host, and for his ability to combine professional expertise and commitment with dedication, generosity, and wit.

Any student at General Seminary from the 1970s on has a story about Doctor Wright. Actually, of course, seminarians know him not as Doctor or Professor Wright but as Father Wright, for his life as priest and pastor shapes his relationship with them. He regularly invites them to meals and cocktail parties in his on-campus apartment, bringing together new M.Div. students with church leaders, theologians, and visiting scholars. Pedagogically he is similarly generous in the care and creativity with which he teaches, always endeavoring to share with his students his own breadth of knowledge, love of learning, and rigorous commitment to getting things right. Known by his students as Doctor Xeroxes for his indefatigable production of class notes, he is unfailing in making all that he knows available to those who wish to learn. Conscious of the practical problems that will face his students once they are priests, he regularly offers an informal class on tax preparation. His commitment to his students continues well past their graduation, leading to new friendships and new professional relationships.

Doctor Wright's teaching method reflects his own integration of learning and experience, as he constantly encourages his students to incorporate their new knowledge into their lives. His class in Eucharistic Celebration involves not only lecturing about the history and theology of the eucharist but also instructing in its praxis, so that future priests may come to understand the sacrament intellectually, practically, and experientially — to know what they are doing and what it means. As a result, GTS students may sometimes be heard chatting over pizza and wine about the reason some celebrating priests join thumb and forefinger, or the precise moment at which the consecration takes place. In other classes Father Wright takes his students on field trips — classes studying medieval Christianity may go to the Metropolitan Museum of Art or the Cloisters — in both of which he has celebrated the eucharist according to medieval rites, joined by GTS students and other faculty.

Doctor Wright's concern to engage students reflects a pattern in his own life. As an ecumenist seeking a fuller understanding of Orthodoxy he not only read and engaged in bilateral dialogue with the Orthodox but also took up the study of the history, creation, and meaning of icons and then began his now-extensive icon collection. Having translated that new area of expertise back into his life as a professor, he teaches a seminary course on iconography, inviting the class to see his icons and then taking them to visit an Orthodox cathedral in New York, where they may watch contemporary iconographers at work, talk with a priest, and remain for an Orthodox liturgy. Those whom Doctor Wright introduces to icons learn about history, doctrine, liturgy, worship, culture, and art, so that what might elsewhere be merely an academic subject becomes for his students as it is for their professor an open window on Christian history and life.

Besides exercising personal hospitality, Doctor Wright has over the years led the General Theological Seminary in generously opening its doors through the creation of the Visiting Sabbatical Professor program. Several of the contributors to this volume have taught in that program, living at the seminary, eating in the refectory with students and faculty, teaching classes, doing research in the GTS library, joining in daily Evensong, preaching in chapel, addressing the faculty association, contributing to the Thanksgiving potluck dinner, and singing in the seminary *schola*. While they are guests of the seminary Doctor Wright extends his hospitality to them, entertaining them with other guests in his apartment and hosting them at events outside the seminary. He also takes particular care to ensure that his students and advisees benefit from visiting professors' presence. The editors of this volume met when Doctor Wright urged doctoral student Patrick Gray to study medieval Cistercian sermons with Marsha Dutton, a visiting sabbatical professor. Their work together led to a conference paper and then a published article for Patrick, a growing friendship between Patrick and Marsha, and collaboration on this book to honor their mutual friend and patron.

First, last, and always Doctor Wright is a man of the church, an Episcopalian, a servant of Christ and the church catholic. Now a regular celebrant at GTS and participant in the seminary's daily services of morning and evening prayer, he is a cradle Episcopalian with a B.A. with honors from Sewanee. While a Fulbright scholar and D.Phil. student at Oxford, he was ordained a priest in the diocese of Indianapolis, with Bishop Mervyn Stockwood of Southwark (England) acting for Bishop John Pares Craine of Indianapolis. As is not usual for most Episcopal ordinations, Doctor Wright's received coverage in both the *Church Times* and the London *Times*. He recalls the two years he spent as a young priest in London, daily celebrating the eucharist, as among his happiest.

Perhaps his own life as a priest and his years of teaching future priests help to explain Doctor Wright's longstanding outspoken support for the ordination of women, a support that has earned him wide admiration and that surely helped to sway many of the early opponents. He remains alert to the topic in ecumenical contexts, always treating women's ordination as an unassailable aspect of Episcopal Church life and teaching.

Doctor Wright is also active in the public service of the Episcopal Church. As a consultant to the Standing Liturgical Commission he helped to lay out the 1979 Book of Common Prayer. Today he serves on numerous church boards and commissions and on the editorial board of *The Anglican Theological Review* and *The Anglican,* for both of which he regularly writes. Among the many books he has edited, mostly on ecumenical topics, are three collections of readings and commentaries for the benefit of Episcopalians at worship: *Prayer Book Spirituality: A Devotional Companion to the Book of Common Prayer; Readings for the Daily Office from the Early Church,* and *They Still Speak: Readings for the Lesser Feasts.*

As a representative of the Episcopal Church in ecumenical consultations, Doctor Wright has spent an incalculable amount of time in ecumenical meetings, dialogues, and conferences (and traveling to and from such meetings) to join with representatives of the churches as together they seek to recognize, realize, and celebrate the shared faith that brings them together. In these often difficult, often tedious, often apparently hopeless hours of negotiation, Doctor Wright is always there, engaged, knowledgeable, and ready to redirect the conversation. His familiarity with the substance and phrasing of previous dialogues and documents, his broad grasp of the issues, and his articulate tenacity in argument all contribute to finding new ways forward. He is at his most effective when he inquires about the significant detail that no one else has noticed or thought to question: "Why *governor* instead of *a governor*? Why does the later version add the word *perhaps*?" No one who knows him can forget the incisive pleasure of his wit in such conversations, his ironic proposals for a new phrasing or a more candid public response. Indeed one of the aspects of his writing most familiar to those who know him is the sharp edge of perilous humor that runs beneath the surface — an edge that is often just the thing needed to sever the linguistic veils that keep the churches apart.

Doctor Wright's professional and ecclesiastical responsibilities would seem to leave him little in the way of spare time, but he also manages to give tours of art museums, churches, cathedrals, and his own seminary, to consult or be featured on video and audio tapes, to write letters to the *New York Times* regarding air travel (a subject with which he has ample familiarity) or to *The Living Church* about those who may receive communion in the Episcopal Church, to attend programs and receptions at the Grolier Club — and to coach the General Theological Seminary basketball team, which he guided through three undefeated seasons. He is, after all, a polymath. Not only a brilliant scholar and committed teacher and colleague, not only a tireless ecumenist and worker in the vineyard of the Lord, but also a delightful companion and conversationalist, a Midwestern Anglophile who has spent his adult life in New York City, a staunchly orthodox iconoclast, an abstemious lover of art, books, and good food, a man of forceful outspokenness and reliable kindness, a friend — and a gift to the one church holy, catholic, and apostolic.

The Articles Honoring J. Robert Wright

The breadth of Doctor Wright's knowledge, the quantity and range of his contributions to historical, ecclesial, and ecumenical understanding, his quick insight, and his multifaceted acumen have prompted the planning and writing of this volume. The writers are his friends, of recent acquaintance and decades-old intimacy, colleagues past and present, fellow historians and ecumenists, and former and present students. So many scholarly colleagues and friends here join to honor Doctor Wright through their contributions and their praise for his work, their expressions of gratitude for his guidance and friendship, and the topics they have chosen that the volume nearly bursts with learning, all honoring Doctor Wright's intellectual, ecumenical, and collegial reach. Each article demonstrates appreciation for his work for and in the church; each writer represents hundreds of other admirers and friends. Thus while he can certainly not hang the book around his neck or probably display it on his mantle among icons and basketball trophies, we hope he will receive it and daily re-receive it as truly meet and right.

The twenty-one articles below fall into two broad categories, Christian ecclesiality and ecumenism. Both categories represent Doctor Wright's own life and scholarship; both are as intertwined here as in his work. They explore people, events, and texts from the biblical and patristic periods, the Middle Ages, the eighteenth, nineteenth, and twentieth centuries, and the spring of 2005. They overlap, they echo one another's subjects and concerns, and they resonate with the fundamental questions of Christian life and understanding, exploring how Christians have through the centuries understood who they are and who God is. Ultimately all reach toward an understanding of Christians as one people in shared faith and shared desire to live together as members of one body, to join in one communion as in one faith, one hope, one baptism — that they may be truly one as Christ and the Father are one.

The book begins with five articles that have to do with the early church; the first four examine the echoes and influence of the New Testament in the development of the early church and patristic writing. Walter R. Bouman examines New Testament texts on the role of women in the apostolic period. From scriptural evidence that in the church both men and women exercised the essential ministry of prophet/presider, Bouman argues that the ordained ministry of women as of men is ancient and orthodox, and is God's gift to the church. With its new insights about women in the life of the early church, this article also provides new ways of addressing a critical point of ecumenical conflict. Richard A. Norris, Jr., also considers scriptural passages for insight into developments in the early church, exploring the relationship between New Testament affirmations of faith in Christ and their echoes in the confessional and catechetical formulas of the first and second centuries. He concludes that creedal declarations appeared in both catechetical and confessional formulations, exercising a mutual influence on one another and jointly leading to the three-clause creed of the later centuries.

The next two articles turn from the evidence of scripture for the life of the early church to patristic writers' use and interpretation of scripture. Petra Heldt examines the use of Galatians 4:21-31 in patristic formulations of group identity, paying particular attention to authors' use of allegory and the way in which their *skopos,* their heuristic lens, determines their constructions of their own group's identity. Her article considers works by a number of patristic writers but gives particular attention to Origen's use of the Galatians passage. Patrick Terrell Gray also examines Origen's use of scripture, exploring Origen's confidence in the Holy Spirit as the inspirer of scripture as the basis of his scriptural interpretation. For Origen, Gray points out, the purpose of scripture is moral, bringing the reader to Christ, who is the Word of God, and so to conversion of life.

The last in this series of studies of the early church is Joanne McWilliam's consideration of Augustine's teaching on the incarnation and the person of

Christ and the correspondence of that teaching to the decisions of the fifth-century Council at Ephesus. McWilliam concludes from her examination of Augustine's works that he would probably have agreed with the Christology of the Antiochenes — but that ultimately he was fortunate to have missed Ephesus.

The next two articles explore writers from the church of the Middle Ages. John V. Fleming explicates Dante's portrait of the classical monster Geryon, who transports Dante-pilgrim and his guide Virgil across the abyss into the eighth circle of the *Inferno,* the Malebolge, the *locus* of the fraudulent and malicious. Fleming shows that Dante plumbs the works of scripture and patristic authors as he develops Geryon as an image of Satan, snared, bound, ridden, and finally trampled underfoot as Dante and Virgil ascend to Purgatory, manifesting God's victory over evil and death. Marsha L. Dutton examines the fourteenth-century laywoman Julian of Norwich as an Anglican before Henry VIII, finding in Julian's writing characteristic aspects of the Anglican ethos — scripture, tradition, revelation, reason, and faith searching for understanding. She also emphasizes the way Julian's writing of theology anticipates the ministry of the laity in Anglican tradition.

The next three authors examine the shaping and development of the Episcopal Church. R. William Franklin considers ways in which the eighteenth-century separation of the Episcopal Church from the Church of England and the church's polity reflecting that separation explain characteristics of the Episcopal Church today and bear on conflicts between the Episcopal Church and the Anglican communion. Robert Bruce Mullin discusses the developing distinctiveness of the Episcopal Church in the nineteenth century, focusing on Bishop John Henry Hobart's encouragement to the young church to identify with the struggling church of the first centuries instead of with the rich and powerful Church of England.

Another Episcopal priest and bishop, the great Phillips Brooks, contributed in a different way to the development of the Episcopal Church, guiding it toward increasing openness to other Christian churches and so to the ecumenical movement. Joseph Britton explains Brooks's view of Christian orthodoxy as centered in the person of Jesus and extending ever outward, dynamic, expansive, and inclusive rather than fixed, restrictive, and exclusive, with God's love as an ever-widening circle. Brooks's understanding of orthodoxy and his engagement with non-Episcopal churches offer valuable insights for the church's doctrine and life as well as for today's ecumenical movement.

Robert W. Prichard looks at early-twentieth-century changes in the Episcopal church in Virginia. Using a wide variety of parish minutes and records, he presents a church where at first blacks and whites and rich and poor worshiped together but separately, then moved toward physical and financial integration of the white members but increased racial segregation.

Finally Victor Lee Austin analyzes the Christology of Pope John Paul II as revealed in his social encyclicals. Austin argues that John Paul presented Christ's function as revelatory rather than political and taught that Christ is united with each human being and that the church is to bring Christ to Christ, to bring the gospel to all of those with whom Christ is already one.

The next two articles, both by Anglican bishops, suggest ways forward in the churches' search for unity. The Right Reverend S. W. Sykes examines Anglicanism with particular attention to its ecumenical potential, identifying four Anglican characteristics as particularly ecumenically valuable: a quiet and confident catholicism, an openness to a plurality of spiritual traditions, authority with consent, and a developing baptismal ecclesiology. He warns, however, against the Anglican tradition's susceptibility in its "eclectic openness" to a culpable "triviality and superficiality." Bishop Sykes's combination of encouragement to ecumenical progress and concern for what is sometimes called indifferentism reflects the ambivalence between enthusiasm and caution inherent in the ecumenical movement. Next the Right Reverend C. Christopher Epting explicates six challenges recently put to the churches and to the ecumenical movement by Cardinal Walter Kasper, president of the Roman Catholic Church's Pontifical Council for Promoting Christian Unity. By articulating what each of those challenges would require of the churches and some of the ways in which progress is already taking place, Bishop Epting's article offers a practical introduction to Christian ecumenism in the twenty-first century and anticipates the concerns and responses of the articles that follow.

Two authors address issues of particular difficulty in ecumenical conversations. Ellen K. Wondra examines the ordination of women and the ordination of gay men and women as a way of considering how the churches may move toward full communion while temporarily leaving certain topics undecided. She proposes a solution based on the way churches with unresolved differences have worked out relationships through approaches already familiar in ecumenical experience, such as unity by stages and the hierarchy of truths. Mary Tanner then examines an issue of longer-recognized ecumenical difficulty, the place in the church of the bishop of Rome and the Petrine ministry. She provides a historical overview of bilateral and multilateral discussions on the topic since the mid-1970s and urges that the ecumenical movement as a whole address the question more urgently, for the benefit of "a world that desperately needs a ministry of reconciliation in each and every place."

The next four articles concern bilateral dialogues and conversations over the past two hundred years. E. Rozanne Elder provides a historical summary of the nineteenth- and early-twentieth-century efforts by Orthodox and Anglicans to recognize their common faith and so to move toward communion. Her exploration of the changes that have taken place between the early hopeful expectation of easy accommodation — "The Age of Illusion" — and the present, "The Age of Disillusionment," is a kind of paradigm for much of the history of ecumenism, as is her call for "a new age" in which the churches may join "in proclaiming Christ's gospel to the world." William G. Rusch also looks toward Orthodoxy, noting the parallels between Orthodox and Lutherans in their "common appreciation, indebtedness, and recognition of authority in the patristic tradition of the church of the first five centuries." His examination of the place of the Fathers of the church in the writings of Luther and in the Lutheran Confessions offers a way forward for Lutheran-Orthodox relations, grounded in a shared reverence for the early church.

Two articles examine significant ecumenical progress during the past decade. Michael Root examines three Lutheran-Anglican agreements establishing full communion, in Northern Europe, Canada, and the United States. Limning the similarities and differences among the three agreements, he especially explores the way each of the three agreements resolve the question of the historic episcopate, one of the four elements required for church unity by the Anglican Communion's Chicago/Lambeth Quadrilateral. Jon Nilson then reviews *The Gift of Authority*, the 1999 agreed statement of the International Anglican–Roman Catholic dialogue, which declares the value to the churches of the Petrine ministry and of synodality in supporting that ministry. Nilson focuses on the tacit challenges *Gift* poses to the churches, identifying problems that remain to be solved before the church can receive universal primacy.

The great ecumenist George Tavard concludes the volume with an exploration of the ecumenical effect of the Vatican's 2000 instruction from the Congregation for the Doctrine of the Faith on interreligious dialogue, *Dominus Jesus*, and its footnote restricting use of the term *sister-church* to Orthodox churches. Exploring the history of the term *sister-church*, Tavard notes that in 1897 the Archbishops of Canterbury and York called the Roman Catholic Church "a sister Church of Christ" and that as recently as 2001 Pope John Paul II spoke of "our brothers and sisters of the Anglican Communion." He concludes by pointing to the religiously pluralistic world in which Christianity lives, the challenges that pluralistic context poses to Christian ecumenism, and Christians' common reaffirmation "of Jesus Christ as the one Savior of the world."

Acknowledgments

The editors wish to express our gratitude to all those who have helped us bring this book into being. We are most grateful to all the contributors for their graciousness in helping us create and complete it, and we thank them for their great patience and courtesy throughout the process. For editorial and computer assistance we thank Richard W. Bailey, David Bullock, Todd Gardner, Stephen Hays, The Reverend Susan C. Mills, William Owen, and Laura Reams, without whom we could not have created and published this volume. We are deeply obliged to the resources of and the patient, reliable, and often imaginative support of OhioLink, of the librarians and staff of Ohio University's Alden Library — especially Ms. Lorraine Wochna — and the Interlibrary Loan Department, and of the University of Michigan's Harlan Hatcher Graduate Library. We express our special thanks to Sister Mary DeVries and her community at Nazareth Hermitage for the Index to the volume. We are also grateful in this endeavor as in so many others to our families, who have supported us with very little irritation, great patience, and true enthusiasm for the project and our reason for doing it: Ezra Gray, David Stuckey, Emily Stuckey, Naomi Gray, and R. T. Lenaghan.

We are particularly grateful to those who have shared in honoring Doctor Wright through financial gifts: The Right Reverend Frank Griswold, Presiding Bishop of the Episcopal Church; The Reverend Andrew Mead, Rector of Saint Andrews Church, Fifth Avenue, New York; The Reverend Allan B. Warren III, Rector of The Church of the Advent, Boston; The Reverend Dirk C. Reinken, St. Luke's Episcopal Church, Trenton, NJ; The Very Reverend Ward Ewing, President and Dean of The General Theological Seminary, New York City; The Right Reverend M. Thomas Shaw, SSJE, Episcopal Bishop of Massachusetts, and The Reverend Wendel Meyer, Associate Minister, The Memorial Church, Harvard.

Above all, however, we thank J. Robert Wright for his many gifts to us as to so many, of wit, wisdom, generosity, hospitality, and affection. We offer him this book on behalf of and together with all those who have through the years benefited from his insights and his teaching, his thoughtfulness and his friendship — in the communion of the many who know and value his gifts to the *ecclesia universalis* as it seeks to be one in life as it is already one in hope, faith, and baptism.

The Feast of   Marsha L. Dutton &
William Reed Huntington, 2005   Patrick Terrell Gray

Curriculum Vitae: The Reverend Canon J. Robert Wright

D.Phil., D.D., D.Cn.L., Dr.Theol., F.R.Hist.S., F.S.,
St. Mark's Professor of Ecclesiastical History,
The General Theological Seminary

Education

- University of the South, Sewanee, TN. B.A. 1958 *(optime merens)*.
  George F. Baker scholar, history major, Phi Beta Kappa, Omicron Delta
  Kappa, Blue Key, Pi Gamma Mu, editor of weekly campus newspaper,
  chairman of debate society, Beta Theta Pi
- Emory University, Atlanta, GA. M.A. in History 1959 (honors). University
  scholar
- The General Theological Seminary, New York, NY. M.Div. 1963 *(cum
  laude)*. Prizes for ecclesiastical history, public speaking, and best honors
  thesis
- Oxford University, England. D.Phil. 1967. Fulbright scholar, fellow of the
  Episcopal Church Foundation, member of Wadham College, Arnold Historical Prize Grant

Honors

- Named Honorary D.D., Episcopal Theological Seminary of the Southwest, Austin, TX, 1983
- Elected a life Fellow of the Royal Historical Society (London), 1981
- Awarded the Syrian Orthodox Patriarchal Cross of Distinction, 1 July
  1990, in Hassake, Syria, by His Holiness Ignatius Zakka I Iwas, Patriarch
  of Antioch and all the East

- Appointed and installed as Honorary Canon Theologian to the Bishop of New York, in the Cathedral of St. John the Divine, 30 December 1990
- Named Honorary D.D., Trinity Lutheran Seminary, Columbus, Ohio, 1991
- Awarded the doctoral title of "Honorary Vartabed" or "Teacher for the Armenian Orthodox Church" by the Armenian Patriarch of Jerusalem, together with the pectoral cross of the Holy See of Etchmiadzin, 21 April 1992
- Inducted as a Chaplain of the Royal Order of St. John of Jerusalem, 15 November 1992
- Awarded the pectoral cross of the Patriarch of Moscow and All Russia, 2 July 1993, in the Dormition Cathedral of the Moscow Kremlin by His Holiness Aleksy II
- Awarded the pectoral cross of the Phanar by his All-Holiness Bartholomew I, the Ecumenical Patriarch of Constantinople, in Istanbul, 6 February 1994
- Awarded the gold cross of the Malankara Indian Orthodox Church by the Catholicos, Baselios Marthoma Matthews II, 19 August 1994
- Named Honorary D.Cn.L. (Doctor of Canon Law), University of the South, Sewanee, TN, 23 January 1996
- Nominated "Historiographer of the Episcopal Church" by the Presiding Bishop of the Episcopal Church; confirmed by unanimous vote of the House of Bishops, General Convention, 5 July 2000
- Named Honorary Dr. Theol., University of Berne (Switzerland), 2 December 2000
- Elected a Life Fellow of the Society of Antiquaries, London, 2001

Ordination in the Episcopal Church

- Deacon: June 11, 1963, by Bishop John Pares Craine of Indianapolis
- Priest: June 29, 1964, by Bishop Mervyn Stockwood of Southwark (England) acting for Bishop Craine
- Canonically resident in the Episcopal Diocese of New York since 1970

Professional Experience

- Littlemore Mental Hospital, Oxford, England. Part-time assistant chaplain 1963-64

- Our Most Holy Redeemer, Clerkenwell, London, England. Honorary curate 1964-65
- St. Peter's, Streatham, London, England. Honorary curate 1965-66
- St. Andrew's, Belmont, MA. Part-time assistant 1967-68
- Episcopal Divinity School, Cambridge, MA. Instructor in Church History 1966-68
- General Theological Seminary, New York, NY. Assistant Professor of Church History 1968-71; Professor of Church History 1971-present; granted tenure 17 January 1973; named St. Mark's-Church-in-the-Bowerie Professor of Ecclesiastical History by the Board of Trustees on 20 May 1974
- Nashotah House, Nashotah, WI. Visiting Professor, summer session, 1970, 2002
- Philadelphia Divinity School, Philadelphia, PA. Visiting Professor, spring term 1972
- Union Theological Seminary, New York, NY. Visiting Lecturer, fall term 1974
- Pontifical Institute of Mediaeval Studies, Toronto. Research Associate 1976 and 1981
- Claremont School of Theology, Claremont, CA. Visiting Professor, summer session 1977
- Huntington Library, San Marino, CA. Research Scholar, summer 1977
- St. George's College, Jerusalem. Visiting Professor, spring sessions 1982, 1992, 1995, 1996
- Trinity College, University of Toronto. Provost's Visiting Professor in Divinity, fall term 1989

Professional Academic and Church Work

- Associate Director of the Graymoor Ecumenical Institute, 1970-80
- Member of the Fellowship Screening Committee of the Episcopal Church Foundation, 1970-77
- Member of/consultant to Anglican–Roman Catholic Consultation in the USA, January 1971-present
- Member of The Anglican-Orthodox Consultation in the USA, 1972-76
- Member of the Board of *The Anglican Theological Review,* 1976-2005
- Member of the Commission on Faith and Order of the World Council of Churches, 1977-91
- Member of/consultant to the Standing Commission on Ecumenical Relations of the Episcopal Church, 1977-present

- Member of the Board of Directors of the Historical Society of the Episcopal Church, 1978-96, 2000-present
- Chaplain to the Guild of Scholars of the Episcopal Church, 1978-present
- Associate of The Anglican Centre, Rome, 1978-present
- Delegate from the Episcopal Church to the World Council of Churches' Faith and Order Commission meetings in Accra, Ghana, summer 1974; Bangalore, India, summer 1978; Lima, Peru, January 1982; Stavanger, Norway, summer 1985, and Budapest, Hungary, summer 1989
- Delegate from the Episcopal Church to the World Conference on Faith and Order, Santiago de Compostela, Spain, summer 1993
- Consultant to the Standing Liturgical Commission of the Episcopal Church, in preparation of the 1979 Book of Common Prayer
- Former Chaplain to the British Schools and Universities Club of New York City
- Member of "The Club," New York City
- Harvey Lecturer for the Episcopal Seminary of the Southwest, Austin, TX, 1979
- Speaker at over 150 ecumenical, historical, and liturgical conferences
- Coordinator of The General Theological Seminary–New York University Joint Doctoral Program, 1969-73
- Coordinator of Junior Tutorial Seminar program (cross-disciplinary introduction), The General Theological Seminary, 1976-96
- Member of the Ministries Commission of the Episcopal Diocese of New York, 1974
- National Secretary-Treasurer, Catholic Clerical Union of the Episcopal Church, 1971-72
- Guest lecturer at Woodstock College, Rutgers University, City University of New York, University of Toronto (Canada), and the University of Melbourne, the University of Newcastle, and Moore Theological College (Australia)
- Celebrant and Director, Solemn Votive Mass of St. Thomas Becket according to the Use of Sarum *c.* A.D. 1200, celebrated by students and faculty of The General Theological Seminary by invitation of the Metropolitan Museum of Art at The Cloisters, 23 March 1970, in connection with the "Year 1200" Symposium
- Celebrant and Director, Solemn Gothic Requiem Mass according to the Use of Paris *c.* A.D. 1300, celebrated by students and faculty of The General Theological Seminary at The Cloisters, 14 February 1972
- President of The Anglican Society, May 1994-present; member of the Executive Committee 1983-present

- Member of the Advisory Council of the Institute of Theology of the Cathedral Church of St. John the Divine, New York City, 1981-91
- Member of The Anglican/Roman Catholic International Commission (ARCIC II), 1983-91
- Member of Final Drafting Committee, January 1982, for the "Lima Statement" on Baptism, Eucharist and Ministry (BEM) of the Faith and Order Commission of the World Council of Churches; drafting chair and first celebrant of the Lima Liturgy
- Dahlberg Ecumenical Lecturer for Colgate Rochester Divinity School, Rochester, NY, 1984
- Acting Sub-Dean for Academic Affairs, General Seminary, spring term 1984
- Debate Forum Lecturer, St. John's University, Collegeville, MN, 1987
- Board Member of the Archives of the Episcopal Church, 1985-91
- Board member of *Anglican and Episcopal History,* 1991-present
- Member of the Editorial Board and Honorary Associate Editor, *Journal of Ecumenical Studies,* 1989-present
- Theological Consultant to the Ecumenical Office of the Episcopal Church, 1982-present
- Chair of Drafting Committee for House of Bishops' Pastoral Letter, "The Ministry of Bishops," 1991
- Chair of the General Seminary Faculty Association, 1993, 1998-99
- Convenor of the Conference of Anglican Church Historians, 1995-present
- Member of the Nikaean Club (London), March 1996-present
- Member of the Grolier Club (New York City), 1996-present
- Member and then chair of the New York Diocesan Russia Committee, 1992-2001
- Chair of Drafting Committee for House of Bishops' Pastoral Study on the Priesthood, 1997-2000
- Fellow of the J. Pierpont Morgan Library (New York City), 1999-2001
- Morpeth Lecturer (32nd annual), University of Newcastle, NSW, Australia, 10 May 1999
- Principal Episcopalian Architect and Drafter, *Concordat of Agreement* and *Called to Common Mission,* for full communion with the Evangelical Lutheran Church in America, 1982-2000
- Historical speaker, First Fellows Forum of the Episcopal Church Foundation, New York City, February 2000
- Member/consultant of the Inter-Anglican Standing Commission on Ecumenical Relations, 2000-present
- Consultant to the Inter-Anglican Theological and Doctrinal Commission, 2001-present

- Principal Drafter of the Ministry document for Churches Uniting in Christ, 2002-5
- American consultant for *The Bibliography of the Book of Common Prayer 1549-1999*, ed. D. N. Griffiths, British Library, 2002
- Editorial Advisory Board for *Ecclesiology,* 2004-present

Publications

Books

Co-editor and co-author, with Herbert J. Ryan, S.J. *Episcopalians and Roman Catholics: Can They Ever Get Together?* Denville, NJ: Dimension Books, 1972.

Editor. *Handbook of American Orthodoxy.* Cincinnati: Forward Movement Publications, 1972.

Author. *The Church and the English Crown, 1305-1334: A Study Based on the Register of Archbishop Walter Reynolds.* Toronto: Pontifical Institute of Mediaeval Studies, 1980.

Editor and co-author. *A Communion of Communions: One Eucharistic Fellowship.* New York: Seabury Press, 1979.

Editor and co-author. *Lift High the Cross* (New York City 1983 Commemoration of the Oxford Movement Sesquicentennial). Cincinnati: Forward Movement Publications, 1984.

Co-editor, with Joseph W. Witmer. *Called to Full Unity: Documents on Anglican-Roman Catholic Relations 1966-1983.* Washington, DC: USCC, 1986.

Editor and co-author. *Essays in Memory of Powel Mills Dawley. Anglican and Episcopal History* 56 (1987).

Editor and co-author. *Quadrilateral at One Hundred: Essays on the Centenary of the Chicago-Lambeth Quadrilateral 1886/88-1986/88.* Cincinnati: Forward Movement Publications; London and Oxford: Mowbray, 1988. Repr. as supplementary series no. 10, ATR, March 1988. Trans. to Japanese in *The Voice of Theology* (Journal of Central Theological College, Tokyo) 30.61 (1990).

Editor and author. *Prayer Book Spirituality: A Devotional Companion to the Book of Common Prayer Compiled from Classical Anglican Sources.* New York: Church Hymnal Corporation, 1989.

Editor and author. *Readings for the Daily Office from the Early Church.* New York: Church Hymnal Corporation, 1991.

Co-editor and co-author, with G. R. Evans. *The Anglican Tradition: A Handbook of Sources.* London: SPCK; Minneapolis: Fortress Press, 1991.

Editor and author. *On Being a Bishop: Papers on Episcopacy from the Moscow Consultation 1992.* New York: Church Hymnal Corporation, 1993.

Editor and author. *They Still Speak: Readings for the Lesser Feasts.* New York: Church Hymnal Corporation, 1993.

Author. *Saint Thomas Church Fifth Avenue.* Grand Rapids: William B. Eerdmans Publishing Company, 2001. 2001 selection of the Episcopal Book Club.

Editor and author, with Edward Kasinec. *Russo-Greek Papers 1863-1874.* New York: Norman Ross Publishing, 2001.

Author and editor. *Patristic Commentaries on Proverbs, Ecclesiastes, and Song of Solomon.* Ancient Christian Commentary on Scripture series. Leicester: Inter-Varsity Press, 2005.

Articles

1. Editorial columns written as Editor-in-chief. *The Sewanee Purple* (weekly campus newspaper of the University of the South, Sewanee, TN) 55.1-26, n.s. 1198-1223, 4 October 1956-29, May 1957.
2. "Religion at Oxford." *Fulbright Courier,* May 1960: 8-13.
3. "Lambert of Auxerre: the ETS Codex." *Bulletin de Philosophie Médiévale* 8-9 (1966-67): 123-26.
4. "The Supposed Illiteracy of Archbishop Walter Reynolds." In *Studies in Church History V.* Ed. G. J. Cuming. Leiden: E. J. Brill, 1969. Pp. 58-68.
5. "The Confraternity of the Blessed Sacrament: From Past to Present and Future." *The Living Church* 1 October 1967: 14-15.
6. "St. Mary's Conference on the Liturgy." *The Living Church* 5 July 1970: 5-6.
7. "The Last Supper — The First Eucharist: You Are There." *The Lamp* Nov. 1970: 6-11.
8. Five articles in *Encyclopedia Americana.* 1971 ed.
9. "Yes, Ordain Women." *Episcopal New Yorker* June 1972.
10. "Contours for Tomorrow: The Graymoor Conference." *The Living Church* 18 June 1972: 8-10.
11. "The Graymoor Conference: Episcopalians and Roman Catholics View Their Future." ATR 54 (1972): 351-59.
12. "Arthur Michael Ramsey, Archbishop of Canterbury." In *Pilgrim from Canterbury.* Ed. Joseph P. Egan. Garrison, NY: Graymoor, 1972. Pp. 5-6.
13. "Anglicans and the Papacy." In *Episcopalians and Roman Catholics: Can They Ever Get Together?* Co-edited and co-authored with Herbert J. Ryan. Denville, NJ: Dimension Books, 1972. Pp. 138-62.
14. "An Address in Favor of the Ordination of Women to the Priesthood." ATR 55 (1973): 68-72.

15. "Anglican Orders in Ecumenical Dialogue." ATR supp. series no. 2, Sept. 1973: 62-67.

16. "We Shall See Him as He Is." *The Messenger* July-August 1973: 3-6.

17. "Holy Russia and Soviet Russia — A Recent Impression." *Cowley* 44.2-4 (Oct. 1973 and Jan. 1974): 40-51, 57-71.

18. "The Priesthood in New York." *Bulletin of the General Theological Seminary* 60.1 (1974): 8-12.

19. "The Priesthood in New York." *Tract: Theological Review of the Association for Creative Theology* Winter-Spring 1974: 23-28.

20. "The Canterbury Statement: Background and New Dynamics." In *Conversations* (Garrison, NY: Graymoor) May 1974, pp. 2-10.

21. "An Irenikon to Dean Holmes." ATR 57 (1975): 56-59.

22. "Prayer Book Studies 26: Considered Objections." *The Anglican* 4 (1974): 7-18; expanded and corrected version in ATR 57 (1975): 60-71.

23. "Report: Faith and Order at Accra." *The Anglican* 4 (1974): 79-81.

24. "The Canterbury Statement and the Five Priesthoods." *One In Christ* 11 (1975): 282-93.

25. "The Canterbury Statement and the Five Priesthoods." ATR 57 (1975): 446-56.

26. "Ministry in New York: the Non-Stipendiary Priesthood and the Permanent Diaconate" (originally a working paper prepared for the Bishop and Ministries Commission of the Diocese of New York, fall 1974). *Saint Luke's Journal of Theology* 19 (1975): 18-50.

27. "Anglicans and the Papacy." *Journal of Ecumenical Studies* 13 (1976): 379-404.

28. "Anglicans and the Papacy." In *A Pope for All Christians?* Ed. Peter J. McCord. New York: Paulist Press, 1976; London: SPCK, 1977. Pp. 176-209.

29. "Luther outside Lutheranism: an Anglican Viewpoint." *Concilium* no. 118 (1976): different paginations in German, French, Spanish, Italian, Dutch, and Portuguese editions.

30. "Women Priests: Continued Dialogue." *The Ecumenist* 14.6 (1976): 92-96.

31. "Die Anglikaner und das Papsttum." *Una Sancta* 4 (1976): 310-19.

32. "New Work on Thomas Aquinas." ATR 59 (1977): 454-58.

33. "Anglican Comprehensiveness and the Limits of Conscience." *Ecumenical Trends* 6.11 (Dec. 1977): 169-71.

34. "The Rev. Rowland Johns Cox, D.D., 1928-1977" (Requiem homily). *Seminary News* [GTS] 3.3 (1977): 3.

35. "Documentation and Reflection — the Venice Statement." ATR 60 (1978): 306-32.

36. "Bangalore 1978 — A Report on Faith and Order." *Ecumenical Trends* 7.11 (Dec. 1978): 170-74, and 8.1 (Jan. 1979): 5-7.

37. "Le Dialogue entre Anglicans et Catholiques aux États-Unis durant ces treize dernières années." *Irenikon* 51 (1978): 492-508.

38. "The Turin Shroud — Miracle or Forgery?" *The Living Church* 4 March 1979: 8-9, 14.

39. "Anglicani e Cattolico-Romani in U.S.A." *Vita Sociale* 36.186 (May-June 1979): 247-58.

40. "Theological Response." In *The Lived Experience.* EDEO-NADEO Joint Task Force, 1979.

41. "Anglican–Roman Catholic Dialogue in the U.S.A. — A Survey of Thirteen Years." *One in Christ* 15.1 (1979): 73-84.

42. "Anglican Peculiarities Affecting Anglican Evangelism." ATR, supp. series no. 8 (Nov. 1979): 104-19.

43. "Faith and Order at Bangalore, 1978." ATR 61 (1979): 498-507.

44. "The Accounts of the Constables of Bordeaux 1381-1390, with Particular Notes on Their Ecclesiastical and Liturgical Significance." *Mediaeval Studies* 42 (1980): 238-307.

45. "Anglican–Old Catholic Conference." *The Living Church* 25 May 1980: 5-6.

46. "Ecumenical Actions of the Episcopal Church's 1979 General Convention." *Journal of Ecumenical Studies* 17 (1980): 580-87.

47. "Questions of the Roman Church's Sincerity." *Newsday* 25 August 1980: 37.

48. "An Anglican Commentary on Selected Documents of Vatican II." *Ecumenical Trends* 9.8, 9.9 (Sept., Oct. 1980): 124-31, 138-43.

49. Seventeen biographical sketches in *Lesser Feasts and Fasts.* 3rd ed. New York: Church Publishing Co., 1980.

50. "Documentation: Anglican/Old Catholic Theological Conference." ATR 63 (1981): 72-73.

51. "Bishop Myers: A Personal Remembrance." *Trinity News* 28.4 (1981): 5, 12-13.

52. "Ordination in the Ecumenical Movement." *Review and Expositor: A Baptist Theological Journal* 78 (1981): 497-514.

53. "Maundy Thursday at the General Seminary." *The Anglican* 11.4 (1981): 8-12.

54. "Evangelism in Anglican Perspective: Historical and Ecumenical Considerations." *Trinity News* 28.5 (1981): 10-11; 29.1 (1982): 7, 12-13; 29.3 (1982): 10, 14.

55. "An Anglican Response to the Canadian ARC Statement on Infallibility." *Journal of Ecumenical Studies* 19 (1982): 85-93.

56. "Mary's Purification: Christ's Presentation." Sermon in *AVE* (of Church of St. Mary the Virgin, New York) 51.4 (1982): 55-59.

57. "The Emergence of the Diaconate: Biblical and Patristic Sources." *Liturgy* 2.4 (1982): 17-23, 67-71.

58. "An Anglican Commentary" (on the ARCIC Final Report). *Ecumenical Trends* 11.10 (1982): 149-57.

59. "Documentation and Reflection: Faith and Order at Lima, 1982." ATR 65 (1983): 66-77.

60. "Anglican and Old Catholic Theology Compared." In *Old Catholics and Anglicans 1931-1981*. Ed. Gordon Huelin. Oxford: Oxford University Press, 1983. Pp. 125-40.

61. "Evangelism and a Scottish Saint" (on St. Ninian). *The Living Church* 18 September 1983: 8-9.

62. "Boswell on Homosexuality: A Case Undemonstrated." ATR 66 (1984).

63. "The ARCIC Final Report: An Annotated Bibliography." ATR 66 (1984): 177-87.

64. "The Oxford Movement and the American Church." In *Lift High the Cross*. Ed. J. Robert Wright. Cincinnati: Forward Movement Publications, 1984.

65. "Reflections on Lutheran/Episcopal Interim Eucharistic Sharing." *Ecumenical Trends* 13.10 (1984): 147-50.

66. "The Testament or Last Will of Walter Reynolds, Archbishop of Canterbury, 1327." *Medieval Studies* 47 (1985): 445-73.

67. "Open Letter to the Members of ARCIC-II." *Journal of Ecumenical Studies* 23 (1986): 354.

68. "Responses to the ARCIC Final Report: A Comparison of Methodologies." *Ecumenical Trends* 15.5 (May 1986): 74-76. Letter to Editor about same, *Ecumenical Trends* 15.6 (June 1986): 100.

69. "Ecumenism and Mission: Together Not Apart." In *Beyond the Horizon*. Ed. Charles R. Henery. Cincinnati: Forward Movement Publications, 1986. Pp. 97-116.

70. "A Christian Reflection on the Statue of Liberty." *Trinity News* 33.3 (August 1986): 11, 14.

71. "Christmas Traditions: An Interview with Dr. J. Robert Wright." *Trinity News* 33.5 (December 1986): 8-10.

72. "The Chicago-Lambeth Quadrilateral: Heritage and Vision." *Ecumenical Bulletin* 80 (1986): 16-39.

73. "The 1983 Code of Canon Law: An Anglican Evaluation." *The Jurist* 46 (1986): 394-418.

74. "An Anglican Comment on Papal Authority in the Light of Recent Devel-

opments." In *Authority in the Anglican Communion.* Ed. Stephen W. Sykes. Toronto: Anglican Book Centre, 1987. Pp. 236-63.

75. "Martin Luther: An Anglican Ecumenical Appreciation." In *Essays in Memory of Powel Mills Dawley.* Ed. J. Robert Wright. Pp. 319-29 (= *Anglican and Episcopal History* 56 [1987]).

76. "Provisional Bibliography: The Published Writings of Powel Mills Dawley." In *Essays in Memory of Powel Mills Dawley.* Ed. J. Robert Wright. Pp. 331-35 (= *Anglican and Episcopal History* 56.3 [1987]: 331-35); and *Anglican and Episcopal History* 58 (1989): 437.

77. "The Authority of Chalcedon for Anglicans." In *Christian Authority: Essays in Honour of Henry Chadwick.* Ed. G. R. Evans. Oxford: Clarendon Press, 1988. Pp. 224-50.

78. "Authority and The Anglican/Roman Catholic Dialogue." *Phos* (Pentecost 1988): 12-15.

79. "Heritage and Vision: The Chicago-Lambeth Quadrilateral." In *Quadrilateral at One Hundred.* Ed. J. Robert Wright. Cincinnati: Forward Movement Publications; London and Oxford: Mowbray, 1988; ATR, supp. series no. 10, March 1988. Pp. 8-46.

80. "Anglicanism, *Ecclesia Anglicana,* and Anglican: An Essay on Terminology." In *The Study of Anglicanism.* Ed. Stephen Sykes and John Booty. London: SPCK; Philadelphia: Fortress Press, 1988. Pp. 424-29.

81. "Salvation and the Church: A Response to David Scott." *Journal of Ecumenical Studies* 25 (1988): 437-44.

82. "Communion and Episcopacy: An ECUSA Perspective." In *Communion and Episcopacy — Essays to Mark the Centenary of the Chicago-Lambeth Quadrilateral.* Ed. Jonathan Draper. Ripon College Cuddesdon [UK], 1988. Pp. 57-78.

83. "An Ecumenical Salutation to Bishop Peter." *Jacob's Well* (NY/NJ Diocese, Orthodox Church in America) Fall/Winter 1988: 2.

84. "The Authority of Lambeth Conferences 1867-1988." *Anglican and Episcopal History* 58 (1989): 278-90.

85. "Prolegomena to a Study of Anglican Ecclesiology." In *This Sacred History: Anglican Reflections for John Booty.* Ed. Donald S. Armentrout. Cambridge, MA: Cowley Publications, 1990. Pp. 243-56.

86. "Chicago-Lambeth Quadrilateral" and "William Reed Huntington." In *Dictionary of Christianity in America.* Ed. Daniel G. Reid, et al. Downers Grove, IL: InterVarsity Press, 1990. Pp. 248, 562.

87. "Fundamental Consensus: An Anglican Perspective." In *In Search of Christian Unity.* Ed. J. A. Burgess. Minneapolis: Augsburg Publishing House, 1991. Pp. 168-92.

88. "Festival Morning Prayer and the Restoration and Rededication of St. Michael's Church, New York City." *Anglican and Episcopal History* 60 (1991): 191-95.

89. "L'Académie Nord Américaine des Oecuménistes." *Unité des Chrétiens* 83 (July 1991): 7-8.

90. "Sermon on the Eve of the Visit of Patriarch Aleksy" and "Anglicans and Orthodox Then and Now." *The Anglican* 21.2 (1992): 4-8.

91. "Vatican Response to Dialogue Squelches Hope." *Episcopal Life* February 1992: 22.

92. "Grundkonsens — eine anglikanische Perspektive." In *Grundkonsens — Grunddifferenz. Studie des Strassburger Institut für Ökumenische Forschung: Ergebnisse und Dokumente.* Ed. André Birmelé and Harding Meyer. Frankfurt am Main: Lembeck; Paderborn: Bonifatius Verlag, 1992. Pp. 145-54, 283-88.

93. "The Genesis of a Book: Readings for the Daily Office from the Early Church." *Worship* 67 (1993): 144-55.

94. "The 'Official Position' of the Episcopal Church on the Authority of Scripture." ATR 74 (1992): 348-61, 478-89.

95. "Sequential or Cumulative Orders vs. Direct Ordination." ATR 75 (1993): 246-51. Reprinted in *The Orders of Ministry.* Ed. Edwin F. Hallenbeck. Providence, RI: North American Association for the Diaconate, 1996. Pp. 47-51, 99.

96. "Richard Hooker and the Doctrine of Cumulative or Sequential Orders." *Sewanee Theological Review* 36 (1993): 246-51.

97. "The Origins of the Episcopate and Episcopal Ministry in the Early Church." In *On Being a Bishop.* Ed. J. Robert Wright. New York: Church Hymnal Corporation, 1993. Pp. 10-32.

98. "The Reverend Father Sergei V. Melnikas." *The Army Chaplaincy* Spring 1993: 41.

99. "Translating the Tradition." In *How Shall We Pray? Expanding Our Language about God.* Ed. Ruth A. Meyers for the Standing Liturgical Commission (Liturgical Studies Two). New York: Church Hymnal Corporation, 1994. Pp. 76-84.

100. "The First Seventy-Five Years of the 'ATR': Its Purpose and Contents, 1918-1993." ATR 76 (1994): 132-59.

101. "Ekklesiologischer Kommentar zu den orthodox-altkatholischen Dialogtexten und Überlegungen zu möglichen Folgerungen für das neue Europa." *Internationale Kirchliche Zeitschrift* 406 (April-June 1994): 77-91.

102. "The Problem of Tradition in the Definitive Response of the Vatican to the Final Report of ARCIC-I." In *The Quadrilog: Tradition and the Future*

of Ecumenism (Essays in Honor of George H. Tavard). Ed. Kenneth Hagen. Collegeville: Liturgical Press, 1994.

103. "Intercommunion and Full Communion: The Meanings of These Terms for Anglicans and for Their Relations with Old Catholics." In *Christus Spes: Liturgie und Glaube in oekumenischen Kontext: Festschrift für Bischof Sigisbert Kraft*. Ed. Angela Berlis and Klaus-Dieter Gerth. Frankfurt am Main: Peter Lang, 1994. Pp. 335-45.

104. "Anglican Recognition of the Augsburg Confession: An Actual Possibility?" In *Concordat of Agreement: Supporting Essays*. Ed. Daniel F. Martensen. Minneapolis: Augsburg Publishing House; Cincinnati: Forward Movement Publications, 1995. Pp. 127-43.

105. "The President's Message" (inaugural). *The Anglican* 24:1 (1995): 1.

106. "The Anglican Doctrine of Priesthood." *The Anglican* 24.1 (1995): 9-14.

107. "The Priesthood in Anglicanism." In *A Speaking Life: The Legacy of John Keble*. Ed. Charles R. Henery. Leominster [UK]: Gracewing: Fowler Wright, 1995. Pp. 67-107.

108. "The Reception of ARCIC I in the USA: Latest Developments." In *Communion et Reunion: Mélanges Jean-Marie Roger Tillard*. Bibliotheca Ephemeridum Theologicarum Lovaniensium 121. Ed. G. R. Evans and Michel Gourgues. Leuven: Leuven University Press, 1995. Pp. 217-30.

109. Eleven articles in *The Encyclopedia of New York City*. Ed. Kenneth Jackson. New Haven: Yale University Press, 1995.

110. "An Historical and Ecumenical Survey of the Church of the Holy Sepulchre in Jerusalem, with Notes on Its Significance for Anglicans." *Anglican and Episcopal History* 64 (1995): 482-504.

111. "The Dimension of Ecumenical Consensus in the Revision of Ordination Rites: A Response to Professor Paul Bradshaw." ATR 78 (1996): 117-21.

112. "The Meaning of the Four Chalcedonian Adverbs in Recent Ecumenical Agreements." *St. Nersess Theological Review* 1.1 (1996): 43-49.

113. "Taylor Stevenson as Editor: A Tribute." ATR 78 (1996): 379-81.

114. "Comments on the Righter Court Decision and Its Implications for Historic Episcopate in the Chicago-Lambeth Quadrilateral." *The Anglican* 25.1 (1996): 2.

115. "The Implications of Ecclesiology for Proselytism and Evangelism" (Conference with Russian Orthodox). *The Anglican* 25.1 (1996): 19-22 (+ photo); corrected in *The Anglican* 25.2 (1996): 30.

116. "Comments on the Report of the Joint Standing Commission on the Structure of the Church." *The Anglican* 25.2 (1996): 2.

117. "Who Should Vote in the House of Bishops?" *The Anglican* 26.1 (1997): 3-4.

118. "Reflections on 'Armenian Church Historical Studies' by Archbishop Tiran Nersoyan." *The Armenian Church* 11.2 (1997): 15-17.
119. "Central American Lutherans and Episcopalians Inspired by Concordat." *The Anglican* 26.2 (1997): 3-4.
120. "An Olivetan Benedictine Breviary of the Fifteenth Century." In *A Distinct Voice: Medieval Studies in Honor of Leonard E. Boyle, O.P.* Ed. Jacqueline Brown and William P. Stoneman. Notre Dame: University of Notre Dame Press, 1997. Pp. 143-54.
121. "In Support of the Concordat: A Response to Its Opponents." *Sewanee Theological Review* 40.2 (1997): 165-73.
122. "Annual Report to The Anglican Society." *The Anglican* 26.3 (1997): 3.
123. "Heraldry in The Anglican/Episcopal Tradition." *The Coat of Arms*, n.s. 12.178 (Summer 1997). Originally published with illustrations in *The Anglican* 26.3 (1997): 1, 17-21.
124. "The Concordat of 1997 for 2000?" *The Anglican* 26.4 (1997): 3-5.
125. "The Nature and Mission of the Church in Interchurch Dialogue, Especially the WCC" (with Victor Lee Austin). *The Anglican* 26.4 (1997): 10-14.
126. "On Communion, Catholicity, Dialogue, and Dissent." *The Anglican* 27.1 (1998): 3-4.
127. "La Signification des quatres adverbes chalcédoniens dans les accords oecuméniques récents." *Irénikon* 1998: 1, 5-16.
128. "Papal Questions." *The Anglican* 27.2 (1998): 3-4.
129. "Lay Eucharistic Presidency, and the Blessing of an Icon." *The Anglican* 27.3 (1998): 3-6.
130. "The Episcopal Church and the Historic Episcopate: An Episcopalian Speaks to Lutherans." Guest Editorial in *EDEO News* 6.3 (Fall 1998): 1, 3-12.
131. "William Reed Huntington." In *The SPCK Handbook of Anglican Theologians.* Ed. Alister E. McGrath. London: SPCK, 1998. Pp. 146-52.
132. "The Book of Common Prayer: 1549-1999 and Beyond" (and the Mission of St. Mary Magdalene of The Anglican Province of Christ the King, New York City). *The Anglican* 27.4 (1998): 3-4.
133. "Lambeth 1998 and the Question of Authority." *The Anglican* 28.1 (1999): 4-5.
134. "An Episcopalian View of the Historic Episcopate"; "A Response to the Responses." *Dialog: A Journal of Theology* 38.1 (1999): 53-61, 68-69.
135. "Called to Common Mission: Our Best Opportunity." *Word and World* 19.2 (Spring 1999): 180-83.
136. "Guest Editorial: Called to Common Mission — The Bottom Line as I See It." *Lutheran Forum* 33.1 (1999): 9-10.

137. "An Anglican Response" (to the Lutheran–Roman Catholic Agreement on Justification). *Lutheran Forum* 33.1 (1999): 45-47.

138. "Gloria Dei" (sermon on Glory). *Trinity Seminary Review* 21.1 (1999): 35-38.

139. "The Book of Common Prayer and Those to Its Left and Right." *The Anglican* 28.2 (1999): 3-4.

140. "Why Believe Still in the Trinity?" *The Living Pulpit* 8.2 (1999): 38-39.

141. "The Historic Episcopate: An Episcopalian Viewpoint." *Lutheran Partners* 15.2 (March/April 1999): 20-29. Follow-up and Response in *Lutheran Partners* 15.4 (July/August 1999): 9-16.

142. "The First Prayer Book of 1549 and the New York Commemoration of 1999." In *But One Use: An Exhibition Commemorating the 450th Anniversary of the Book of Common Prayer* (St. Mark's Library, General Theological Seminary, 1999; Isaac Gewirtz, Curator). Pp. 16-35.

143. "The Episcopal Church and the Historic Episcopate: An Episcopalian Speaks to Lutherans." *Anglican and Episcopal History* 68 (1999): 188-214.

144. "Observations on Australian Anglicanism." *The Anglican* 28.3 (1999): 3-4.

145. "In Memoriam H. Boone Porter January 10, 1923-June 5, 1999." ATR 81 (1999): 547-49.

146. "Theology in the Service of the Church's Pastoral Life: A Proposal." In *A New Conversation: Essays on the Future of Theology and the Episcopal Church*. Ed. Robert B. Slocum. New York: Church Publishing, 1999. Pp. 184-89.

147. "The Gift of Authority: Contents and Questions." *The Anglican* 28.4 (1999): 3-4.

148. Fifty-five articles in *An Episcopal Dictionary of the Church*. Ed. Don S. Armentrout and Robert B. Slocum. New York: Church Publishing, 1999.

149. "The Biblical and Theological Basis for Ecumenism." In *One Household — Many Hearts: A Study in Ecumenism*. Richmond, VA: Ecumenical and Interfaith Commission of the Episcopal Diocese of Virginia, 2000. Pp. 17-19, 25.

150. "Differing Gifts of Lutherans." *The Living Church*, 16 January 2000: 13-14.

151. "Different Lutherans Bring Different Gifts." *The Anglican* 29.1 (2000): 3-4.

152. "Singapore and the Authority of Bishops." *The Anglican* 29.2 (2000): 3-4.

153. "Good News from Toronto." *The Anglican* 29.3 (2000): 3-4.

154. "Those Singapore Ordinations." [Lutheran] *Forum Letter* 29.8 (August 2000): 6-8.

155. "Tradition and Innovation in Anglicanism: Is Tradition Always the Enemy of Innovation? Some Historical and Ecumenical Examples" (address

for the First Fellows Forum of the Episcopal Church Foundation). ATR 82 (2000): 765-78.

156. "The Ecumenical Ministry of Catholicos Karekin I (+1999)." *St. Nersess Theological Review* 5-6 (2000-2001): 1-6.

157. "Questioning the Promise of Toronto." *The Anglican* 30.1 (2001): 3-4.

158. "Holy Spirit in Holy Church: From Experience to Doctrine." ATR 83 (2001): 443-54. Reprinted in *Engaging the Spirit: Essays on the Life and Theology of the Holy Spirit.* Ed. Robert Boak Slocum. New York: Church Publishing, 2001.

159. "Ecumenical Breakthrough between Episcopalians and Lutherans in the United States: An Ecclesiological Reflection." *Internationale Kirchliche Zeitschrift* 91 (2001): 196-208.

160. "Sermon at the Deposition of the Relic of Saint Thomas Aquinas in the High Altar of the Chapel of the Apostles." *Sewanee Theological Review* 44 (2001): 374-77.

161. "When a 'host' is not a 'Host'." *The Anglican* 31.2 (2002): 3-4.

162. "Supplemental Episcopal Pastoral Care." *The Anglican* 31.3 (2002): 3-4.

163. "The Case for Charles." *SKCM News* (June 2002): 7-10; *The Anglican* 31.3 (2002): 20-22.

164. "Charles Hale and the Russian Church: The Biography of Innokentii"; "Archival Report: Charles Reuben Hale (1837-1900), Bishop of Cairo and Coadjutor of Springfield 1892-1900" (both with Edward Kasinec). *Anglican and Episcopal History* 71 (2002): 1-16, 17-21.

165. "Challenges for Canterbury's New Archbishop." *The Anglican* 31.4 (2002): 3-4.

166. "Charles and the Book of Common Prayer." *The Anglican* 32.1 (2003): 3-5.

167. "And Now the Moravians!" *The Anglican* 32.2 (2003): 2-3.

168. "The Ecclesiology of *Called to Common Mission.*" In *Discovering Common Mission: Lutherans and Episcopalians Together.* Ed. Robert B. Slocum and Don S. Armentrout. New York: Church Publishing Company, 2003. Pp. 1-26.

169. "Historical Prints of English Divines." *Anglican and Episcopal History* 72 (2003): 255-58.

170. "Sex and Ecumenism." *The Anglican* 32.3 (2003): 2-3.

171. "Charles Reuben Hale and Urs von Arx: Two of a Kind." In *Die Wurzel aller Theologie: Sentire cum Ecclesia. Festschrift zum 60.Geburtstag von Urs von Arx.* Ed. H. Gerny, H. Rein, and M. Weyermann. Bern: Stämpfli Verlag, 2003. Pp. 292-300.

172. "Bishops Rejected at Previous General Conventions." *The Anglican* 32.4 (2003): 3-4.

173. "General Convention Confirmation of Bishops-elect Is Not Pro Forma." *The Historiographer* 41.3 (2003): 18.

174. "At the Grolier Commemoration of 9/11" (address given on 9/11/2002). *Gazette of the Grolier Club,* n.s. 54 (2003): 103-8.

175. "On I Timothy 3:2 and the Difficulties of Being Fundamentalistic." *The Anglican* 33.2 (2004).

176. "The Possible Contribution of Papal Authority to Church Unity: An Anglican/Episcopal Perspective." In *The Ecumenical Future: Background Papers for "In One Body through the Cross: the Princeton Proposal for Christian Unity."* Ed. Carl E. Braaten and Robert W. Jenson. Grand Rapids: William B. Eerdmans Publishing Company, 2004.

177. "The Three Holy Oils: Their Origins & Their Uses." *The Anglican* 33.3 (2004): 3-4.

178. "Historiographer Challenges EWHP to Blandina Commemoration." *Timelines* (Newsletter of the Episcopal Women's History Project) 24.2 (2004): 7, 11.

179. "Walter Reynolds, Archbishop of Canterbury, 1313-1327." In *Oxford Dictionary of National Biography.* Oxford (UK): Oxford University Press, 2004.

180. "The Transfiguration and Dual Citizenship." *The Anglican* 33.4 (2004): 3-4.

181. "What Does Scripture Plainly Deliver?" *The Anglican* 34.1 (2005): 3-4.

182. "Prayer Shapes Our Belief" (review of *The Book of Divine Worship*). *The Anglican* 34.2 (2005): 3-4.

183. "Anglicanisme." In *Dictionnaire de Théologie.* Ed. Jean-Yves LaCoste, *et al.* Paris: Presses Universitaires de France, 1998.

184. "The Windsor Report: Two Observations on Its Ecumenical Content." ATR 87 (2005): 629-35.

185. "Early Prayerbook Translations in Foreign Languages." In *The Oxford Companion to The Book of Common Prayer.* Oxford: Oxford University Press, 2005.

Dr. Wright's full *curriculum vitae* is available on the website of The General Theological Seminary: http://www.gts.edu.

CHRISTIAN ECCLESIALITY

Catholic Ministry and the Ordination of Women

Walter R. Bouman

The full communion of the Episcopal Church in the U.S.A. and the Evangelical Lutheran Church in America, which was celebrated and begun on January 6, 2001, with a festive Eucharist in the (National) Cathedral of Saint Peter and Saint Paul in Washington, D.C., is only one in a series of agreements between Lutherans and Anglicans throughout the world. In 1996 the Porvoo Agreement established communion between the Anglican churches of the United Kingdom and Ireland and the Lutheran Churches of Norway, Sweden, Finland, Iceland, Estonia, Lithuania, and Latvia. In the summer of 2001 the Anglican Church of Canada and the Evangelical Lutheran Church in Canada celebrated their full communion. Anglican and Lutheran churches in Africa, Asia, and Latin America are in various stages of entering into communion with each other. Some of these churches have had a continuous catholic form of ordained ministry from their first evangelization. Over the course of the next several decades, all of the churches from these two traditions that are in full communion with each other will have a catholic form of ordained ministry, that is, they will share in a succession that goes back to early Christianity and priests/pastors who are ordained with a bishop in succession presiding.

Both Lutheran and Anglican churches have made catholic claims for their ordained ministry. The catholic form of ordained ministry was continuous in Anglican churches even after the Act of Supremacy of 1534 separated the Church of England from the Church of Rome. Anglicans have required the catholic form in England at least since the 1661 revision of the ordinal in the Book of Common Prayer and have required it of dialogue partners since the Chicago-Lambeth Quadrilateral of 1886/1888. Some Anglicans have always stressed the catholicity of their ordained ministries, and most have done so since the Oxford Movement in the nineteenth century (1833-45).[1] Similarly Lutherans identified their desire to retain the catholic form in their confessions:

> Concerning this subject we have frequently testified in the assembly that it is our greatest desire to retain the order of the church and the various ranks in the church — even though they were established by human authority. . . . Thus the cruelty of the bishops is the reason for the abolition of canonical order in some places despite our earnest desire to retain it. Let the bishops ask themselves how they will give an answer to God for breaking up the church. We have clear consciences on this matter since we know that our confession is true, godly, and catholic.[2]

Emphasis on the catholic character of their ordained ministry has been a characteristic of the Lutheran confessional renewal movement since the middle decades of the nineteenth century.[3]

Neither the Anglican churches nor the Lutheran churches thought that they were surrendering the catholic character of their ministries when they began to ordain women to the priesthood or the pastoral (presbyteral) office in recent decades. Most of the member churches of the Lutheran World Federation ordain women to the pastoral office, and many of these member churches now have women who are bishops. Many of the member churches of the Anglican World Communion ordain women to the priesthood, and some have also ordained women to the episcopal ministry. However, the Roman Catholic Church and the Orthodox churches have regarded the ordination of women as an action that calls into question the catholic character of the ministries involved. In 1975 Pope Paul VI warned the Archbishop of Canterbury that ordaining women to the priesthood would create a grave new obstacle in the quest for Christian unity. The pope characterized the position of the Roman Catholic Church as follows:

1. Cf. William P. Haugaard, "From the Reformation to the Eighteenth Century," Perry Butler, "From the Early Eighteenth Century to the Present Day," and Richard A. Norris, Jr., "Episcopacy," in *The Study of Anglicanism*, ed. Stephen Sykes and John Booty (London: SPCK, 1988), pp. 3-47, 296-309.

2. "Apology of the Augsburg Confession," Article XIV, in *The Book of Concord: The Confessions of the Evangelical Lutheran Church*, ed. Robert Kolb and Timothy J. Wengert (Minneapolis: Fortress Press, 2000), p. 222. Cf. *"Toward Full Communion" and "Concordat of Agreement": Lutheran-Episcopal Dialogue Series III*, ed. William A. Norgren and William G. Rusch (Minneapolis: Augsburg Press, 1991), pp. 43-54.

3. Holsten Fagerberg, *Bekenntnis, Kirche und Amt in der Deutschen Konfessionellen Theologie des 19. Jahrhunderts* (Uppsala: A. B. Lundequistska Bokhandeln, 1952), pp. 271-312.

She holds that it is not admissible to ordain women to the priesthood, for very fundamental reasons. These reasons include: the example recorded in the sacred Scriptures of Christ choosing his Apostles only from among men; the constant practice of the Church, which has imitated Christ in choosing only men; and her living teaching authority which has consistently held that the exclusion of women from the priesthood is in accordance with God's plan for his church.[4]

The concern of the Roman Catholic Church and the Orthodox churches, both of which are in serious ecumenical dialogue with Anglicans and Lutherans, makes it incumbent upon Anglicans and Lutherans to give an account as to why their churches have decided to ordain women and to address in some appropriate way the major objections to the orthodoxy, that is, the catholicity, of this action. This essay is an attempt by a Lutheran theologian to do so.

1. The Origin of the Church as Messianic Movement

There are two dimensions to the task of making a positive case for the ordination of women. The first dimension is historical, the historical origins of the church and its ministry. The second is theological, the calling and mission of the church as the basis for the ordination of women. There are more difficulties involved in addressing the historical origins of church and ministry than in addressing the question of the historical Jesus. The sources are modest at best. The apostolic letters in the New Testament give us tantalizing glimpses into the historical development. The Acts of the Apostles is useful, but even if it is regarded as in the main historical, it is episodic, not a full-blown account of the origins of the church and its structures.

What is today almost universally acknowledged is that Jesus cannot be said to have founded the church in the sense that Joseph Smith and Mary Baker Eddy founded religious institutions, complete with doctrines, rituals, scriptures, and

---

4. Paul VI, *Response to the Letter of His Grace the Most Reverend Dr F. D. Coggan, Archbishop of Canterbury, concerning the Ordination of Women to the Priesthood* (30 November 1975), AAS 68 (1976): 599. These concerns were expanded in the Congregation for the Doctrine of the Faith's Declaration *Inter Insigniores* on the Question of the Admission of Women to the Ministerial Priesthood (15 October 1976), AAS 69 (1977): 98-116. Pope John Paul II reemphasized this teaching and focused on the consistency and inviolability of the tradition in *Ordinatio Sacerdotalis* on Reserving Priestly Ordination to Men Alone, issued on 22 May 1994. The text available to me is in Lavinia Byrne, *Woman at the Altar: The Ordination of Women in the Roman Catholic Church* (London: Mowbray, 1994), pp. 127-30.

systems of governance. Nothing like that can be attributed to Jesus. There are only two sayings ascribed to Jesus in which the term *church* is used, Matthew 16:18 and Matthew 18:17.[5] The latter reference assumes a community but does not refer to its founding. Whatever Jesus means by the saying in Matthew 16, it refers to a future action. Jesus himself, before his resurrection, did not found a new religious institution separated from the Jewish synagogue and temple.[6]

After the resurrection of Jesus, his disciples understood themselves to be a messianic movement within Judaism. Raymond Brown best sums up this position:

> Many of our assumptions about the early Christian community flow from the erroneous supposition that Christianity was thought of as a new religion with its own religious institutions. But our best evidence is exactly to the contrary: at the beginning Christians constituted a movement within Judaism, differing only in some features (especially in the belief that Jesus was the Messiah, that with him God had inaugurated the eschatological times, and that therefore Gentiles could now participate fully in the blessings of Israel without formally adopting all the precepts of the Law of Moses). The Christians understood themselves as the renewed Israel, not immediately as the new Israel; and they expected that soon all . . . of Israel would join this renewal movement.[7]

Understanding the earliest disciples of the risen Jesus as a messianic movement within Judaism means that the documents that make up our present

---

5. Matt. 16:18: "And I tell you, you are Peter, and on this rock I will build my church, and the gates of Hades will not prevail against it." Matt. 18:17: "If the member refuses to listen to them, tell it to the church; and if the offender refuses to listen even to the church, let such a one be to you as a Gentile and a tax collector."

6. Hans Küng, *The Church,* trans. Ray and Rosaleen Ockenden (New York: Sheed and Ward, 1967), p. 73. Küng writes: "the gospels do not report any public announcement by Jesus of his intention to found a Church or a new covenant or any programmatic call to join a community of the elect. Such statements would have been interpreted as the founding of a separate synagogue and would have minimized and confused the uniqueness of Jesus' preaching. . . . Not until Jesus is risen from the dead do the first Christians speak of a 'Church'. The Church (and in this sense the new people of God) is therefore a post-Easter phenomenon."

7. Raymond Brown, *Priest and Bishop: Biblical Reflections* (Paramus, NJ: Paulist Press, 1970), p. 17. Brown states that not until the *Epistle of Barnabas,* written perhaps around A.D. 100, is there explicit mention of Christians as a "new people." Cf. J. Severino Croatto, *Biblical Hermeneutics: Toward a Theory of Reading as the Production of Meaning,* trans. Robert R. Barr (Maryknoll, NY: Orbis Books, 1987), p. 59: "the infant church had no consciousness of a distinctive 'founding'; it understood itself as the reinterpretation *of Israel.*"

New Testament are movement literature. They do not give us the texts for sacramental rites, doctrines, or systems of leadership and governance. The roots of these eventual structures of the church are found in the documents of the New Testament, but not with the kind of specificity and content that later emerged.[8]

The documents do reveal that from the beginning the disciples of Jesus gathered for a meal designated as "the breaking of bread." The term is used seventeen times in Acts, and Joachim Jeremias makes the case that it is a designation for the church's eventual eucharist.[9] What they do *not* indicate is who presided at these meal rituals of the gathered disciples. Raymond Brown states:

> There is simply no compelling evidence for the classic thesis that the members of the Twelve always presided when they were present, and that there was a chain of ordination passing the power of presiding at the Eucharist from the Twelve to missionary apostles to presbyter-bishops.[10]

Insofar as early Christian literature gives any indication about who presided, the evidence in the second-century Didache 10:7 is that prophets presided.[11]

Because the earliest disciples of Jesus understood themselves to be a messianic movement within Judaism, the role and meaning of the Twelve are especially important. Acts 1:15-26 indicates that the number twelve was so significant that it seemed necessary to replace Judas so that there would again be twelve. The significance of the Twelve is not that they were the first ordained leaders of the Christian community. The Twelve was a "creation" by Jesus early in his own messianic mission (Mark 3:14-16),[12] because the renewal of Israel in its twelve-tribe character was an expectation of the eschatological time of salvation.[13] They are also called "apostles" (Mark 3:14 and parallels), but there are more apostles than the Twelve. The James who is the obvious leader of the church in Jerusalem (Acts 12:17, Acts 15:13, Gal. 1:19) was not one of the Twelve, although he and others were apostles. The fact that all of the Twelve were men

---

8. L. William Countryman, "The Gospel and the Institutions of the Church with Particular Reference to the Historic Episcopate," ATR 66 (1984): 402-15.

9. Joachim Jeremias, *The Eucharistic Words of Jesus,* trans. Norman Perrin (Philadelphia: Fortress Press, 1966), pp. 117-22.

10. Brown, *Priest and Bishop,* p. 41.

11. "In the case of prophets, however, you should let them give thanks in their own way." Cf. Didache 13:3 and 15:1-2, *Early Christian Fathers,* ed. Cyril C. Richardson, The Library of Christian Classics vol. 1 (Philadelphia: Westminster Press, 1953), pp. 176-78.

12. Mark uses the Greek verb ποιέω 'to make' or 'to create', which the NRSV translates as "appoint," as if Jesus were appointing to an office already there instead of creating a new entity.

13. Gerhard Lohfink, *Jesus and Community,* trans. John P. Galvin (Philadelphia: Fortress Press; New York: Paulist Press, 1984), pp. 9-12.

has most probably to do with their symbolic significance as the new "sons of Jacob" in the eschatological renewal of Israel. It does not mean that only men were to be apostles, nor is it evidence that Jesus intended only men to give eventual ordained leadership to the church or to preside at the eucharist.

2. Women as Leaders in Early Christianity

Historically it is also necessary to look at the evidence of leadership roles occupied by women in the church during the first centuries of its existence. The most careful attention to this evidence to date has been given by Ute E. Eisen. Addressing first the apostolic office, she notes that there was at least one woman who was an apostle. In Romans 16:7, Paul sends greetings to a person named Junia (or Julia), whose name is clearly feminine. Eisen has demonstrated that despite some attempts at altering the text, Paul refers to a woman apostle who shared his imprisonment and who was a disciple (apostle?) before Paul himself became one.[14]

Eisen's extensive work on women who functioned as prophets is important because it seems from the Didache that prophets presided at the community's eucharist. Their importance in the messianic movement that became the church is evident from the four "lists" of ministries in the New Testament: 1 Corinthians 12:4-11, 1 Corinthians 12:27-30, Romans 12:4-8, and Ephesians 4:11. Prophets are the only ministry mentioned in all four lists. The ministry of prophets was more like what we today understand by preaching, as described at some length in 1 Corinthians 14:1-33, where prophecy/preaching is contrasted with ecstatic speech. Paul uses λαλέω for the speaking that can also be ecstatic and προφητεύω for proclamation. The prophets did not so much *predict* the future as *proclaim* the future that had been revealed in the resurrection of Jesus; in other words, they proclaimed the gospel.

Paul's concern that women pray and prophesy with their heads covered in 1 Corinthians 11:5 is evidence that women functioned as preachers and quite probably as those who prayed the prayer of thanksgiving at eucharist. This view is not contradicted by 1 Corinthians 14:34-35, for the silence enjoined by Paul refers to the wives of male members of the congregation, not to the women officeholders who engaged in prophecy/proclamation or in prayer leadership. Scholars have long noted that this passage's present location in the text is a matter of some uncertainty. It may quite probably have been inserted at this point

---

14. Ute E. Eisen, *Women Officeholders in Early Christianity*, trans. Linda M. Maloney (Collegeville: The Liturgical Press, 2000), pp. 47-49.

because it was regarded as intended for those who expressed themselves in ecstatic speech, the topic that Paul is addressing in 1 Corinthians 14.[15] Acts 21:9, which speaks of the four daughters of Philip as prophets, is further evidence of women functioning in this office.

Other offices also included women. Paul identifies Phoebe as a deacon in Romans 16:1. Prisca is a missionary leader mentioned not only in Romans 16:3 but also in Acts 18:18, when she and her husband Aquila accompany Paul to Ephesus. Paul identifies them as co-leaders of "the church in their house" in 1 Corinthians 16:19. He greets them again in 2 Timothy 4:19. Apphia apparently functions in a similar way as house church co-leader with her husband Philemon (Philem. 1-2). There is considerable weight to the argument that Paul is addressing *leaders* in his admonition to Euodia and Syntyche in Philippians 4:2. It may be that they are officeholders among the "bishops and deacons" who are addressed in Philippians 1:1.

The development of the Christian messianic movement into the institutional church was both inevitable and necessary. The proliferation of leadership groups (the Twelve, the Seven), individual leaders (Paul, Barnabas, and others), leadership "teams" (Prisca and Aquila, Philemon and Apphia), and local prophets gave way to presbyter-bishops, at first in Asia Minor and then in churches throughout the empire. Raymond Brown's brief but authoritative history says that the presbyter-bishops were not the successors of the Twelve.[16] Rather, some of them were successors of a Pauline type of apostolic leadership, a pattern of governance and eucharistic presidency that came to be regarded as normative by the end of the second century.[17]

It is impossible to determine just when women ceased to be officeholders in leadership roles as presbyters or bishops. With the possible exception of Philippians, there is no explicit reference to women presbyters and bishops in the New Testament, perhaps because these offices were in the earliest stages of development. But Eisen gives evidence of women serving both as presbyters and as bishops well into the history of Christianity, including an extended discussion of Theodora, mother of Pope Paschal I (A.D. 817-24). Her grave inscrip-

---

15. Antoinette Clark Wire, *The Corinthian Women Prophets: A Reconstruction through Paul's Rhetoric* (Minneapolis: Fortress Press, 1990), pp. 135-58.

16. Brown, *Priest and Bishop*, p. 55, states, "There can be no successors to the Twelve as such. . . . Rather, as the founders of the renewed Israel they are immortalized. . . . They have an eschatological role to play."

17. Brown, *Priest and Bishop*, p. 38. Brown notes that, without calling into question the eventual Petrine ministry of the Bishop of Rome, "in mid-2nd century, if that is when the *Shepherd of Hermas* was written, the Roman church seems still to be ruled by a presbyterate (Vision II iv 3)."

tion refers to her as ἐπίσκοπα, a reference that cannot mean that she was the wife of a bishop.[18]

The emergence of women in leadership roles as presbyters/priests and as bishops in the twentieth century does not challenge the development of normative Catholic structures of ministry and governance in the church. Nor is this emergence a correction of abuses or a restoration of rights. Ordained ministry in the church is not a legal or constitutional right. It is always a gift of the risen Lord (Eph. 4:7 and 11) through the Holy Spirit. The emergence of women in ordained ministry is due rather to attention (*renewed* attention) to the church's calling and mission as eschatological community in the past half century. That is its theological grounding.

3. The Church as Eschatological Community

The earliest "gospel" or "good news" of the disciples of Jesus was simply that Jesus was risen from the dead, and according to Acts 1:22 the earliest disciples of Jesus understood themselves to be first and foremost witnesses to his resurrection. Peter states this understanding in the Pentecost narrative: "This Jesus God raised up, and of that all of us are witnesses" (Acts 2:32). Later, at the Temple, Peter says, "You killed the Author of life, whom God raised from the dead. To this we are witnesses" (Acts 3:15). To Cornelius Peter says, "They put him to death by hanging him on a tree; but God raised him on the third day and allowed him to appear, not to all the people but to us who were chosen by God as witnesses" (Acts 10:39-41). For Paul as well, the earliest proclamation is not about the cross as God's saving act (that comes later), but about the resurrection (1 Thess. 1:10; compare 1 Thess. 2:15 with Acts 2:23, 3:15, 4:10, 7:52, and 10:39). In Romans 1:4 Paul summarizes his "gospel" as having to do with David's heir, who "was declared to be the Son of God with power according to the spirit of holiness by resurrection from the dead."

The resurrection was good news not because it was a personal vindication for Jesus, the righteous sufferer (as, for example, in 2 Maccabees 7:9, 14, etc.), but because in his resurrection Jesus was revealed to be the eschatological Messiah: "Therefore let the entire house of Israel know with certainty that God has made him both Lord and Messiah, this Jesus whom you crucified" (Acts 2:36). The disciples of Jesus have been let in on the secret of history! They know the identity of the Messiah, the final judge of the universe. They are like people who have read the last chapter of cosmic history. They do not know all the de-

18. Eisen, *Women Officeholders*, pp. 116-42 and 199-216.

tails of the plot, but they know the outcome of the story: Jesus, not Satan, will have the last word! Life, not death, will be history's last chapter! The Reign of God, not the reign of the power of sin and evil, will finally be victorious!

What is more, they have the experience of the Holy Spirit animating the entire community of Jesus' disciples. Before Jesus' resurrection the Holy Spirit is given to individuals in Israel but not to the people as a whole. However, in Isaiah and in the exilic and post-exilic prophets, the expectation is that in the eschatological future (the "day of salvation") the Spirit will be given "to the whole house of Israel" (Ezek. 37:11-14), and indeed the Spirit will be poured out "on all flesh" (Joel 2:28-29).[19]

The meaning of this experience of the Holy Spirit by the entire community is best expressed by the term ἀρραβών 'down payment'. The Holy Spirit is "down payment" on the reality of God's eschatological promises in Jesus (2 Cor. 1:22), on the final eschatological triumph of life over death (2 Cor. 5:5), and on "our inheritance toward redemption as God's own people" (Eph. 1:14). A "down payment" on a house enables one to live in the house as if one already owned it. The experience of the Holy Spirit means that the Christian community is set free to live as if the eschatological victory of the Reign of God were in fact already here, as if God's justice, God's peace, God's compassion, God's redemption of all of creation were already in place. The experience of God's Spirit is present where the community is already anticipating the ἔσχατον, the outcome, the final victory of the Reign of God. The church is called and liberated to anticipate in its language and being, in its structures and life, the gathering and reconciliation of the whole of humanity, the whole of the cosmos.

That is why the church invokes the Holy Spirit in its eucharistic celebration. If death has been defeated in the resurrection of Jesus, if the last chapter of history as the victory of life has been revealed, then there is more to do with our lives than to preserve them. We are free to offer our lives into the service of the Reign of God. The eucharist is the meal in which the Messiah takes us up into the once and final offering of himself for the sake of the Reign of God, makes us one with his offered body and blood, and sends us to be the offering of ourselves — the Body of Christ — for the world (Rom. 12:1-2). In the meal we are already anticipating the Messianic banquet, the meal in which all nations are gathered because death has been defeated (Isa. 25:6-8). In the eucharist the Messiah is sharing the eschatological meal as he promised (Matt. 26:29 and parallels).

When we forgive debts (Matt. 6:12) we signify that the age of jubilee, the messianic age, is here. When we forgive our enemies, those who sin against us

---

19. Arland J. Hultgren, *Christ and His Benefits* (Philadelphia: Fortress Press, 1987), pp. 31-37.

(Luke 11:4), then we anticipate God's final eschatological verdict on our sins. As Jesus is the grounding and consummation of the Reign of God, its ἄλφα and ὤμεγα, so the Holy Spirit is the dynamic of the Reign of God in history and its down payment in the community, the church. The eucharist as the presence of Christ's offering in the power (δύναμις) of the Holy Spirit thus gives the church its identity and its mission: to be witness to and anticipation of the eschatological victory of the Reign of God.

This is why the Pentecost narrative becomes the grounding for the shared ministry of prophet/presider by both men and women. Peter quotes the words of the prophet Joel, but with one significant change. Joel celebrates the pouring out of the spirit "afterward," that is, after the plague ends, after fertility returns, after the covenant is restored (Joel 2:18-27). Peter changes the "afterward" to "in the last days," that is, when the messianic age has arrived, when the ἔσχατον has been revealed. Just this has taken place in the resurrection of Jesus. The disciples of Jesus have experienced the promised outpouring of the Spirit. The sign of the messianic age is that "your sons and your daughters shall prophesy." "Even upon my slaves, both men and women, in those days I will pour out my Spirit; and they shall prophesy" (Acts 2:17-18). Both men and women will be prophets, proclaiming God's eschatological salvation, presiding at God's eschatological eucharistic feast.

The ordained ministry of women and men as deacons, priests/presbyters, and bishops belongs essentially to the church's identity and mission as eschatological anticipation of all humanity. Their shared ministry is a sign that the church is called to embody the coming of the messianic age, that the church is called to anticipate the victory of the Reign of God, that the church is called to be a witness to Jesus' resurrection. For the resurrection of Jesus is the grounding and consummation of God's eschatological salvation (1 Cor. 15:24-28).

Thus the inclusion of women in the ordained ministries of the church is not destructive of catholic tradition. Charles Peguy once said, "One must always tell what one sees. Above all, which is more difficult, one must always *see* what one sees."[20] In the last century we have begun to see again what was always in the tradition but was invisible to our eyes: the women officeholders grounded in the eschatological resurrection of Jesus. The ordination of women is the renewal and eschatological expression of what has always been present in catholic tradition. Authentic catholic tradition is the development and embodiment of the normative structures necessary for the church's institutional life between the resurrection of Jesus and the consummation of the Reign of God. The structures of sacramental liturgy and ordained polity, of scriptural canon

---

20. Quoted in Ernest Becker, *Angel in Armor* (New York: The Free Press, 1969), p. 157.

and orthodox doctrine, have their roots in documents of the New Testament even though they are not spelled out in the New Testament. Authentic catholicity can once again see the historical content and catholic presence of women officeholders in the documents of the New Testament and early Christianity.

Thus the ordained ministry of women and men is present from the beginnings of the Christian church as a messianic movement within a Jewish matrix.

This position is orthodox ecclesiology. For the sake of catholic tradition Lutherans and Anglicans are required to bear witness that the Lord Jesus, the Messiah, has given the gift of the ordained ministry of women to their communions. Professor J. Robert Wright has been an ardent advocate of the ordination of women and an eloquent witness to the catholicity of such ordination.

Confessional and Catechetical Formulas in First- and Early-Second-Century Christian Literature

Richard A. Norris, Jr.

In the opening chapters of *Early Christian Creeds* J. N. D. Kelly makes clear what the English word *creed* properly denotes when employed in an ecclesiastical sense. Derived as it is from the Latin *credo*, the first word of the so-called symbol of the Apostles and of the Constantinopolitan symbol, it refers to a certain kind of profession of faith in the first person, what Kelly calls a "declaratory" formula. This first-person profession of faith, he explains, is the phenomenon whose origins he is interested in investigating. Furthermore, he takes great care — and rightly so — to distinguish creeds understood as proof of faith from the baptismal confession of faith. The distinction, he points out, consists not merely in their form (the creed proper being declaratory, while the baptismal confession took the form of a set of questions with affirmative responses) and in their relative length (the baptismal confession being generally much shorter than a creed) but also in their original function. The creed was an instrument of catechesis, and the baptismal confession was a part of the sign of the believer's new relation to God — or else, perhaps, the terms of the *pactum* or covenant that constituted this relation.[1]

The discussion in which Kelly makes these points locates the subject firmly in the period between the beginning of the third century and its halfway mark, as is clear from the fact that the evidence Kelly adduces comes for the most part from people like Tertullian, Hippolytus, and Cyprian. Their testimony establishes the fact that the baptismal confession was never a formula of

---

1. J. N. D. Kelly, *Early Christian Creeds*, 3rd ed. (New York: David McKay Co., 1972), pp. 1-61.

declaratory form. The question naturally arises, therefore, of what precedents or ancestors before the third century can be discovered for either of these types of formula and what the relation between them might be.

Adolf von Harnack's classic article on the Apostles' Creed,[2] which traced that formula's beginnings back to the middle of the second century, hardly ever raised the question of the origins or anticipations of the symbol in earlier Christian literature. In eschewing such questions, Harnack was acting in accord with the earlier judgment of Ferdinand Kattenbusch. The latter acknowledged that the New Testament contained parallels and analogues of certain phrases in what he called simply "the creed," but he doubted whether there was any continuity of development between the primitive confession "Jesus is Lord" and the earliest form of the Apostles' Creed. This formula, whose appearance he located at a date roughly half a century earlier than that assigned by Harnack, he took to be a new composition, deriving from the church at Rome, and he thought that its appearance marked the true beginning of the history of creedal or confessional formulas.[3]

Since the days of Kattenbusch and Harnack, however, a great deal of water has flowed under the bridge of inquiry into the history of what is today known as the creed. For one thing, it is now easier to recognize and appreciate the variety of kinds of formulaic utterance that occur in early Christianity. For another, a suspicion has grown up among scholars that the use of such terms as *composition* in connection with primitive creedal materials represents something of an anachronism. The study of creedal antecedents is a study of oral and traditional materials: the earliest creed that one has the right to think of as in some sense composed (that of the *Apostolic Tradition,* attributed to Hippolytus) dates from the third century, and the very fact that it is, or may well be, an individual composition has led to doubts whether it was ever actually used in the form we know. Most important of all, however, a whole series of studies has attempted to relate later, explicitly creedal, materials to more primitive slogans, catchwords, or patterns of speech.

The principal stimulus to such inquiry was the now forgotten work of Alfred Seeberg, *Der Katechismus der Urchristenheit.*[4] In this work, Seeberg tried to reconstruct the text of a possibly creedal formula that he thought could be shown to underlie a group of widely scattered New Testament passages, each of which he judged to exhibit unmistakable signs of containing or alluding to

2. Adolf von Harnack, "Apostolisches Symbolum," in *Realencyklopädie für protestantische Theologie und Kirche* 1:741-55.

3. Ferdinand Kattenbusch, *Das apostolische Symbol,* 2 vols. (Hildesheim: G. Olms, 1962), 2:346-47; cf. 2:341-43.

4. Leipzig: A. Deichert'sche Verlagsbuchhandlung Nachf. (Georg Böhme), 1903.

fixed confessional expressions. In Seeberg's opinion,[5] the text of this creed defined at once the content of preaching, the object of belief, and the material of catechesis and confession in the churches of the apostolic age. Critics of Seeberg swiftly agreed that he had tried to prove far too much, but they also agreed that he had made a significant advance by establishing the presence in the New Testament of statements and expressions with a *prima facie* claim to have functioned as teaching summaries or as vehicles of confession. Thus Hans Lietzmann, writing some two decades later, noted the absence of confessional formulas in the age of the apostles:

> There are no confessional formulas, but rather "confessional patterns" [*Bekenntnistypen*], schemas if you will, which determine the point and the essential topical heads of their content. Such confessional patterns are clearly recognizable in the New Testament, and it is the abiding contribution of A. Seeberg to have pointed out the traces of this confessional element in the New Testament.[6]

It was left to Lietzmann himself, however, not only to attempt to classify such confessional patterns in the New Testament but also to develop what should probably be called the classical theory of the evolution of confessional forms.[7] The basis of Lietzmann's classification — as his use of the term *Bekenntnistypen* indicates — was not primarily the use or function of the materials in question but rather their abstract form as that was determined by their subjects, i.e., by the heads of confession or teaching or preaching they included. Accordingly he distinguished three types of formula-like expressions in the New Testament writings.

The most obvious of these are simple characterizations of Jesus as Messiah, Lord, or Son of God. These, he thought, reflected the earliest shape of the baptismal confession. Such one-member statements are also found in more elaborate forms that in effect constitute summaries of the churches' customary preaching or teaching about the status of Jesus as it was attested by the events of his life, death, and resurrection. Lietzmann saw this pattern of what has been called Christological confession as persisting in the church of the second century and afterward in various settings and uses, but especially in formulas of praise and in teaching summaries.

Alongside this one-member confessional pattern, according to Lietzmann,

---

5. Seeberg, *Der Katechismus*, p. 85.
6. Hans Lietzmann, "Symbolstudien X," ZNW 22 (1923): 263.
7. Lietzmann, "Symbolstudien X-XII," ZNW 22 (1923): 262-79.

a second pattern appears, in which proclamation of Jesus as Lord and Messiah is organically connected with the mention or confession of God, who figures not primarily as creator of the cosmos but as the vindicator of his Messiah. This two-member schema not only continued in use after the close of the New Testament period but also, in Lietzmann's view, represented the form whose expansion through the addition of a third member produced the three-clause pattern that eventually became normative for the baptismal profession of faith.

Finally, Lietzmann recognized in the New Testament itself, notably at Matthew 28:19 and 2 Corinthians 13:13, the presence of a three-member pattern of ritual speech that supplemented acknowledgment of Jesus and his Father with mention of the Holy Spirit.[8] He pointed out, however, that neither the terminology of Matthew 28:19 nor the order of names in 2 Corinthians 13:13 was directly reflected in later three-member formulas; for this reason he insisted on the formal derivation of the latter from the two-member type of confession.

This account of the nature and evolution of early formulaic materials has guided standard treatments of the subject since Lietzmann's time. His scheme of classification provided the basis on which Kelly handled the New Testament evidence.[9] Furthermore, Oscar Cullmann presupposed Lietzmann's position in the working out of his own hypothesis concerning the evolution of creedal forms in the first and second centuries. On this hypothesis, the most primitive communities expressed their belief in a simple, one-clause confession of Jesus. The triadic shape of later confession, therefore, has been envisaged as the product of a two-stage development from the simple to the complex. From a one-clause Christological formula, sufficient for Jewish Christians who did not need to be reminded of their faith in the one God, Christian formulas expanded as the gospel was preached to pagan Gentiles, to include an announcement or expression of faith in God. The Holy Spirit was added to the standard topics of confession at a still later stage by reason of its close association with baptism.[10]

Criticisms of the Traditional View

Kelly was at pains to emphasize against Cullmann's form of the hypothesis that dyadic and triadic forms of expression are as firmly rooted in primitive sources

---

8. Matt. 28:19: "Go therefore and make disciples of all nations, baptizing them in the name of the Father and of the Son and of the Holy Spirit"; 2 Cor. 13:13: "The grace of the Lord Jesus Christ, the love of God, and the communion of the Holy Spirit be with all of you."

9. Kelly, *Early Christian Creeds,* pp. 13-29.

10. Oscar Cullmann, *The Earliest Christian Confessions,* trans. J. K. S. Reid (London: Lutterworth Press, 1949), esp. chap. 3.

as are Christological affirmations. He ventured the critical observation that "scholars . . . have been mesmerized by the evolutionary axiom that the less complex must always precede the more complex, and that there must be a line of progressive development."[11] Yet Kelly himself offered no explanation of the currency of the dyadic and triadic patterns of language to which he called attention in the New Testament; nor did he suggest how one might connect them with later creedal forms.

On the other hand, and from an entirely different angle, Hans von Campenhausen has argued that to speak of confessional formulas in the New Testament requires an awareness that they are distinct both in function and in content from other types of formulas — and most particularly from summaries of historical tradition or of doctrine, which, he insists, "went their own way."[12] The history of confession must confine itself — at least where the early period is concerned — to the progeny of formulas like "Jesus is Lord," "Jesus is the Christ," and "Jesus is the Son of God," expressions that, moreover, had no specific *Sitz-im-Leben* but were employed indiscriminately, if only occasionally. If von Campenhausen is right, the developmental hypothesis originally suggested by Lietzmann has been far too eager to assimilate and associate materials that are in fact separate in function and belong to different streams of tradition. In the end, then, it seems that there is little direct connection to be discerned between New Testament confessional utterances and later creeds.

What is interesting in these two criticisms of the classical theory of creedal evolution is the fact that each calls in a different way for a more complex appreciation of the development that led up to the appearance of declaratory formulas — i.e., creeds proper. The idea of the simple, linear expansion of a one- or two-member *Bekenntnistyp* needs to be modified, for at least two reasons. First, the term *confession* (*Bekenntnis* = ὁμολογία) cannot properly be applied to much of the formulaic material in the New Testament. Much — even most — of it had other functions. Hence the history of the development of creeds cannot be envisaged simply as the evolution of confessional formulas. Second, all three of Lietzmann's *Bekenntnistypen*, whether or not all or always confessional in function, occur in early literary sources.

The question then becomes how to get from the various primitive summaries, slogans, and catchwords, in all their variety of form and of function, to a later era's baptismal confessions and declaratory creeds — both triadic in form but having, at least to some extent, different functions.

Obviously, to start with, it is important to follow von Campenhausen —

11. Kelly, *Early Christian Creeds*, p. 27.
12. Hans von Campenhausen, "Das Bekenntnis im Urchristentum," ZNW 63 (1972): 211.

and, even earlier, V. H. Neufeld[13] — in making a firm functional distinction between ὁμολογία in the strict sense and formulaic materials that set out the ground or subject of confession. In the strict sense, the term ὁμολογία refers to acts of public self-commitment or of praise, while the formulaic materials embody namings or accounts of the circumstances or agents that evoke self-commitment or praise. Obviously both of these activities tend naturally to generate stable, if not necessarily fixed, forms of expression.

Two Types of Speech Patterns in the Primitive Sources

Confessional response occurs in a variety of settings in the New Testament. Liturgical praise, for example, appears in the statement "Jesus Christ is Lord" at Philippians 2:11, and the setting of theological debate appears at 1 John 4:2-3, in the confession that "Jesus Christ has come in the flesh." There is also the possible case of confession as a condition of, or a moment in, Christian initiation — that is, baptism.[14]

At the same time, the New Testament uses an almost technical vocabulary to denote the act of setting forth the ground or subject of confessional response. One thinks of verbs like εὐαγγελίζεσθαι, παραδιδόναι, κηρύσσειν, and διδάσκειν, whose customary objects amount to little more than catchphrase summaries of the Christian message: "Jesus and the resurrection," "Jesus as Lord," "the things concerning Jesus," or simply "the faith," "the word," "the teaching concerning Christ."

Summaries in this latter class plainly cannot be classified as confessions. On this point von Campenhausen is correct. Yet they may be closely related to confessional expressions as far as both content and form are concerned: it was this circumstance to which Lietzmann called attention. The reason is obvious. What is preached or taught on the one hand and what is confessed on the other generally amounts — and, what is more, is understood to amount — to much the same thing. The fact that two patterns of speech perform different functions, then, does not in itself mean that they are not correlative or, as von Campenhausen argues, that their development will necessarily follow separate paths. If they are correlative, they may well influence one another.

The way that functionally different formulas may be correlative is exempli-

---

13. V. H. Neufeld, *The Earliest Christian Confessions* (Grand Rapids: Eerdmans, 1963). Neufeld's discussion of *didache* contributes materially to awareness of the distinction between confessional formulas and teaching patterns.

14. See for example Rom. 4:24-25, 1 Pet. 2:24, Tit. 2:13, Acts 22:16.

fied in the two passages in the Pauline corpus that have the most obvious claim to be some sort of teaching formulas. In Romans 1:3-4, Paul speaks of "the gospel concerning [God's] Son, who was descended from David according to the flesh and was declared to be Son of God with power according to the spirit of holiness by resurrection from the dead. . . ." Then in 1 Corinthians 15:3b-5, Paul speaks of the message that he had "received" and also "delivered" (παρέδωκα) to his Corinthian converts: "that Christ died for our sins in accordance with the scriptures, and that he was buried, and that he was raised on the third day in accordance with the scriptures, and that he appeared to Cephas, then to the twelve."

Inspection shows that these formulas are summaries whose whole attention is focused on the figure of Christ and that thus fall into the class of Lietzmann's "one-member" types. They answer exactly, therefore, to confessional utterances like "Jesus is the Son of God" or "Jesus is the Christ." On the other hand, they are by no means so terse as such confessions. They show a tendency to outline a story about Jesus and by so doing to intimate theological frameworks within which his significance can be understood. Furthermore, even though they are logical correlates of a one-membered confession, both introduce figures other than Jesus himself. The formula in Romans 1 tacitly acknowledges both the God whose son Jesus is and the "spirit of holiness." By its use of the passive ἐγήγερται, 1 Corinthians 15:4 alludes unmistakably to God, who raised Jesus from the dead.

It is hardly surprising, therefore, to find other Christological preaching and teaching summaries or catchphrases that touch more briefly on the same themes as Romans 1:3-4 and 1 Corinthians 15:3b-5. Whether they are reminiscences of formulas or mere summary reiterations of standard preaching schemes (as seems the more likely alternative), they obviously represent patterns of talk that are becoming customary and authoritative through repetition. The second of them, interestingly, is barely distinguishable in function from a confession of faith:

> Remember Jesus Christ, raised from the dead, a descendant of David (2 Tim. 2:8);

> . . . we believe that Jesus died and rose again (1 Thess. 4:14);

> It was Christ Jesus, who died, yes, who was raised (Rom. 8:34).

Virtually equivalent to these in function are other summary turns of phrase that develop the idea suggested by 1 Corinthians 15:4, explicitly identifying God's action:

Jesus Christ and God the Father, who raised him from the dead (Gal. 1:1);

. . . you were also raised with him through faith in the power of God, who raised him from the dead (Col. 2:12);

. . . this man . . . you crucified and killed. . . . But God raised him up (Acts 2:23-24).

In this primitive and widespread summary pattern of speech it becomes clear that to announce the resurrection of Jesus from the dead is at the same time to proclaim the God who thus vindicated him. Yet this form of words, which in Lietzmann's classification is a rudimentary two-member formula, does not merely co-exist with but is also the direct correlative of the "simple" Christological confession. The confession "Jesus is the Christ" is not the response to some remark about Jesus alone but rather to a proclamation in which Jesus' resurrection is either explicitly or implicitly set forth as the work of God. The distinction between the one-member and the two-member teaching summary is not one of function or of content, then, but merely of form.

If, however, the Christological confession answers to a proclamation or teaching in which God figures either openly or implicitly, it is understandable that circumstances might arise in which it becomes necessary to embody the full content of such teaching in a properly confessional utterance. It is in this way, I judge, that one must understand Paul's language at 1 Corinthians 8:6: "yet for us there is one God the Father, from whom are all things and for whom we exist, and one Lord Jesus Christ, through whom are all things and through whom we exist." In this instance the form of habitual preaching and teaching summaries is carried over into confessional utterance.

It is clear that the intent of Paul's formulation here is polemical. Functionally speaking, his words represent an act of confession, but they belong to the category of what might best be called reflexive confession. That is, the confession in question grows out of reflection on the terms and implications of already accepted and established forms of teaching. In a situation where teachings conflict, they tend to formulate the clear but hitherto implicit sense of traditional patterns of instruction — patterns that in their original shape did not address the issues that are currently being argued.

If one asks, however, what these traditional patterns of teaching were, it is not enough to allude solely to Paul's inherited monotheism (i.e., to Deuteronomy 6:4 or 5:6-7), as though for him these represented something on the order of a supplement or addition to the claim that Jesus is "Christ" and "Lord." For the claim embodied in a confession like "Jesus is the Christ" presupposed a teaching-pattern that presented Jesus as embodying the salvific act of the one God. The two-membered form of this reflexive confession therefore immediately reflects the "Christ-and-God" or "God-and-Christ" structure of primitive teaching-summaries or preaching-schemas, and it renders explicit what these patterns of teaching imply for the problem of "Gods many" and "lords many."

Here then is a confessional utterance — occasional in its immediate context but precedent-setting for later creeds — that departs from the standard one-member pattern of New Testament ὁμολογία by incorporating into its terms the full content of the preaching and teaching patterns to which all confessional utterance answered. Despite their functional difference, these two forms of speech interacted with and influenced each other.

If this conclusion is correct, might it be possible that the origins of the three-member baptismal confession known from the second and third centuries are likewise to be sought not in an early confessional form but in a habitual schema of teaching or preaching? Consider the following series of passages:

> . . . chosen and destined by God the Father and sanctified by the Spirit to be obedient to Jesus Christ and to be sprinkled with his blood (1 Pet. 1:2);

> But you were washed . . . sanctified . . . justified in the name of the Lord Jesus Christ and in the Spirit of our God (1 Cor. 6:11);

> But it is God who establishes us with you in Christ and has anointed us, by putting his seal on us and giving us his Spirit in our hearts as a first installment (2 Cor. 1:21-22);

> And because you are children, God has sent the Spirit of his Son into our hearts, crying "Abba! Father!" (Gal. 4:6);

> God our Savior . . . saved us . . . through the water of rebirth and renewal by the Holy Spirit. This Spirit he poured out on us richly through Jesus Christ our Savior (Tit. 3:4-6);

> . . . God chose you as the first fruits for salvation through sanctification by the Spirit and through belief in the truth . . . so that you may obtain the glory of our Lord Jesus Christ (2 Thess. 2:13-14).

Each of the passages refers (in one setting or another and for one purpose or another) to what can be called the situation or the circumstances or the status of believers. In other words, each of them refers to what has come to pass, or comes to pass, for those who find themselves in the ἐκκλησία. Moreover, each of the passages does so by referring — though in different orders and with slightly varying nomenclature — to three figures or agents: God, Christ, and the Spirit. In other words, all the passages characterize the believer's situation or status through reference to a relationship that has three terms. Except in Matthew 28:19, however, these terms are not set alongside one another in a co-ordinated list of the form "A and B and C." They occur in complex expressions or sentences, whose effect is to suggest that the relationship itself is complex even though it comes down to one thing. One might, therefore, refer to these passages as having a three-membered structure, as long as one did not intend to suggest them to have three parts or, for that matter, to assert the tri-unity of God, even though they stand at the beginning of the historical development that produced that doctrine.

Finally, most if not all of these passages occur in contexts where the subject of baptism is either under discussion or hovering immediately in the background. Baptism is certainly inherent in 1 Peter 1:2, and the two passages from Paul's Corinthian correspondence focus even more clearly on the imagery of baptism. The full passage from Titus, from a later period, explicitly declares the relationship between God's goodness and Christian baptism:

> But when the goodness and loving kindness of God our Savior appeared, he saved us, not because of any works of righteousness that we had done, but according to his mercy, through the water of rebirth and renewal by the Holy Spirit. This Spirit he poured out on us richly through Jesus Christ our Savior. (Tit. 3:4-6)

Writing to the Galatians, Paul employs such a pattern of reference not to refer directly to the meaning of initiation but rather to refer to its permanent effect as a once-for-all event: "And because you are children, God has sent the Spirit of his Son into our hearts, crying 'Abba! Father!'" (Gal. 4:6). In Ephesians, he employs this manner of speech in ethical exhortation (5:18-20) and again in a possible liturgical formula (4:4-6). Its essential relation to baptism, however, and so to the structuring realities of the Christian life, appears clearly again in 2 Thessalonians 2:13-14.

One- and two-membered teaching-patterns seem to grow out of the proclamation itself, with its recital of the work of God in the sending, the dying, and the rising of Christ. The same is not true, however, with these triadic ways of talking. If the evidence is to make any sense, one must conclude that the functional context of this mode of speech (and so of the formulas that grew out of it) is neither ὁμολογία in the strict sense nor proclamation/teaching (if by that is meant an immediate setting-forth of the ground of faith's confession), but rather explication of the new situation in which faith and baptism locate the believer. It thus seems that the three-membered pattern of speech belongs originally to some form of doctrinal catechesis associated with baptism rather than to confession or proclamation.

Does this hypothesis, though, cohere with the evidence of the instruction of the risen Christ to his disciples at Matthew 28:19? For here — or so it has seemed to generations of Christians — a triadic form of words is prescribed as an essential form of the baptismal rite:

> Go therefore and make disciples of all nations, baptizing them in the name [εἰς τὸ ὄνομα] of the Father and of the Son and of the Holy Spirit, and teaching them to obey everything that I have commanded you.

Whatever interpretation is put on this text, there can be no question of its central importance for the history of creedal forms. By the middle of the second century at the latest, baptismal formulas that conformed to the structure if not to the exact language of the expression "in the name of the Father and of the Son and of the Holy Spirit" seem to have become prevalent in the churches, and it is difficult not to suppose that these words of Matthew had some, even if not exclusive, responsibility for this development. On the other hand, if they are taken as prescribing the language — the precise words — of some baptismal formula, their presence in Matthew is difficult to account for in view of the fact that the practice they seem to inculcate is not obvious in any of the records of the first-century Christian movement. This difficulty, moreover, is not eased by the obvious step of discounting the truth-claim of Matthew's story. Even if one reads Matthew 28:19 not as *ipsissima verba Domini* but as an allusion to later ecclesiastical practice attributed to Jesus by the tradition on which the author drew, the verse could be understood as enjoining a baptismal formula only if the use of such a triadic formula were a practice so settled and unquestioned that it could be given dominical authority without appearance of innovation. Yet there is no reason to suppose that this explanation is the case. The question of how to take Matthew 28:19 therefore still remains.

To investigate the question, one must inquire more closely what might be meant by describing Matthew's words as a baptismal formula. This description of his expression can of course mean two quite different things. It may on the one hand be taken to denote what might be called a performative formula spoken by the officiant at a baptism — perhaps in the form of the declaration that came to be used at Antioch in the fourth century: "*N* is baptized in the name of. . . ." On the other hand, it may be taken to denote a baptismal confession, whether spoken by the baptizand or (on the model of what we know was later usage) spoken by the officiant in the form of questions to which the candidate responded affirmatively.

In fact, however, neither of these alternatives will do. For one thing, there is no positive evidence from the New Testament period, or for any period before the fourth century, for the use of performative baptismal formulas. There is, it is true, evidence that taken in itself is not inconsistent with the use of such formulas — most notably that of James 2:7, taken with that of Hermas's *Shepherd*.[15] These texts, however, are ambiguous. As S. New argued many years ago, they almost certainly do not make a clear reference to baptism. Furthermore, the custom that was prevalent in the later second and the third centuries seems from all indications to have been that of employing an interrogatory confession. It is therefore best, as Kelly has argued, to interpret any ambiguous testimonies, if in fact they refer to baptism, in a sense consonant with this later practice.

But even where confession — whether declaratory or interrogatory — is concerned, there is great doubt about whether such a practice was uniformly associated with baptism during the greater part of the first century. Von Campenhausen has argued eloquently that the earliest Christian baptism was "dumb" — that confession of faith was presupposed in the act itself, or preliminary to it. But this argument discounts the evidence of allusions like that of Acts 22:16, where Paul is commanded to "Rise and be baptized . . . , calling on his name" — language that suggests that in some places and at some times baptism was accompanied by Christological confession. Even with this qualification, however, von Campenhausen's thesis is true to the great mass of New Testament evidence.

Furthermore, the very language of Matthew 28:19 dispels the notion that it was intended to legislate some kind of confessional formula. As long ago as 1903, Wilhelm Heitmüller pointed out that there was originally a difference of meaning between the phrases ἐν (or ἐπὶ) τῷ ὀνόματι and εἰς τὸ ὄνομα.[16] The former regularly means 'with naming or invocation of', while the latter (to paraphrase von Campenhausen) specifies the sense or meaning of an act, that with which it involves or identifies a person. One can hardly suppose, therefore, that Matthew 28:19 is prescribing something to be said; rather, it is speaking of baptism in a way that does not merely name the act ("washing") but also gives a summary clue to its meaning.

---

15. *Similitudes* 8.1.1, 9.14.3.

16. Wilhelm Heitmüller, *"Im Namen Jesu": Eine sprach.- u. religionsgeschichtliche Untersuchung zum Neuen Testament, speziell zur altchristlichen Taufe* (Göttingen: Vandenhoeck & Ruprecht, 1903), pp. 1-127.

If this view is true, however, then Matthew 28:19 must be taken in much the same way as the other triadically shaped texts cited above. Again a triadic mode of speech is being employed to define the meaning of baptism. It is an act that directly involves the convert with Father, Son, and Holy Spirit. A number of critics have called attention to the fact that neither the terms Matthew uses (i.e., *Father, Son,* and *Spirit*) nor the precise serial order in which he sets them is reproduced in other New Testament formulations (and in particular not at 2 Corinthians 13:13). That fact is significant only if one supposes that Matthew's expression lays claim to being a fixed formula of some sort. This supposition, however, is clearly based on what later liturgical usage made of the text. As one more example of a prevalent and typical way of explaining the meaning of baptism, it occasions no difficulties at all.

My initial conclusion from this review, then, is clear. Matthew 28:19 is one of a number of instances of triadic speech, widespread in the churches of the first century, which summarize or encapsulate a way of explaining the meaning and consequences of baptism and so of the structure of Christian life. This pattern of speech cannot be regarded as a formula in any sense. Though it recurs, it is never in the proper sense repeated, and it exhibits no signs of verbal fixity. Its stability can best be accounted for by reference to the habits of understanding and exposition that lie behind it. In this respect, it is not unlike a phrase like *faith and morals,* which has a traditional and formulaic quality about it but which in fact simply epitomizes a habitual way of characterizing two structural aspects of Christian life. It is simply a catechetical commonplace.

How, though, does this catechetical commonplace enter into the prehistory of declaratory creeds? Hans-Jochen Jaschke, in his discussion of the doctrine of the Holy Spirit in Irenaeus, has argued convincingly that the triadic shape of many formulations of the so-called "Rule of Faith" in the late second and early third centuries must be attributed to the influence of a three-member baptismal formula.[17] If he is right (and I believe that in substance he is), then what this later era reveals is the gradual shaping of catechetical summaries by the baptismal confession, and the ultimate product of the process turns out to be a confessional form with a catechetical function — in a word, the declaratory creed. It is unlikely, however, that one can presuppose the existence of a triadic confession behind Matthew 28:19. Like the other first-century statements that assume such a threefold shape, this text is a distillation of catechetical practice. It appears, therefore, that in this more primitive phase of the development of Christian formulas, things were moving in a converse

---

17. Hans-Jochen Jaschke, *Der Heilige Geist im Bekenntnis der Kirche,* Münsterische Beiträge zur Theologie 40 (Münster: Aschendorff, 1976).

sense: that is, the baptismal formula (by which I mean here the baptismal confession) was growing out of the structure of the catechesis, which explained the meaning of the baptismal act.

For such a process there is, as I have tried to show, some precedent or parallel. In Paul's polemical confession at 1 Corinthians 8:6, the implicitly or explicitly dyadic form of teaching and preaching summaries has shaped a reflexive profession of faith. It is not unlikely, then, that as the tendency grew to fix the confessional moment in baptism in a form of words, the formula used should have been molded to the shape of the instruction by which the meaning of baptism was ordinarily explained. Already in Acts, as von Campenhausen has noted, there is an indication that oral confession is becoming part of the baptismal action — though the confession presupposed there seems to have been Christological. Apparently a period of transition took place during which confession was gradually ritualized as an element in the baptismal action while at the same time the triadic form embedded in the traditional explication of baptism came gradually to prevail over the one-member shape known to the author of Acts.

The phrase *from catechesis to confession and back* might then serve usefully to summarize the processes involved in the pre-history of declaratory creeds. Thus one must not exaggerate the functional distinction between what was taught (in the broadest sense of that term) and what was confessed. There are indeed two streams of development, but they mingle not infrequently, and the clearest testimony to this fact is the term that their interaction reaches, the declaratory creed itself. The debate — by now almost traditional — about whether the content of the creeds was shaped primarily by polemical and reflexive needs or simply by popular traditional processes is itself evidence of the twofold character and function of the creeds. As successors to the catechetically grounded Rule of Faith, they show every sign in their content and language of reflecting the polemical concerns that in the conditions of the second century influenced much of the content of Christian catechesis. On the other hand, as formulas whose outline and heads are determined by the tradition of confession, they also incorporate elements — including their very form — that are polemically irrelevant or neutral. It is precisely this merging of catechesis and confession, renewed at many points in the pre-history of the creeds, that constitutes the creeds as we know them.

To the extent that this statement is true, however, lucid and linear schemes of development are unlikely to fit the pre-history of declaratory creeds. The idea that the churches moved from a one- or two-member to a three-member "confession of faith" simply does not seem to fit the evidence. What is one generation's catechesis is another's confession, and *vice versa*. The triadic pattern visible in declaratory creeds is visible also in much earlier sources, though not in the form of a confession and not in a verbally fixed shape. Dyadic teaching-summaries are visible in New Testament sources and persist in certain versions of the Rule of Faith. Yet in 1 Corinthians 8:6, as later in the declaration of the Smyrnaean elders, even these are transmuted into a confessional form and seem in that guise to have influenced the content of interrogatory as well as of declaratory formulas. It is a process of mutual interaction rather than one of addition or supplementation that eventually produces the three-clause creed of the third and later centuries.

Constructing Christian Communal Identity in Early Patristic Writers

Petra Heldt

(21) Tell me, you who desire to be subject to the law, will you not listen to the law? (22) For it is written that Abraham had two sons, one by a slave woman and the other by a free woman. (23) One, the child of the slave, was born according to the flesh; the other, the child of the free woman, was born through the promise. (24) Now this is an allegory: these women are two testaments. One woman, in fact, is Hagar, from Mount Sinai, bearing children for slavery. (25) Now Hagar is Mount Sinai in Arabia and corresponds to the present Jerusalem, for she is in slavery with her children. (26) But the other woman corresponds to the Jerusalem above; she is free, and she is our mother. (27) For it is written,

> *Rejoice, you childless one, you who bear no children,*
> *burst into song and shout, you who endure no birth pangs;*
> *for the children of the desolate woman are more numerous*
> *than the children of the one who is married.*

(28) Now you, my friends, are children of the promise, like Isaac. (29) But just as at that time the child who was born according to the flesh persecuted the child who was born according to the Spirit, so it is now also. (30) But what does the scripture say? "Drive out the slave and her child; for the child of the slave will not share the inheritance with the child of the free woman." (31) So then, friends, we are children, not of the slave but of the free woman.

Galatians 4:21-31

This study concerns the reading of scripture in the second and third century A.D. in Greek texts in the Mediterranean area, exemplified in the reading of Paul's letter to the Galatians 4:21-31. This passage has long been regarded as a key text for Christians' understanding of Jews in history, especially because of its use of allegory as a method for reading scripture. Scholars have generally assumed that these writers used Galatians primarily to define Christians' understanding of Jews, so laying a foundation for blaming anti-Judaism on Paul and on this passage. But examination of patristic writers' use of the passage shows that it was not a seminal text for claiming that Christians replaced Jews.[1] Indeed patristic writers' use of the text reinforces the shift in reading Paul argued by scholars such as Krister Stendahl, Lloyd Gaston, and John Gager, who deny that Paul intended a polemic against the Jewish people or against the observance of Torah by Jews, including Jewish adherents of Jesus.[2] Rather, they explain, with this passage Paul sought to reject attempts by Judaizers to impose observance of the whole Torah upon Gentiles.

While correct in their interpretation of Paul, these same scholars are incorrect in asserting that the use of the passage for anti-Jewish purposes began as soon as Paul left the scene.[3] A Christian anti-Judaic reading of those eleven verses and their use in so-called triumphalist theology did not begin with the first authors who employed them, such as Clement of Alexandria, or indeed with any of the ancient authors discussed here. By their time, the issue of Judaizing was no longer so acute, and the anti-Jewish polemics of later times had not yet begun.[4]

Rather, these authors were fundamentally concerned with questions such as how to read scripture, how to distribute knowledge, how to establish communities, how to safeguard individualism, and how to obtain entrance to an elite. They shared a common interest in delineating an identity for their own groups of religious adherents. All of them aimed at providing identity for the Gentiles, by starting from something like the triadic cosmological concept of the Middle Platonists and then concentrating on explaining how their own group participated in salvation. Their works thus develop diverse schemes of identity that allow an informative glimpse of the process of form-

---

1. Cf. Hans Lietzmann, *An die Römer* (Tübingen: Mohr, 1971), p. 91.

2. Krister Stendahl, *Paul Among Jews and Gentiles* (Philadelphia: Fortress Press, 1976); Lloyd Gaston, *Paul and the Torah* (Vancouver: University of British Columbia Press, 1987); John Gager, *Reinventing Paul* (Oxford and New York: Oxford University Press, 2000).

3. Petra Heldt, "The Epistle of Paul to the Galatians 4:21-31 in the Reading of the Early Church: Research in Patristic Exegesis," diss., Hebrew University, pp. 16-17. Gager claims that "two thousand years of readers have misread Paul" (*Reinventing Paul*, p. 74).

4. Heldt, "The Epistle of Paul," p. 17.

ing identity in the complex and multifaceted society of political transition in the Roman Empire.

Patristic Writers and Galatians 4:21-31

Twenty-nine patristic texts of the late second and early third centuries A.D. and fifty-four texts of Origen (*c.* A.D. 185–*c.* 251) discuss Galatians 4:21-31, but no one of those eighty-three texts considers the entire passage.[5] Although one text (Tertullian's *Against Marcion* 5:4.8) employs six of the eleven verses, only three verses are significant for him.[6]

From a systematic study of these patristic texts I draw two conclusions: in all the texts the authors' literary approach is an important consideration, and each verse or group of verses is typically attached to a specific subject. The pre-Origen authors employ verses 22-24, 28, and 30 for constructing their communal identity in contemporary Roman and Greek society, but when Origen discusses the passage he develops his subject more than do his predecessors. He continues their effort, using almost the same verses — 21-24, 28, and 29 — to discuss the question of how to read the law, thereby creating an identity for the Christ-people amidst the existing peoples of the Roman Empire in the second and third centuries A.D.[7] Notions of identity already present at the time Origen and his predecessors were writing help to illuminate their intent in using these verses from Galatians.

Literary Approach: Mimesis, *skopos,* and Allegory

As the oratory of Aelius Aristides and the *Corpus Hermogenicum* (both from the Antonine Age) show, the standards of the Second Sophists influenced literature of the second century A.D. in both content and quality of approach.[8] One of the main features of the authors' approach is mimesis, a kind of imitation of

---

5. This article is based on a lecture given at the Swedish Theological Institute, Jerusalem, 6 December 2001.

6. Cf. the discussion in Heldt, "The Epistle of Paul," pp. 78-100.

7. Pre-Origen authors and Origen all employ verse 26 for discussing the place of salvation and verse 27 for discussing access to salvation. Salvation in pre-Origen authors is a metaphysical notion and in Origen a present reality; cf. Heldt, "The Epistle of Paul," pp. 140-44, 291-93, 321-28, 330-31.

8. The Antonine Age includes the reigns of Hadrian (A.D. 117-38), Antoninus Pius (A.D. 138-61), Marcus Aurelius (A.D. 161-80) and Commodus (A.D. 180-92). See Ian Rutherford, *Canons of Style in the Antonine Age* (Oxford: Clarendon Press, 1998).

the best of tradition, with figures, heroes, and events of the past presented for imitation by the present culture. B. P. Reardon says that mimesis is "un concept d'une importance capitale pour la compréhension de la littérature de cette epoche surtout."[9] It is a reference to the tradition; it is "quasi-historical," "une déja-vue"[10] that makes the present appear eclectic in its inclusion of elements from a variety of sources or periods. B. A. van Groningen pronounces a harsher verdict: "Reading the bulk of second century literature, that is to say such writings as reflect general tendencies, one is not transported into a real world, but into a sham one, in a museum of fossiles."[11]

Recent research, however, takes a kinder view of mimesis. The individual author of a period decides what is "the best of tradition" and how the "best" is presented. Analysis of a second-century author's decisions about presenting precursor texts allows the period now to be recognized as innovative rather than eclectic; mimesis can even alter culture. This point has been demonstrated by David Dawson, whose study focuses on the *skopos* — the heuristic lens or intended outcome — of three authors, Philo, Valentinus, and Clement of Alexandria. Dawson establishes that an author's *skopos* determines his reading of precursor texts.[12] The precursor texts carry an author's *skopos;* each author chooses his texts from a previous culture for mimesis but through his *skopos* adapts them to the present. Identifying an author's *skopos* reveals the way that author has read a text and shows that his reading actually expresses the understanding with which he began rather than being merely his neutral interpretation of the text. The authors shape the real world by selective use of the past.[13]

Frances M. Young has argued that this reading pattern is not arbitrary.[14] The *skopos* steers the matter of interest, which a verse in the text expresses mimetically. More often than not, the resulting verse respects the coherence of the precursor text, though, if necessary, authors may adapt a word or phrase to the subject matter through any number of rhetorical tropes, such as metaphor, par-

9. B. P. Reardon, *Courants littéraires grecs des IIe et IIIe siècles après J.-C.* (Paris: Les Belles Lettres, 1971), p. 7.

10. Cf. J. Bompaire, *Lucien écrivain: imitation et création,* Part 1: *La doctrine de la mimésis* (Paris: E. de Boccard, 1958).

11. B. A. van Groningen, "General Literary Tendencies in the Second Century A.D.," *Mnemosyne* 4th series (1965): 41–56, here 52.

12. David Dawson, *Allegorical Readers and Cultural Revision in Ancient Alexandria* (Berkeley: University of California Press, 1992).

13. This result is somewhat similar to the restoration of the Cardo in the Old City of Jerusalem. The Cardo is now both a living quarter of the present, embellished with selected features from the past, and a monument of the past, presented in modern dress.

14. Frances M. Young, *Biblical Exegesis and the Formation of Christian Culture* (Cambridge [UK]: Cambridge University Press, 1997).

able, syncrisis, hypodeigma, periphrasis, anakephalaiosis, prosopopoeia, hyperbole, and paraenesis. In the fourth or fifth century, Adrianus, of the Antiochene tradition, compiled a list of around two dozen such tropes in his *Isagoge ad sacras scripturas.*[15]

Although Adrianus includes allegory only briefly in the middle of his list, it is one of the common tools used by the pre-Origen authors to assist them in their use of precursor texts. Adrianus wrote some two centuries after these authors, but his list and the place of allegory in that list confirm what study of their writing reveals, that they employed allegory as a tool, not a method, to "read something else" for a word or two in a precursor text in order to adjust that text to the mimesis and the *skopos,* so imitating previous events and adapting them to the present. Thus the reality of the present seems to be part of another reality, as if one looked into a mirror, always seeing reality laterally inverted. But this reality is far from inventing one's own reality and imposing it upon the present reality, as is the case when one uses allegory not merely as an occasional tool but as a systematic method. Neither pre-Origen authors nor Origen employs allegory as a method in reading Galatians 4:21-31. Origen might be thought to be on the way of developing an imaginary reality and imposing it on present reality, but the method he uses is still that of mimesis.[16]

While mimesis is a basic element of these authors' literary approach, their literary content is governed by *paideia,* the concept of educating the leadership of Greek society by means of reading lists of classic works known from the Second Sophists and Middle Platonists. The Second Sophists revived Plato, in particular the cosmology of his dialogue *Timaeus.* Themes such as ethics, physics *(Logos),* and the Platonic underworld dominate the thought of the Middle Platonists,[17] culminating in the traditions of the Valentinian school, traditions that provided a starting point for reference to verses from Galatians 4:21-31.

The Notion of Identity in the Second Century A.D.

Identity is the subject matter typically attached to Galatians 4:22-24, 28, and 30. This is a topic of great concern in the second century A.D. Most of the pre-

15. Frances M. Young, "The Fourth Century Reaction Against Allegory," *Studia Patristica* 30 (1997): 120-25.

16. Cassian's fifth-century invention of Origen's threefold or fourfold method found its way into the western tradition and has influence even today. For an extensive discussion of this topic see Heldt, "The Epistle of Paul," pp. 198-204.

17. John Dillon, *The Middle Platonists, 80 B.C. to A.D. 220* (Ithaca: Cornell University Press, 1996), pp. 384-89.

Origen authors write within the Antonine period. In that time, characteristics of Roman citizenship changed rapidly, from being a citizen by being part of the military, to being a citizen despite not having a public function, to — a high point, in the *Constitutio Antoniana* (Act of Caracalla, A.D. 211-17) — all free inhabitants of the empire being offered Roman citizenship.[18] This last event took place during the very time that Origen was writing.

These shifting regulations regarding citizenship created new realities.[19] Identity came to be seen not as an eternal given, says Rebecca Preston, "but as something actively constructed and contested, based on subjective, not objective criteria. The formation of identity is a process of self-definition in opposition to other identities; it relies as much on differences from others as on similarities."[20] That is, identity involves an objective reality, but identifying it is a subjective process. Struggle for the control of meaning is central to the distribution of power in society. The cultural authority is bound up with political authority. Presenting identity is, as Preston points out, "a complex process of construction, negotiation, and contestation,"[21] fully employing mimesis and *paideia* for creative imitation and ultimately altering culture. An example is Plutarch's *Parallel Lives,* historical biographies juxtaposing famous Greeks and Romans, with Plutarch (*c.* A.D. 40-120) encouraging his peers to imitate their examples. He expresses his concern about identity by showing a complex struggle between the classical Greeks and the Romans, and between past and present identity. His work is thus a paradigm for the process of searching for identity in the second century.

Pre-Origen authors and Origen are part of this tradition. In fact, the pre-Origen authors' use of Galatians 4:22-24, 28, and 30 and Origen's use of Galatians 4:21-24, 28, and 29 give insight into the process of building identities. A number of different groups can be identified in the texts of pre-Origen authors, including Theodotus, Valentinians, millenarians, philosophers, Judeans, Gentiles, different parties of the church, Marcionites, and adherents of "the *Logos* [that] became flesh." Some of these groups already had a place in the world, while others wished to gain a place in the world. The single question of

18. A. N. Sherwin-White, *The Roman Citizenship,* 2d ed. (Oxford: The Clarendon Press, 1996), pp. 264-74, 279-87.

19. Tim Whitmarsh, "'Greece Is the World': Exile and Identity in the Second Sophistic," in *Being Greek Under Rome: Cultural Identity, the Second Sophistic and the Development of Empire,* ed. Simon Goldhill (Cambridge [UK] and New York: Cambridge University Press, 2001), pp. 269-305, here p. 272.

20. Rebecca Preston, "Roman Questions, Greek Answers: Plutarch and the Construction of Identity," in Goldhill, ed., *Being Greek under Rome,* pp. 86-122, here p. 87.

21. Preston, "Roman Questions," p. 88.

what identified a group got any number of answers. Most of these answers were incomplete, since the reporting author (e.g., Clement) often did not represent the reported author (e.g., Theodotus) extensively or accurately. The pre-Origen authors were also highly concerned with determining the means to and nature of salvation, which played a key element in their construction of identity.

Identity in Pre-Origen Authors

Clement of Alexandria (A.D. 150-215) reported on Theodotus, the head of the Valentinian school in the East in the second century A.D.[22] Theodotus *per se* seems to have been rooted in the Middle Platonic triadic cosmology, which, however, according to Clement's reporting, he obviously read anthropologically, thus reducing it to a dual cosmology. In his reading the Middle Platonic triadic cosmology mutated into the three anthropological classes: the spiritual class saved by nature, the intellectual class choosing whether to be saved, and the material class lost by nature. The three classes now face two cosmological realms, namely saved or lost. Theodotus ascribed identity to the first two classes by mimesis from a precursor text, Romans 11:17 and 24, in which the saved intellectuals "are grafted into the olive tree." He identified Israel with the first class and believing Gentiles with the second, yet he integrated such Gentiles into the first class, which he said needed the Gentiles for completion, though he did not explain what kind of completion he understood. For him Gentiles were identified through Israel, and Israel was identified by the integration of the Gentiles.

Clement of Alexandria, who transmitted Theodotus's teaching, quotes Theodotus's work in order to disagree with it, for "Israel" allegorically reading "to see God," as in Genesis 33:10: "And Jacob [Israel] said: . . . I see your face as one sees the face of God." So Clement presents the spiritual class by way of mimesis from Galatians 4:22, identifying that class with the "rightful son of Abraham, of the free woman." He identifies the fleshly or material class, which is thus lost, with the "son according to the flesh, of the Egyptian slave woman" (Galatians 4:23). On the one hand, Clement abolishes the triadic cosmological system and works with a dual one, categorized by saved and lost; on the other hand, he adopts Theodotus's triadic anthropology but modifies the division.

---

22. The text under discussion is Clement of Alexandria, *Excerpts from Theodotus* 56:2. The Greek text is in *Clemens Alexandrinus*, vol. 3: *Stromata. Bücher VII und VIII, Excerpta ex Theodoto–Eclogae Propheticae. Quis Dives Salvatur–Fragmente*, ed. Otto Stählin, GCS 17 (Leipzig: J. C. Hinrichs'sche Buchhandlung, 1909), pp. 103-33; cf. the English rendition of Robert Pierce Casey, ed. and trans., *The Excerpta ex Theodoto of Clement of Alexandria*, Studies and Documents 1 (London: Christophers, 1934).

Where Theodotus has three groups — Israel, saved Gentiles, and lost Gentiles — so dividing the Gentiles into two groups, Clement divides the category "Israel" into two classes, "to see God" and "not to see God." Both classes are of the same origin, from Abraham, but are divided according to their mothers, because identity comes from the mother. The *skopos* of Clement presents the embodied *Logos,* which works for all mankind. Thus the two classes have the same origin but a different upbringing, a point he elaborates in his *Miscellanies.*

In *Miscellanies* 1.53.2 Clement draws attention to the identity of adherents of the embodied *Logos* as against the identity of philosophers.[23] Both depend on the *Logos*[24] but live with it differently, so that adherents of the embodied *Logos* are saved and philosophers are not saved. He presents this position through the mimesis of the two women in Galatians 4:30. Philosophers have no part of salvation; they are children of the slave woman, presenting *propaedeutica.* But believers — those who will be saved — receive the *Logos* as a free gift, detached from past or future and thus from inheritance. Adherents of the embodied *Logos* will be saved, for they are the result of a promise that includes both past and future and thus inheritance. Thus whether or not the *Logos* is embodied determines the identity of the saved class.

In *David and Goliath* 7:2, Hippolytus (*c.* A.D. 170-236) also roots identity in a triadic cosmology turned into a triadic anthropology, in which the first two classes (those of concern here) are defined by an end-time battle, with the redeemer (the first class) standing on a mountain and his supporters (the second) fighting with him from another mountain. Some of them will survive. According to this reading the third class has already perished in the valley.[25] The first class is the one with the redeemer standing on one mountain, and the second class is those fighting with him from another mountain, some of whom will survive.

Hippolytus's end-time battle has two precursor texts. The first, which provides the mimesis for the three classes, is 1 Samuel 17: "And the Philistines stood on the mountain on one side while Israel stood on the mountain on the other side, with the valley between them." The second precursor text is Galatians 4:24: "Now this is an allegory: these are two covenants. One is from

23. The Greek text is in Stählin, *Clemens Alexandrinus;* cf. the English rendition of John Ferguson, trans., *Stromateis: Books One to Three,* FOC 85 (Washington, DC: Catholic University of America Press, 1991).

24. On Middle Platonic notions of the *Logos,* see Dillon, *The Middle Platonists,* pp. 160-66.

25. The text is edited by Gérard Garitte, *Traités d'Hippolyte sur David et Goliath, sur le Cantique de Cantiques et sur l'Antéchrist,* CSCO 263 (Louvain: Sécretariat du CSCO, 1965), pp. 1-23.

Mount Sinai, bearing children for slavery; she is Hagar." This verse provides the allegorical tool for reading the "two testaments" in the verse as the "two mountains," the mimesis for the two classes that will be part of salvation. The first class mimetically shows David, from whom the redeemer comes. The second class mimetically shows the foreigners — unbelieving Gentiles — preparing for war. The first testament entails the story of David; the second shows the grace that the name of the redeemer brings to the unbelieving Gentiles. The identity of Gentiles is that of being reached out to by grace and kept apart from Israel in the time of salvation. Thus the triadic cosmology remains intact. This representation differs from Theodotus's concept, in which a dual cosmology results from the absorption of the saved Gentiles into Israel.

Irenaeus (*c.* A.D. 130-200) develops another aspect of identity in *Against Heresies* 5:32.2, in response to the question of whether divine promises are also valid for Gentile martyrs.[26] His affirmative answer runs like this: God gave promises to Abraham but has not yet fulfilled some of them. Those who have faith like Abraham's, however, will see the promises fulfilled in the end. The mimesis for Gentiles' faith comes from the reference to Isaac in Galatians 4:28; for Gentiles their faith counts the same as for Isaac, for believing in the promises is having a part in them. But unlike Isaac, the Gentiles are not of Abraham's seed in the fleshly sense.

Irenaeus gives three definitions of what it means to be of Abraham's seed.[27] Fear and belief in God, he says, are the first meaning of being of Abraham's seed, as is seen in the church. A second way to be of Abraham's seed is to be adopted to God through Christ, because believing in Christ means receiving Christ, and as Christ is of Abraham's seed, he is the seed for Gentiles. Those of faith are also the children of Abraham, and therefore the Gentiles are blessed in Abraham. Thus Gentile martyrs will also receive the divine promises.

For Irenaeus, then, the identity of the Gentiles lies in their faith in the promises given to Abraham. They are adopted by Christ, who is of Abraham's seed; through this seed they also are of Abraham's seed. Abraham's faith defines Gentile identity, developed mimetically from the heroes Abraham and Isaac. As this kind of faith prepares for salvation, Irenaeus employs neither a cosmological nor an anthropological classification.

In *Against Marcion* 5:48, Tertullian (*c.* A.D. 200) reports on the *Apostolicon* of Marcion (d. *c.* A.D. 154).[28] Marcion's argument lies in the mimesis of

26. The text is published by Adelin Rousseau, Louis Doutreleau, and Charles Mercier, eds., *Irénée de Lyon: Contre les Hérésies. Livre 5.1, 2*, SC 152, 153 (Paris: Éditions du Cerf, 1969).

27. Note that Judeans are not mentioned in this passage.

28. The text is in Ernest Evans, ed. and trans., *Tertullian: Adversus Marcionem, Books 1 to 3* (Oxford: Clarendon Press, 1972).

Galatians 4:22-24. Tertullian, however, quotes the text not as it is known today but in the following form, probably interlacing it with his own comments, which appear here within parentheses:

[22b, c] Abraham had two sons, one by the slave woman and the other by the free woman, [23] but he that was by the slave woman was born after the flesh while he that was by the free woman was by promise, [24a] which things are allegorical (which means indicative of something else); [24b] for these are the two revelations, [24c] the one from Mount Sinai (referring to the synagogue of the Judeans), which (according to the law) engenders slavery: (the other engendering [Eph. 1:21] "above all principality, power, and domination, and every name that is named not only in this world but also in that which is to come": [26c] for she is) "our mother."

Marcion's text probably followed verses 22-24 but contained the change in 24 without the insertion of Ephesians 1:21: "which things are allegorical [*allegorica*] . . . for these are the two revelations [*ostensiones*], the one from Mount Sinai . . . engenders slavery."[29] Thus the "two sons" become "two revelations" of two gods, creating two peoples. Marcion's group develops its identity by belonging to a newly revealed god. In contrast, Tertullian presents the *skopos* of the adaptation of Gentiles by God and their particular obligation to the law explained to them by Christ. The "two sons" are the two peoples, Judeans and Christians, set parallel to each other and with different obligations.

All of these authors are involved in the process of providing identity for Gentiles, starting from something like the triadic cosmological concept of the Middle Platonists and then concentrating on the means to salvation for their own group. A picture of diverse schemes of identity emerges from their views:

- Gentiles are grafted into Israel, being cosmologically one with them (Theodotus, from the Romans 11:17 imagery of being grafted into the olive tree);
- Humankind is divided by its upbringing according to the *Logos* (Clement of Alexandria, from the two women of Galatians 4:22–23);
- Embodied *Logos* adherents and philosophers differ according to the way they understand the *Logos* and so whether or not they share in salvation (Clement of Alexandria, from the two women of Galatians 4:30);
- Gentiles are saved by grace but cosmologically separated from Israel (Hippolytus, from the two testaments of Galatians 4:24);

29. *ostensiones* = 'revealing', not *testamentum* = *fixum*.

- Gentiles are sons of Abraham by faith and by adoption (Irenaeus, from Isaac in Galatians 4:28);
- A new God brings new identity (Marcion, from the two sons in Galatians 4:22);
- Two sons of Abraham produce two peoples, the one defined by the law from Sinai, the other by the law of Christ. Both laws are valid but not interchangeable (Tertullian, from the two sons of Galatians 4:22).

Origen

Origen (*c.* A.D. 185–*c.* 251) employed Galatians 4:21-24, 28, and 29[30] for establishing an identity of the Christ-people.[31] Unlike his predecessors, who established identity largely through a process of negotiating and contesting, Origen concentrated on constructing by similarity, with two focal points: the Greek and Roman political culture concerning the law, and Scripture. He aimed to establish an identity for the present life, not for the time of salvation. Yet salvation remained a key element in his construction of identity.

Greek and Roman Political Culture

In Greek and Roman culture, the law defined identity. Origen adapted four central aspects of this concept for constructing identity for the Christ-people:

1. As Aristotle had noted, for the Greeks *nomos* was of divine origin, delivered by wise men and divinely inspired. Thus hearing *(akouein)* the divine voice was important for "understanding" the law. The scribe *(grammateus)* must read out the *nomos* in public, but he should be hearing and not merely reading *(anaignōskein)* it. Origen makes much use of this feature when employing verse 21. His conflation of two existing textual variants results in: "Tell me, you who read the law, do you not hear the law?" His phrasing expresses qualities for the reading of scripture expected to be like those of public readers of the law (Gal. 4:21).

2. Greek culture, as seen for example in Aristotle and Xenophon, distinguished between the written law and the unwritten law (natural law), both be-

---

30. The following is a summary of the analysis of twenty-six texts in the *corpus* of Origen that employ Gal. 4:21-24, 28, and 29; see Heldt, "The Epistle of Paul," pp. 248-47. For text editions see Henri Crouzel, *Origen* (Edinburgh: T&T Clark, 1989), pp. xiii-xiv.

31. When employing Gal. 4:27, Origen constantly speaks of the Christ-people as the *ethnos* but calls the non-Christ people *laos*.

ing of divine origin. Origen, however, presented both written law and natural law as Scripture, through which people are defined (Gal. 4:22-23).

3. In Greek and Roman culture, the Greek *nomos* meant 'constitution' and the Latin *lex* meant 'the authoritative law' of a sovereign power in the state, enforced by the state. A similar difference appears in Origen's texts. Some of them present parts of Scripture as *nomos;* those parts rule and function like a constitution and are not meant to be kept like individual *leges,* items of authoritative law. Origen regards the laws of marriage and circumcision as *nomos* (Gal. 4:21-24).

4. The Attic context distinguishes between the *koinon,* a united body of citizens of equal standing under the law, and the *perioikoi,* provincials, serfs, and slaves who could gain certain privileges. The Torah distinguishes between the rights of Jewish and non-Jewish people. Origen draws on both Greek-Roman and Hebrew concepts of exclusion and division when defining a Christ-people and a non-Christ people. By this approach, the way the law is read defines the people (Gal. 4:21-24).

Origen mimetically constructs his methodology for developing a people according to the Greek and Roman culture yet keeps it always connected with Hebrew culture. His description of the features of the Christ-people and the non-Christ people derives from the mimesis in Galatians 4:22-24.

Scripture

According to Origen's interpretation the two testaments of Galatians 4:24 provide the mimesis for the two peoples. By divine choice, one testament leads through Christ to water by the spirit and to freedom for those who are heirs of the divine promise by adoption: the Christ-people. The other testament leads to the desert for fleshly people who, although a great nation with divine blessings and gifts, are in both sensate and literal slavery: the non-Christ people. In one text Origen calls them Judeans, but in other texts he does not make such a specific identification.

Tensions exist between the two peoples. Origen describes the non-Christ people as troublemakers who stir up malicious charges, lie in ambush, contrive hostilities, and persecute. Who are the non-Christ people? With the exception of the one time he calls them Judeans, the characteristics he gives them indicate a general if conservative collection of law-obeying cultures, e.g. Valentinians, Judeans, Ebionites, etc. But the precise identification of the non-Christ people is of no great interest to Origen, as his goal is to give an identity to a new people, the Christ-people.

Origen discusses three kinds of difficulties for preserving the identity of the Christ-people: (1) dualism between flesh and spirit in each individual (Galatians 4:29), (2) dualism between love and fear of God within the Christ-people (Galatians 4:22, with its two sons, one of whom serves God from fear and one from love, the latter superior to the former), and (3) the Christ-people's forgetting that their origin lies in the divine promise of adoption (Galatians 4:23). Each of the three kinds of challenges has the potential to disrupt the Christ-people, he says, through neglect of the law.

Summary

In works both by predecessors of Origen and by Origen, the use of Galatians 4:21-24 as a mimesis of the authors' self-definitions of their groups' identities, suiting those definitions to their own needs and goals, exposes readers to the complexities of negotiating identity in the Roman Empire at the time of the Second Sophists and shortly after. None of the writers eliminates any category of people — any believing or unbelieving group — nor do they oppose insiders to outsiders, believers to unbelievers. Rather, those debating employ differences and similarities in ways of reading the verses from Galatians creatively, thus constructing, negotiating, and contesting positions. Each employs precursor texts to establish his own *skopos* in the form of mimesis. The present reenacts past events, times, and heroes, and the past is changed by each author's intentional use of precursor texts.

A Meaning Worthy of God: Origen and Scripture in a Pre-Constantinian Age

Patrick Terrell Gray

The increased recent interest in the patristic period is not without reason. In an age of theologically diverse opinions, it is natural for Christians to seek some justification for their beliefs in the work of their predecessors. The writings of Athanasius and the Cappadocian Fathers have been of immense value in current debates, particularly in those surrounding the doctrine of the Trinity.[1] Yet those who deal with doctrine must also examine the patristic use of scripture, as almost all patristic literature is in some way concerned with interpreting the Bible.[2] The hermeneutics of Athanasius and the Cappadocians surely merits the attention it has received, but what of Origen, their predecessor?[3] The evidence

---

An earlier version of this article appeared in *Quodlibet Journal* 4.4 (2002); http://www.Quodlibet.net/gray-origen.shtml.

1. See *The Forgotten Trinity: The Report of the B.C.C. Study Commission on Trinitarian Doctrine Today* (London: British Council of Churches, Inter-Church House, 1989); Thomas F. Torrance, *The Trinitarian Faith: The Evangelical Theology of the Ancient Catholic Church* (Edinburgh: T&T Clark, 1988); John D. Zizioulas, *Being as Communion: Studies in Personhood and the Church* (Crestwood, NY: St. Vladimir's Seminary Press, 1985); Colin E. Gunton, *The Promise of Trinitarian Theology* (Edinburgh: T&T Clark, 1991).

2. Joseph W. Trigg, *Biblical Interpretation* (Wilmington, DE: Michael Glazier, 1988), p. 11. Trigg later notes, "Origen's work was the single most significant influence on the later development of Patristic biblical interpretation, not only in Alexandria, but in the church as a whole" (p. 26).

3. Torrance hardly mentions Origen in his recent collection of essays on patristic hermeneutics, perhaps judging his essay on Clement of Alexandria to encompass all that is best (or worst) in Origen as well (Thomas F. Torrance, *Divine Meaning: Studies in Patristic Hermeneutics*

of Origen's great impact on them is unmistakable in the compilation that the Cappadocians Basil (the Great) and Gregory Nazianzen made of the *Philocalia,* an anthology of Origen's writings. But today's question is whether Origen's writings are equally compelling and relevant in the first decade of the twenty-first century.

This paper briefly reviews the theological diversity of Origen's era, examines Origen's view of scripture, and explores the implications of Origen's view of scripture for Christian life and morality.

Origen's Theologically Diverse Age

Origen, born in Egypt *c.* 185, came from an age that did not experience the benefits of Constantine's victory at the Milvian Bridge. It was in fact a time when belief in Christianity could result in martyrdom, as the Christian process of spiritual conversion was hostile to the pagan religions of the Roman Empire. The Empire therefore viewed Christianity as a personal threat and often violently demonstrated its hostility towards Christianity. One result was the killing of Origen's father, a Christian, during the persecution in Alexandria in 202. As Eusebius of Caesarea explains, Origen, even as a young boy, had a longing also to be martyred:

> His one ambition was to come to grips with danger and charge headlong into the conflict. Indeed, he was within a hair's breadth of arriving at the end of his days, when for the benefit of mankind the providence of Almighty God used his mother to defeat his ambition. She first appealed to him in words, begging him to spare his mother's feelings for him; then, when the news that his father had been arrested and imprisoned filled his whole being with a craving for martyrdom, and she saw that he was more determined than ever, she hid all his clothing and compelled him to stay at home.[4]

[Edinburgh: T&T Clark, 1995]). Torrance, however, does give Origen credit for being the first "to discern the philosophical significance of [the] reversal of Aristotelian and Stoic concepts, in establishing the connection between the transcendence of God and the rationality of nature, thus delivering the universe from being shut up in the futility of being unable to offer any explanation of its own rationality" (Thomas F. Torrance, *Space, Time and Incarnation* [London and New York: Oxford University Press, 1969], p. 12).

4. Eusebius, *The History of the Church from Christ to Constantine,* trans. G. A. Williamson (New York: Penguin Books, 1989), VI.2, p. 180. Origen's wish for a true testing of his faith was fulfilled in 250 during the persecution of Decius, when Origen was "imprisoned and subjected

Benjamin Drewery remarks of this story that "one is reminded of the felon who walked to the gallows under an umbrella, lest he should catch cold!"[5]

Despite the threat of martyrdom, Origen consistently engaged his culture. He was the greatest thinker of his day, always writing to convince others, says John Clark Smith, of "the importance of Christian life and why a person should become a Christian."[6] His great work *Contra Celsum* was a reasoned answer to the attacks of the pagan philosopher Celsus, who in his *True Discourse* criticized the exclusive claims of Christianity as well as the doctrine of the incarnation. Certainly many of Origen's theological works, particularly *De Principiis (On First Principles)*, need to be seen as attempts to speak apologetically to the educated Greco-Roman culture around him, with its menagerie of pagan philosophies, mystery cults, Gnostic groups, and oriental religions.[7] His methodology was defined not by this culture but rather by mission to it. And his constant reference to pagan philosophies brought him success at this venture. The Alexandrian school at which he was the instructor (dubbed by Drewery the "first Christian University")[8] attracted not only Christians but pagans as well.

Nor was Origen a stranger to Christian sects and heresies. Much of his biblical work was written in response to the Marcionites, who believed, as the *Oxford Dictionary of the Christian Church* puts it, that "the Christian Gospel was wholly a Gospel of Love to the absolute exclusion of Law."[9] This belief implied that the God of the Old Testament (the Creator God or Demiurge) had nothing to do with the God of Jesus Christ. Origen attempted to maintain the integrity of the Bible by showing that the Creator God and the Redeeming God are one and the same.[10] Other heretics whom Origen opposed included the

---

to prolonged torture, which he survived only a few years" ("Origen," *The Oxford Dictionary of the Christian Church,* ed. F. L. Cross and E. A. Livingstone, 3rd ed. [Oxford: Oxford University Press, 1997], p. 1193). Origen wrote his ascetical work, *Exhortation to Martyrdom,* during the persecution of Maximin in 235. See *Alexandrian Christianity,* trans. John Oulton and Henry Chadwick (London: SCM Press, 1954), pp. 388-429.

5. Benjamin Drewery, *Origen and the Doctrine of Grace* (London: The Epworth Press, 1960), pp. 1-2.

6. John Clark Smith, *The Ancient Wisdom of Origen* (Cranbury, NJ: Associated University Presses, 1992), p. 15.

7. Was Origen a Platonist? Yes; what else would he have been? But he was not interested in converting people to Platonism (or any other philosophical system) but rather in converting people to Christ. In fact, an argument can be made that whenever Origen talked about philosophy, he criticized it.

8. Drewery, *Origen and the Doctrine of Grace,* p. 2.

9. "Marcion," in *The Oxford Dictionary of the Christian Church,* p. 1034.

10. Origen was not the only one to challenge Marcion and his followers. The defenders of

Anthropomorphites, who took literally the anthropomorphisms that the Bible attributes to God and the soul and therefore pictured God as corporeal.[11] Henri Crouzel describes the "Great Church" as full of Gnostic sects, Marcionites, Montanists, Modalists, Adoptionists, and Chiliasts, just to name a few.[12] Origen's situation may not have been as bad as Athanasius's, calling forth *Origen contra mundum,* but it was certainly a theologically diverse time, even within the "Great Church."

Despite the theological diversity of Origen's time, the argument might be made that that era, one of violence and martyrdom, is entirely different from today's, when Christianity is often considered irrelevant to the world, by those both outside and inside the church. If only someone were martyred for their faith in our day and age, someone might say. If the world would only pay attention to us. Yet despite the abuses of Christian religious rights in the world today,[13] Christianity is today a global religion; Origen's insights may be more relevant than citizens of the West may recognize. For the life of faith makes an impact on the world and on its inhabitants, whether they notice it or not.

Origen's View of Scripture

How much of a biblical scholar was Origen? He was certainly not merely a philosopher, as some of his critics would argue, but a trained grammarian.[14] Unfortunately only fragments survive of his famous *Hexapla,* a massive compilation of the Old Testament[15] with the Hebrew text in one column,[16] a Greek transliteration of the Hebrew in another, and the four Greek translations of Aquila, Symmachus, the Septuagint, and Theodotion, all similarly in parallel

---

orthodoxy against this heresy included Irenaeus of Lyons, Theophilus of Antioch, Tertullian at Carthage, and Hippolytus at Rome ("Marcion," p. 1034).

11. Henri Crouzel, *Origen,* trans. A. S. Worrall (San Francisco: Harper & Row, 1989), p. 155.

12. Crouzel, *Origen,* pp. 153-56.

13. See Paul A. Marshall, *Their Blood Cries Out* (Dallas: Word Publishing, 1997).

14. Gerald Watson, "Origen and the Literal Interpretation of Scripture," in *Scriptural Interpretation in the Fathers: Letter and Spirit,* ed. Thomas Finan and Vincent Twomey (Cambridge [UK]: Cambridge University Press, 1995), p. 80.

15. Eusebius, however, writes that the *Hexapla* consisted of the Psalms, with no mention of the complete Old Testament (*History of the Church* VI.16, p. 194).

16. Eusebius commented, "So meticulous was the scrutiny to which Origen subjected the Scriptural books that he even mastered the Hebrew language, and secured for himself a copy, in the actual Hebrew script, of the original documents circulating among the Jews" (*History of the Church* VI.16, p. 193).

columns.[17] But Origen was more than an editor. The main body of his work comprised commentaries and homilies on books of the Bible, all generally expounding the biblical texts line by line.[18] It was such exposition of the scriptures that was, as Gerald Watson puts it, "the centre of his life."[19] Origen was also prolific. Epiphanius claimed that Origen wrote approximately six thousand volumes during his career![20] Although the number is no doubt an exaggeration, Origen's output was undoubtedly vast, covering most of the biblical books.

Origen gave such meticulous attention to each letter of scripture because he considered every jot and tittle important, for each word was the very word of God. In this sense, he had an exalted view of scripture. According to him the Bible was indeed inspired, and Origen thought of it, as Crouzel has pointed out, as being rather like dictation from the Holy Spirit.[21] The Bible, then, could not be treated like any other human book. There was nothing useless in scripture, since the Holy Spirit, the author of the Bible, would not give anything useless, and therefore everything in scripture had meaning.[22] Origen scholar Ronald Heine notes Origen's insistence on this role of the Holy Spirit: "We will not understand the way Origen reads the Bible if we miss this basic point, that it is always the Holy Spirit who speaks in the text of the Bible."[23]

17. Crouzel writes, "Scholars are not agreed on the motives that led Origen to undertake such a gigantic task: to facilitate the controversy of the Christians with the Jews by showing the former the text which the latter accepted; to recover, behind the various mistakes of the copyists, the primitive text of the Septuagint by choosing variants from the other versions, or even through the literal translation of Aquila and the more literary one of Symmachus to try to get back to the primitive Hebrew text itself" (Crouzel, *Origen,* p. 41).

18. Much of Origen's work was destroyed after he was condemned (unfairly, some argue) as a heretic at the Fifth Ecumenical Council, but 279 homilies survive, on such books as Genesis, Judges, Jeremiah, the Song of Songs, and the Gospel of Luke.

19. Watson, "Origen and the Literal Interpretation of Scripture," p. 78.

20. C. Bammel, "Origen's Pauline Prefaces and the Chronology of His Pauline Commentaries," *Origeniana Sexta* [*Origen and the Bible*] (Leuven: Leuven University Press, 1995), p. 495.

21. Crouzel, *Origen,* p. 71.

22. Origen gives as a proof of the Holy Spirit's authorship of the Bible the rapid spread of Christianity. He writes, "Now we can see how in a short time this religion has grown up, making progress through the persecution and death of its adherents and through their endurance of confiscation of property and every kind of torture. And this is particularly wonderful since its teachers themselves are neither very skillful nor very numerous" (Origen, *On First Principles,* trans. G. W. Butterworth [London: SPCK, 1936], p. 258).

23. Ronald Heine, "Reading the Bible with Origen," in *The Bible in Greek Christian Antiquity,* ed. Paul M. Blowers (Notre Dame, IN: University of Notre Dame Press, 1997), p. 132.

But Origen's idea of inspiration differs dramatically from a modern fundamentalist approach to scripture. For one thing, Origen did not believe that the inspiration of the scriptures guaranteed the accuracy of the historical and scientific information in the Bible.[24] In fact, even to produce certainty on almost certain events was extremely difficult, he declared in *Contra Celsum:* "we must say that an attempt to substantiate almost any story as historical fact, even if it is true, and to produce complete certainty about it, is one of the most difficult tasks and in some cases is impossible."[25] He recognized the presence in scripture of historical and textual discrepancies, such as the difference in chronology and geography concerning the story of Jesus' cleansing the temple.[26] Yet since the scriptures are inspired by the Spirit, they cannot contain errors, he declared, and three times in his commentaries, according to Robert M. Grant, he "explicitly states that inspiration implies freedom from error."[27]

One difficulty that Origen had to resolve was how the scriptures could be free from error, even if inspired by the Holy Spirit, when they contain such obvious problems. He held that the apparent distortion of historical information resulted not from some scribal or other literary error but was purposefully put into the text by the Holy Spirit as a reminder that readers must not depend on a purely historical reading:

> . . . the divine wisdom has arranged for certain stumbling-blocks and interruptions of the historical sense to be found therein, by inserting in the midst a number of impossibilities and incongruities, in order that the very interruption of the narrative might as it were present a barrier to the reader and lead him to refuse to proceed along the pathway of the ordinary meaning: and so, by shutting us out and debarring us from that, might recall us to the beginning of another way, and might thereby bring us, through the entrance of a narrow footpath, to a higher and loftier road and lay open the immense breadth of the divine wisdom.[28]

24. Heine, "Reading the Bible with Origen," p. 132.

25. Origen, *Contra Celsum* 1.42, trans. Henry Chadwick (Cambridge [UK]: Cambridge University Press, 1965), p. 39.

26. The Synoptics (Matt. 21:12-17; Mark 11:15-19; Luke 19:45-48), compared with John (2:13-25).

27. Robert M. Grant, *The Earliest Lives of Jesus* (New York: Harper & Brothers Publishers, 1961), p. 54. According to Karen Jo Torjesen, the basic criticism of Origen in the seventeenth century was not that his allegories were fanciful but rather that his interpretations depreciated history (*Hermeneutical Procedure and Theological Method in Origen's Exegesis* [Berlin: Walter de Gruyter and Co., 1985], p. 2).

28. *De Principiis* IV.II.9, in Butterworth, trans., *On First Principles*, p. 286.

Thus what may appear as errors is intended by the Holy Spirit to call the reader's attention to "the impossibility of the literal sense" and therefore to signal the need for "an examination of the inner meaning."[29]

The inner meaning of scripture is what the Spirit intends to communicate in the words of the Bible, and it is the job of the interpreter to seek this spiritual meaning. The interpretive method employed by Origen is one that was already popular as he began to expound scripture, a rhetorical approach that Heine explains as used by the philosophers "to find symbolic meaning in the texts of Homer and the other poets," the allegorical method.[30] So for example in a commentary on the Psalms of which only a fragment survives, Origen uses allegory to explain the spiritual meaning of Psalm 68:13 ("Though they stay among the sheepfolds — the wings of a dove covered with silver, its pinions with green gold"): "Some people say that the lots [sheepfolds] and feathers are the Old and New Testaments; others the practical and contemplative life; others knowledge of corporeal and incorporeal substances; others the knowledge of God and of Christ who was sent by him."[31] In his era, allegory was in the air; he used it as an instance of "spoiling the Egyptians," or, in this case, spoiling Greek philosophy.[32] But Origen does not accept allegory because of its use by the phi-

29. *De Principiis* IV.II.9, p. 287. At the time, however, many condemned Origen for a too-literal reading of scripture, perhaps leading him to castrate himself. Eusebius wrote, "Origen did a thing that provided the fullest proof of a mind youthful and immature, but at the same time of faith and self-mastery. The saying 'there are eunuchs who made themselves eunuchs for the kingdom of heaven's sake' he took in an absurdly literal sense, and he was eager both to fulfil the Saviour's words and at the same time to rule out any suspicion of vile imputations on the part of unbelievers. For in spite of his youth he discussed religious problems before a mixed audience. So he lost no time in carrying out the Saviour's words, endeavouring to do it unnoticed by the bulk of his pupils" (*History of the Church*, VI.8, p. 186). Most Origen scholars, however, consider Eusebius's story spurious.

30. Heine, "Reading the Bible with Origen," p. 135. Perhaps *method* is the wrong term to use in association with Origen's use of allegory, for as Torjesen writes, "Allegory, understood as method, appears to make the claim of being an instrument or technique for research. But as a scientific method it fails to conform to canons of method — objectivity, consistency, repeatability. The problem with allegory is that it is an utterly unscientific method for interpreting Scripture" (Torjesen, *Hermeneutical Procedure*, p. 2).

31. Quoted in R. P. C. Hanson, *Allegory and Event: A Study of the Sources and Significance of Origen's Interpretation of Scripture* (Richmond, VA: John Knox Press, 1959), p. 133.

32. Porphyry, who claimed to know Origen as a young man, targeted Origen's method of interpretation in his treatise against the Christians: "In their eagerness to find, not a way to reject the depravity of the Jewish Scriptures, but a means of explaining it away, they resorted to interpretations which cannot be reconciled or harmonized with those scriptures, and which provide not so much a defence of the original authors as a fulsome advertisement for the interpreters. 'Enigmas' is the pompous name they give to the perfectly plain statements of Moses, glorifying them as oracles full of hidden mysteries, and bewitching the critical faculty by their extravagant nonsense. . . . This absurd method must be attributed to a man whom I met

losophers; rather, in "practicing" allegory Origen understood himself as standing in the tradition of the apostle Paul.[33]

According to Origen, Paul taught the church how to interpret the books of the Law. Origen's fifth homily on Exodus explains the difference between the Jews' literal reading of the story of the departure of the Israelites from Israel and the Pauline spiritual or allegorical reading:

> The Jews . . . understand only this, that "the children of Israel departed" from Egypt and their first departure was "from Ramesse" and they departed from there and came "to Socoth," and "they departed from Socoth" and came "to Etham" at Epauleus next to the sea. Then, next, they understand that there the cloud preceded them and the "rock" from which they drank water followed; and furthermore, they crossed the Red Sea and came into the desert of Sina.
>
> Let us see, however, what sort of rule of interpretation the apostle Paul taught us about these matters. Writing to the Corinthians he says in a certain passage, "For we know that our fathers were all under the cloud, and all were baptized in Moses in the cloud and in the sea, and all ate the same spiritual food, and all drank the same spiritual drink. And they drank of the spiritual rock which followed them, and the rock was Christ." Do you see how much Paul's teaching differs from the literal meaning? What the Jews supposed to be a crossing of the sea, Paul calls a baptism; what they supposed to be a cloud, Paul asserts is the Holy Spirit.[34]

Origen goes on to say that Christian readers should apply this kind of rule of interpretation to other passages in a similar way, to read the Bible as Paul did, in order to cultivate "the seeds of spiritual understanding received" from him.[35]

Origen appeals to a series of Pauline texts as evidence for this type of interpretation.[36] From these texts he draws out the principle that is later called

---

while I was still quite young, who enjoyed a great reputation and thanks to the works he has left behind him, enjoys it still. I refer to Origen, whose fame among teachers of these theories is widespread" (Porphyry, quoted by Eusebius, *The History of the Church* VI.19, p. 196).

33. For another discussion of Origen and his predecessors' use of allegory to interpret Scripture, see Petra Heldt, "Constructing Christian Communal Identity in Early Patristic Writers," pp. 29-41 above.

34. Origen, "Homily V on Exodus," trans. Ronald E. Heine, FOC 71 (Washington, DC: Catholic University Press, 1982), p. 276.

35. Origen, "Homily V on Exodus," p. 277.

36. Rom. 7:14: "For we know that the law is spiritual"; 1 Cor. 9:9-10: "For it is written in the law of Moses, 'You shall not muzzle an ox while it is treading out the grain.' Is it for oxen that God is concerned? Or does he not speak entirely for our sake? It was indeed written for our sake, for whoever plows should plow in hope and whoever threshes should thresh in hope of a share

"interpreting Scripture by Scripture." This principle, according to Heine, "was a common procedure among exegetes of all types in the ancient world. It was used by the Greek grammarians to interpret Homer, by philosophers to interpret Aristotle or Plato, and by Hellenistic Jews such as Philo, but also by the rabbis, to interpret the Old Testament."[37] Origen himself claimed to have learned this principle from a Jewish teacher.[38]

In Origen's view readers are taught by the Spirit "by comparing one text with another."[39] If it is truly the Spirit who speaks in all the texts of the Bible, then one arrives at the meaning of a text "by comparing other Biblical texts containing similar terminology," so that the Spirit's speaking in the auxiliary texts teaches the meaning of the text in question:[40] "for indeed we are taught out of scripture itself how we ought to think of it."[41]

Origen is deeply concerned with the grammatical quality of the text. But allegory has been criticized for its easy decision of allegorizing a text if it proves too difficult. Origen himself warns against the dangers of allegorizing in a way that does not do justice to the original meaning of words in their context. In his *Peri Pascha (Treatise on the Passover)* Origen criticizes those who are "rashly attempting to interpret things written in Hebrew without first knowing the Hebrew meaning."[42] The situation that warrants such a criticism is the Greek word for *passover.* Origen writes:

---

in the crop"; 1 Cor. 10:11: "These things happened to them as an example, and they were written down to instruct us, on whom the ends of the ages have come"; 2 Cor. 3:6: "Who has made us competent to be ministers of a new covenant, not of letter but of spirit; for the letter kills, but the Spirit gives life"; 2 Cor. 3:15-16: "Indeed, to this very day whenever Moses is read, a veil lies over their minds; but when one turns to the Lord, the veil is removed."

37. Heine, "Reading the Bible with Origen," p. 136.

38. Trigg explains Origen's use of allegory to confront the Jews as well as the heresies of his day: "Allegory enabled him [Origen] to appropriate the Old Testament from the Jews by giving even the most arcane provisions of the Law a Christological interpretation. It also enabled him to purge the Bible of the morally offensive elements which estranged the Gnostics and to demonstrate to pagans that it contained teachings consistent with the deepest insights of Greek philosophy. Since prejudice against the supposed barbarities of Scripture often made Gnosticism more appealing to classically educated persons than was orthodox Christianity, the two latter concerns often merged. Origen won over his patron, Ambrose, from Gnosticism by means of his allegorical interpretation much as the allegorical interpretation of a later Ambrose, the bishop of Milan, weaned the classically educated young Augustine from Manichaeism" (*Biblical Interpretation,* pp. 25-26).

39. Text in C. Jenkins, ed., "Origen on I Corinthians," *Journal of Theological Studies* (Old Series) 9 (1908): 240.

40. Heine, "Reading the Bible with Origen," p. 137.

41. Origen, *De Principiis* IV.II.4, p. 275.

42. Origen, *Treatise on the Passover,* trans. Robert J. Daly, Ancient Christian Writers vol. 54 (New York: Paulist Press, 1992), pp. 27-28.

Most of the brethren, indeed perhaps all, think that the passover (πάσχα) takes its name from the passion (πάθος) of the Savior. Among the Hebrews, however, the real name of this feast is not πάσχα but *fas* — the three letters of *fas* and the rough breathing, which is much stronger with them than it is with us, constituting the name of this feast which means 'passage' (διάβασις). For since it is on this feast that the people come out of Egypt, it is thus called *fas,* that is, 'passage' (διάβασις). Because it is not possible in the Greek language to pronounce this word the way the Hebrews do, since the Greeks are unable to pronounce *fas* with the stronger breathing in force among the Hebrews, the word was Hellenized: in the prophets it is called *fasek,* and when Hellenized more completely, the word becomes πάσχα. And should one of us in conversation with Hebrew people too rashly mention that the passover takes its name from the suffering of the Savior, he would be ridiculed by them as one totally ignorant of the meaning of the word.[43]

This passage shows that Origen does not want allegory to distort the historical and grammatical meaning of a passage by giving the words an improper meaning. Allegory, then, is not a substitute for historical criticism. But Origen does require readers to search for the spiritual meaning in the text, for through this spiritual meaning the Bible becomes accessible in new historical contexts, leading the hearer of the word to a true meeting with the Logos of God.[44]

Origen is deeply concerned with the relevance of God's word to one's own time and place, because he regards it as always relevant to all times and all places. Put simply, the scriptures are where one meets Christ, so the interpretation of scripture must not point to itself but instead to him in whom all things were made, in whom is salvation. Christ is literally the exegesis of both the Old and the New Testaments.[45] In *Peri Pascha,* Origen makes a fascinating connec-

43. Origen, *Treatise on the Passover* 1, p. 27.

44. Trigg finds some modern philosophical tendencies to approve of allegorical interpretation. He writes, "Paul Ricoeur refers sympathetically to Patristic interpretation; allegory helps resolve what he calls the first and second moments in the hermeneutical problem that faces us today, the relation between the Old and the New Testaments and the mutual adjustment of the interpretation of the book and the interpretation of life" (*Biblical Interpretation,* p. 51).

45. Concerning the unity of the Old and New Testaments, Origen thinks the usage of allegory is more than just reading the New Testament meaning back into the Old Testament. Torjesen writes, "When Origen speaks of the unity of the two Testaments he is not giving instructions on interpretation. The most that can be deduced from these passages [concerning the unity of the two Testaments] is that the subject matter of both Testaments is Christ. If he

tion with the lamb at Passover mentioned in Exodus 12:8-9,[46] the scriptures, and Christ:

> If the lamb is Christ and Christ is the Logos, what is the flesh of the divine words if not the divine Scriptures? This is what is to be eaten neither raw nor cooked with water. Should, therefore, some cling just to the words themselves, they would eat the flesh of the Savior raw, and in partaking of this raw flesh would merit death and not life — it is after the manner of beasts and not humans that they are eating his flesh — since the Apostle teaches us that the letter kills, but the Spirit gives life (2 Cor. 3.6). If the Spirit is given us from God and God is a devouring fire (Deut. 4.24; Heb. 12.29), the Spirit is also fire, which is what the Apostle is aware of in exhorting us to be aglow with the Spirit (Rom. 12.11). Therefore the Holy Spirit is rightly called fire, which it is necessary for us to receive in order to have converse with the flesh of Christ, I mean the divine Scriptures, so that, when we have roasted them with this divine fire, we may eat them roasted with fire. For the words are changed by such fire, and we will see that they are sweet and nourishing.[47]

The scriptures, inspired by the power of the Holy Spirit, bring those who read them to Christ, the very Word of God. Scholar Karen Jo Torjesen clarifies Origen's position on this point: "Origen's doctrine of Scripture would read as follows: Scripture is nothing other than the teachings of Christ; the divinity of Scripture is nothing other than the divine power and effectiveness of these teachings. The inspiration of Scripture is nothing other than the divine origin of these teachings."[48]

---

wanted to make a hermeneutical principle out of the unity of the two Testaments he would need to say that the exegetical movement from letter to spirit is a movement in both Testaments from Christ concealed in the letter to Christ revealed in the spiritual sense" (*Hermeneutical Procedure*, pp. 7-8).

46. "They are to eat the flesh the same night, roasted with fire, and they are to eat unleavened bread with bitter herbs. Do not eat any of it raw or boiled with water, but roasted with fire, the head with the feet and the entrails" (apparently Origen's translation).

47. Origen, *Treatise on the Passover* 26-27, pp. 41-42. Later in the same treatise Origen writes, "His flesh and blood . . . are the divine Scriptures, eating which, we have Christ; the words becoming his bones, the flesh becoming the meaning from the text, following which meaning, as it were, we see in a mirror dimly (1 Cor. 13.12) the things which are to come, and the blood being faith in the gospel of the new covenant" (33, p. 45).

48. Karen Jo Torjesen, "'Body,' 'Soul,' and 'Spirit' in Origen's Theory of Exegesis," ATR 67 (1985): 1, 288.

The Value of Scripture

For Origen the end of the study of scripture is moral: it is to bring its hearer or reader to conversion of life. Origen never reads scripture merely as disinterested study. Rather, he regards the interpretation of scripture as "a participation in the divine pedagogy, a process that purifies, instructs, and transforms the person whom scripture addresses."[49] For Origen, it is not enough that someone is convinced that the teachings of Jesus are true, because, says Torjesen, the power of those teachings is such that it should compel its hearers "to change their way of life and become adherents and dedicated followers of the truth. This latter point is how the task of teaching was understood in antiquity, an ideal effectively realized only by the Christians."[50] The Bible, then, Origen would say, is really about living a life of virtue. Hearing the Word is one thing, but knowing the Word is quite another.

In so knowing the Word, a life of virtue is possible, for the Word is all virtue. John Clark Smith explains this moral essence of Origen's teaching: "True virtue . . . is absolute for Origen. There are no grades of growth. However, there is a path toward that virtue, and this is popularly called virtue. In other words, there is no place for vice; there is only more and more virtue."[51] Just as the Lord is, according to Origen, "total virtue, animated and living,"[52] so men and women become like him as they move in virtue towards him, who is that very virtue by which we move. As Christ is each of the virtues absolutely, so insofar as what people do is righteous and holy, they share with Christ.

Not everyone in this movement with and to Christ is in the same location, however. Origen insists on the effect of differing human capacity: "we partake of the true Lamb according to our capacity to partake of the Word of God."[53] He does not mean that those who partake in the Lamb to a lesser extent do not partake of the Lamb truly. Rather, his concern is the difference between salvation and conversion. Salvation is given before conversion is completed. Smith explains the distinction as one of time and process: "Salvation is possible

---

49. Trigg, *Biblical Interpretation*, p. 24. Origen writes in *De Principiis*, "For we have been overcome and conquered, we who come from the nations and are as it were the spoils of his victory, we who have bowed our necks to the yoke of his grace" (*De Principiis* IV.I.5, p. 263).

50. Torjesen, "'Body,' 'Soul,' and 'Spirit,'" p. 287.

51. John Clark Smith, *The Ancient Wisdom of Origen* (Cranbury, NJ: Associated University Presses, 1992), p. 94.

52. Quoted in Smith, *The Ancient Wisdom of Origen*, p. 113.

53. Origen, *Treatise on the Passover* 30, p. 43.

even for the one of little faith, but conversion continues."[54] Origen explains conversion as grounded in the scriptures:

> The true conversion, therefore, is to read the old [books], to see those who were justified, to imitate them, to read those [books] to see those who were reproached, to guard oneself from falling into those reproaches, to read the books of the New Testament, the words of the apostles; after reading, to write all these things into the heart, to live in accordance with them, lest a "book of divorce" is also given to us.[55]

Thus for Origen scripture is not only the very center of belief but also the very center of behavior. If scripture plays such an important role in both knowing and doing, a tremendous burden (or blessing) is placed on the exegete, a reality through which the essential task of exegesis is decisively organized around "the figure of the hearer/reader."[56] Exegesis, then, becomes for Origen an essential process of redemption for the soul. He is no stranger to the immensity of this task. In his *Dialogue with Heraclides,* his ambivalence emerges, concerning a question asked him by a student:

> I am worried about speaking; I am worried about not speaking. For the sake of the worthy, I want to speak so as not to be guilty of defrauding of the Word those able to hear it. Because of the unworthy, I hesitate to speak . . . so as not to throw holy things to dogs and cast pearls before swine. It was for Jesus alone to know how to distinguish among his hearers between those without and those within, and thus to speak to those outside in parables and to explain the parables to those who came into his house. . . . I hesitate to put off speaking, and when I do speak I change my mind again. What is it I really want? To treat the matter in a way that heals the souls of my hearers.[57]

These comments reveal that, for Origen, the true teacher is one who morally improves his or her listeners.[58] The one who sees in scripture a meaning worthy of God will explain it to others, not only in words but also in deeds.

---

54. Smith, *The Ancient Wisdom of Origen,* p. 107.

55. Quoted by Smith, *The Ancient Wisdom of Origen,* p. 137.

56. Torjesen, *Hermeneutical Procedure,* p. 12.

57. Origen, *Dialogue with Heraclides* 15, trans. Robert J. Daly, Ancient Christian Writers vol. 54 (New York: Paulist Press, 1992), p. 69.

58. Smith, *The Ancient Wisdom of Origen,* p. 135.

Conclusion

Origen has a deep concern for both the salvation of the hearers of the Word and for their conversion, so that they may become doers of the Word. Movement towards the end, which is Christ, is his main concern, rather than a continuous perfect condition without sin.[59] It is in and through the very words of scripture that human beings are brought into the presence of Christ.

In this theologically diverse early twenty-first century, Origen would no doubt encourage readers not to forget to read scripture spiritually, since scripture contains both the human and the divine, and by way of the human one arrives at the divine. As the process that the incarnation manifested, it gives more worth to that which is human, rather than diminishing it. He would also surely encourage Christians to continue to "spoil the Egyptians," arguing that they must engage the culture if they are to keep the conversation going. That means bringing the Word to where people are in their cultural situation. The teachings of Christ turned the world upside down in Origen's time, and they can do (and, from Origen's view, probably are doing) the same today. But the current situation, in which the world regards the church as irrelevant, is, in a sense, unimportant. Christians must simply strain onward towards Christ.

As Eusebius writes in his *Ecclesiastical History,* Origen left "messages full of help for those in need of comfort."[60] For Origen this message is Christ, for he is our help, he is our comfort. He is one who gave to the things of God — scripture and the human life — "a meaning worthy of God."[61]

---

59. Smith, *The Ancient Wisdom of Origen,* p. 127.
60. Eusebius, *The History of the Church* VI.39, p. 209.
61. Origen, *De Principiis* IV.II.9, p. 287.

Augustine at Ephesus?

Joanne McWilliam

Augustine, of course, was not at the first Council of Ephesus, held in the summer (June to September) of 431. He died almost ten months before, in August 430.[1] But if he had been there he would have found it difficult, if not impossible, to join either side wholeheartedly. On the one hand, his understanding of how Jesus Christ could be both God and man differed radically from that of Cyril and his followers, as did his practice of Christological predication. On the other, the Antiochenes had ties, both personal and theological, to the Pelagians, and that fact in itself could have been enough to turn Augustine away from Nestorius. These three topics — the manner of the co-existence of divinity and humanity in Christ, the manner of Christological predication, and (very briefly) the Nestorian-Pelagian connection — and the correspondence of all three with the decisions taken at Ephesus are examined here.

There were no official Acta from the Council.[2] Eduard Schwartz organized the bits and pieces of surviving documents in *Acta Conciliorvm Oecvmenicorvm* II.1.1-6. Concerning Cyril's second letter to Nestorius and Nestorius's reply, Aloys Grillmeier wrote, "The reading of these two letters and the verdict of the council upon them is the decisive dogmatic act of the

---

1. There were no bishops from North Africa at Ephesus; Capreolus of Cartharge sent a letter excusing himself (*Acta Conciliorvm Oecvmenicorvm* [hereafter ACO], ed. Eduard Schwartz [Berlin and Leipzig: Walter de Gruyter and Co., 1933], 1.1.2.52-54). One bishop from Illyria attended, and two Roman legates. The rest were Easterners.

2. For the details see P. Th. Camelot, *Ephèse et Chalcédoine: Actes des conciles*, trans. A. J. Festugière (Paris: Éditions de l'orante, 1962), pp. 241-42.

Synod."[3] Although Cyril's third letter and his anathemas did not receive the same support from the Synod, the anathemas most clearly reveal the theology of Cyril and his followers.

Mode of Union

Augustine never insisted on one description of the incarnation as the only correct one. For him it remained a mystery, eluding formulas. As late as the early 400s he wrote, "So a man was coupled and even in a certain sense compounded, with the Word of God as one person."[4] But the amorphous "in a certain sense" did not prevent his use of many metaphors to describe the Christological union; some prevailed at one time, some at another. In his early writings the use of "taking up" *(susceptio)* and "assumed" *(assumptus)* is especially frequent, as in "the man assumed by the almighty, eternal, immutable Son of God"[5] and "a complete man was indeed taken up by the Word."[6] *The Homilies on the Psalms* 1-32 (A.D. 392) have many instances: "[Christ], the man taken up, who offered himself as a sacrifice," and "'You, Lord, are the one who lifts me up' is spoken to God by the man, Christ, because the taking up of a man is the Word made flesh."[7] This usage continued throughout his life.[8] (It provoked a lively controversy in the early twentieth century between the Franciscan Déodat de Basly and several Dominicans.)

3. Alois Grillmeier, *Christ in Christian Tradition,* vol. 1, *From the Apostolic Age to Chalcedon (451),* trans. John Bowden, 2 vols., 2d rev. ed. (London and Oxford: Mowbrays, 1975), p. 485. See also W. H. C. Frend, *The Rise of the Monophysite Movement* (Cambridge [UK]: Cambridge University Press, 1972), p. 20.

4. De trin 4.5.30 (A.D. 400-420); trans. Edmund Hill, *Saint Augustine. The Trinity,* Works Aug (Brooklyn: New City Press, 1991), p. 175.

5. De quant animae 76 (A.D. 388); trans. John J. McMahon, *The Magnitude of the Soul,* FOC, vol. 4. Augustine's works are dated parenthetically after their first mention in the text or notes.

6. S 14.6 (A.D. 391). To my knowledge there is no English translation. The translation here as often elsewhere is my own.

7. En in Ps 2.7, trans. A. Cleveland Coxe, *Expositions on the Book of Psalms* (condensed from the Oxford translation), NPNF 8; trans. Maria Boulding, *Homilies on the Psalms,* 6 vols., Works Aug, vols. III/15-20 (Hyde Park, NY: New City Press, 2000-2005). The Latin numbering of the Psalms is used here and throughout.

8. E.g., De agone 16.20 (A.D. 396), trans. *The Christian Combat,* FOC 2; C Faust 13.8 (A.D. 400), trans. R. Stothert, *Reply to Faustus the Manichaean,* NPNF 4; Ep 169.7 (A.D. 415), trans. W. Parsons, in *Letters,* FOC 12, 18, 20, 30, 32; In Ev Ioann 74.3 (ca. A.D. 420), trans. John Gibb and James Innes, *Tractates on the Gospel of John,* NPNF 8; Ench 36.11 (A.D. 424), *Enchiridion,* NPNF 2; De corr et gratia 11.30 (A.D. 426), trans. Benjamin B. Warfield, *On Rebuke and Grace,* NPNF 5.

Augustine also used more graphic figures: clothing ("the man was apparent, God hidden; they saw the clothing and despised the wearer"[9]) and inhabitation ("that abode of the taking up of the human"[10]). Sometimes the inhabitation was military; in the war on evil, he wrote that the Word "set up his military headquarters (that is, the economy of his incarnation) in time."[11] Sometimes the habitation is in a tabernacle or temple.[12] The spousal metaphor is a common one, with God joined *(copulatus)* to the man as husband to wife.[13] Another favorite analogy is that of body and soul: "You are a human person because of [the union of] soul and body; he is Christ because of [that of] God and man."[14] Whatever the metaphor, Augustine, like Origen, saw Christ's human soul as the means by which divinity is united to the material world. Sometimes that hinge becomes a protection. Thus in *De fide et symbolo* (A.D. 393) he asks rhetorically, after pointing out that light is not polluted by whatever it passes through:

> How much less could the Word of God . . . have been polluted by the body of a woman when he assumed human flesh along with a human soul and spirit, within which the majesty of the Word was hidden away from the weakness of the human body?[15]

Augustine often uses Colossians 2:9 to explain how Christ differs from others, stating that God is everywhere, but divine inhabitation is not the same for all. It is not that God does not inhabit others, "but in Christ 'all the fullness of the Godhead dwells in bodily wise', not in a shadowy way . . . but *bodily,* that is to say substantially and truly." A few lines later he writes: "humanity was united to the Word to become the one person of Christ."[16]

From his earliest writings Augustine presents Christ as the recipient of grace: "The favor of your grace lifted me up" and "Inasmuch as he favors me I remain steadfast in him."[17] Throughout his writings he depicts Christ as receiv-

---

9. In Ev Ioann 37.1.
10. En in Ps 32.14.
11. En in Ps 18.6.
12. In Ev Ioann 18.2.
13. En in Ps 18.6.
14. Ep 137.11; In Ev Ioann 19.15.
15. De fide et symbolo 10; trans. J. H. S. Burleigh, "On Faith and the Creed," *Augustine: Earlier Writings,* Library of Christian Classics (Philadelphia: The Westminster Press, 1953), p. 359.
16. En in Ps 67.20; cf. In Ev Ioann 74.3.
17. En in Ps 17.36, 15.8.

ing divine help, sometimes phrased as a singular excellence of anointing.[18] But during the second and third decades of the fifth century, as the controversy with Pelagius and Julian grew more intense, he increasingly explained the Christological perfection in terms of grace: "Great fullness of grace is given to our Lord and Savior."[19] So, Augustine stated, Christ was sinless from infancy "not by his fellowship with other infants, but by his own excellent and singular grace,"[20] and "in taking up human nature the grace itself somehow became so natural to the man as to admit no possibility of sin."[21]

Augustine's Epistle 187 (A.D. 417), devoted to the presence of God, describes that singular grace given to Christ, comparing it to grace received by others. Clearly the two kinds of grace are not the same, "because, by the singular taking up of this man, one person is made one with the Word." By this taking up "divine grace has been plainly and clearly made evident."[22] In no way can this grace of union be said to be shared by other human persons, he says, and it would be sacrilegious to suggest that it could be merited. In a more specific comparison, he writes:

> All graces were conferred on Paul, but there are other graces in addition to these. . . . For it is not to be supposed, however greatly the apostle Paul excelled others as a member of Christ's body, that the very Head of the entire body himself did not receive more and ampler graces, whether in his flesh or in his soul as man, his own creature which the Word of God assumed into the unity of his own person.[23]

In the same year he wrote in *On the Trinity:* "For that the Unbegotten is equal to the Father belongs to his nature, not to grace; however, that a man was assumed into union with the person of the Unbegotten belongs to grace, not nature."[24] The anti-Pelagian background is clear in this passage from the same work:

> [The incarnation] in the man Christ advertises the grace of God towards us without any previous deserts on our part, as not even he won the privilege

18. In Ev Ioann 7.13; En in Ps 88.22.

19. En in Ps 18.2.

20. C duas ep 4.2.2; trans. Benjamin B. Warfield, *Against Two Letters of the Pelagians,* NPNF 5.

21. De trin 15.26.46; Ench 12.39.

22. Ep 187.40.

23. De gestis 14.32; trans. Benjamin B. Warfield, *On the Proceeding of Pelagius,* NPNF 5.

24. De trin 13.17.22; cf. In Ev Ioann 105.4.

of being joined to the true God in such a unity of person, Son of God, by any previous merits of his own.[25]

And, a few years later, "his being the only-begotten, the equal of the Father, is not of grace but of nature, but the assumption of the man into the personal unity of the only-begotten is not of nature, but of grace."[26]

Augustine gives great weight to Christ's human will. That Christ did not sin, he said, was not because he was not free to do so but because of the exceptional graces he received. Yet he was truly tempted: "When I was examined, I was found righteous."[27] Christ does not coerce "but converts human persons to imitate him in liberty. . . . He taught not what he did not."[28] The dereliction in Gethsemane was real: Christ's human will cried out, but it yielded to the divine will.[29] There Christ showed the human will as it should be.[30] Augustine points out to Faustus that Christ chose to suffer, that as man "he became obedient unto death."[31] And, again quoting Paul, he writes, "By the obedience of one man, many shall be made righteous."[32]

Grillmeier finds Augustine's way of describing the union of God and a man in Christ — fullness of grace enabling perfect and salvific obedience (what today is called "a call and response" Christology) — unsatisfactory, lacking a basis in philosophy or speculative theology.[33] It is, in his view, at best accidental. This criticism is valid only within an Aristotelian/Thomistic ontology of substance and accident. Augustine was not a systematic theologian, and his philosophical leanings were to Neoplatonism, but his theology was nonetheless coherent; that is, his understanding of the Christological union as one of grace and obedience, as one of love, was consistent with his understanding of the trinitarian unity. He writes in the *Treatises on the Gospel of John*: "If therefore my soul and your soul become one soul when we think the same thing and love one another, how much more must God the Father and God the Son be one God in the fountain of love." Equally, in Augustine's eyes, the

---

25. De trin 13.17.22.

26. In Ev Ioann 74.3.

27. En in Ps 16.3.

28. En in Ps 18.9; see En in Ps 30.1.10.

29. En in Ps 32.2: "In his human will he embodies our advance. . . . 'Father,' he said, 'if it is possible let this cup pass from me.' It was his human will speaking here. . . . But he wanted the rest of us to be right of heart, . . . and therefore he added, 'Yet not what I will, but what you will be done.'" See also En in Ps 31.26, 93.19, 100.6.

30. See En in Ps 32.12.

31. C Faust 27.2.

32. In Ev Ioann 18.4.

33. Grillmeier, *Christ*, p. 412.

Christological union is one of mutual love, of (in R. V. Seller's phrase) "reciprocal presence."[34]

Augustine had no doubt that Christ was one person, not two. He often, though not consistently, identified that person with the eternal Word: "It is clear that by some unique taking up of that man one person with the Word resulted,"[35] and ". . . which creature [the man] the Word of God assumed . . . into the unity of his person."[36] But sometimes he identifies the person with the God-man, Christ: "that form of the man who was taken up is the person of the Son," and "the man is joined to the Word in the one person of Christ."[37] This inconsistency in usage shows that the "location" of Christ's person was not a problem for Augustine. He would certainly have offered no objection to identifying the person of Christ as the person of the Word, and as has been shown, he sometimes did so (although, it will be recalled, he did not like *person* applied to the Trinity).[38]

But Augustine would not have identified the union of divine and human in Christ as hypostatic *(kath' hypostasin)*. He would have had the objection that Luigi Scipioni attributes to Nestorius: a hypostatic union is a natural union, and Augustine's understanding was definitely one of grace and response.[39] Frances Young points out that the problem posed for the Antiochenes by *hypostatic union* was that it implied Apollinarianism, a confusion of natures, and a *natural union*, "that is, one brought about by something inherent in the nature of things and so by necessity, rather than one voluntarily undertaken by the gracious will of God."[40] Augustine's Christological union of grace and response would have been radically challenged by Cyril's second anathema:

> If anyone does not confess that the Word of God the Father was united to flesh hypostatically, and that he is one single Christ with his own flesh, to

34. R. V. Sellers, *Eustathius of Antioch* (Cambridge [UK]: Cambridge University Press, 1928), pp. 106-7. See Joanne McWilliam Dewart, "Moral Union in Christology before Nestorius," *Laval Théologique et Philosophique* 32 (1976): 283-99.

35. Ep 187.40.

36. S 14.6.

37. De trin 2.5; Hill translates this phrase as "that form of the man who was taken on is the person or guise of the Son only" (*Saint Augustine*, p. 103). He also explains, "to call the man Jesus the *persona* of the Son is an unusual use of the word. It must here have its primitive meaning of a mask" (*Saint Augustine*, pp. 124-25, n. 19).

38. De trin 7.9-11.

39. Luigi I. Scipioni, *Ricerche sulla Cristologia dell "Libro di Eraclide" di Nestorio* (Fribourg: Edizioni Universitarie, 1956), p. 74.

40. Frances M. Young, *From Nicaea to Chalcedon* (Philadelphia: The Westminster Press, 1983), p. 222.

the extent that the same [Word] is at once God and man, let him be anathe-matized.[41]

For Cyril and his followers any mode of Christological union other than hypostatic could not establish the oneness of Christ.

Predication

Concern over what can and cannot be said of Christ as God and as man goes back at least to the Gnostics and was critical in the Arian controversy. It is fundamen-tally a trinitarian question.[42] The Arians argued that because human attributes (e.g., suffering and death) were predicated of Christ, he could not be fully divine. In countering them, Athanasius gave little if any salvific import to Christ as man, predicating everything, even death, of the eternal Word in his human nature. This hegemony of the Word, without reference to the role of Christ's humanity in sal-vation, endured in the Alexandrian tradition. Thus the tenor of Cyril's argument in his second letter to Nestorius insists that incarnation, suffering, death, and res-urrection must be predicated of the Word, co-eternal with the Father. The Coun-cil endorsed this position, as Nestorius pointed out in his response to Cyril:

> The great and holy synod stated that the unique Son himself — naturally begotten out of God the Father, true God out of true God, light out of light, through whom the Father made everything that exists — descended, was enfleshed, became human, suffered, and rose.[43]

Although the Council did not adopt the anathemas following Cyril's sec-ond letter, the twelfth particularly shows how greatly Augustine's manner of Christological predication differed from Cyril's:

> If anyone does not confess that the Word of God suffered in the flesh, was crucified in the flesh, and that in the flesh he tasted death and that he has

41. "Cyril of Alexandria's Second Letter to Nestorius," in *The Christological Controversy*, ed. and trans. Richard A. Norris, Jr. (Philadelphia: Fortress Press, 1980), pp. 131-35. The anathemas were attached to Cyril's second letter to Nestorius; they do not however appear in Norris's translation.

42. Michael Slusser, "The Exegetical Roots of Trinitarian Theology," *Theological Studies* 49 (1988): 461-76; Robert Wilken, "Tradition, Exegesis, and the Christological Controversy," *Church History* 34 (1965): 123-45.

43. "Nestorius's Second Letter to Cyril," in Norris, *Christological Controversy*, pp. 135-40, here p. 135.

become the first begotten of the dead, and that in as much as he is God he is life and life-giving, let him be anathematized.

The Antiochene tradition and the Western were different from the Alexandrian. Nestorius, in his reply to Cyril, argued that "the Fathers" understood Jesus Christ as the basis of their Christology:

> Observe how [the Fathers] first of all establish, as foundations, the titles which are common to the deity and the humanity — "Lord" and "Jesus" and "Christ" and "Only Begotten" and "Son" — and then build on them the teaching about his becoming human and his passion and resurrection, in order that . . . the things which pertain to the sonship and lordship are not divided and the things peculiar to the natures within the unitary sonship do not get endangered by the suggestion of a confusion.[44]

Nestorius saw himself in this tradition, and Paul as its instigator. Paul, he says, "used the Word *Christ,* an appellation which signifies in one person [*prosōpon, hypostasis*] both a passible and an impassible substance [*ousia*]." The usage avoids ascribing passibility to the divine or impassibility to the human. For example, the apostle predicated the descent described in Philippians 2:6-8 of Christ, not the Word, because it culminates in Christ's death, and surely the Word cannot die.[45]

Augustine faced two problems when it came to what could and could not be said of Christ, first that of Christ in himself and as head of the church, and second that of Christ as God and Christ as man. Nowhere is his practice better demonstrated than in the *Homilies on the Psalms.* For example, he says in the space of a few lines that "In the Lord I trust" is spoken by Christ as man, that "The Lord is in his holy temple" is applicable either to the Word incarnate or to the glorified man, and that "His eyes look upon the poor" can be said either by the Word about the man, Christ, or by Christ as man about those for whom he suffered.[46]

I deal here only with what Augustine predicated of Christ as God and as man, but not as head of the church. The psalms or parts of psalms that he ascribes to Christ personally are divided into three groups: (1) those dealing with his relationship to God the Father, (2) those relating to his birth, life, death, and resurrection, and (3) those describing him as eschatological judge.

44. "Nestorius's Second Letter to Cyril," p. 136.
45. Letter of Nestorius to Cyril, read at the Council of Ephesus.
46. En in Ps 10.12.

Augustine's assertions of the full divinity of Christ as Word are frequent and unequivocal and are found in his earliest writings. He is the eternally generated "Power and Wisdom of God, the only begotten Son."[47] Psalm 9 "is sung for the hidden things of the only begotten Son of God,"[48] and Psalm 5 places him in a trinitarian context: "Inasmuch as both the Son and the Father are God, and at the same time they are one God, and if we ask about the Holy Spirit nothing other should be understood than God."[49] He consistently attributes this sharing of divine being with the Father and the Holy Spirit to the Word.

In the second category, those things assigned to Christ as man are physical and mental suffering (but not ignorance[50]), joy, temptation and successful resistance to temptation, all the virtues (notably humility and obedience), and prayer. Augustine was unusual in his time in the importance he placed on petitionary prayer in Christ's life. He portrayed him, particularly in these *Homilies,* as a man whose hopes and fears found expression in turning to God for personal strength and in imploring God not to withdraw from him: "I cry to you, Lord, my God, do not separate the unity of your Word from the man that I am, lest at any time you turn away from me in silence, and I shall be like those that go down into the pit."[51]

For Augustine, Christ's soul is unambiguously a human soul and therefore dependent on divine help. In Christ's mouth the words "I have cried out, for you have heard me, O God" mean:

> With a free and strong effort I have directed my prayers to you. That I might have this power [of strong prayer] you heard me when praying more weakly. "Incline your ear to me and hear my words." Do not let your hearing desert my humility.[52]

Psalm 3, Augustine explains, "is to be understood as in the person of Christ," and the most straightforward interpretation of verse four ("With my voice have I cried unto the Lord, and he heard me out of his holy mountain") is that God heard that prayer: "For it was just that he should raise from the dead the innocent man who was killed, and to whom evil had been returned for good."[53] Christ prayed that that resurrection not be delayed: "But Thou, O

47. En in Ps 5.8.
48. En in Ps 9.1.
49. En in Ps 5.3.
50. En in Ps 6.1.
51. En in Ps 27.2.
52. En in Ps 16.6.
53. En in Ps 3.1, 3.4.

God, raise me up again, not . . . at the end of time, like others, but immediately."[54]

On the question of Christ's resurrection Augustine is not entirely consistent. He frequently portrays Christ beseeching the Father for immediate resurrection, but in the homily on Psalm 15 the Word appears to be the agent of resurrection: "The humanity of my divinity has profited them that I might die and the divinity of my humanity that I might rise again."[55] It is as man that Christ ascended[56] and as human person that he provides the criterion of judgment: "By Christ's human life God distinguishes between the righteous and sinners."[57] As man Christ will judge at his second coming: "[B]y patience the man purchased heaven. . . . That is the hidden judgment. . . . [At his second coming] he will openly judge the world in equity."[58] Accepting death the humble Christ endured the unjust judgment, his "hidden judgment," while the open, final judgment will be that of the glorified Christ "in the manifest splendor of his brilliance."[59] Finally, it is as man that he will rule.[60]

Despite the care with which he distinguishes what should be said of Christ as Word and as human person, Augustine is as fully aware as Nestorius that both divine and human attributes are predicated of the one person, whether Augustine identifies that person as the Word or as Christ. He writes (*c.* A.D. 420) in the *Treatises on the Gospel of John,* "What is there to wonder at then . . . if, in reference to this servant form, the Son of God says, 'The Father is greater than I' and, in speaking in the form of God, the self-same Son of God declares, 'I and the Father are one'?"[61]

And what of *theotokos?* Here Augustine makes the same distinction: "Christ was born of a woman not as he is, the blessed God over all, but in that feeble [nature] which he took from us."[62] "As man, born of Mary, God was his god. As God the Word, eternally born, the relationship was to a Father."[63]

---

54. En in Ps 21.20.
55. En in Ps 15.3.
56. En in Ps 75.17.
57. En in Ps 16.8.
58. En in Ps 9.9.
59. En in Ps 7.13.
60. En in Ps 109.7-10.
61. Tract 36.2.
62. C Faust 3.6.
63. En in Ps 21.10-11. "I speak now as a human being, as a weakling, as Word made flesh. From my mother's womb you have been my God. Not from my birth from you are you my God, for from my eternal birth you are my Father. But from the womb of my mother you are my God." See En in Pss 1.58.2, 54.20. Augustine never uses the Latin equivalent of *theotokos* (Daniel E. Doyle, "Mary, Mother of God," in *Augustine through the Ages: An Encyclopedia,* gen. ed.

Again, what is to be noted here is not only that divine and human characteristics can be predicated of the same subject, but that as often as not for Augustine that subject is Christ.

Pelagianism in the East

A notional compatibility between the Pelagians and the Antiochenes has often been remarked. For example, Young writes: "It was no mere accident of Church politics that Nestorius hesitated to condemn the Pelagians. . . . One side in each case emphasized the human effort required for salvation, the other attributed all to God."[64] But is such compatibility enough to label the Eastern church Pelagian, or even, anachronistically, semi-Pelagian? Lionel Wickham has argued that the Eastern church was neither Pelagian nor Augustinian, and that Cyril, while aware of the Western dispute over grace and free will, appears to have tolerated "Pelagian" refugees in Alexandria. When Cyril wrote to Celestine in the late 420s, Wickham alleges, his complaint about Pelagianism was really "a means of stirring up Celestine against Nestorius."[65]

It has been pointed out that the question of grace and free will had a different ambience in West and East. In the West, the question was how human persons are saved. What role, if any, does human response play? For the Easterners it was a question of divine intentionality, of "the purposeful actions of a gracious God."[66] Against this background it is perhaps futile to ask whether Nestorius or any other Greek theologian was Pelagian in the sense Augustine understood the term — that is, as a denial of the need of God's grace. But if any kind of voluntary human cooperation with divine grace is seen as Pelagian, then it was rife in the East, as can be seen in the writings of Chrysostom, Theodore, and Theodoret.

Modern scholarship has shown that Nestorius did not teach two persons, or "two sons," in Christ. To my mind, there is nothing in Nestorius's letter to

---

Allan D. Fitzgerald [Grand Rapids, MI: William B. Eerdmans Publishing Company, 1999], pp. 542-45).

64. Frances M. Young, "A Reconsideration of Alexandrian Christology," *The Journal of Ecclesiastical History* 22 (1971): 103-14, here 104.

65. Lionel Wickham, "Pelagianism in the East," in *The Making of Orthodoxy: Essays in Honour of Henry Chadwick*, ed. Rowan Williams (Cambridge [UK] and New York: Cambridge University Press, 1989), pp. 200-13, here p. 204.

66. Robert Wilken, "Free Choice and Divine Will in Greek Christian Commentaries on Paul," *Paul and the Legacies of Paul*, ed. William S. Babcock (Dallas: Southern Methodist University Press, 1990), pp. 123-140.

Cyril to which Augustine would have taken exception. And as late as 428 Augustine thought Theodore an instance of right thinking.[67] But Elizabeth Clark has shown how important personal relationships, both positive and negative, were in the late-fourth- and early-fifth-century controversies.[68] Augustine surely could not have known, praising Theodore, that Julian had taken refuge with him (as had Celestius with Nestorius). It would require a long journey through Augustine's conviction of the transmission of sin and guilt in procreation and the consequent total depravity of the human will, and the role of the virgin conception in Christ's sinlessness, to understand how Augustine could give such prominence to Christ's response to grace and so despair of all others. On the basis of Christology alone the bishop of Hippo would have sided with the Antiochenes at Ephesus. But for the last decade of his life Augustine was obsessed with Pelagianism, and the Antiochenes would have been blackened by their association with Nestorius. I think Augustine was fortunate to miss Ephesus.

---

67. C Iul 3.111.

68. Elizabeth A. Clark, *The Origenist Controversy. The Cultural Construction of an Early Christian Debate* (Princeton: Princeton University Press, 1992), *passim*.

The Flight of Geryon

John V. Fleming

The medieval Christian cultural enterprise was to a surprising degree an extended series of accommodations, appropriations, and syncretism. Christianity came into a Greco-Roman world that it utterly transformed from a spiritual perspective while at the same time leaving large monuments of the cultural edifice virtually undisturbed. The phenomena present us with paradoxes rich enough for nearly endless speculation. Christians were aware of, and they articulated, the essentially revolutionary newness of the *kerygma*. Yet its cultural implementation was everywhere channeled through socially conservative tradition.

What is often regarded as the humanistic impulse in medieval literature was an inevitable implication of the institutions of Latinity into which the western church was distributed in the fourth and fifth centuries, the age of Jerome, translator of the Vulgate, and of Augustine, the permanent giant of catholic thought. Those institutions, especially those of law and education, were deeply conservative, and they were founded upon a written canon of great power and authority. So far as education was concerned, the canon was decidedly "literary" and poetic. At its heart was the *Æneid* of Virgil, which enjoyed among the Latins the remarkable prestige that the Homeric poems had enjoyed among the Greeks.

The church's cultural accommodation of Latin literature had been in a sense foreshadowed by its earlier accommodation of the Hebrew scriptures. In the Book of Acts we find the historical traces of the halting journey by which a Jewish sect, the Jesus Movement, penetrated the larger Mediterranean world, in which its Jewishness was no less foreign than its "Jesusness." The debate concerning the claims of "circumcision" — shorthand for the plenary demands of the Mosaic law — might focus as well on the claims of the Jewish texts in which the law was enshrined. Once a great historical decision has been made it is difficult for us to imagine other outcomes. Christianity without the Hebrew scriptures, though it was once a lively historical possibility, is now culturally unimaginable.

What about a Christianity without Virgil? The question may seem absurd, since in the modern context it is impossible to imagine a Christianity in any significant sense *with* Virgil. But until Europe's definitive cultural break with the Latin language, a gradual development with no fixed date but clearly belonging to modern times, the question was often a lively one. The competing claims of the great Latin pagan writers and the Latin Christian scriptures are frequently dramatized in patristic biography, in such famous episodes as Saint Jerome's dream in the letter to Eustochium and Augustine's account of his reading of Cicero's *Hortensius* in the *Confessions*.

As the two contrasting anecdotes suggest, the meeting between the Bible and classical authority could be the occasion of dramatic confrontation or fruitful cooperation. Indeed we may perhaps oversimplify grossly but usefully by defining two opposing medieval cultural attitudes as the Hieronymite and the Augustinian. The former wanted to banish pagan poetry altogether, seeking its literary refreshment solely in the Scriptures. The latter searched, diligently if at times warily, for the "Egyptian gold" of ancient wisdom to be found in the pagan writings.

There are repeated medieval episodes of the debate between the two, but its richest documents are probably to be found in fourteenth-century Italy, in the period of early or "pre"-humanism, in the writings of Boccaccio, Petrarch, Salutati, and, for the opposition, Giovanni Dominici.[1] Their enterprise of classical accommodation was in many respects analogous to the "humanistic" movement in theology, and particularly in the attempts of the Schoolmen to reconcile an inherited theology based almost exclusively in biblical exegesis with the newly available moral philosophy of Aristotle. Unlike the Greek texts of the Stagyrite, the great poetic patrimony of Latinity, especially in Virgil and Ovid, had never been lost.

The great humanist poets of the vernacular Middle Ages — Jean de Meun in France; Dante, Petrarch, and Boccaccio in Italy; Chaucer in England — were all in this sense Augustinian poets, active and imaginative practitioners of a poetics of classical accommodation that I might for the purpose of this essay call medieval poetic ecumenism. That purpose, of course, is to join in honoring

---

1. See Concetta Carestia Greenfield, *Humanist and Scholastic Poetics, 1250-1500* (Lewisburg, PA: Bucknell University Press, 1981).

Professor J. Robert Wright, an important medieval historian who has made significant contributions to our understanding of the church in the age of Dante, a Christian ecumenical leader, and, for the half century since we first met in the golden autumn of our freshman year at Sewanee, a personal friend. Some degree of the "humanistic spirit" could be found even in unexpected places in the age of Dante, even in the household of much-maligned Archbishop Walter Reynolds, whom Wright cites as taking "as our highest responsibility that the care for those persons reading in holy writ be stimulated and the fervour of their study be augmented, so that, from this, rich fruits may come for God's church in due time."[2]

The stakes were very high in the confrontation of the secular and sacred scriptures, for the principal issue was truth itself. In this regard a medieval pedagogical document of the highest importance is the so-called "Eclogue" of Theodulus, a poem for which I recently advanced ambitious claims with respect to medieval monastic culture.[3] This Carolingian schoolbook, which enjoyed a significant prestige in the propaedeutic pedagogy of Latin for well onto a thousand years, is a pseudo-Virgilian poem of about three hundred and fifty lines dating from the Carolingian period.[4] The name *Theodulus* is of course a philological fiction suggesting that the author is a true worshipper of God. A similar grammatical allegory commands the names of the two principal interlocutors Pseustis (Falsehood) and Alithea (Truth), who participate in a curious poetical competition.

The "Eclogue" of Theodulus may be the first known instance of what is now called a poetry slam. In parallel quatrains the two pastoral contestants utter competing gobbets of mythology on parallel themes, those of Pseustis drawn from profane literature and those of Alithea from the Hebrew Bible, mainly from the book of Genesis. The contest begins, for example, with contrasting versions of prelapsarian bliss. Pseustis tells of the Golden Age under Saturn, Alithea of Adam in his "green Paradise." Within the fictive structure of the "Eclogue" Phronesis, the moderator of the "debate," naturally decides the contest in favor of Alithea. Yet at the same time the poem preserves rather than condemns pagan mythology, providing young students with numerous imitative models. The eclogue is Virgilian not merely in form but in much of its content, including the exotic pastoral setting revealed in the opening lines

---

2. J. Robert Wright, *The Church and the English Crown, 1305-1334* (Toronto: Pontifical Institute of Mediaeval Studies, 1980), p. 253.

3. John V. Fleming, "Muses of the Monastery," *Speculum* 76 (2003): 1071-1106, esp. pp. 1086-89.

4. Theodulus, *Ecloga: Il canto della verità e della menzogna*, ed. Francesco Mosetti Casaretto (Florence: SISMEL-Edizioni del Galluzzo, 1997).

("Æthiopum terras iam fervida torruit æstas/In Cancro solis dum volvitur aureus axis . . ."), closely imitating Virgil's tenth eclogue.[5]

The "Eclogue" became so authoritative as to attract several academic commentaries. That of Conrad of Hirsau speaks thus of the poet's intention: "intentio eius est sacrae paginae veritatem commendare et fabularum commenta dissuadere, non quidem ut non legantur, sed ne lectae credantur vel in actum transferantur."[6] Just as medieval commentators sometimes warn their readers against thinking in the Age of Grace about practicing such biblical cultural conventions as polygamy, acceptable before or under the Law, the commentator is here saying, in effect, "Do not try this at home." And the textual parallels between sacred and secular scripture licitly suggest another analogy: that of Biblical typology. It is not wrong to suggest that the pagan Golden Age is a "type" of which the brief reign of bliss in Paradise is the "antitype."

Many of the greatest Christian poets of the vernacular Middle Ages became experts at "classical typology" or what I am here calling poetic ecumenism, but Dante Alighieri alone makes it one of the central structural techniques of a great poem. He was entirely aware of the revolutionary novelty of his enterprise in the *Commedia,* a novelty that on the whole he chose to dramatize rather than to disguise. The poem is replete with what can only have been intended as intentionally shocking moments, but perhaps none is more shocking than the reverent introduction of ancient, pagan Virgil as the guide, in matters moral no less than those topographical, to the Christian pilgrim. In the first canto of the *Inferno* the narrator, falling back in alarm and dejection from his encounter with the three menacing beasts, becomes aware in the vast wilderness of "one who seemed faint through long silence" (Inf 1.63).[7] This is the poet Virgil, who identifies himself in an elliptical fashion with sufficient clarity but also with a notable historical diffidence: "I . . . lived at Rome under good Augustus, in an age of false and lying gods. I was a poet, and I sang the just son of Anchises come from Troy" (Inf 1.71-73).

The phrase "false and lying gods" is a remarkable one. Commentators have rightly seen in it Augustine's adjectives *falsus* and *fallax* as he used them in

---

5. "Aethiopum versemus ovis sub sidere Cancri" (Virgil, "Eclogue 10," l. 68).

6. "His intention is to commend the truth of the sacred page and to warn against the inventions of the poets, not that they should not be read, but so that what is read there should not be believed or imitated" (*Accessus ad auctores,* ed. R. B. C. Huygens, 2nd ed. [Leiden: E. J. Brill, 1970], p. 94).

7. Except as noted all references to the *Inferno* (abbreviated Inf) are from the edition and translation of Robert and Jean Hollander (New York: Anchor Books, 2002). Pending the publication of the Hollanders' *Paradiso* (abbreviated Par), I have used the edition of John D. Sinclair, *Dante's Paradiso* (New York: Oxford University Press, 1939).

the *City of God* to describe the official Roman deities.[8] What is *falsus* is untrue, and that is bad enough; what is *fallax* is intentionally deceptive, and that is worse. Both kinds of falsity characterized pagan practice and belief. What should be the posture of the poet when confronted with a giant? The poet David had slain Goliath with a slingshot, then decapitated him with his own sword. That image became a particularly robust exegetical emblem of the victory of Christianity over pagan culture, parallel to that of Augustine's Egyptian gold, whereby the literary weapons of darkness are appropriated to the service of light. But we know as well the famous and gentle proverb of Bernard of Chartres, that the Christian scholar is a dwarf raised higher by the shoulders of the pagan giant.

In the introduction of Virgil in Dante's first canto we find both voices, that of censoriousness and that of adulation. Dante's Virgil is a tragic figure, as one born out of time, a Moses allowed to know of the Promised Land but not to enter it. For all his poetic deference, Dante can finally suggest that though Virgil was only sixth among "the fair school of the lord of loftiest song" (Inf 4.94-95), he is yet the greatest of them all, having the greatest subject of all, and the most true. His attitude, indeed, may perfectly typify a certain kind of ecumenical outlook, eager for accommodation, yet supremely confident of its own foundation.

To us medieval intellectual life may seem slavishly subservient to received tradition and authority. In actuality Dante criticizes Virgil in the fashion of a scholar trying to revalidate a revered source by bringing it up to date with the most recent developments in the field and recently edited primary sources. In human moral education the most recent development is the stupendous fact of the incarnation, attested to in texts Virgil could not have known. Religious revelation was the principal basis for medieval self-confidence, but it was not the only one. Several of the translators of the ancient matters of medieval romance — the stories of Thebes, of Troy, of Rome itself — had access to what they regarded as better secular historical materials than the ancient poets had had. Thus at the very end of the *Historia destructionis Troiæ*, Guido delle Colonne states as his principal motive the correction of factual errors made by Ovid and Virgil. The latter was the master of a "glorious style," and nothing can ever replace him, but he lacked the eye-witness account of the Trojan War that Guido had found in Dares the Phrygian.[9]

---

8. Dante Alighieri, trans. Charles S. Singleton, *Inferno, Translated with a Commentary*, 2 vols. (Princeton: Princeton University Press, 1989), 2:14.

9. Guido de Columnus, *Historia Destructionis Troiæ*, ed. Nathaniel Edward Griffin (Cambridge: Medieval Academy, 1936), pp. 275-76.

The typical ecumenical gesture of medieval Christian poetry is one that, like the matched quatrains of the "Eclogue" of Theodulus, silently collates the classical and the scriptural. Dante's reading in the classical poets was very wide, but it is not without reason that he chooses Virgil as his particular guide, for Virgil is Dante's poet *par excellence.* In the second canto of the *Inferno* the pilgrim Dante balks at the daunting journey that Virgil has proposed: "Poeta che mi guidi,/guarda la mia virtù s'ell' è possente,/prima ch'all'alto passo tu mi fidi" (Inf 2.10-12).[10] He makes an implicit contrast between his own debility and the strength of two predecessors on otherworldly journeys — Æneas, who went to the Underworld, and Saint Paul, who was lifted in rapture to the Third Heaven (2 Cor. 12:2). He deals with them chronologically, so to speak, first Æneas, then Paul, but with a scarcely noticeable want of equality. Of Æneas he says to Virgil "Tu dici" — *You say* that the father of Silvius went to the other world. As Singleton notes, the phrase subtly but unmistakably identifies the story as something told by a poet, that is, a fiction.[11] Of Paul's ascent to the Heavens, on the other hand, he says simply that "The Chosen Vessel went there . . ." (Inf 2.28). Such an attitude is entirely consistent with the spirit of Theodulus's "Eclogue." The story of the journey of Æneas is beautiful and inspiring. The story of the journey of Paul is beautiful and true. The pilgrim expresses his own hesitations in terms of both the beautiful fiction and the beautiful truth: "Io non Enëa, io non Paulo sono," "I am not Æneas; nor am I Paul" (Inf 2.32).

The collation of the beautiful fiction, which is Virgilian, with the beautiful truth, which is biblical, is a technique often repeated in the *Commedia.* Yet unlike Theodulus, whose method is ever confrontation, Dante very often seeks accommodation. That is, he seeks to redeem the poetic lie by insulating it with the scriptural truth. One such instance involves one of Dante's greatest poetic whoppers, the flight of the monster Geryon. Geryon was perhaps the classical monster least likely to be familiar to Dante's readers and therefore the one offering him the greatest opportunities for invention. Certainly the role Geryon is made to play — that of the steed or beast of burden that physically transports Virgil and Dante to the Malebolge, a destination apparently lacking the convenience of road access — is unprecedented and extraordinary.[12]

---

10. "Poet, you who guide me, consider if my powers will suffice before you trust me to this arduous passage."

11. Singleton, *Inferno,* 2:25.

12. The bibliography relevant to the Geryon episode is of course large. Fairly comprehensive up to the time of its publication is Roberto Mercuri, *Semantica di Gerione: Il motivo del viaggio nella "Commedia" di Dante* (Rome: Bulzoni, 1984). There is further valuable information in Paolo Cherchi, "XVII," in *Dante's Divine Comedy: Introductory Readings: I, Inferno,* ed. Tibor Wlassics (Charlottesville, VA: University of Virginia Press, 1990), pp. 222-34.

1. The Cord

Toward the end of the sixteenth canto of the *Inferno* the pilgrim Dante stands with his master Virgil beside a noisy cascade of *acqua tinta* — "dark water" or "tainted water," depending upon your translator of choice. As not infrequently happens in the *Inferno*, the narrator seems to pause briefly to wonder what can possibly happen next:

> Io avea una corda intorno cinta,
> e con essa pensai alcuna volta
> prender la lonza alla pelle dipinta.
>
> Poscia che l'ebbi tutta da me sciolta,
> sì come 'l duca m'avea comandato,
> porsila a lui aggroppata e ravvolta.
>
> Ond'ei si volse inver lo destro lato,
> e alquanto di lunge dalla sponda
> la gittò giuso in quell'alto burrato.
>
> "E' pur convien che novità risponda,"
> dicea fra me medesmo "al novo cenno
> che 'l maestro con l'occhio sì seconda."
>
> Ahi quanto cauti li uomini esser dienno
> presso a color che non veggion pur l'ovra,
> ma per entro i pensier miran col senno!
>
> El disse a me: "Tosto verrà di sovra
> ciò ch' io attendo e che il tuo pensier sogna;
> tosto convien ch'al tuo viso si scovra."[13] (Inf 16.106-23)

13. "I had a cord around my waist with which I once had meant to take the leopard with the painted pelt. After I had undone it, as my leader had commanded, I gave it to him coiled and knotted. Then, swinging round on his right side, he flung it out some distance from the edge, down into the depth of that abyss. 'Surely,' I said to myself, 'something new and strange will answer this strange signal the master follows with his eye.' Ah, how cautious we should be with those who do not see our action only, but with their wisdom peer into our thoughts! He said to me: 'Soon what I expect and your mind only dreams of will appear. Soon it shall appear before your eyes.'"

What is this cord? With it at the beginning of the next canto Virgil seems to catch or at the very least summon up Geryon, perhaps the most remarkable and original of Dante's infernal monsters, an embodiment of fraud with a long serpentine body with a sharpened tail but with a human head. The cord is perhaps a clue. Certainly it is a clew in that etymological sense of a filament or string that, like the thread left by Ariadne for Theseus, can lead us through a labyrinthine textual thicket.

Dante's medieval commentators, like his modern ones, shed sometimes light and sometimes obscuring dust. To make a thorough review of the exegetical history of the *corda* and/or of Geryon would too greatly distend this essay, but it should be possible to enter the discussion *in medias res* in a fashion that focuses on selected themes and issues, the first of which is the possible "Franciscanism" of the passage. It was the early commentator Francesco da Buti (late fourteenth century) who first recorded the rather obvious interpretative suggestion, practically inevitable to a medieval Italian and not easily avoided even by a modern American, that the cord could be a reference to the habit of the Friars Minor, or Franciscans, of which it was such a distinctive feature that the denominator "Cordelier" eventually became standard in the French language and is not unknown in medieval Italian.[14] Buti actually makes two remarks on this subject. The first is "biographical" and dubious, the second artistic and illuminating. The "biographical" claim is that "questa corda ch'elli [Dante] avea cinta significa ch'elli fu frate minore; ma no vi fece professione nel tempo della sua fanciullezza."[15] This is clearly a claim at the level of history that Dante entered the Franciscan novitiate, though he never went on to make his profession. If we make the validity of the commentator's "Franciscan" suggestion dependent upon our acceptance of the biographical claim, we shall probably reject it. For as the anonymous hand of the excellent, learned, and economical notes in the venerable Dent bilingual edition of the *Commedia* notes, "The symbolism here would be quite clear, if we could credit Buti's statement that Dante joined the Franciscans in his youth; but unfortunately the story has every appearance of having been fabricated for the purpose of elucidating this passage."[16]

Other modern commentators have found the suggestion wanting on ei-

---

14. See the *Storia di fra Michele minorita,* ed. Francesco Flora (Florence: F. Le Monnier, 1942), p. 55.

15. "This cord that he had wrapped around himself means that he was a Friar Minor; but he did not go on to make his [final] profession in his youth" (*Commento di Francesco da Buti sopra la Divina Comedia di Dante Allighieri,* ed. Crescentino Giannini [Pisa: Fratelli Nistri, 1858], 1 [*Inferno*]: 438).

16. See the note by H. Oelsner in his edition for the Temple Classics, *The Inferno of Dante Alighieri* (London: Dent, 1932), p. 178.

ther philological or historical grounds. My friend and *maestro* Robert Hollander thinks that the more authentic medieval Italian word for the Franciscan girdle was *capestro*.[17] That is the word used by Guido Minore, among the false counselors, when alluding to his own status as a Franciscan (Inf 27.92). When he speaks of actually joining the Order, however, he says simply "e poi fui cordigliero" (Inf 27.67).[18] The principal meanings of *capestro* seem to be an animal leash or lead, a bridle or a halter, or a hangman's rope for executions. An attempt to save the biographical appearances by suggesting that though the young Dante was never professed, he may have been a member of the Third Order was successfully rebuffed by Michele Barbi's demonstration that the Tertiaries of Dante's day wore not the cord but a leather cinch.[19]

Yet that may not be all there is to the matter. We are often required to read Dante's early readers with the care demanded by Dante's text itself. We must try to understand not merely what they expressly state but also the unstated assumptions on which their statements may rest. What Buti goes on to say is that "in these six *terzini,* our author makes a noble and beautiful fiction."[20] The fiction need not be the device of the cord, but rather the fictive history toward which the cord points. That fiction is that the first-person narrator had "once upon a time [*alcuna volta*] thought to capture with this the leopard-bitch with the piebald skin" (Inf 16.106-9).

In Dante one allegory leads to another, so that the question of the meaning of the *lonza* 'she-leopard' arises. Buti identifies it with the beast that, together with a lion and a she-wolf, blocked the pilgrim's path at the very beginning of the poem (Inf 1.32). Its specific allegorical meaning is lust *(lussuria)*.[21] Like most commentators, Buti associates the three beasts in a general sense with the three "enemies" (the world, the flesh, and the Devil) against which every Christian brought to the baptismal font promises to fight manfully. They are also to be associated with the "three temptations" (the lust of the eyes, the lust of the flesh, and the pride of life, or *avaritia, luxuria,* and *vana gloria*) conquered by Jesus in the desert (Matt. 4) and enumerated in the first of the catholic epistles of Saint John (2:16). The imagery is thus consistent with a generally ascetic reading of the first canto, in which the pilgrim "à dimonstrato sotto la poetica fizione com'era uscito della vita mondana e volea montare all'altezza delle virtù significata per lo monte."[22]

17. *Inferno,* ed. Robert and Jean Hollander, p. 307.

18. "And then I became a Franciscan."

19. Michele Barbi, *Problemi di critica dantesca,* 2 vols. (Florence: G. C. Sansoni, 1965), 1:241.

20. Buti, *Commento,* 1:438.

21. Buti, *Commento,* 1:33.

22. Buti, *Commento,* 1:33.

It may be a fiction that the young Dante ever had any formal connection to the Franciscans. But that a man of his spiritual temperament once entertained the idea of the religious life is highly plausible. For a Florentine youth of the final quarter of the thirteenth century, furthermore, the exemplary role of the Franciscans as emblems of religious life generally would have been very natural. In fact, the possibility that he once entertained the idea of overcoming the sins of the flesh through ascetic life is very easy to believe. If what we know of his biography suggests that, like most medieval Christians, he sought the solution to *luxuria* in committed matrimony rather than in votive chastity, that is no impediment to our crediting that at one time [*alcuna volta*] he had contemplated a more Augustinian course.

If the Franciscan cord is a dead-end lead, a general ascetic allegory is almost too easy to adduce. The biblical phrase "to gird up one's loins" means to prepare for action, a meaning that in hackneyed speech it retains until this day. When that action is interpreted spiritually, as it is so often by medieval exegetes, the ascetic allegory is nearly inescapable. Most male religious of the Middle Ages wore some kind of belt or girdle, the typical technical terms being *cingulum* and *zona*. Teufelsdruck was not the inventor of the "philosophy of clothes," and there is a rich literature of commentary on the various items in the repertory of monastic dress. The girding of the loins in particular took on a wide variety of ascetic meanings, from donning the armor for spiritual combat with devils to symbolic self-castration "for the kingdom of God's sake."[23] The wearing of the cord, therefore, need not be regarded as particularly strange. More pressing, perhaps, is the need to understand the thinking behind the strange purpose to which Virgil puts it — as signal, lasso, bridle, or fishing line.

Though the monster will indeed prove to be to Dante a *novità*, something never before seen, its arrival is described with an image from closely observed commercial and maritime life. Dante sees "come swimming up . . . a shape most like a man's who, having plunged to loose the anchor caught fast in a reef or something other hidden in the sea, now rises, reaching upward and drawing in his feet" (Inf 16.131-36).[24] There was a technical word for the diver whose task it was to free the anchor: *palombaro*.[25] In his commentary Benvenuto da Imola

---

23. See Philippus Oppenheim, *Symbolik und religiöse Wertung des Mönschskleides im christlichen Altertum* (Münster: Verlag Aschendorff, 1932), pp. 59-82.

24. "venir notando una figura in suso,/maravigliosa ad ogni cor sicuro,/sì come torna colui che va giuso/talora a solver l'àncora ch'aggrappa/o scoglio o altro che nel mare è chiuso,/ che 'n sù si stende, e da piè si rattrappa."

25. Ignazio Baldelli, "Un errore lessicografico: 'palombaro' e Gerione palombaro," in *Omaggio a Gianfranco Folena* (Padua: Editoriale Programma, 1993), [3]: 2243-49. The word is recorded by Alberto Guglielmotti in *Vocabolario marino e militare* (Rome: Voghera Carlo, 1889),

uses the Latin word *palumbarius,* and he finds the image particularly just because the *palumbarius* returns to the surface with the aid of a cord.[26] So the
cord may have a very practical as well as a symbolic purpose.

Buti, who directs our attention to the possibly Franciscan association of
the *corda* used to summon Geryon, has illuminating things to say about Geryon
himself. After telling us that Dante intends Geryon as a figure of worldly wisdom (*astuzia*), he goes on to consider three aspects of the monster:

> Et a figurarlo à posto tre varie forme: imperò che prima li à dato il capo con
> la faccia d'uomo giusto, le branche pilose di fiera, e l'altro fusto di serpenta;
> e doviamo notare che l'autore prese questa figura della santa Scrittura . . .
> Pone lo Genesis, che è lo primo libro della Bibbia, che lo Lucifero andò
> tentare li nostri primi padri in questa prima figura; col volto vergineo e con
> l'altro fusto di serpente. . . .[27]

Buti is a typical medieval exegete in the important respect that he frequently collates or buttresses his own "readings" with the opinions of other
commentators. He is here alluding to a curious and persistent gloss on the Book
of Genesis and the story of Satan's successful temptation of Eve in the Garden of
Eden. He is further typical in his tendency to blur distinctions between the primary scriptural sense and its exegetical commentary. According to him "As we
find in Genesis, which is the first book of the Bible, Lucifer went to tempt our
first parents in this first guise: with a maiden's face, but with the rest the body of
a serpent." Of course the hybrid serpent, part human, part beast, will be found
not in the primary text of Genesis but in its medieval exegetical elaborations. In
particular the first literary evidence of the woman-headed serpent appears in a
problematical passage of the twelfth-century *Historia Scholastica* of Peter
Comestor. Commenting on Genesis 3:1, "Now the serpent was the most crafty
[*callidior*] . . . ," Peter writes that Satan "elegit etiam quoddam genus serpentis, ut
ait Beda, virgineum vultum habens, quia similia similibus applaudunt. . . ."[28]

---

s.v. "palombaro," 2. See further Faustolo Rambelli, "Palombaro: una parola misteriosa,"
H[istorical]D[iving]S[ociety] *Notizie* 9.26 (April 2003): 26-28.

26. Cited by Baldelli, "Un errore lessicografico," pp. 2446-47.

27. "And to depict him he has presented three forms: first of all he has given him the face
of a just man, the hairy arms of a wild beast, and finally the trunk of a serpent; and we ought to
observe that the author takes this image from the Holy Scriptures . . ." (Buti, *Commento,* 1:461).
See also Enrico Proto, "Gerione," *Giornale dantesco* 8 (1900): 65-105.

28. ". . . he chose, as Bede says, the form of a serpent with the face of a young virgin, because like attracts like . . ." (Peter Comestor, *Historia scholastica,* "Liber Genesis," cap. 21, PL
198:1072).

I think that there can be little doubt that Dante, in his imaginative construction of the monster Geryon, has in his mind, as one of several thematic strands, the diabolical human-headed serpent of scriptural tradition. I use the rather vague word *tradition,* because we cannot be sure whether the idea first appeared in the visual arts or in literature and, if the latter, when it first appeared. The immediate problem is with the citation of Bede, in whose works it has proved impossible to find the idea Peter seems to attribute to him. So far as scholars have yet been able to determine, the *Historia Scholastica* itself is our first textual source.

There are many possible solutions to this puzzle. Peter may have mistaken his source or even, God forbid, made the whole thing up. He may have remembered the idea from a work falsely ascribed to Bede or from one, though genuinely by Bede, that has not survived. We can hope that further research may find an answer, though fortunately the argument of this essay can in the meantime proceed. There are two points worth noting briefly. The first is that the legend of the human-headed tempter was in the thirteenth century very widely diffused by one of the most important and learned books used by classicizing medieval poets, the *Historia destructionis Troiæ* of Guido delle Colonne. Guido includes the material in the important digression in his tenth book, in which he speaks of the origins of idolatry. "Because this material is not known to many," he writes, "we have decided to describe it in a short account in this place."[29] He, too, cites Bede, though his fuller engagement with Peter's *Historia Scholastica* makes it clear that the latter is his actual source. The language in which he speaks of what we would call "text" and "gloss" is most interesting. The first, the actual scriptural text, is the story "secundum Mosaycam tradicionem." The second, with the supplementary detail of the maiden-headed serpent, is the story "secundum tamen traditionem sacrarum scripturarum catholice vniuersalis ecclesie."[30]

A second observation is that the phrase used to underscore the apparent innocence and guilelessness of the tempter, *virgineus vultus,* a phrase attributed by Peter Comestor to Bede, then used again by Guido delle Colonne, then repeated again by Buti in the vernacular [*volto vergineo*], is specifically Virgilian and Ovidian. It is probable that "Bede" in his description of the woman-headed serpent is recalling an apt passage from the *Metamorphoses,* in which Ovid describes the punishment of the sirens upon the occasion of the rape of

---

29. *Historia Destructionis Troiæ,* trans. Mary Elizabeth Meek (Bloomington: Indiana University Press, 1974), p. 93; Guido de Columnis, *Historia destructionis Troiae,* p. 96: "Et quia plerisque material non est nota, ideo sub compendio de eo dicere decreuimus in hoc loco."

30. Guido de Columnus, *Historia destructionis Troiæ,* p. 97.

Proserpina (Met 5.551-63). Medieval mythographers frequently invoked the story of Proserpina, captured unaware by the King of Hell while she was gathering flowers in a *locus amoenus,* as a parallel to the story of the seduction of Eve in Eden. The punishment of the biblical serpent was that he should forever slither upon the earth (Gen. 3:14). The punishment of the sirens, the daughters of the River Acheolus found culpably inattentive, is their transformation into birds — but birds with human heads, the heads being necessary for the retention of their beautiful voices:

> Vobis, Acheloides, unde
> Pluma, pedesque avium, cum virginis ora geratis? . . .
> *Virginei vultus,* et vox humana remansit. (Met 5.552-53, 563)

The "maidenly countenance" is probably not a conscious "allusion," but one example from among a large number that might be adduced of the unconscious or semi-conscious way that classical themes and classical language inform the style of medieval exegetes deeply trained in *grammatica.*

Whether any iconographic instance of the theme is to be found from the age of Bede or earlier is uncertain. The oldest and still one of the best of several studies dealing with the human-headed serpent is that of John K. Bonnell, published in 1917.[31] He concluded that "it is not until the thirteenth or the beginning of the fourteenth century that we find the tempter represented with a human head." This statement is not strictly speaking accurate. Louis Charbonneau-Lassay claims that the theme will be found among "the first Christian artists," meaning presumably paleo-Christian artists, but his vague statement lacks detailed support.[32] I can think of one notable example in a widely admired masterpiece of the twelfth century, the so-called "Verdun altarpiece" at Klosterneuburg in Austria.[33] Yet it is certainly true that it is the fourteenth century, and probably the efflorescence of the religious drama of Europe, that witnesses the popularity of the iconographic subject.

Returning to the specific remarks of Buti, we must note the depth of the commentator's Virgilianism. Geryon is not a particularly familiar mythological

---

31. "The Serpent with a Human Head in Art and in Mystery Play," *American Journal of Archæology* 21 (1917): 255-91. The other indispensable essay is Henry Ansgar Kelly, "The Metamorphoses of the Eden Serpent during the Middle Ages and Renaissance," *Viator* 2 (1971): 301-27.

32. Louis Charbonneau-Lassay, *Le bestiaire du Christ: la mystérieuse emblématique de Jésus-Christ* (Bruges: Desclée, de Brouwer et Cie, [1940]), p. 771.

33. Helmut Buschhausen, *Der Verduner Altar* (Vienna: Tusch, 1980), plate 28. Here the head is crowned and androgynous.

creature. Lodovico Castelvetro becomes testy in discussing Geryon. No other poet or historian, he says, reports any of these things about the monster. The whole invention is for him a "vanity," and one that cannot be justified by recourse to the allegory of fraud, since to find an allegory without the help of a sensible literal sense is to fly without wings or cross the ocean without a boat.[34] At the same time it is not entirely clear how Dante could have been true to the poets and historians of a tradition so fragmentary and vague. Geryon is to be found in Hesiod and Lucretius, but Dante is certainly dependent on Virgil, in whose poem Geryon is twice named and once alluded to. Even his most prominent appearance, in the eighth book, where he is incidentally mentioned in a recital of the exploits of Hercules, is hardly emphatic:

> Nam maximus ultor
> Tergemini nece Geryonae spoliisque superbus
> Alcides [Hercules] aderat. . . . (*Æneid* 8.201-3)[35]

But Buti is also entirely aware that it is to Geryon that Virgil alludes in his sixth book, in a catalogue of the monsters at the portals of hell, as the "forma tricorporis umbræ" (*Æneid* 6.289). He notes that it is Dante's Virgil who addresses Geryon by name at Inf 17.97 and suggests that this passage in the sixth book is the source of the sinister repertory of monsters taken by Dante from Virgil: ". . . come Virgilio dice nel sesto dell'Eneida: Et forma tricorporis umbræ."[36] He then goes into a learned discussion of whether Geryon had three bodies and three souls or three bodies and a single soul. It is of course by no means readily apparent what it would mean to have "three bodies" or to be "tricorporal" in any case. As we have already seen, Buti interprets it to mean in Dante a monster combining *tre varie forme:* face of a man, hairy limbs of a feral beast, and trunk-like tail of a serpent.[37]

Dante shows very considerable originality in transforming Virgilian

---

34. *Sposizione di Lodovico Castelvetro a XXIX canti dell'Inferno dantesco,* ed. Giovanni Franciosi (Modena: Tipi della Società tipografica, 1886), p. 218. My attention was drawn to this passage, as to so much else, by the Hollanders' notes.

35. "Then came the great avenger Alcides [Hercules] himself, exulting in the killing and despoiling of three-bodied Geryon" (Virgil, *Opera,* ed. R. A. B. Mynors [Oxford: Clarendon, 1969]).

36. "As Virgili says in the sixth book of the Æneid: *Et forma tricorporis umbræ*" (Buti, *Commento,* 1:460).

37. For suggestions of the way in which the tricorporality fits in with the very large "Trinitarian" scheme of the poem see Paul Priest, *Dante's Incarnation of the Trinity* (Ravenna: Longo, [1982]).

Geryon, but the transformed monster itself, incorporating suggestions of serpent, fish, bird, and feral beast, is actually rather commonplace, as classical monsters go, at least classical sea-monsters.[38] Indeed within the taxonomy of classical monstrosity Geryon's only really distinctive feature — a very striking one to be sure — is the monster's *human head*. It is the human head, I believe, that allowed Dante to accommodate the vague data concerning Virgilian Geryon — his monstrosity, his tricorporality, and his implicit association with fraud — while at the same time preparing another agenda that included, quite particularly, some consideration of the problem of fraud in language. The human-headed serpent is, from Dante's perspective, a *biblical* fact, a fact *secundum traditionem sacrarum scripturarum catholice vniuersalis ecclesie*, in the words of Peter Comestor. The "novelty" of the human head, indeed, is a poetic supererogation or correction of a classical pagan monster. Here Dante is playing the precise role of Truth in the debate between Truth and Falsehood in the *Eclogue* of Theodulus.

2. *Humano capiti*

Geryon is in the broadest sense an emblem of fraud, that is to say an emblem of what is not merely *falsus* in deed but positively *fallax* in intention: hypocrisy, dissimulation, evil guile. This is "the beast with pointed tail, that leaps past mountains, shatters walls and weapons!" (Inf 17.1-2).[39] Such dissimulation was that practiced by the ancient Tempter in using a benign human face that might better conceal the falseness of his human words.

Among the iconographic monuments of the human-headed reptilian Tempter is a rare one in which the figure actually has *two* heads, one male, one female. Though Dante's Geryon has but a single human head, the poet's strategy may nonetheless be duplex, as befits a literary attempt to deal with duplic-

38. There was a rich classical iconography of sea-monsters generally reminiscent of Geryon, for which the usual word was the Greek *kētos*, a word of much wider suggestion than Latin *cetus* ('whale'). See John Boardman, "'Very Like a Whale' — Classical Sea Monsters," in *Monsters and Demons in the Ancient and Mediaeval Worlds: Papers Presented in Honor of Edith Porada*, ed. Ann E. Farkas, Prudence O. Harper and Evelyn B. Harrison (Mainz on Rhine: Philipp von Zabern, 1987), p. 71. Much of this iconography was carried over into Christian art in terms of the story of Jonah. See Marion Lawrence, "Ships, Monsters, and Jonah," *American Journal of Archaeology* 62 (1966): 289-96. On one famous monument, the paleo-Christian "Projecta Casket" in the British Museum, the Nereid riding the *kētos* holds a stretched-out length of — of what? Rope, chain, netting? See Kathleen J. Shelton, *The Esquiline Treasure* (London: British Museum Publications, 1981), plate 5 and p. 73.

39. "la fiera con la coda aguzza,/che passa i monti e rompe i muri e l'armi."

ity. The description of "classical" tricorporal Geryon is that of Siamese triplets: three upper bodies and three pairs of legs that share a single midsection. Dante gives us instead a single body composed of conjoined parts of three different *kinds* of body, human, quadruped, and reptilian, in which the singular novelty is the union of the human and the animal.

Surely the most famous "polycorporal" image in world literature is that in the opening lines of one of the world's most famous poems — the *Ars poetica* of Horace:

> Humano capiti cervicem pictor equinam
> iungere si velit se varias inducere plumas
> undique conlatis membris, ut turpiter atrum
> desinat in piscem mulier formosa superne. . . .[40]

"If a painter were to graft a human head onto a horse's neck, apply harlequin plumage, and finish off as an ugly black fish what began as a beautiful woman" — if he were to do that, would he not invite our scornful laughter?

Is it possible that Dante has Horace in mind? More than a century ago the great British *dantista* Edward Moore wrote what is still the best synoptic essay on Dante's use of the classical Latin poets.[41] He devoted only ten pages to Horace, finding that Dante offers "little evidence of familiarity with his works, at any rate beyond the limits of the Ars Poetica."[42] To that work he adduces several citations or borrowings. He does not include the description of Geryon, but the intellectual context of the monster's appearance suggests that we are not wrong to do so.

Though striking, the comparison of a verbal construction with an organic, animate being is a very ancient one in Greek thought. Perhaps the classical expression of the idea comes near the end of Plato's *Phædrus*, where Socrates says that a discourse should be constructed in the form of a living being, revealing the harmonious, functional shape of a body.[43] More than one of Plato's readers, baffled by the challenge of finding such a coherent structure in

---

40. *Ars poetica* ll. 1-4.

41. Edward Moore, *Studies in Dante. First Series: Scripture and Classical Authors in Dante*, 2nd ed. (Oxford: Clarendon, 1969), pp. 197-206.

42. Moore, *Studies in Dante*, p. 197.

43. *Phædrus* 264c: "Every speech must be put together like a living creature, with a body of its own; it must be neither without head nor without legs; and it must have a middle and extremities that are fitting both to one another and to the whole work." Trans. by Alexander Nehamas and Paul Woodruff, in *Plato, Complete Works*, ed. John M. Cooper (Indianapolis: Hackett, 1997), p. 541.

the *Phædrus* itself, has commented on it with some irony. The analogy was also widely used to identify harmonious unities of other kinds. There is a cognate reflection of the idea in a well-known image of Saint Paul, in 1 Corinthians 12, where he speaks of the harmonious participation in a unified body of a disparity of bodily members.

What makes it very probable, in my judgment, that Dante is here engaging Horace is the striking thematic context in which Geryon is introduced. Virgil is perhaps particularly wordy in explaining in the eleventh canto the microeconomics of the seventh circle, the circle of the Violent. And though Dante praises the clarity of the account (Inf 11.67-69), the reader may remain somewhat less sanguine. Violence may be done, says Virgil, with regard to three different objects: against God, against self, against neighbor. One species of violence against God occurs when we "scorn nature and her bounty" (Inf 11.48). But Art *(arte)* follows Nature as an offspring, so that Art "is God's grandchild, as it were" (Inf 11.105). Hence the usurers of the seventeenth canto, who are associated with Geryon, with whom Dante has brief, private colloquy while Virgil speaks to Geryon, also privately — these usurers are the emblems of "violence against art." Horace too is concerned with violence against art, the violation of the *ars poetica.*

That is one congruence, and there is another. The opening lines of the *Ars Poetica* are usually invoked in terms of the classical doctrine of poetic decorum, and there is good evidence that that doctrine was recognized and honored by medieval poets. One very amusing testimony is found in Chaucer, in the gracefully comic scene in which Pandarus tries to teach the tongue-tied Troilus how to write a love letter:

> Ne jompre ek no discordant thing yfeere,
> As thus, to usen termes of phisik
> In loves termes; hold of thi matere
> The forme alwey, and do that it be lik;
> For if a peyntour wolde peynte a pyk
> With asses feet, and hedde it as an ape,
> It cordeth naught, so were it but a jape. (TC 2.1037-1043)[44]

Here the central injunctions are "hold of thi matere the forme alwey, and do that it be lik" — that is, "stick to a single subject, and make sure that the work is unified" in subject, tone, and style. That is indeed a defining tenet of

---

44. Geoffrey Chaucer, "Troilus and Criseyde," *The Riverside Chaucer,* ed. Larry D. Benson, 3rd ed. (Boston: Houghton Mifflin, 1987), p. 503.

"Horatian decorum" as later formulated by the eighteenth-century theorists of the "unities," but within Chaucer's context, as within Dante's, it can hardly be innocent or unironic. Pandarus's distinctive increment to the advice of Horace, illustrating the prohibition of throwing together discordant subjects of themes, is the hypothetical combination of medical and amatory "terms." But medieval poets mix amatory and medical language very frequently, following the lead of Ovid, one of whose works most widely cited by medieval writers is after all entitled *Remedia Amoris,* and no major vernacular poem, even including the *Roman de la Rose,* does it more schematically than does the *Troilus and Criseyde,* where "love sickness" plays a major role in the plot as well as in the thematic structure.

There is, I think, a similar indirection in the *Commedia.* The poet Dante seems to be addressing not decorum but a slightly different though cognate issue, that of poetic truth. The arrival of Geryon at the end of the sixteenth canto is accompanied by an important authorial reflection on truth-speaking, that there are times when it is wiser to say nothing. Perhaps for the poet all things are lawful, but not all are expedient:

> Sempre a quel ver c' ha faccia di menzogna
> de' l'uom chiuder le labbra fin ch'el pote,
> però che sanza colpa fa vergogna. (Inf 16.124-26)

"To a truth that bears the face of falsehood a man should seal his lips if he is able lest he not be believed although he tell the truth."

Good advice, no doubt, "But here I cannot be silent":

> ma qui tacer nol posso; e per le note
> di questa comedìa, lettor, ti giuro,
> s'elle non sien di lunga grazia vòte,
> ch'i' vidi. . . . (Inf 16.127-30)[45]

The language here is far from diffident. Dante fully recognizes just how fantastic and fabulous his description of Geryon must be. His adjective is *maravigliosa* (Inf 16.132), 'astonishing, amazing'. We are reminded of our recent encounter, in the previous canto, with Brunetto Latini, who cried out upon recognizing Dante "Qual maraviglia!" (Inf 15.22). Indeed that a living poet should descend to the Underworld and there hold converse with the damned requires a

---

45. "But here I can't be silent. And by the strains of this Comedy — so may they soon succeed in finding favor — I swear to you, Reader, that I saw. . . ."

poetic credulity of the same order as that required to "believe in" what is perhaps the most outrageous of Dante's monsters.

It is one thing to say, as the sacred authors repeatedly do, "My testimony is true." It is quite another to swear extravagantly that it is true. After all, Jesus himself warned against swearing at all, either by heaven, or by earth, or by Jerusalem, or even by your own head, "for you cannot make one of your own hairs black or white" (Matt. 5:36). Yet Dante does swear, and whatever the strange phrase "by the *note* of this Comedy" is meant to convey, he is in effect swearing by heaven, earth, Jerusalem, and, perhaps above all, by his own head.

The narrator-pilgrim is certainly protesting much, yet I am not prepared to say "too much." After all, he confronts the difficulty of describing that accomplished and artful falseness that is, according to Milton, "the only evil that walks invisible, except to God alone."[46] If it is risky to report the truth that has the "face" of a lie, what of the lie that has the "face" of truth? That is, in effect, what Geryon is, a false face. Indeed, Dante emphasizes his "faceness." It is the word *faccia* that links the thought about poetic tact at the end of canto sixteen with the actual appearance of the monster at the beginning of seventeen:

La faccia sua era faccia d'uom giusto,
tanto benigna avea di fuor la pelle. . . . (Inf 17.10-11)[47]

The opposite of the truth that has the face of a lie is presumably a lie that has the face of the truth. Geryon is the embodiment of Fraud, or a lie that has the face of truth, at least the face of a "uom giusto." The paradox Dante orchestrates is that to achieve truth he must offend against the prudence of literary decorum. This is just one of the many places in the *Commedia* when Dante "goes on the offensive" in insisting that his fiction is not a fiction, but it is possibly the most dramatic. It appears that the poet will be satisfied with nothing short of his readers' active belief. As the Hollanders note, "Dante has put the veracity of the entire Comedy . . . upon the reality of Geryon."[48] And he has reimagined the monster in a fashion that confronts Horace even more brusquely than it does Virgil, Geryon's "inventor." Truth is stranger than fiction, says the poet. There are more things in Hell and Earth, Orazio, than are dreamt of in your philosophy. Once again Alithea trumps Pseustis. The decorum of plausibility may be required by fiction; God's reality submits to no such petty restrictions.

46. John Milton, *Paradise Lost* 3.682, in *The Riverside Milton*, ed. Roy Flannagan (Boston: Houghton Mifflin Company, 1998), p. 436.
47. "It had the features of a righteous man, benevolent in countenance. . . ."
48. Hollander and Hollander, ed. and trans., *Inferno*, p. 308.

3. The Leviathan

In terms of medieval biblical theory, a figure like Geryon reverses the dialectic of the exegetical process. Instead of moving from a harsh exterior (the "letter") to a sweet interior (the "spirit"), in the unveiling of untruth we confront a deceptive sweet exterior that masks a harsh interior truth. I speak of a figure "like Geryon" because there are numerous analogous literary figures that offer us instruction. Even Horace's image contains a suggestion of a deceptive surface attractiveness, an appealing outside that disguises an unappealing inside, so that what begins as a beautiful woman ends in a foul black fish. That suggestion becomes dominant in the false face of Geryon. In the background of Horace's image there are memories of harpies and sirens. The distinction between Harpies and Sirens in ancient literature is hardly a fine one. The ambiguity is that of woman/bird and woman/fish, the more ancient siren being the former. Here Horace plays a kind of medial position, since his grotesque has a woman's head and a fish's tail, but also feathers.

Dante's poem has both Harpies and a/the Siren. The former make a brief appearance in the wood of suicides in Inferno 13, where they gloomily chomp the leaves of the arborified suicides. The Siren has a more extended and also, for our purposes, more relevant role in the nineteenth canto of *Purgatorio,* where she appears to Dante in a dream. It is more relevant in that it deals with the theme of overcoming or unmasking Fraud, a theme that is also important in the Geryon episode. Here, in Purgatory, and indeed at an advanced station on the road to purgation, the false exterior of female beauty has fallen away from the Siren. What Dante sees is a woman deformed, ugly, unappealing. Despite that — despite "seeing what she really is" — Dante is still susceptible to her song. Only the intervention of the "holy lady" followed by a sharp rebuke from Virgil, who rips her garment to expose the Siren's putrid belly, saves Dante from the fate of Ulysses.

We may gain some insight by comparing Dante's treatment of Fraud with that of a later moral allegorist, Edmund Spenser. In the first book of the *Faerie Queene* Spenser develops at considerable length the figure of Duessa — that is, Doubleness, or Duplicity herself:

> I that do seeme not I, Duessa am . . .
> Duessa I, the daughter of Deceipt and Shame. (FQ 1.5.26)[49]

Duessa plays a major and complex role in Spenser's poem, but one consistent aspect of her presentation is a captiously attractive exterior, often achieved through

---

49. *The Poetical Works of Edmund Spenser,* ed. J. C. Smith and E. de Selincourt (Oxford: Oxford University Press, 1932), p. 26.

enchantment, that masks a repellent interior. The very strong element of sexual licentiousness that characterizes her clearly links her with the Siren. The fish-tail on the mermaid, apparently regarded as rather cute by Hallmark Cards, was in ancient tradition regarded as disgusting. That is why Horace wrote of the grotesque image that begins as a beautiful woman and ends in a foul black fish, and it is why medieval mermaids displayed only their upper bodies. Spenser's Fradubbio, one of Duessa's victims, understands her true nature only when it is too late:

> Her neather partes misshapen, monstruous,
> Were hidd in water, that I could not see. (FQ 1.2.41; p. 13)

Notwithstanding the fact that the *Faerie Queene* contains a sustained and at times violent polemic against Roman Catholicism, Spenser had read his Dante and remembers that in a similar fashion Geryon "beached its head and chest but did not draw its tail up on the bank" (Inf 17.8-9).

4. Sacred and Secular Exegesis

In the letter to Can Grande Dante famously used the fancy word "polysemous" to describe the nature of allegory in the *Commedia*. Within the context of an invocation of the "allegory of the theologians" this adjective has rightly been understood to refer to the so-called "fourfold" exegetical method that approached a text from literal, "allegorical," tropological, and anagogical perspectives. That might be called vertical or hierarchical polysemousness. But there is also in Dante a notable horizontal or distributive polysemousness by which we find a plurality of complex, competitive, perhaps unresolvable literal suggestions. Thus is Geryon a monster of the deep or of the air? Is he fish-like or bird-like? He rises like a diver to the surface of a deep declivity, yet he seems to fly back through the same medium whence he has emerged as a dragon through the air.

Dante is above all an artist, and his imagery is an artist's imagery. It often finds its sources of scriptural inspiration not in a naked reading of scriptural text but in the more complex associations of that text within its already established exegetical penumbra. There is a graceful little essay by theologian J. B. Bauer in which he demonstrates — especially with regard precisely to what we would call "animal imagery" — the powerful influence of the patristic exegetical enterprise on the visual arts.[50]

---

50. J. B. Bauer, "L'exégèse patristique, créatrice des symboles," in *Sacra Pagina: Miscellanea*

As we see from a hundred examples throughout his poem Dante's exegetical imagination is hardly sluggish; it needs only the slightest hint or prod. There is now a general consensus among *dantisti* that a single somewhat cryptic verse about God's terrible power in the prophecy of Isaiah — "irrita faciens signa divinorum et ariolos in furorem vertens, convertens sapientes *retrorsum* et scientiam eorum stultam faciens" (Isa. 44:25) — is the "source" of the poet's very remarkable and horrible image of the "retrofacial" carriage of the diviners in *Inferno* 20.[51] This bit of sacred exegesis is perhaps paralleled by a similarly remarkable example of profane exegesis in *Paradiso* 20. The obscure Trojan warrior Ripheus is a spear-bearing "extra" in the drama of the *Æneid,* his only narrative role to die amid the general slaughter; but Virgil says of him

> Cadit et Ripeus, iustissimus unus
> Qui fuit in Teucris et seruantissimus æqui. (Æneid 2.426-27)[52]

That is not very much, but it is enough for Dante. The ancient Trojans were the ancestors of the ancient Romans, and the "most just" member of that tribe must have been very just indeed. So Dante, who could make rather heavy weather of last-minute repentance in the *Purgatorio,* here simply ignores any suggestion that *extra ecclesiam nulla salus.* "Who would believe it" he asks ("Chi crederebbe" [Par 20.67]), that Ripheus is right there in Heaven, in the very eye of the Eagle?

Buti knew his Virgil, but of course he also knew his Bible. As he thought about Geryon, his mind naturally turned to the figure of the fallen Lucifer.[53] I believe that Dante, too, was thinking about Lucifer, and about one of Lucifer's particularly relevant exegetical associations — that of Leviathan, a monster of the deep. Indeed though Leviathan is not textually present in Dante's poem, I believe that he is there by exegetical inference and as the catalytic image that "christianizes" Geryon. We are wont to think of Leviathan as a huge fish, the largest of whales, and indeed one of the biblical words for Leviathan is *cetus,* 'whale'. Yet Dante, instinctively relying upon the medieval iconographic and exegetical traditions, would probably have first thought of a creature monstrous not only in size but also in composition: scaly, serpentine, elongated.

---

biblica congressus internationalis catholici de re biblica, Actes du Congrès International Catholique de Sciences Bibliques: Bruxelles-Louvain, 1958, ed. J. Coppens, *et al.,* 2 vols. (Gembloux: J. Duculot, 1959), 1:180-86.

51. ". . . that frustrateth the tokens of the liars, and maketh diviners mad, that turneth wise men *backward* and maketh their knowledge foolish."

52. "Ripheus also falls, the most just one among the Trojans, and the most observant of justice."

53. Buti, *Commento,* pp. 440, 461.

Leviathan is named only three times in the Vulgate — twice in the Book of Job (3:8 and 40:20), once in the prophecy of Isaiah (27:1) But there are allusions to Leviathan, if not the name of Leviathan, in some other places, most notably in the seventy-third psalm. When we examine these scriptural sites we shall find the clews that Dante, too, followed in the peculiar construction of his hybrid monster. The Vulgate rendering of Psalm 73 follows the Septuagint's "dragon in the waters," moving from the plural "the heads of the dragons" to the singular "the heads of the dragon": "tu confirmasti in virtute tua mare, contribulasti capita draconum in aquis; tu confregisti capita draconis . . ." (Ps. 73:13-14). In the Hebrew the second, the singular beast, was named "Leviathan," but whether the beast itself is one or several, there are a plurality of heads *(capita)*. The meaning of the plural form, while not absolutely obvious, suggests a monster, like Cerberus, that is polycapital.

A second text, that in Isaiah, perhaps more specifically suggests a parallel with the tricorporality of Geryon, for though it refers to a single monster, it refers to him under three aspects: "in die illa visitabit Dominus in gladio suo duro et grandi et forti super Leviathan serpentem vectem et super Leviathan serpentem tortuosum et occidet cetum qui in mari est" (Isa. 27:1).[54] This *serpentem vectem,* the "bar serpent" of the Douay translation, is somewhat difficult. The Authorized Version gives us "piercing serpent," the RSV "fleeing serpent." The Douay translators of course see *vectem* as a noun (*vectis,* 'a stout pole or crowbar') in apposition to the accusative *serpentem.* The meaning of "bar serpent" is therefore 'a serpent strong and rigid as an iron bar'. On the other hand the meaning of the image in the exegetical tradition of moral allegory is quite stable and uniform from the time of Gregory on. The rigidity *(vectis)* of the beast is combined with a certain supple flexibility *(tortuositas),* because the maliciousness of Lucifer is masked by a superficial gentleness.[55] Never was it more so, of course, than when like Geryon, who presents the fraudulent face of a just man, Lucifer adopted a virgin's head, the better with which to deceive Eve.

There is also convincing evidence in the strange details of the narrative that Dante has in mind the exegetical associations of Leviathan. These derive from two references in the book of Job and from Gregory's extraordinary treatment of them in his *Moralia* — a book that can without exaggeration be said to

54. "In that day the Lord with his hard and great and strong sword shall visit Leviathan, the bar serpent, and Leviathan the crooked serpent, and shall slay the whale that is in the sea."

55. Thus Herveus of Deols (twelfth century), *Commentaria in Isaiam:* "Sed propheta, qui nunc *serpentem* dixerat, *tortuosumque* subjunxit, interposit vectem, quia in serentis tortitudine fluxa mollities, in vecte autem est diritia rigiditatis. Ut ergo hunc et durum signaret, et mollem, etiam *vectem* nominat, et *serpentem.* Durus quippe est per malitiam, mollis per blandimenta" (PL 181:252). Most of Herveus is taken virtually verbatim from Gregory's *Moralia in Job* 4.9 (PL 75:645).

be one of the fundamental wellsprings of the imagery of medieval literature. The first reference to Leviathan, or rather to "a leviathan," is in the terrible curse uttered by Job at the beginning of the third chapter. The curse, to be sure, is not against God but against the day of Job's very conception: "Maledicant ei qui maledicunt diei, qui parati sunt suscitare Leviathan" (Job 3:8).[56] It is in commenting on this verse that Gregory gives his highly influential interpretation of the word *leviathan*. It means *additamentum*, 'an addition, an increase, a supplement', for what Lucifer gave to our unhappy parents in Eden was the bitter "supplement" of sin. In promising to add to them divinity, he actually subtracted their immortality.[57] What we should perhaps note here is the curious Vulgate phrase *suscitare Leviathan*. The verb *suscitare* suggests raising up from a depth, or awakening from torpor, and it would be highly apt in describing the strange command given and the strange action effected by Virgil: the throwing of the cord into the abyss in order to "raise" Geryon.

It is thence only a fairly small imaginative step to other connections between a cord and Leviathan. As the book nears its end, the Lord famously answers Job from the whirlwind. It is hardly a comforting response. The distance between God and man is immeasurable, as is the inequality of their powers. The enormity of God's power is suggested by his creation of two colossal beasts: the behemoth and the leviathan. With rhetorical sarcasm God asks whether Job can master Leviathan: "an extrahere poteris Leviathan hamo, et fune ligabis linguam eius; numquid pones circulum in naribus eius? . . . numquid inludes ei quasi avi, aut ligabis illum ancillis tuis?" (Job 40:20-21, 24).[58]

Now there are three ideas here that seem to me relevant to Dante's fiction of Geryon. Two of them involve a cord *(funis)*. The first is the idea of fishing for Leviathan in a body of water, and the second is of roping or bridling Leviathan like a domestic beast. As is so often true in Dante's poem, a surface of apparently concrete specificity becomes blurred and ambiguous under close investigation. How, for instance, does Virgil cast the cord into the abyss? Dante hands it to him "coiled and knotted together" (*aggroppata e ravvolta,* Inf 16.111). Coiled and knotted like a snare or a lasso? And when Virgil casts it "some distance out from the edge" (*alquanto di lunge dalla sponda,* Inf 16.113), does he or does he not continue to hold onto one end? When Geryon responds to the strange "signal" *(cenno)*, does he rise by means of the cord?

56. "Let them curse it who curse the day, who are ready to raise up a leviathan."

57. "Sed dum blande non habita se daturum perhibuit, callide et habita subtraxit" (PL 75:645).

58. "Canst thou draw out the leviathan with a hook, or canst thou tie his tongue with a cord? Canst thou put a ring in his nose . . . shalt thou play with him as with a bird, or tie him up for thy handmaids?"

From the point of view of spiritual understanding such questions are not unimportant. Yet vivid though the scene seems, and is, only the reader's imagination can answer them. In reading a text the reader must always bring something to it. The poet can do some of the work, even most of the work, but he cannot do all of the work. If Dante has triggered in our minds associations of Leviathan, we are likely to see certain possibilities. The first is that the cord is metaphorically a kind of fishing line. The second is that the cord is metaphorically a kind of bridle or halter. The first "catches" Geryon; the second controls him. Certainly when Virgil and Dante fly off on the monster's back, one might say that they are playing with him as with a bird.

Of all the books of the Bible, with the possible exception of the Canticle, no text was in the later Middle Ages more inseparably wed to an authoritative allegorical gloss than was the book of Job. Wherever Job was read it was almost certain to be read in the expository light of Gregory's *Moralia in Job,* one of the three or four greatest and most enduring monuments of patristic exegesis. We know that Dante was, as we would expect, familiar with some of the works of Gregory, who was the authoritative source for the legend of Trajan's conversion and from whose *Moralia* Dante first borrowed, then amusingly corrected (in *Paradiso* 28.133-35), the hierarchies of angels.[59] Gregory did not invent the arguments that exploited the imagery of Leviathan within the theological doctrines of the incarnation and of soteriology. The Greek Fathers, and especially Gregory of Nyssa, seem to have been their inventors. But Latin Gregory gave them their definitive elaboration and their popular diffusion.

"Canst thou draw out Leviathan with a hook?" God asks of the miserable Job (Job 40:20). This is rhetorical *sarcasmos.* One implication of the question is that it is absurdly beyond the petty powers of man even to imagine the power of God. But of course a cognate implication is that in fact God *can* catch Leviathan with a hook. Many medievalists will be familiar with an extraordinary illustration preserved from the now lost *Hortus Deliciarum* of Herrad of Hohenbourg.[60] In the upper left-hand quarter of a vertical rectangle God the Father stands with fishing-pole in hand. The lengthy fishing line, which descends to the bottom of the illustration, looks something like a rosary, composed as it is of seven linked roundels containing bearded male heads and ending with the large "gaud" of a Crucifix (Christus Rex). The Crucifix ends in a large fishhook, which has pierced the jaw of Leviathan, a classical *kētos* with

---

59. I here follow Simonetta Saffiotti Bernardi, "Gregorio I," in the *Enciclopedia Dantesca.*

60. This was first brought into the discussion of cantos 16-17 in the illuminating article of John Block Friedman, "Antichrist and the Iconography of Dante's Geryon," *Journal of the Warburg and Courtauld Institutes* 35 (1972): 108-22.

monstrous head, lion's paws, feathered wings, and long and *tortuosus* serpentine body. Leviathan has been caught with a hook on which the attached bait is the crucified Christ![61] The following captions describe the theological action. "Divinitas hamum in mare seculi mittit." The fishing-line "rosary" ending in Christ is composed of roundels of "Patriarche et prophete." Leviathan is thus identified: "Leviathan est piscis marinus similis draconi et significat diabolum."[62]

If we pause momentarily to summarize the implied theological argument, it is this: God the Father goes fishing for Leviathan, an emblem of the monstrous ancient enemy of mankind, who appears in another form as the human-headed sweet-talking serpent of the Garden of Eden. Like all angling, God's activity involves a certain kind of fraud, the concealing of the danger of the iron barb with the superficial attractiveness of the wiggling worm. But this piscatorial fraud answers the older and fatal fraud through which the Old Enemy defeated our first parents using a fruit "fair to the eye" (Gen. 3:6). Thus writes Gregory of Nyssa, one of the inventors of this remarkable exegetical image: "Nor would this deception have succeeded had not the fishhook of evil been furnished with the outward appearance of good, as with a bait. Of his own free will man fell into this misfortune and through pleasure became subject to the enemy of life."[63]

The classic medieval exegesis of the passage, that in Gregory's *Moralia,* is too extensive to summarize here, but we may note certain features that seem particularly relevant to Dante's Geryon. Jahweh's speech from the whirlwind centers on two stupendous creatures, the comparison with which dramatizes human puniness: Behemoth, a land animal, and Leviathan, an animal of the sea. Indeed *Behemoth,* according to Gregory, literally means 'animal', but the figurative meaning is the Devil.[64] Hence in his extended exegesis Gregory often seems to think of Behemoth and Leviathan as alternative images of the same monstrous evil. We have already noted Dante's artful ambiguity in *Inferno* 16 and 17, which leaves us uncertain whether to regard Geryon as fish or as fowl.

In considerably amplifying the piscatorial metaphor of salvation Gregory

---

61. Herrad of Hohenbourg, *Hortus Deliciarum,* ed. Rosalie Green *et al.,* 2 vols. (London: Warburg Institute, 1979), 1:135, plate 94.

62. "Divinity throws the hook into the sea of the world"; "Leviathan is an ocean fish similar to a dragon, and it signifies the Devil" (Herrad of Hohenbourg, *Hortus Deliciarum,* 2:134).

63. *Christology of the Later Fathers,* ed. Edward Rochie Hardy (Philadelphia: Westminster Press, 1954), p. 298. For the Greek text see Gregory of Nyssa, *Discours catéchétique,* ed. Louis Méridier (Paris: A. Picard, 1908), p. 104.

64. "Quem sub Behemoth nomine, nisi antiquum hostem insinuat?" (Gregory, *Moralia* 23.12.16, PL 75:1055b).

naturally has a good deal to say about the cord or line *(funis)* used to capture, hook, or tame Behemoth and Leviathan. The idea of a restraining rope is implicit in several of the verses of this extended medley, and, as *funis,* it is explicit in Job 40:20: "an extrahere poteris Leviathan hamo, et *fune* ligabis linguam eius." Gregory comments on the "polysemousness" of the cord as it appears in Scripture. In Psalm 15:6 it means a measuring line. In the curse of Isaiah 5:18 it means "sins," as also at Psalm 108. On the other hand, the "three-stranded cord" of Ecclesiastes 4:12 means "faith," founded in the knowledge of the Trinity. The various allegorical meanings of the cord justify Gregory's own complex series of alternative readings *in malo* and *in bono,* the most remarkable of which is the source of the painted illustration in the *Hortus Deliciarum.* In the vastness of the watery abyss, that is, in the immensity of the human generations doomed to death, God goes fishing for the Enemy, hooking him on the barb hidden beneath the bait of the human flesh of Christ.[65] The little Latin rubrics or captions to the illustrations in the *Hortus Deliciarum* refer in elliptical form to this strange theological allegory: "The fishing line itself is indicated in the Gospel by the generation of the ancient fathers" — that is, by the forty-two links in the genealogy that prefixes Matthew's gospel.[66]

There is a cognate patristic exegetical image, this one Augustinian, that probably entered Dante's imagination in his framing of the Geryon episode: that of the "devil's mousetrap."[67] In medieval literature the image of Satan as a predator, a hunter or a fowler, is too commonplace to require documentation. The image is founded both in scripture itself and in aspects of a material culture of long duration that the rural alimentary economies of medieval Europe shared with the ancient world, economies in which hunting and trapping birds and animals was a common feature of daily life. The hunting of birds could involve nets, liming (spreading glue on places where small birds might walk or perch), or snares. Since hunting normally involves stealth and deception, it was very natural that "hunting images" would be applied to the frauds of the devil. Dante memorably uses the verb *invescare,* meaning to coat with birdlime, to describe the moral confusion of the ancients bewildered by the intentionally ambiguous language of the oracles (Par 17.32).[68] The word *snare* has nearly disap-

---

65. Christ's human flesh is that of a "worm" because of the application to him of the psalm verse (21:7) "Ego autem sum vermis et non homo" ("I am a worm and no man").

66. "Hujus hami linea illa est per Evangelium antiquorum patrum propago memorat" (Herrad, *Hortus Deliciarum,* 2:134).

67. See J. Rivière, "'Muscipula Diaboli': Origine et sens d'une image augustinienne," *Recherches de théologie ancienne et médiévale* 1 (1929): 484-96.

68. For the background see John V. Fleming, *Classical Imitation and Interpretation in Chaucer's Troilus* (Lincoln: University of Nebraska Press, 1990), pp. 45-71.

peared from common use in its literal sense in the English language, but it remains common in the ossified moralizing phrase *a snare and a delusion,* founded in traditional biblical exegesis.

Among the many passages in the Bible in which the idea occurs is Psalm 123:7: "anima nostra sicut passer erepta est de laqueo venantium; laqueus contritus est, et nos liberati sumus."[69] The Latin *laqueus* means a knotted rope or noose, especially one laid out as a snare. According to J. Rivière the word appeared even more frequently in the African psalter with which Augustine was familiar than it does in the Vulgate, a circumstance that encouraged its rich development in the *Enarrationes in Psalmos.* Now Dante's description of Geryon includes the striking feature of the decoration of the beast's torso:

> lo dosso e 'l petto e ambedue le coste
> dipinti avea di nodi e di rotelle. (Inf 17.14-15)[70]

This is the only passage in Dante recording any form of the word *rotella,* but *nodo* is a fairly common word meaning 'knot, loop, noose,' as well as an animal or bird trap so constructed; *nodo* is in Dante's Italian what *laqueus* is in Augustine's Latin. Of course it is in the nature of a successful trap that the trap disguise its dangerous function with a neutral or attractive exterior. The decoration of Geryon's body is compared with beautiful and attractive textiles, the finest of panchromatic Eastern cloth, or the tapestries from Arachne's very own loom. "It is clear," writes Giuseppe Giacalone, summarizing the general exegetical consensus, "that these *nodi* and *rotelle* signify the deceptions with which the fraudulent capture their victims."[71]

There is a pointed theme in Augustine's exegetical essay that would have particularly appealed to Dante, the theorist of the *contrapasso.* We have already seen that Gregory of Nyssa himself drew attention to a certain ironic justice in the hooking of Leviathan. The story has a so-called "biter-bit" plot. The master of snares becomes himself ensnared. The dramatic irony of this nearly whimsical operation of the *lex talionis* as acted out on stage of the drama of human salvation Augustine called a "magnificent retribution": *magnifica retributio, nihil iustius.*[72]

In a fine essay entitled "Tradition and the Individual Talent," T. S. Eliot

---

69. "Our soul hath been delivered as a sparrow out of the snare of the fowlers: the snare is broken; and we are delivered."

70. "The back and chest and both its flanks were painted and inscribed with rings and curlicues."

71. *Inferno,* ed. Giuseppe Giacalone (Rome: Signorelli, 1972), p. 254.

72. Cited, amid rich documentation, by Rivière, "Muscipula Diaboli," p. 491 n.

gave a classic explication of the fundamental dynamism of the literature of the western cultural tradition. He there suggested the dynamic commerce of the artistic imagination, in which ambitious invention works in cooperation with a learned and respectful engagement of the poetic past.[73] Ralph Waldo Emerson had anticipated him in slightly different terms in a neglected gem entitled "Quotation and Originality": "Original power is usually accompanied with assimilating power . . . ," writes Emerson. "Genius borrows nobly."[74] My own essay has sketched a number of the sacred and secular exegetical traditions with which Dante engages in the episode of Geryon. These include the exegesis of a seminal biblical narrative, the "Fall of Man," and a striking biblical image, Leviathan, and, from secular letters, the doctrine of literary verisimilitude enshrined in Horace's *Ars Poetica*. These are some of the *traditional* ideas with which the poet works, but the transformations wrought upon them by the operations of his *individual talent* are, as so often with Dante, astonishing.

We began our investigation with a literal and metaphorical clew — the cord thrown by Virgil into the depth dividing the seventh and eighth circles. Thomas Bergin takes the cord as a representative of a whole class of "incidental" or "anecdotal" or "subsidiary" allegories that lie prominent but unresolved on the textual surface, tempting a reader to hermeneutical gapper delay, though without too seriously impeding the progress through the poem: "Another special allegory is the very vexing one of the cord tossed into the gulf of Lower Hell to ensnare — or entice — Geryon."[75]

We may ask ourselves what becomes of the cord after it sinks from visibility beneath the text. There are tradition and individual talent in reading as well as in writing, and every reader is allowed an individual answer. Mine is that the cord never really vanishes, for Virgil continues to hold one end of it firmly. Its purpose is not of the either/or sort ("to ensnare — or to entice — Geryon"). Its function is dual — enticement *and* ensnarement — because those are the two principal aspects of Fraud that from the moral perspective here interest the poet, and because enticement and ensnarement are the two actions suggested by two verbs in the Vulgate — *suscipere* and *extrahere* — that have *Leviathan* as their direct object. Nor, in my reader's eye, does the matter end there. Dante may convince me in the name of truth that Virgil

73. "Tradition and the Individual Talent," in *The Sacred Wood: Essays on Poetry and Criticism,* 2d ed. (London: Methuen, 1928), pp. 47-59.

74. Ralph Waldo Emerson, *Letters and Social Aims* (Boston: J. R. Osgood, 1876), pp. 169-70.

75. Thomas G. Bergin, *Perspectives on the Divine Comedy* (New Brunswick: Rutgers University Press, 1967), p. 102.

and Dante rode Geryon bareback, but surely even Virgil would not have attempted that without a bridle or halter. There the Latin verb is *ligare* (Job 40:24) and the Italian noun *capestro!* When Gregory the Great thought of the capture of Leviathan he thought also of the millennial binding of Satan: "And I saw an angel coming down from heaven, having the key of the bottomless pit and a great chain in his hand. And he laid hold on the drago, the old serpent, which is the devil, and Satan, and bound him for a thousand years" (Rev. 20:1-2).

The apprehension of Dante's allusions or "noble borrowings" forces no particular interpretation upon Dante's text, but it does help clarify the poet's tone. If we allow ourselves access to the theological themes associated with the exegesis of Leviathan, the Geryon episode, terrifying as it is and is meant to be, adumbrates a final victory. The episode picks up a number of themes introduced in the narrative of the eighth canto, in which Virgil and Dante arrive before the gates of Dis. There are numerous similarities shared by these two episodes. In both instances the Pilgrim and his guide face an apparently impassable barrier at a significant landmark in hell's incrementally penal geography. In both Virgil seeks private colloquy with the demonic forces, and in both Dante suffers a near paroxysm of fear. In both a palpable irony characterizes their mode of transportation, one of which arrives with the speed of a flying arrow, the other of which departs with the speed of a flying arrow.

Despite the apparent failure of Virgil's parley with the demons, who "slammed shut the gates against my master," he remains, though temporarily shaken, confident. He has already said, has he not, "Non temer, che 'l nostro passo/non ci può tòrre alcun: da tal n' è dato" (Inf 8.104-5).[76] This confidence echoes Christ's assurance, perhaps no less unlikely in its given context, concerning the foundation of the church: "The gates of hell shall not prevail against it" (Matt. 16:18).

All the monstrous and demonic sentinels of Hell are types of, participants in, the Great Enemy. Satan is simply too big, poetically speaking, to be exhausted by the treatment Dante gives him in the thirty-fourth canto, brilliant as that treatment is. So we get bits and pieces of Satan in Cerberus, in the Minotaur, in the Harpies, in the Furies, in Geryon. And even for Dante some ideas and phrases were too good not to use more than once. The promise to the saints is that they will trample Satan beneath their feet. Perhaps only Dante could imagine an actual staircase, but he does so twice. Referring to Geryon's body Virgil tells Dante "Omai si scende *per sì fatte scale*" (Inf 17.82).[77] Of Satan him-

76. "Have no fear. None can prevent our passage, so great a power granted it to us."
77. "From here on we descend *such stairs as these.*"

self he says "Attienti ben, ché *per cotali scale* . . . conviensi dipartir da tanto male" (Inf 34.82, 84).[78] There is a verse from the Psalms that throughout the Middle Ages was widely cited in relation to the ascetic ascent: "conculcabis leonem et draconem," "Thou shalt trample underfoot the lion and the dragon" (Ps. 90:13). Hybrid Geryon offers the opportunity of trampling both with a single tread and, at the same time, correcting the inadequacy of Horace's ideas about "violence against art."

78. "Hold on tight, for *by such rungs as these* . . . must we depart from so much evil."

Julian of Norwich, Medieval Anglican

Marsha L. Dutton

> *They argued that God . . . has power to act wherever he chooses, whenever he chooses, to whom he chooses, and through whom he chooses.*
>
> Aelred of Rievaulx, *The Life of Saint Edward, King and Confessor*[1]

In about 1372 an English laywoman wrote a book describing a series of visions in which God revealed his eternal love to humankind. Twenty years later she revised it, adding a visionary parable showing Adam's fall to be one with Jesus' descent into human flesh and an extended passage on the divine motherhood of Jesus. The author, now known as Julian of Norwich, portrayed herself as her books' visionary protagonist, a woman in dialogue with God, struggling not only to accept God's promises of enduring love and protection for his creation but also to understand those promises and reconcile them with her knowledge of human sin and belief in the judgment to come.

As an author and theologian, Julian seeks to reconcile the inherent conflict between the doctrines that God both greatly loves his children and condemns them for sin. Structuring her argument through *ratiocinatio*, 'reasoning by question and answer',[2] she portrays her visionary *persona* as troubled by

---

1. *The Life of Saint Edward,* in Aelred of Rievaulx, *The Historical Works,* trans. Jane-Patricia Freeland, ed. Marsha L. Dutton, CF 156 (Kalamazoo: Cistercian Publications, 2005), pp. 123-243.

2. Edmund Colledge and James Walsh, Introduction, in *Julian of Norwich, Showings,*

God's assurance that "Alle maner a thing shalle be wele," until finally through insistence, argument, and demonstration God persuades her to believe "that synne shalle be no shame, but wurshype to man" and that "all that is made . . . lasteth and ever shall, for god loueth it."[3]

Intellectually free and courageous in her exploration of the church's teaching, Julian dramatizes believers' search to understand God's will. Although her first book recommends that the believer accept the church's teaching rather than questioning it, in the revised version she shows that God desires that believers engage in rational inquiry of the faith, that reason is God's gift to humankind, and that when God fails to blame humans for sin, he himself acts in accord with reason. As a laywoman writing theology in English, incorporating and integrating scripture, tradition, revelation, and reason in her search for new answers to old questions, Julian demonstrates the accuracy of J. Robert Wright's judgment that well before the sixteenth century the living expression of Christianity in England was Anglican.

The Ecclesia Anglicana

As Wright and others have explained, the Church of England — and through it the Anglican Communion — has long understood itself historically and doctrinally as a continuation of the *ecclesia anglicana* established in England in 597. Although the first OED citation for the term comes from 1215, in the Magna Carta, it was already in use in the mid-twelfth century, signifying geographical but not theological distinctiveness.[4] Thus Wright argues that the historical study of Anglicanism ought to begin not after Henry VIII declared himself

---

trans. Edmund Colledge and James Walsh (New York, Ramsey, Toronto: Paulist Press, 1978), p. 29. Julian's use of *ratiocinatio* reinforces the importance she places on reason as shared by God and his human creatures. According to her editors she at least once uses the word *reson* within the text to mean *ratiocinatio* (Colledge and Walsh, eds., *Showings*, p. 266, n. 17).

3. Julian of Norwich, *A Book of Showings to the Anchoress Julian of Norwich*, ed. Edmund Colledge and James Walsh, 2 vols. (pages numbered consecutively), Studies and Texts 35 (Toronto: Pontifical Institute of Mediaeval Studies, 1978), LT pp. 422, 445, 300. In this article I cite the early short version of Julian's book as ST (Short Text) and her longer revision as LT.

4. J. Robert Wright, "Anglicanism, *Ecclesia Anglicana,* and Anglican: An Essay on Terminology," in *The Study of Anglicanism*, ed. Stephen Sykes, John Booty, and Jonathan Knight, rev. ed. (London: SPCK; Minneapolis: Fortress Press, 1988) (hereafter Study), pp. 477-83, here pp. 480-81; see also Paul Avis, "What Is 'Anglicanism'?" in Study, pp. 459-76, esp. 460-61.

head of the English Church in 1529-34 but rather "in the 'patristic' period of 'Anglican' church history."[5]

Certainly Christians in England before the Reformation were already shaping the English church, defining what would later be seen as Anglican distinctiveness in life, teaching, and worship. But what characterizes that distinctiveness? What did it mean to be an Anglican then, and what now? How does one investigate Wright's claim other than tautologically?

Scholars generally agree that Anglicanism lacks a distinctive doctrine, that, as Elizabeth I said, its faith is "that very religion which is ordained by Christ, sanctioned by the primitive and Catholic church, and approved by the consentient mind and voice of the most early Fathers."[6] Thus Anglicanism is usually defined as an ethos, a way of being that involves common prayer, use of the vernacular in worship, and reliance on scripture, tradition, and reason. Anglican distinctiveness is regularly explained in such abstractions as "a synthesis of catholic, protestant, and liberal elements" or "an attempt at a *via media,* a balancing act between various factors based on compromise and mutual concessions."[7] Archbishop of Canterbury Michael Ramsey defined even Anglican theology as "a method, a use and a direction."[8]

Certain characteristics appear consistently in discussions of post-Reformation Anglicanism. Paul Avis summarizes them in his discussion of "the essence of Anglicanism":

Scripture and tradition, revelation and human reason, "credal orthodoxy and liberty in non-essentials, the appeal to antiquity and the welcome to new knowledge, the historic continuity of the Church and the freedom of national churches" — all were held together to form the distinctive spirit of Anglican theology. . . .

The Bible is open: available, unchained, not subject to control, monitoring and binding interpretation by ecclesiastical authority. The pre-eminent place accorded to Holy Scripture in the Anglican formularies . . . is matched by the freedom enjoyed by Anglican laity since the Reformation to read and to study the Bible in the vernacular and to arrive at their own convictions and to express them. . . .

Finally, Anglicanism's love of the truth is fearless. The scholarly pursuit

5. Wright, "Anglicanism, *Ecclesia Anglicana,* and Anglican," p. 483.
6. In *Calendar of State Papers, relating to English Affairs, Preserved Principally at Rome in the Vatican Archives and Library,* ed. J. M. Rigg (London: H. M. Stationery Office, 1916-26), pp. 154-55; quoted in Wright, "Anglicanism, *Ecclesia Anglicana,* and Anglican," p. 481.
7. Avis, "What Is 'Anglicanism'?" p. 468.
8. Quoted in Avis, "What Is 'Anglicanism'?" p. 469.

of truth and the conscientious witness to it are safeguarded in Anglicanism.[9]

W. Taylor Stevenson further identifies worship and prayer as essential for Anglican faith and life. In worship itself, he suggests, Anglicans join reason to revelation, as well as love of and search for truth: "In Anglicanism, the worship of the people of God plays a very distinctive role, being the principal arena not only of supplication and praise but also of theological experimentation and formulation."[10] For Anglicans, then, faith, prayer, and understanding are interwoven, a mutual means of knowing and worshipping God. One particular link between worship and the Anglican search for understanding of the faith, Stevenson suggests, is its characteristic starting point in the "symbols and mythic narratives which present the life, death and resurrection of Jesus of Nazareth":

> "Symbol gives rise to thought." . . . *Lex orandi* has the priority, *lex credendi* is essential but logically and ontologically derivative. . . . It is this order which is expressive of the intrinsically Anselmic character of Christian faith: faith in search of understanding, understanding in search of an adequate articulation of the faith which undergirds it, which in turn alters what is received.[11]

Little attention has yet been given to whether these characteristics of Anglican distinctiveness existed before the Reformation or emerged only in the new Church of England with its English head, English Bible, English liturgy, and incorporation of the laity into the governance of the Church. Whatever Anglican identity endures from the early *ecclesia anglicana,* whatever distinctiveness in Anglicans' method, use, and direction, it must be sought in the people of that time.

Most of the best-known members of the early *ecclesia anglicana* were priests, and many were also bishops: Augustine of Canterbury, Cuthbert, Bede, Wilfrid, Dunstan, Wulfstan, Aelred of Rievaulx, and John Wyclif. English kings also identified themselves personally and publicly with the church;[12] King Al-

---

9. Avis, "What Is an 'Anglicanism'?" pp. 469-70. As expensive objects, Bibles like other books in the Middle Ages were chained for protection from thieves, just as gold and silver vessels were locked in treasuries. The fact that Bibles were in Latin was for most people sufficient restriction on interpretation.

10. Stevenson, "Lex Orandi — Lex Credendi," in Study, pp. 187-201, here p. 187.

11. Stevenson, "Lex Orandi — Lex Credendi," p. 196.

12. For Aelred of Rievaulx's insistence on the appropriate relationship between king and

fred, who visited Rome as a boy and received a blessing from Pope Leo IV, later translated Augustine's *Soliloquies* and Gregory the Great's *Pastoral Prayer* into English. One well-remembered female Christian is Hilda, seventh-century abbess of Whitby, where the English church in synod adopted the rite and calendar of the Roman church. Any of these figures would be a place to start in looking for pre-Reformation Anglicanism. But their lives and works show the public face of Latin learning and clerical authority rather than the private face of ordinary Christians, who then as now comprised the majority of the faithful.

A more representative member of the medieval *ecclesia anglicana* is Julian of Norwich (*c.* 1342–*post* 1429), laywoman, anchorite, writer, and theologian. Although next to nothing is known of her life, her two books exploring the vexed question of God's mercy and human sin reveal the essence of her faith and of her thoughtful intelligence and fidelity to the church. Julian's theology is grounded in scripture and church doctrine. Her method and her subject echo the books of the Hebrew prophets, and most of her visions originate in the gospel accounts of the crucifixion.

Julian frames both versions of her work autobiographically, developing them dialectically in a series of visions. The short first version — twenty-five chapters written in about 1372 — explores the scriptural and doctrinal contradiction between God's love and God's punishment of sin. The later long revised text is more insistent than the short one about the conflict between the doctrines of God's love and of God's readiness to condemn sinners; it also offers a compelling resolution to the problem. This version also affirms, as the short version does not, the importance of knowledge and the necessity of understanding the faith.

Julian's books are usually classified as works of spirituality or manuals of popular devotion, and most writers explain Julian herself in biographical and experiential terms, as a devout woman who on what seemed to be her deathbed received a series of visions. Books and articles about her thus tend to identify the visions as the facts from which the books derive. Kerrie Hide's study of Julian's soteriology begins: "In 1373 a woman known as Julian of Norwich experienced a series of *showings* or visions that she believed were a revelation from God."[13] Benedicta Ward plumbs the visions to discern something about Julian's life, concluding in part from the works' discussion of the nature of God that

church, see Marsha L. Dutton, "*Sancto Dunstano Cooperante*: Aelred of Rievaulx's Advice to the Heir to the English Throne in *Genealogy of the Kings of the English*," in *Religious and Laity in Northern Europe 1000-1400: Interaction, Negotiation and Power*, ed. Janet Burton and Emilia Jamroziak, Europa Sacra series (Turnhout: Brepols, 2006).

13. Kerrie Hide, *Gifted Origins to Graced Fulfillment: The Soteriology of Julian of Norwich* (Collegeville, MN: The Liturgical Press, 2001), p. 3.

Julian had probably been married, borne a child, and seen her child and husband die, perhaps of the plague or in war.[14]

Over the years, however, a number of writers have studied Julian as a writer and theologian. In 1967 Thomas Merton referred to her as "one of the greatest English theologians in the ancient sense of the word."[15] More recently scholars such as Hide, Simon Tugwell, Grace Jantzen, and Christopher Abbott have explored the substance of her books, though often subordinating her theology to her experience.[16] Thus Abbott's study of Julian's incarnational theology takes the two books as above all autobiographical:

> Julian writes in the first person about her own experiences, and directly out of her reflection on those experiences comes a remarkably bold theological vision. It is the central claim of this book that, in Julian's case, the personal and the theological are best taken together, and we will call upon a certain broad concept of autobiography in order to explore the relationship between Julian's personal experience as she records it and the incarnational theology which she develops out of it. The intention is finally to show that the witness Julian's writing gives of a life lived is inextricable from, and in a sense illustrative of, her mature theological vision.[17]

Like all visionary works, Julian's books are framed narratives, introducing the visionary, her circumstances, and the events leading to the visions in the frame, and narrating the visions in the body.[18] The frame twice intrudes into the body when the visionary briefly awakens from her visions. The books end with no explicit return to the frame.

However based on personal experience the books may be (a question inaccessible to scholarly inquiry), Julian is writing not autobiography but theology, using an ancient conventional genre particularly popular in her time[19] to

---

14. Benedicta [Ward], "Julian the Solitary," in Kenneth Leech and Benedicta [Ward], *Julian Reconsidered* (Fairacres, Oxford: SLG Press, 1988), pp. 24-25.

15. Thomas Merton, *Mystics and Zen Masters* (New York: Delta, 1967), p. 140.

16. Simon Tugwell, *Ways of Imperfection* (London: Darton, Longman and Todd, 1984); Grace M. Jantzen, *Julian of Norwich: Mystic and Theologian* (London: SPCK, 1987); Christopher Abbott, *Julian of Norwich: Autobiography and Theology* (Cambridge: D. S. Brewer, 1999).

17. Abbott, *Julian of Norwich*, p. 3.

18. To distinguish between author and her *persona* in the books I refer to the author as Julian and to the woman who reports on her visions as the visionary.

19. A number of fourteenth-century authors wrote visionary works; in addition to *Pearl* and *Piers Plowman*, which also resolves the paradox of justice and mercy, several of Geoffrey Chaucer's works are visions (e.g., *Parlement of Foules* and *Book of the Duchess*). A lesser-known visionary work of the time is John Whiterigg's "Meditacio ad Crucifixum" (*The Meditations of*

explore theological concepts — the incarnation, the Trinity, human sin — and problems such as the conflict between divine justice and divine mercy. The theme of both books is the same: God's love for his creatures will endure always, and God desires that they have knowledge of that love.

The Justice-Mercy Paradox

The central theological issue addressed by Julian is human salvation. Both texts struggle to explain the relationship between human sin and Christ's atonement, and the apparent conflict between God's justice and God's mercy, topics of passionate concern to fourteenth-century theologians. Of central concern to Julian as to others of her time was what Jaroslav Pelikan calls "the paradox of justice and mercy":[20] divine justice demanded that God impose eternal death — damnation — as the penalty for human sin, while divine mercy promised beatitude. How could both be true?

Paul is the source for both positions. In the Epistle to the Romans he writes:

> Is God to be charged with injustice? Certainly not! He says to Moses, "I will show mercy to whom I will show mercy, and have pity on whom I will have pity." Thus it does not depend on human will or effort, but on God's mercy. . . . he not only shows mercy as he chooses, but also makes stubborn as he chooses. You will say, "Then why does God find fault, if no one can resist his will?" Who do you think you are to answer God back? Can the pot say to the potter, "Why did you make me like this?" Surely the potter can do what he likes with the clay. (Rom. 9:14-21)

Augustine, the great shaper of medieval church doctrine, interpreted Paul's words as a statement of God's predestination, his election of the blessed for salvation and the damned for eternal death. As all have sinned in Adam, Augustine argues, all are condemned in Adam. Only God's unmerited goodness saves any, and that salvation is as truly God's mercy as the condemnation of the others is God's justice. This doctrine inevitably troubled many theologians and believers, perhaps above all those who recognized themselves and their friends

---

the Monk of Farne, ed. Hugh Farmer, Studia Anselmiana 41, *Analecta Monastica*, 4th series [Rome: Herder, 1957], pp. 158-215).

20. Jaroslav Pelikan, *The Christian Tradition: A History of the Development of Doctrine*, vol. 3, *The Growth of Medieval Theology (600-1300)* (Chicago and London: University of Chicago Press, 1978), pp. 108-18.

and relatives as the Pauline pots. If Christ's crucifixion and resurrection manifested God's mercy and atoned for human sin and yet God condemned most sinners, where was the mercy? And where the justice?

The two versions of Julian's work show the development of her answers to these questions as well as a growth in her abilities as a writer and theologian. The first book is tentative, establishing her genre and method and briefly exploring the apparent conflict between God's justice and God's mercy in scripture and doctrine, but the argument concludes well before the end of the book with an assertion that the believer should accept God's assurances rather than trying to understand. The second book shows a matured intellect at work, a sharpened understanding of the resources of the genre, and increased theological incisiveness and originality.

Here Julian reveals her increasing conviction that God's mercy will not allow him to damn his children for sin or even to blame them. She articulates this position in a vision that is really a parable, showing God's refusal to blame men and women as itself justice, not a violation of justice.[21] This revised text also shows a change in Julian's view on the place of human inquiry into God's intention. Whereas the first book says that the faithful should for the most part simply receive and accept the teachings of the church, trusting in God to make all well, in the revision Julian insists that believers must know and understand their faith in order to know and love God.

The Visions: Faith Seeking Understanding

Julian explores the paradox of justice and mercy in a work rhetorically formed by vision — in bodily sight and spiritual sight — and in dialogue between God and the visionary, "be worde formede in myne vndyrstandynge" (ST p. 224). In the dialogue God declares that his love for his creation will endure forever and that he does not blame anyone for sin. In response the visionary protests that she cannot understand how God's promises will be fulfilled when she knows that many will be condemned, citing both the church and her own experience for her knowledge, so combining knowledge of church doctrine, scripture, and reason in her attempt to understand God's revelation. The visionary thus affirms Pauline/Augustinian orthodoxy while God rejects it; he is the authority

---

21. The other visions in the work are essentially static, though with some movement and dialogue, as when blood runs down Jesus' head. This one, however, is both vision and parable, a narrative with setting, costume, characters, and dramatic action, as well as an extended interpretation.

and the teacher, while she is his pupil, who disclaims any responsibility for what she has learned in her visions or what she is about to report:

> Botte god for bede that ȝe schulde saye or take it so that I am a techere, for I meene nouȝt soo, no I mente nevere so; for I am a womann, leued [un-learned], febille and freylle. (ST p. 222)

But despite her lack of ability, she says, God desires that she make known to others what he taught her:

> Botte I wate wele, this that I saye, I hafe it on the schewynge of hym tha(t) es souerayne techare. . . . Botte for I am a womman, schulde I therfore leve that I schulde nouȝt telle ȝowe the goodenes of god, syne that I sawe in that same tyme that is his wille, that it be knawenn? . . . Thane schalle ȝe sone forgette me that am a wrecche, and dose so that I lette ȝowe nought, and behalde Jhesu that ys techare of alle. (ST p. 222)[22]

The visionary returns to this point in the long text, interrupting her inter-pretation of the work's central vision to recall that all that she came to under-stand was of God's teaching: "Also in thys merveylous example I haue techyng with in me, as it were the begynnyng of an A B C, wher by I may haue some vnderstondyng of oure lordys menyng, for the pryvytes of the reuelacion be hyd ther in, not withstondyng that alle the shewyng be full of prevytes" (LT p. 539).

The visions themselves begin with three revelations, two from the gospel and the third recalling God's creation, all making known the same point: God's ev-erlasting love for his creatures. First the crucified Christ is seen with blood running from under the crown of thorns, and then Mary appears as "a simple mayden and a meeke, yong of age, a little waxen aboue a chylde, in the stature as she was when she conceivede." Finally God shows to the visionary, in the palm of her hand, "a lit-tle thing, the quantitie of an haselnott." In the bleeding Christ she comprehends that "The trinitie is our maker, . . . our keeper, . . . our everlasting louer, . . . our endlesse ioy and our bleisse," and in Mary she recognizes "the greatnes of her maker and the littlehead of her selfe that is made" (LT pp. 294-300).

The third image in this vision, that of the "little thing," is essential to Julian's method and argument. After the appearance of the two central symbols of Christian faith, this tiny object would seem to be of no significance, nothing, too small to last.[23] With it however Julian introduces both the grand theme of

---

22. Colledge and Walsh indicate their emendations with parentheses.
23. Although studies of Julian often refer to this showing as "the vision of the hazelnut"

the work and its dialectical method, as for the first time the visionary inquires and God replies:

> I looked theran with the eye of my vnderstanding, and thought: What may this be? And it was answered generaelly thus: It is all that is made. I marvayled how it might laste, for me thought it might sodenly haue fallen to nawght for littlenes. And I was answered in my vnderstanding: It lasteth and ever shall, for god loueth it; and so hath all thing being by the loue of god. (LT p. 300)

The visionary's anxiety here for creation, "all that is made," and God's promise to preserve it provide the paradigm for their interaction in the rest of the visions: he provides the vision, she questions its meaning, and he answers her in her understanding. Furthermore, here God articulates for the first time the thesis of Julian's books, that God the creator is God the preserver and lover, the Trinity, whose love for his creation will never end. This revelation thus succinctly states the meaning of all the visions to follow, of the crucifixion, the Virgin Mary, and the lord and the servant, all revealing that God is a loving God who will save all that he has made.

The passage also reveals Julian's reliance on scripture not only for the most familiar symbols and narratives of the faith, such as Adam's fall, the incarnation, and the atonement, but also for genre and rhetorical approach. Her source for the apparently insignificant vision of the "little thing," and for its meaning, is a vision of the prophet Amos. When God shows an approaching swarm of locusts approaching Israel, Amos cries out, "Lord God, forgive, I pray you. How can Jacob survive? He is so small." God speaks reassurance to Amos, saying: "This will not happen" (Amos 7:1-3). Here Julian identifies herself and the visionary with a great prophet of Israel, who sees visions of God's plan to destroy his nation for its wrongdoing, intercedes with God, and obtains God's promise that a remnant of the nation will survive.

The conflict between God's punishment and his mercy that Julian struggles to resolve is thus centrally present in this revelation, in scripture as in doctrine. But Julian adapts the message of Amos's vision to her own purpose. In *Showings* God promises not destruction but salvation, not damnation "for crime after crime of Damascus" (Amos 1:3), but love. Although Julian remains imprecise on the question of how many God will condemn, everything in her

---

(see e.g. Hide, *Gifted Origins*, pp. 65-66), it is not even that — merely a small unrecognizable object. Its description echoes the description of Mary a few lines earlier: "the littlehead of her selfe that is made."

books indicates her rejection of the Augustinian view that all but 144,000 will be damned, saving the doctrinal appearances merely by occasional references to "them that shalle be savyd" (LT p. 323). But it is clear that Julian's soteriology allows for damnation of only a few, with the majority receiving honor in heaven. Julian thus translates Amos's vision of certain destruction for all but a few into a New Testament promise of salvation for almost all.

Julian again raises the concern about justice and mercy later, in another exchange between God and the visionary. This exchange recurs in both works, with God promising that "alle schalle be wele, and alle maner of thynge schalle be wele" and the visionary unable to believe (ST p. 245). God's words are simple but sweeping, and the double or triple repetition each time he speaks them emphasizes their significance.[24] Julian's treatment of God's promise as a stumbling block, not only unbelievable but an offense to those who, knowing their sin, expect damnation for themselves or those they love, gives pointed urgency to her exploration of the contradiction between sin and God's promise.[25]

The visionary expresses her anxiety for creation and then more specifically for a friend, "a certayne personn that I lovyd" (ST p. 252), because in the vision she has recognized the insignificance of creation beside the grandeur of God. She is thus herself the devil's advocate, insisting against God's promise that damnation is sure. She pleads not for mercy or forgiveness but merely to know the truth, so that she can make sense out of God's incomprehensible words.

This conflict creates the most intense exchange between God and the visionary in both books. In the short text she explicitly explains her anxiety about God's promises as tied to her knowledge of sin, and God attempts to reassure her. Were there no sin, she thinks, then all would be well. When God replies that despite sin all will be well, she begs for understanding:

> Bot in this (I) schalle studye . . . sayande thus to oure lorde in my menynge with fulle grete drede: A, goode lorde, howe myght alle be wele for the grete harme that is comonn by synne to thy creatures? And I desired as I durste to

---

24. T. S. Eliot's inclusion of the phrase three times in "Little Gidding," the last of his *Four Quartets,* has received little study. See, however, Amy Hume, "'Expanding of Love beyond Desire': Repetition, Return, and the Use of Memory in T. S. Eliot's Collaboration with Julian of Norwich in 'Little Gidding,'" M.A. essay, Ohio University, 2005.

25. Many readers have misinterpreted God's statement here as evidence of Julian's easy optimism. See, e.g., Greta Hort: "'All shall be well . . .' Dame Julian might be content to assert of 'all that shall be saved'. But Langland had a deeper love of men and a deeper knowledge, and thus a harder struggle" (*Piers Plowman and Contemporary Religious Thought* [London: SPCK, n.d.], p. 111).

hafe sum mare open declarynge whare with I myght be hesyd in this. (ST
p. 247)

Here, however, having answered her objection and assured her of his ability to
make all well, God tells her to stop questioning, to accept his promise without
further explanation. He explains only that while some things may be known —
such as "oure savioure and oure saluacionn" — others must remain hidden:

> that is to saye alle that is besyde oure saluacionn. For this is oure lordys
> prive consayles, and it langes to the ryalle lordeschyp of god for to haue his
> prive consayles in pees, and it langes to his seruanntys for obedyence and
> reuerence nought to wille witte his councelle. (ST p. 248)[26]

Elsewhere in the short text Julian reiterates that Christians should not
question their faith but hold tightly to the church's teaching. So the visionary
expresses her understanding of obedience to God's restriction as no hardship
for her and pleasing to God, who is one with the church and the provider of all
its teaching:

> God schewyd me fulle grete plesannce that he has in alle men and womenn
> that myghttelye and mekelye and wyrschipfullye takes the prechynge and
> the techynge of haly kyrke, for he is haly kyrke. For he is the grownde, he is
> the substannce, he is the techynge, he is the techare, he is the ende, he is the
> myddes [reward] wharefore ilke trewe sawlle trauaylles; and he is knawen
> and schalle be knawenn to ylke saule to whame the haly gaste declares it.
> (ST pp. 251-52; LT p. 431)

Thus in the first version of *Showings* Julian raises her essential questions
— how does human sin measure up against Christ's atonement? how can God
not damn his creatures? how can God see no blame in sin? — but stops there.
She has addressed and sought to resolve the central problems of fourteenth-
century soteriology, and perhaps that seems to her all it is possible or indeed
necessary to do. Apparently concluding that there are some things she cannot
understand, she ends her theological essay with the visionary accepting God's
promises, without understanding.

26. The suggestion that one should not inquire into God's secrets must have been a com-
monplace in the fourteenth century and a hindrance to Julian's theological project. In Chaucer's
Canterbury Tales, the Miller twice warns not to question, e.g.: "Men sholde nat knowe of
Goddes pryvetee," "The Miller's Tale," in *The Riverside Chaucer,* ed. Larry D. Benson, 3rd ed.
(Boston: Houghton Mifflin Co., 1987), I.3454, p. 71; cf. I.3153-64, p. 67.

By the time Julian revises her book twenty years later, however, she has reached a resolution to the justice-mercy paradox and figured out how to explain her solution. In this book, therefore, the visionary pushes her inquiries further, and God answers more of them than before. This time when God promises that all will be well, she expands her explanation of the way what she has learned from the church hinders her ability to accept his promise:

> And in this syght I marveyled gretly, and be held oure feyth, menyng thus: oure feyth is groundyd in goddes worde, and it longyth to oure feyth that we beleue that goddys worde shalle be sauyd in alle thing. And one point of oure feyth is that many creatures shall be dampnyd, as . . . many that hath receyvyd cristondom and lyvyth vncristen lyfe and so dyeth ou3te of cheryte. All theyse shalle be dampnyd to helle withou3t (e)nde, as holy chyrch techyth me to byleue.
>
> And stondyng alle thys, me thought it was vnpossible that alle maner of thynge shuld be wele. (LT pp. 424-25)

The visionary does not here or elsewhere imply that the church is right and God wrong, or the contrary, but instead insists that as God is the church, his promises that all will be well contradict his own truth, leaving it inaccessible and incomprehensible to human reason. The conflict is not between the two authorities, God and the church, for Julian insists that they are one. Nor is it a conflict between God's justice and God's mercy, for God himself says that he has no need to forgive because he sees no blame in sin, so his justice and his mercy are one. The problem is flawed human understanding, the belief that sin deserves punishment and that the infliction of that punishment is justice. The core of the problem is thus humankind's inability to see sin as honor, to comprehend it as both necessary and nothing. No wonder the visionary cannot accept that God can make all well.

Thus for Julian the core of the justice-mercy paradox lies in the fact that without God's help it is impossible for men and women to comprehend God's promise to preserve his creation. The visionary is thus passionate in declaring her need to know the truth about God's judgment of sin:

> I know truly that we syn grevously all day and be moch blame wurthy; and I may neyther leue the knowying of this sooth, nor I se nott the shewyng to vs no manner of blame. How may this be? For I knew be the comyn techyng of holy church and by my owne felyng that the blame of oure synnes continually hangyth vppon vs, fro the furst man in to the tyme that we come vppe in to hevyn. . . . And betwene theyse two contraryes my reson was

> grettly traveyled by my blyndnes. . . . And yf it be tru that we be synners and blame wurthy, good lorde, how may it than be that I can nott see this truth in the, whych art my god, my maker in whom I desyer to se all truth? (LT pp. 511-12)

The visionary reinforces this request to know the truth by stating that her life and faith depend on it:

> it nedyth me to wytt, as me thyngkyth, if I shall lyve here, for knowyng of good and evyll, wher by I may be reson and by grace the more deperte them a sonder, and loue goodnesse and hate evyll as holy chyrch techyth. I cryde inwardly with all my myght, sekyng in to god for helpe, menyng thus: A, lorde Jhesu, kyng of blysse, how shall I be esyde, who shall tell me and tech me that me nedyth to wytt, if I may nott at this tyme se it in the? (LT p. 512)

In response God shows her a lengthy parable that answers the question, showing the servant who while running to do his lord's service falls, causing himself great injury that extends to his reason: "he was blyndyd in his reson and stonyd in his mynde so ferforth that allmost he had forgeten his owne loue" (LT pp. 515-16). The visionary is invited to interpret this parable for herself, to understand how it explains God's failure to blame. The lord in the parable, whom the visionary understands to be God, asks her to consider what it is right for him to do in response to the fall and injury of his servant. He thus allows her to resolve the conflict she had until that moment perceived between sin and God's failure to blame. In the vision she recognizes at last that Adam's sin was not willful wrongdoing but a painful fall, that human sin is human suffering, which a loving God cannot punish but only repay. The solution she sees here is thus not mercy in place of justice or forgiveness for wrongdoing but recompense for what the servant suffered in serving his lord. It is the reasonable thing for any good lord to do for a servant injured in such a fall:

> Lo my belouyd servant, what harme and dysses he hath had and takyn in my servys for my loue, yea, and for his good wylle. Is it nott reson that I reward hym his frey and his drede, his hurt and his mayme and alle his woo? . . . And in this an inwarde goostely shewyng of the lordes menyng descended in to my soule, in whych I saw that it behovyth nedys to be standyng his grett goodnes and his owne wurschyppe, that his deerworthy servannt, whych he lovyd so moch, shulde be hyely and blessydfully rewardyd withoute end, aboue that he shulde haue be yf he had nott fallen. (LT pp. 517-18)

This vision, the core of Julian's revised book, resolves the paradox of human sin and God's love for the sinner, but not through abstract promises or propositional explanations. Rather, like any parable, it is concrete and filled with the detail of daily life. It requires the hearer to work out its meaning, to interpret it through personal experience and common sense, and then to translate emotional comprehension into understanding, rational acceptance, and faith.

Faith Seeking Understanding

With this visionary parable of the lord and the servant, Julian calls particular attention to the value of reason as part of the substance that humankind shares with God. The servant who falls is injured not only in his body but in his reason and his mind, and the lord says that it is "reson" — rational — that he should reward the servant for that injury. Thus Julian links the servant and the lord not only in emotion and tenderness, not only, as the early showing of the little thing had suggested, in God's creation of and love for his people, but in reason itself. This insistence on God's judgment as rational and linked to human reason helps to explain the significance of the vision in the theology of Julian's book. It resolves the paradox of justice and mercy, but it also reveals Julian's matured understanding of the reason that believers must try to understand their faith. Human reason may be impaired through Adam's fall, but it is still God's gift and an aspect of the image of God persisting in humankind.

As Julian begins her book by defining God as the teaching and the teacher and declaring that the visionary receives the meaning of her visions in her understanding, she continues to insist on the value of reason, knowledge, and wisdom. Ringing the changes on these lexically resonating terms, she points with all of them to human reason as essential to faith and to God's desire that humans know his love. Julian is emphatic that human reason is a gift of God, intended for use in knowing and understanding him, not despised or rejected by but established in God:

> . . . oure reson is groundyd in god, which is substanncyally kyndnesse [humanity, nature]. Of this substancyall kyndnesse mercy and grace spryngyth and spredyth in to vs, werkyng all thynges in fulfyllyng of oure joy. Theyse be oure groundys, in whych we haue oure beyng, oure encrese and oure fulfyllyng. . . . God wylle we vnderstande, desyeryng with all oure hart and alle oure strengh to haue knowyng of them evyr more and more in to the tyme that we be fulfyllyd, for fully to know them and clerely to se them is

not elles but endles joy and blysse that we shall haue in hevyn, which god wyll we begynne here in knowying of his loue. (LT pp. 574-75)

A little later Julian returns to the theme of human knowledge, now making it clear that God desires that believers understand in order that they may do his will. The point is again as earlier moral: one who merely accepts rules without understanding cannot choose rightly:

For the commawndementys of god come there in, in whych we owe to haue two manner of vnderstandyng. That one is that we owe to vnderstand and know whych b(e) his byddynges, to loue them and to kepe them. That other is that we owe to knowe his forbyddynges, to hate them and refuse them. (LT p. 579; cf. LT p. 512)

Even when Julian repeats a passage from the short text that encourages acceptance of church doctrine, her revised text emphasizes rational understanding rather than acquiescence. When in the long text God states his delight in human acceptance of the church's preaching and teaching, Julian alters his earlier encouragement that one accept it "myghttelye and mekelye and wyrschipfullye," substituting a call for wisdom: "God shewde fulle grett plesannce that he hath in alle men and women that myghtly and wysely take the prechyng and the techyng of holy chyrch, for he it is, holy chyrch" (ST p. 252; LT p. 431).

Julian's insistence on a rational effort to understand the faith — what scripture, the church, and revelation all teach — thus leads not away from faith but to it. So the visionary now affirms both her trust in the church as one with God and her certainty of the value of human reason and understanding. In the long text Julian makes it clear that responding to God's love requires knowledge of God's love, that God wants not merely believers' acquiescence, obedience, or even love, but rather understanding and comprehension — for he is the teacher and the teaching.

In her books Julian anticipates the characteristics of post-Reformation Anglican life and thought. She holds throughout to the faith of the church; she shapes her argument through its symbols and myths, dramatizing the believer's search for understanding through the Anglican synthesis of scripture, reason, and revelation. She writes in English, with both Father and Son also speaking English. In her pursuit of truth she interprets scripture independently of the church's teaching, in a fearless desire to understand. She shows her faith as grounded in the interwoven realities of scripture, the church's teachings, and the symbols and narratives of Jesus' life, death, and resurrection. Indeed her books are in many ways exegetical explications of these symbols and narratives, as the visionary sees Christ crucified in the cross held before her and as through those symbols she seeks to understand and articulate God's meaning. And she shows prayer as the place where one learns about God — the place for formulating theology. She and her books exemplify faith seeking understanding.

Finally, Julian writes for her "evyn cristens." As a lay person speaking to the church with the authority given by the Holy Spirit, she anticipates the role of the laity in Anglicanism in the sixteenth century and beyond, resisting clericalism and top-down authority, certain that God chooses those whom he will teach, those whom he wishes to speak for him. So she embodies not only the method and theological synthesis of Anglicanism but also the Anglican understanding of God's call to ministry of the baptized.

Anglicanism and the Laity

Since the appearance of the first Book of Common Prayer in 1549, one characteristic of Anglicanism has been the inclusion of the laity in all aspects of worship and life. A somewhat polemical sermon from the reign of Elizabeth I rejects isolating the authority of the church in bishops, insisting that the Holy Spirit is present throughout the church in all its members:

> But now herein standeth the controversy, Whether all men do justly arrogate to themselves the Holy Ghost, or no? The bishops of Rome have for a long time made a sore challenge thereunto, reasoning for themselves after this sort: "The Holy Ghost," say they, "was promised to the church, and never forsaketh the church. But we are the chief heads and the principal part of the church, therefore we have the Holy Ghost for ever: and whatsoever things we decree are undoubted verities, and oracles of the Holy Ghost." That ye may perceive the weakness of this argument, it is needful to teach you, first, what the true church of Christ is. . . .
>
> The true church is an universal congregation or fellowship of God's faithful and elect people, *built upon the foundation of the apostles and prophets, Jesus Christ himself being the head corner-stone.*
>
> . . . According to which rule, if any man live uprightly, of him it may safely be pronounced, that he hath the Holy Ghost within him. . . .[27]

27. "An Homily Concerning the Coming Down of the Holy Spirit," in *Certain Sermons Appointed by the Queen's Majesty . . . and by Her Grace's Advice Perused and Overseen for the Better Understanding of the Simple People* (Cambridge: John W. Parker, 1850), pp. 457-71.

A document issued by the General Synod of the Church of England in 1985 similarly affirms the place of the laity in the church as equivalent to that of the ordained:

> Because all human beings are made in the image of God, they are called to become the People of God, the Church, servants and ministers and citizens of the Kingdom, a new humanity in Jesus Christ. Though we are tainted by our sinfulness, God's wonderful grace and love offer us all this common Christian vocation. God leaves everyone free to refuse this call; but the call is there for all without exception.
>
> . . . Nor does our calling — our vocation — depend on any kind of *ordination*. There are still many deep controversies about what ordination may signify. . . . But it certainly does not indicate any special "grade" of Christian, more holy than the laity. And for everybody, bishops, priests and laity together, the great sacrament of our common calling is our baptism, which signifies our glorious new life in Christ.[28]

A prominent characteristic of Anglicanism is thus the recognition of all the baptized, both in and out of orders, as equal recipients of the Holy Spirit, called not to look to bishops as "the chief heads and principal part of the church" but to understand themselves as members of the "fellowship of God's faithful and elect people, . . . Jesus Christ himself being the head corner-stone." In Anglicanism throughout much of the world, synodality is a lived reality rather than an element to be desired in a future reformed church. In the Anglican Communion, lay people are in many places canonically required to play policy-making roles as well as being reliably active and heard in others. In the Episcopal Church that is particularly true, recorded in the catechism of the Book of Common Prayer, which defines the ministry of the laity as taking "their place in the life, worship, and governance of the Church."[29] While Anglicans too often revert to an archaic clericalism, as though their polity favored priests and bishops as the real decision makers in the church, officially — legally and practically — ECUSA cannot operate without lay voices and votes.

While the authority of the laity is a time-honored characteristic of Angli-

---

28. Working Party on the Theology of the Laity, *All Are Called: Towards a Theology of the Laity* (London: CIO Publishing, 1985), p. 3. See also Hendrik Kraemer, *A Theology of the Laity* (London: Lutterworth Press, 1958); Fredrica Harris Thompsett, *We Are Theologians: Strengthening the People of the Episcopal Church* (Cambridge: Cowley Publications, 1989); Fredrica Harris Thompsett, "The Laity," in Study, pp. 277-93; Anne Rowthorne, *The Liberation of the Laity* (Wilton, CT: Morehouse-Barlow, 1986).

29. BCP, p. 855.

canism, it remains a distant vision in many other Christian churches and is an area of particular difference (still unexamined) between the Roman Catholic Church and the Anglican Communion that causes predictable gaps in ecumenical understanding.[30] A church in which the laity shares authority with bishops and priests cannot easily accommodate to a church in which laity lack synodal or legislative responsibility or rights; a church in which the laity are expected to accept and obey the *magisterium* but not participate in governance is bound to be puzzled by one in which the election and authority of bishops require lay votes. No wonder authority is a still unresolved issue between Anglicans and Roman Catholics. This difference in tradition and polity — in ethos and method — is as great a barrier to communion between Roman Catholics and Anglicans as such more widely recognized tensions as the validity of Anglican orders, the ordination of women or of gay men and lesbians, or the doctrine of infallibility.

Surprisingly, despite the long Anglican history of lay authority, Anglicans' eagerness to reach agreement with other churches sometimes causes their ecumenical representatives to forget about the laity, to relapse into a theological and ethical indifferentism in this respect, letting go of some fundamentals of Anglican tradition and teaching in exchange for progress in other directions.[31] Thus *Gift of Authority*, the 1999 ARCIC agreed statement on authority in the church, focuses entirely on prelatial authority while ignoring the place of the laity in the structures of authority in the churches.[32] Although *Gift* includes a section on the value of synodality to the church — the obvious place for a paragraph on lay and ordained ministry in church governance — it emphasizes the synodal responsibility of only bishops:

> Forms of synodality, then, are needed to manifest the communion of the local churches and to sustain each of them in fidelity to the Gospel. The ministry of the bishop is crucial, for this ministry serves communion within and among local churches. Their communion with each other is ex-

30. In the fourth of the "Elucidations" to the *Final Report*, ARCIC I acknowledged the charge that the commission had placed "an overemphasis upon the ordained ministry to the neglect of the laity" but declared that "[t]here was no devaluing of the proper and active role of the laity," affirming that "in different ways, even if sometimes hesitantly, our two Churches have sought to integrate in decision-making those who are not ordained."

31. The recognition of "a hierarchy of truths" as developed in ecumenical conversations is indispensable in ecumenical discussion, when observed intentionally rather than inadvertently (see William Henn, "The Hierarchy of Truths and Christian Unity," *Ephemerides Theologicae Lovanienses* 66.1 [1990]: 111-42).

32. *Gift* §39.

pressed through the incorporation of each bishop into a college of bishops. Bishops are, both personally and collegially, at the service of communion and are concerned for synodality in all its expressions.[33]

Although the section on synodality refers several times to "all the faithful" and "believers" and to the important role of the laity in sixteenth-century Anglicanism,[34] it fails to suggest including laypeople (or priests) in the synodal structures recommended for the churches as they move toward communion. Further, of the four "instruments of synodality" in the Anglican Communion that *Gift* identifies — "the Primates' Meeting, the Anglican Consultative Council, the Lambeth Conference, and the Archbishop of Canterbury" — three involve only bishops. Only the Anglican Consultative Council, "which meets every three years or so," officially brings together bishops, priests, and laity from thirty-eight provinces.[35] In fact *Gift* identifies only one role for the laity, that of obedience to bishops:

> The Spirit of Christ endows each bishop with the pastoral authority needed for the effective exercise of *episcope* within a local church. . . . Its binding nature is implicit in the bishop's task of teaching the faith through the proclamation and explanation of the Word of God, of providing for the celebration of the sacraments, and of maintaining the Church in holiness and truth. Decisions taken by the bishop in performing this task have an authority which the faithful have a duty to receive and accept (cf. *Authority in the Church II,* 17). By their *sensus fidei* the faithful are able in conscience both to recognise God at work in the bishop's exercise of authority, and also to respond to it as believers. This is what motivates their obedience, an obedience of freedom and not slavery.[36]

The agreement that *Gift* records between Anglican and Roman Catholic members of ARCIC (only two of whom, both American women, were laity) not only omits an important characteristic of historical Anglicanism but also steps back from the 1983 Roman Catholic *Code of Canon Law.* Canon 208 of the *Code* speaks of the church in language that even Queen Elizabeth might have ap-

---

33. "Synodality: The Exercise of Authority in Communion," *Gift* §§34-40, here §39.
34. *Gift* §39.
35. *Gift* §39. The "four instruments of synodality" have become "organs of unity" in the 2004 *Windsor Report* §§97-104, pp. 41-43, and are also so identified on the Anglican Consultative Council website http://www.aco.org/acc/index.cfm. The website specifies that the ACC meets both "every three years or so" and "every two or three years."
36. *Gift* §36.

proved: "In virtue of their rebirth in Christ there exists a genuine equality of dignity and action among all *christifideles*."[37] Evaluating the new code, J. Robert Wright considers the way the two official English translations handled *christifideles*:

> On canon 208 I note with approval the struggles of both the American and British translators to interpret its meaning as regards the equality of lay persons with clergy and even of women with men: *christifideles*, a new term to canon law, is translated "the Christian faithful" in the American edition, and "Christ's faithful" in the British edition. Whichever way translated, it apparently refers to both laity as well as clergy of the Roman Catholic Church . . . , among all of whom there is predicated here "a true equality."[38]

As a lay woman in the medieval church of England, with its temporal head still in Rome and its lines of authority leading clearly downward from bishops to priests to laity, Julian would surely have welcomed both canon 208 and Wright's interpretation of it as hopeful affirmations for recognition of all the baptized — male and female, ordained and lay — as equal members of Christ's church, equal as recipients of the Holy Spirit and as *christifideles*.

Julian herself seems not to have doubted her equality as one of the baptized, her receipt of the Holy Spirit, and her ability as a laywoman to use her voice and articulate her understanding. Her books make it clear that she understood herself as called not only to believe but to inquire, not only to receive but to reason, not only to accept but to explain, and not only to learn but to understand. She joined the instruction she had received from Holy Church to the revelation and the reason she had received from God, to speak for and to all *christifideles*, all her *evyn crystens*, in her own language, the common language of the *ecclesia anglicana*. For she was, after all, an Anglican.

---

37. *Code of Canon Law, Latin-English Edition* (Washington: CLSA, 1983); quoted from J. Robert Wright, "The 1983 Code of Canon Law: An Anglican Evaluation," *The Jurist* 46 (1986): 394-418, here p. 398.

38. Wright, "The 1983 Code," p. 398.

American, Anglican, and Catholic

R. William Franklin

The remarkable events of April 2005, the gathering of the religious and political leaders of the world and three million pilgrims in Saint Peter's Square in Rome, first for the days of mourning for Pope John Paul II and then for the inauguration of the papacy of Benedict XVI, have been a concrete, visual realization in our time, however fleeting, of the communion among people of faith that is the real goal of the ecumenical movement. It is to this movement that J. Robert Wright has dedicated his labor and scholarship, always from a perspective that has been American, Anglican, and catholic.

The moving scenes shown on the world's television screens were imagined and dreamed of 140 years ago by another American, Phillips Brooks, the greatest Episcopal preacher of the nineteenth century. Just after the Civil War, in April 1866, Phillips Brooks, wrote in a letter from Rome:

> One morning I climbed to the roof and galleries and dome of Saint Peter's. More than ever I seemed to pass beyond the narrowness of the sectarianism of this place, and feel as if it were indeed what one loves to dream it might be, truly Catholic, the great religious home of humanity, where every good impulse, every true charity, every deep faith, every worship, and every benevolence should find a representation, — the great harmony of all the discords of well-meaning and conflicting religious educations and progresses. . . . its very immensity makes it answer vaguely some such purpose even now to those who go there.[1]

1. Quoted in Alexander V. G. Allen, *The Life and Letters of Phillips Brooks*, 3 vols. (New

From Brooks's time this U.S. Episcopalian hope for reconciliation with all people of faith, even with the church of Rome, has marched steadily forward, even toward official recognition. Brooks believed that it was the special mission of the Episcopal Church in the United States to create a new synthesis of catholicism, inherited from the Christian past, with the American democratic tradition of the people, inherited from the eighteenth century. America and catholicism were to be brought into fusion in the United States by the Anglican tradition.[2]

The first official document of the Episcopal Church that expressed this synthesis was the Chicago Quadrilateral, adopted by the House of Bishops in 1886 and crafted by Brooks's close friend from Massachusetts, William Reed Huntington.[3] In the twentieth century, landmarks toward the realization of this synthesis that is American, Anglican, and catholic have been the 1965 founding of the official Anglican–Roman Catholic Dialogue in the United States, the 1985 official reception by the General Convention of the Episcopal Church of the Anglican–Roman Catholic International Commission's Agreed Statements on eucharist and ministry, and the catholic ecumenical witness of the Episcopal Church during the period of admission of women to holy orders. In the twentieth century no one in the United States has played a more consistent role in forwarding a Christian synthesis that is at once American, Anglican, and catholic than J. Robert Wright.[4]

Yet some are now describing this first decade of the twenty-first century as a time of crisis both in the ecumenical relations and in the catholic witness of the Episcopal Church. The commitment of the Episcopal Church and some provinces of the Anglican Communion to the ordination of women has made the relations of the Episcopal Church with the Roman Catholic Church and the Orthodox Churches more complex, while the Episcopal Church remains committed to the goal of full communion. The more visible and open role of gay and lesbian Christians within U.S. Anglican communities has led some prov-

---

York: E. P. Dutton, 1901), 2:46-47; on Brooks and links to Rome see also Phillips Brooks, *Letters of Travel* (New York: E. P. Dutton, 1893), pp. 101-4.

2. On the catholicism of Phillips Brooks as reflected in the architecture of Trinity Church in Boston, see an important new book: Douglass Shand-Tucci, *Ralph Adams Cram: An Architect's Four Quests — Medieval, Modernist, American, Ecumenical* (Amherst: University of Massachusetts Press, 2005).

3. BCP 876-77; J. Robert Wright, "Heritage and Vision: The Chicago-Lambeth Quadrilateral," *Quadrilateral*, pp. 8-46.

4. Joseph W. Witmer and J. Robert Wright, eds., *Called to Full Unity: Documents on Anglican–Roman Catholic Relations, 1966-1983* (Washington, DC: USCC, 1986); J. Robert Wright, "Anglican–Roman Catholic Dialogue in the U.S.A. — A Survey of Thirteen Years," *One in Christ* 15.1 (1979): 73-84.

inces of the Anglican Communion to declare that they are in a state of "impaired communion" with the Episcopal Church, rendering interchangeability in ministry and sacramental life no longer possible. Some primates of the Anglican Communion refuse to receive communion with the Presiding Bishop of the Episcopal Church, and he has resigned as Co-chairman of the Anglican–Roman Catholic International Commission.[5]

From 2003, two actions of the Episcopal Church have led to headlines in the press and have resulted in the development of "impaired" rather than closer communion. First, in August of 2003 the General Convention of the Episcopal Church voted to authorize the Diocese of New Hampshire to proceed to ordain as its bishop Canon V. Gene Robinson, who for many years had been living in a committed, non-celibate relationship with another man. Second, the General Convention authorized parishes that had blessed holy unions of same-sex couples to continue to do so. In November 2003 Bishop Robinson was duly ordained and consecrated, the Presiding Bishop acting as chief co-consecrator. Through 2004 and 2005 some Episcopal Church parishes continued to bless the holy unions of same-sex couples.

In the midst of the resulting alteration of mind and heart in the light of these developments, some Episcopalians came to fear that Holy Scripture had been wrongly interpreted by the General Convention and that the faithful were in danger of being separated from fundamental Christian values. Consequently, some regions of the United States witnessed the rise of a new network of dioceses and parishes, which remained in full communion with the Archbishop of Canterbury but were in "impaired communion" with the Episcopal Church, refusing to recognize the validity of decisions made by the highest Anglican authority in the United States, the General Convention of the Episcopal Church.

By the spring of 2005, with a war of headlines continuing in the press, Anglican life in the United States had reached a point not unlike the early spring of 1861, when individual southern states were seceding from the American union and seeking from England and other foreign powers recognition of their "confederacy," denying that the United States held legitimate sovereignty over all regions of the union. By the end, the eleven southern states had seceded from the American union in reaction against Abraham Lincoln's interpreting the text of the Declaration of Independence as including the whole population of the United States. That spring the text of the Declaration of Independence and the authority of the United States as regarded the unity of the American nation were inter-related questions, with unavoidable implications for conflict and schism.

5. Chris Herlinger, "Top Anglican Leader Quits Dialogue Forum with Catholics over Gay Bishop," *ENI-Ecumenical News International* 24 (2003): 4.

The text of holy scripture and the authority of the General Convention as regards the unity of American Anglicans were similarly inter-related questions in the spring of 2005. Observers from abroad rightly ask what the Episcopal Church believes about the authority of holy scripture that allowed it to ordain the first openly gay U.S. bishop and to bless unions between people of the same sex, and how the Episcopal Church's laws of ecclesiastical polity allow such actions.

Faced with questions from abroad about the events in the United States, in 1861 Abraham Lincoln returned again and again to the example of the generation of leaders who had made the American Revolution to explain to his foreign contemporaries the genesis and the genius of American secular polity. In 2005 the Episcopal Church can follow Lincoln's example by locating the origins of distinctive aspects of its polity in the crisis of the American Revolution in the eighteenth century. But the contemporary crisis provoked by the rejection of the actions of the 2003 General Convention raises the question of whether the internal eighteenth-century polity of the Episcopal Church is adequate to a global age. Even before this crisis, in his writing and his teaching, J. Robert Wright has repeatedly questioned understanding the Episcopal Church only as an eighteenth-century institution. He has located its identity and character in the apostolic and catholic origins of the church, and his scholarship has identified resources that make possible the new understandings of Episcopal polity that are required by internal and external reactions to recent events.

The Eighteenth-Century Origins of the Episcopal Church

The origins of the Episcopal Church lie in an earlier convulsion of church history — the eighteenth-century age of revolution. In retrospect, the early eighteenth century was a golden age of American Anglicanism, not unlike the period of the Episcopal Church from the 1940s to the late 1960s, that time of growth, prosperity, and harmony into which Robert Wright was born and in which he experienced his first Christian formation and education for ministry. But the reversal of Anglican fortunes on the North American continent in the last three decades of the eighteenth century (as in the last three decades of the twentieth century) was unprecedented in Christian history. Until the Russian Revolution, perhaps no church would suffer such extensive deprivations in the aftermath of social and political upheaval as did the Church of England in America, stripped by war of its clergy, its schools, its finances, and its prestige. In the new southern states, American revolutionaries disestablished the Anglican Church, and in Virginia the government seized most of its property. Anglicanism, with its hierarchical ministry, its formal services, and its prescribed liturgy, seemed to reflect a fading European lineage of a vanished era, destined, like warfare, to disappear with the last of the eighteenth-century generation.

In New England, where Robert Wright began his teaching career in theological education, the most influential Anglican parish church, Boston's King's Chapel, moved towards a liberal faith that would abandon the corruptions of European Christianity and recast Anglicanism in a new form, embracing the toleration and the enterprise of American citizens. But despite these bright hopes, the Unitarianism of King's Chapel remained essentially the religion of one provincial region and one small social class.

In the southern states, where Robert Wright was educated for his undergraduate degree and his first graduate degree, by 1784 the Evangelical Revival had led to the formation of the Methodist Church as a separate denomination. But despite its later quickening influence elsewhere, U.S. evangelicalism has never really receded as a regional and provincial expression of the Christian faith.

In this revolutionary period the remarkable contribution of those remaining Anglicans who cast their lot with the new Episcopal Church was to create a body comprehensive enough to encompass an entire nation: all regions, all races, all conditions — north and south, black and white, saints and sinners, beginners and mature Christians. To accomplish this goal of national Anglican unity, by 1792 the Episcopal Church had quickly created new national institutions and structures that transferred to the revolutionary states the old English ideal of the church as an entire nation. These structures were a united episcopate, which maintained the historic apostolic succession derived from the Scottish Episcopal Church and the Church of England; an American version of the Book of Common Prayer, also derived from English and Scottish elements, and, finally, a federal system of church government that in a remarkable way adapted episcopacy and liturgy to a democratic society by vesting ultimate authority in a General Convention made up of the elected representatives of the people.

The eighteenth-century polity of the Episcopal Church crafted by 1792 sought to keep in balance and synthesize two polarities, the catholic structure and authority of a historic faith, and Christian liberty adapted to a new continent. While preserving the apostolic understanding of the authority of bishops, the Episcopal Church modified episcopal government so that the House of Bishops shared its authority with a second House of Lay and Clerical Deputies of the General Convention, who were elected by the people of the dioceses. Holy scripture continued to be the church's primary authority, but interpreted by this elected General Convention. The General Convention was also granted the authority to lead the Episcopal Church forward, through the exercise of the gift of reason and in the light of new developments in knowledge, to a deeper and expanded understanding of the truths of the gospel.

The eighteenth-century founders of the Episcopal Church were convinced that its long-standing historical teaching should interpret scripture. But as children of the rationalism of the eighteenth-century Enlightenment and also as heirs of the sixteenth-century English Reformation and its great theologian of polity, Richard Hooker, they also made room for the role of reason in their interpretation of scripture. The function of reason in the polity of the Episcopal Church was said to determine the way in which holy scripture and tradition would have authority in a new nation. The eighteenth-century founders held that reasonable dialogue in the community of faith would make such determination. They defined the authoritative community of faith to be the General Convention of the Episcopal Church, whose political structures were to bring bishops, priests, and laity into a legislative conversation, where the future parameters of Christian life for the American people were to be determined.

In this legislative and political process, eighteenth-century Episcopalians believed that the interior world of faith was certain about the saving events concerning the life, death, and resurrection of Jesus Christ. But in matters of polity, they did not believe the Episcopal Church to possess a divine pattern. In such matters, they held, the Church lives with probability and reason — a human faculty — and the elected representatives of the Christian community, exercising reason in prayerful conversation, ultimately determine what is authoritative and what is only probable for the interior world of faith and for the public life of the Church.[6]

This was the polity, process, and ecclesiology followed by the Episcopal Church in the 1960s and after, as the church sought to integrate the great movements of Civil Rights in the areas of race and gender into new and legitimate models of Christian life and into an expanded, yet traditional, understanding of Holy Orders. This was the polity, process, and ecclesiology still followed by the Episcopal Church in 2003 in the election and confirmation and then the ordination and consecration of Gene Robinson as Bishop of New Hampshire. Robinson was validly elected as a bishop by a New Hampshire diocesan convention in April 2003; in August 2003 his election was confirmed by majority votes in both Houses of the General Convention of the Episcopal

---

6. R. William Franklin, "The Historical Background of the Current Situation in the Episcopal Church in the United States as a Contribution to Our Ecumenical Dialogue," *Centro pro Unione Bulletin* 66 (Fall 2004): 3-9.

Church. In November 2003, Robinson was ordained as Bishop of New Hampshire, with the Presiding Bishop acting as chief co-consecrator, the Presiding Bishop taking this role not on any independent authority but in his role as chief presiding officer of the General Convention, directed by the action of General Convention.

For in this United States polity of 2003, as in 1792, the Presiding Bishop possesses no independent authority. His authority and office derive solely from the ultimate Anglican ecclesial authority in the United States, the General Convention. Likewise, in 2003 as in 1792, in the United States polity there is no appeal possible to the Archbishop of Canterbury that can go above and beyond this ultimate authority of the General Convention in matters relating to the dioceses of the Episcopal Church in the United States.

What is absolutely clear in this theory and practice is that since the eighteenth century, the Archbishop of Canterbury, the Lambeth Conference, the Anglican Consultative Council, and the primates' meeting — that is, all the "organs of unity" defined by the *Windsor Report* of 2004 — none of these organs of unity currently has any authority according to the polity of the Episcopal Church.[7] This fact is the direct result of the birth of the polity after a bitter war with England within the intellectual constructs of the Enlightenment. The Episcopal Church seeks to address a global crisis of Christianity as still essentially, constitutionally speaking, an eighteenth-century institution.

A strength of this eighteenth-century polity is that the American model represents the first adaptation of Anglican synodality to a democratic society in which Anglicanism was not an established, state religion, as it was in England and Ireland. A second strength may be found in the protection of the synodal authority of the local church, the diocese, within a national federation of dioceses.

The weakness of the American model is that it contains no way in which the local church — even a federation of dioceses — can relate to the universal church. The political realities of the eighteenth century, the deep hostility of Great Britain and the United States toward one another — hostility that extended to legal barriers — made any authoritative communion of American dioceses with the Church of England impossible. American Anglicans still inhabit an eighteenth-century world when it comes to relations with the universal church. Perhaps one unintended consequence of the current crisis about the place of gay and lesbian Christians within national and diocesan structures of the Episcopal Church is that it forces Americans to ask questions now about the place of their dioceses within the world church.

7. *Windsor Report* §§97-104, pp. 41-43.

Rethinking the Polity of the Episcopal Church

At three moments of crisis in the recent past the Church of England has had to rethink its internal polity: in 1833 with the Church Temporalities Act, in 1919 with the Enabling Act, and in 1970 with the Synodical Government Measure. The Temporalities Act restructured the internal finances of the Church of England with the creation of the Church Commissioners. The Enabling Act changed church government in England through the creation of the Church Assembly. The Synodical Government Measure shifted authority over worship and doctrine from Parliament to Church and made possible the publication of modern revised liturgies in the Church of England. The Episcopal Church has never faced such critical reviews of its eighteenth-century polity.

But for forty years, in his teaching and through his scholarship and his representative role in the Ecumenical Movement, J. Robert Wright has asked the Episcopal Church to engage in such a rethinking of its polity. He has asked a series of questions, including: Is the right model of the U.S. church a federation of local churches, as the eighteenth-century Episcopalians thought? Or is the whole creation of the church more than the sum of its individual parts?[8]

Wright has provided answers to these questions in three ways that are relevant to this moment. He has made available historical materials that place the origins of the Episcopal Church and its roots long before the eighteenth century. These ancient roots locate the Episcopal Church's identity primarily as a part of the One, Holy, Catholic, and Apostolic Church of Jesus Christ.[9] As an official representative of the Episcopal Church in ecumenical dialogues, he has negotiated a series of agreements with other churches, agreements that have made the Episcopal Church increasingly part of a coherent world communion and less a loose association of dioceses, as eighteenth-century polity dictated. Now these agreements must be more decisively reflected in the constitutional polity of the American church.[10]

Finally, Wright's scholarship on Anglo-papal and church-state relations in the fourteenth-century Church of England has much to teach the twenty-first century about balancing the autonomy of a local religious community within the coherence of a universal church, about the preservation and development of administrative forms and procedures that could protect the liberties of the church, in a period of considerable domestic crisis. There is a Latin litera-

8. J. Robert Wright, "Challenges for Canterbury's New Archbishop," *The Anglican* 31.4 (2002): 4.

9. G. R. Evans and J. Robert Wright, eds., *The Anglican Tradition: A Handbook of Sources* (London: SPCK; Minneapolis: Fortress Press, 1991).

10. Communion.

ture of the fourteenth century that Wright has explored, also for its contemporary relevance to the question of "communion" that is at the heart of our contemporary domestic crisis.[11] Mining this Latin literature, and that of the whole pre-Reformation Church of England, has provided Wright with a way out of more than one Episcopal Church impasse over the course of the last four decades. I am sure that through his continued reflection on the complex character of the Episcopal Church, the remarkable way in which it combines American, Anglican, and catholic, he will beckon us forward on a sure path that will be a work of time and a work of scholarship, not of headlines.[12]

---

11. J. Robert Wright, *The Church and the English Crown, 1305-1334: A Study Based on the Register of Archbishop Walter Reynolds* (Toronto: Pontifical Institute of Medieval Studies, 1980).
12. J. Robert Wright, "Questioning the Promise of Toronto," *The Anglican* 30.1 (2001): 4.

Finding a Voice, Defining a Space:
John Henry Hobart and the Americanization
of Anglicanism

Robert Bruce Mullin

If Britain and America (according to the old saw) are two peoples divided by a common language, the same can also be said of British Anglicans and American Episcopalians. In many subtle ways, American Episcopalians in the early nineteenth century developed a distinctive vernacular language in order to respond to the new challenges of a republican society. This essay examines the contributions to this new voice of John Henry Hobart, third bishop of the diocese of New York.[1]

Background

What is the church, and what constitutes Anglicanism? These were the questions that peculiarly confronted early-nineteenth-century American Episcopalians. But what made these questions so perplexing for this generation was that they were forced to wrestle with these questions not by means of some idealized *tabula rasa,* but from within the intellectual perspective and sensibilities of late-eighteenth-century Anglicanism. As historians such as J. C. D. Clark have recently noted, from this eighteenth-century Anglican perspective the answer to such questions would have been different from ours now. As the new histories of Hanoverian Anglicanism are demonstrating, in that period the church was

---

1. Some of the following essay is also incorporated in an earlier article, "Serving the Lord in a New Situation: John Henry Hobart and the Americanization of Anglicanism," *The Anglican* 26.2 (1997): 5-8.

viewed not simply as a community of worship but also as a pillar of the society, undergirding law and political sovereignty and being an essential part of the fabric of the social order.[2] This dual stance was part of the genius of classical Anglicanism, as Richard Hooker explained:

> within this realm of England . . . from the pagans we differ, in that with us one society is both Church and commonwealth, which with them it was not; as also from the state of those nations which subject themselves to the bishop of Rome, in which our church hath dependency upon the chief of our commonwealth, which it hath not under him.[3]

One way in which this special relationship was manifested was in the church's concern for the well-being of all of the society. A second mark was the belief that the fullness of the society was reflected in the church. Thus for example in worship, seating patterns usually reflected the hierarchical social order of the community. Finally, one of the roles of the church was instructing its members as to their responsibilities to the different orders of the society. So for example in the traditional Catechism the faithful were instructed to "honour the King, and all that are put in authority under him; To submit . . . to all governours, teachers, spiritual pastors, and masters, [and] To order [oneself] lowly and reverently to all . . . betters."[4]

Colonial Anglicanism in what would become the United States, to be sure, never fully manifested these characteristics, but it did display strong parallels. Current research about the church in southern colonies has increasingly shown that the church prided itself in both affirming and including the various levels and orders of the society.[5] Class distinctions, for example, were emphasized in the Church of Virginia (which was by law established), not only through the form of hierarchical seating but also in the habit of the gentry en-

2. J. C. D. Clark, *The Language of Liberty, 1660-1832: Political Discourse and Social Dynamics in the Anglo-American World* (Cambridge [UK]: Cambridge University Press, 1994). See too Clark's earlier work *English Society, 1688-1832: Ideology, Social Structure, and Political Practice During the Ancien Regime* (Cambridge [UK]: Cambridge University Press, 1985).

3. Richard Hooker, *On the Lawes of Ecclesiastical Polity: Books VI, VII, VIII*, ed. P. G. Stanwood (Cambridge, MA: The Belknap Press of Harvard University Press, 1981), pp. 329-30.

4. BCP (1662) in the "Catechism" in answer to the question "What is thy duty towards thy Neighbour?"

5. Christine Leigh Heyrman, *Southern Cross: The Beginnings of the Bible Belt* (New York: A. A. Knopf, 1997), pp. 11-18; Patricia U. Bonomi, *Under the Cope of Heaven: Religion, Society, and Politics in Colonial America* (New York: Oxford University Press, 1986), pp. 92-97; S. Charles Bolton, *Southern Anglicanism: The Church of England in Colonial South Carolina* (Westport, CT: Greenwood Press, 1982), pp. 123-39.

tering *en masse*. As one observer noted, "It is not the custom for Gentlemen to go into the Church till service is beginning, when they enter in Body."[6] Finally it is possible to see in the language of some colonial Anglicans a hope that as the colonies were brought more closely in line with British practices, the role of the church would become even more regularized. Thus the colonial Anglican Samuel Johnson wrote:

> [T]he most effectual method to secure our dependence on the Crown of Great Britain would be to render our constitution here, both in church and state, as near as possible conformable to that of our mother-country, and consequently to send us wise and good bishops to be at the head of our ecclesiastical affairs, as well as governours (and I could wish a Viceroy) to represent his most sacred Majesty in the affairs of civil government.[7]

Another example of this tendency for colonial Anglicans to elevate their status by an identification with the British establishment can be seen in their use of church architecture. Flemish bond brick work and rounded windows were both symbols of wealth; steeples, as Jon Butler has reminded us, were dramatic statements of laying claim to a landscape; and the place of organs both differentiated Anglican houses of worship from others and reflected a view of religion and culture unlike that of their neighbors. Indeed in the case of organs they could also be symbols of the special political status of Anglicanism. It was not uncommon to have royalist emblems carved on the organ casings themselves.[8]

These parallels should not be surprising, because (with the exception of the Commonwealth period) throughout its history Anglicanism had been an established church reflecting a hierarchical order. The problem for American Anglicans of the early national period was that both realities were profoundly shaken. The legal position of the few Anglican establishments was quickly abolished in the years after 1776. More important, the vision of the comprehensive

---

6. Rhys Isaac, *The Transformation of Virginia, 1740-1790* (Chapel Hill: University of North Carolina Press, 1982), p. 61. On the social nature of the Church of Virginia, see also Dell Upton, *Holy Things and Profane: Anglican Parish Churches in Colonial Virginia* (Cambridge, MA: MIT Press, 1986).

7. Samuel Johnson to John Potter, 3 May 1737, in *Samuel Johnson . . . His Career and Writings,* ed. Herbert and Carol Schneider, 4 vols. (New York: Columbia University Press, 1929), 1:99.

8. Jon Butler, *Awash in a Sea of Faith: Christianizing the American People* (Cambridge, MA: Harvard University Press, 1990), pp. 98-129; Barbara Owen, *The Organ in New England: An Account of Its Use and Manufacture to the End of the Nineteenth Century* (Raleigh: Sunbury Press, 1979), p. 14.

gradated society held together by custom, patronage, and deference was undermined by the republican ideology of the revolutionary generation.[9] What was the Episcopal Church to do? The post-revolutionary era was a critical period for American Episcopalians not simply because of the problems of organization, but also because of the challenge of reconceptualizing their nature and purpose.

The Case of William White

It is the thesis of this essay that John Henry Hobart made bold steps towards this reconceptualization that have heretofore received little discussion. Hobart's radical departure from eighteenth-century Anglican models is further highlighted by comparing him with his older but contemporary colleague, William White. White (1748-1836) was the patriarch of the American Episcopal Church — mastermind of its political organization, its longtime presiding bishop, and author of many of its early pastoral letters. He was also a leading citizen of his time — chaplain to the Continental Congress, participant in the Colonization Society, and advocate of the rights of the persecuted Greeks in their struggle for independence.

Yet despite his active support of American independence, White's vision of the church was still largely tied to eighteenth-century models. The sermons he delivered at the consecration of new church buildings illustrate this fact. During this period the consecration of a church building was a celebrated and formal event, in which the wider public participated. The event was usually an occasion to expound the meaning and purpose of Episcopal practices, and therefore sermons such as these offer a heretofore untapped window into the worldviews of White and Hobart.

Some may immediately question this dichotomy, because (as the story is usually told) White is seen as a leading figure in the Americanization of Anglicanism. He first outlined his vision of the political structure of an American Episcopal Church in *The Case of the Episcopal Church in the United States Considered* (1783), a vision that became largely incorporated into the later reorganization as reflected in the new church's constitution and canons. The principles he elucidated in this treatise were the political separation of the American

---

9. See for example Gordon S. Wood, *The Radicalism of the American Revolution* (New York: A. A. Knopf, 1992); Robert A. Nisbet, *The Social Impact of the Revolution* (Washington, DC: American Enterprise Institute for Public Policy, 1974); and Bernard Bailyn, *The Ideological Origins of the American Revolution* (Cambridge, MA: The Belknap Press of Harvard University Press, 1967).

church from any foreign subservience, government by laity as well as clergy, the election of higher clergy, the equality of all parishes, and the principle that each local congregation ought to retain every power that need not be delegated for the good of the church.

Students of White have noted the clear parallels between White's principles and political theories of his day and the reflection in White of a Whig theory of political sovereignty, in which consensual representation and balanced government predominated.[10] In this way White was able to conform the political organization of the church to the political philosophy of the age. Furthermore, as Robert Prichard has admirably argued, White also set forth a "theological consensus" on questions such as predestination and baptism that served as a shared theological world heritage for early-nineteenth-century Episcopalians.[11]

The picture of White is a standard one for students of both the early national period and the Episcopal Church; it is in many ways true. It is one of the reasons that White was often iconographically pictured in ways strikingly parallel to images of George Washington. But what is often overlooked is that while adapting to the new political culture, on key social and psychological issues White was still strongly tied to the eighteenth century. This truth can be seen in three of his consecration sermons and particularly in his sermon "Of Worshipping in the Beauty of Holiness," preached at the consecration of Trinity Church, Pittsburgh, in 1826. In these works White addressed the purpose and value of public worship.[12]

For White, worship had a number of key functions. One was aesthetic. The aesthetic impulse, he explained, was part of the created order:

> The same Creator who has endowed us with intellectual faculties for the acquiring of knowledge, and with appetites for the preservation of our beings, has also contrived, that there shall be inlets of satisfaction from the

10. See, for example, John F. Woolverton, "Philadelphia's William White: Episcopal Distinctiveness and Accommodation in the Post-Revolutionary Period," *Historical Magazine of the Protestant Episcopal Church* 43 (1974): 279-96.

11. Robert W. Prichard, *The Nature of Salvation: Theological Consensus in the Episcopal Church, 1801-73* (Urbana and Chicago: University of Illinois Press, 1997).

12. These three works of William White are "Of Worshipping in the Beauty of Holiness: A Discourse Delivered at the Consecration of Trinity Church, Pittsburgh . . ." (Pittsburgh: D. & M. Maclean, 1826); "A Sermon, Delivered at the Consecration of Saint James's Church in the City of Philadelphia . . ." (Philadelphia: Printed at the Office of the *United States Gazette*, 1810); and "On Building a New Church," in Bird Wilson, *Memoir of the Life of the Right Reverend William White, D.D. . . .* (Philadelphia: J. Kay, 1839), pp. 353-56.

works of nature and from those of art: for the beauties of nature are not more certainly the beams of his beneficence, than the like impressed on the product of arts, for which he has furnished talents and for which he has provided a correspondent relish.[13]

Since the aesthetic impulse is such a key part of human nature, he argued, it ought not to be excluded from worship. To do so would suggest that "devout sentiments are improperly excited in us by the arch of heaven, and by the inviting colour it displays."[14]

In enumerating the means of aesthetic appeal at the church's command, White emphasized that the aesthetic beauties he appealed to were those of eloquence, poetry, and music. He praised the beauty of eloquence, for example, because it "clothes such thought in language weighty, yet simple, affectionate, yet not familiar, and elevated, yet not pompous."[15] As is evident, a sense of Georgian balance continued to inform White's aesthetic appreciation. White saved his greatest fervor, however, for his defense of instrumental music, and particularly organ music. From the days of ancient Israel, he said, worshippers rightly praised God by songs set to "psaltery and harp, to timbrel and pipe, to stringed instruments and organs."[16] His great pride that the church being consecrated (Trinity Church in Pittsburgh) possessed an organ echoes the eighteenth-century emphasis on the social function of the organ, as representing the wealth, status, and refinement of the congregation.[17]

Two points are worth noting in this consideration of White's aesthetics, both also of relevance for Hobart. In many ways White's emphasis on aesthetics confirms generalizations made by students of refinement in America. What may underlie White's vision is the eighteenth-century interest in a common aesthetic sensibility that did not explicitly differentiate between sacred and secular architectural forms. Accordingly, none of the aesthetic appeals was exclusively religious. Further, White makes no explicit statement about architectural style. This omission is especially noteworthy because Trinity Church was an early American example of use of the Gothic style.[18]

13. White, "Beauty of Holiness," pp. 16-17.
14. White, "On Building a New Church," p. 353.
15. White, "Beauty of Holiness," p. 18.
16. White, "Beauty of Holiness," p. 21.
17. On the continuing social significance of organs, see Owen, *The Organ in New England*, p. 16; and Richard L. Bushman, *The Refinement of America: Persons, Houses, and Cities* (New York: A. A. Knopf, 1992), pp. 177ff.
18. The designer of Trinity, John Henry Hopkins, also wrote the first book in America on the subject of Gothic architecture, *Essay on Gothic Architecture with Various Plans and Drawings*

A second function of worship was its ability both to bolster the religious life of the larger community and to instruct it in the way of true religion. Indeed the building of churches flowed from the social nature of worship in the Anglican tradition. Persons could love God in private but could worship God only in a social setting. The public worship of the church was socially useful in that it allowed for the public expression of religious sentiments, which in turn allowed for the communication of religion from one individual to another.

> In the acquiring of wealth, or in the devising and practicing of the means of retaining of it, there is little danger, that men will uphold their respective exertions. . . . But in the more important work of laying up a treasure in heaven, and of fostering an interest in it, [men] are likely to be hindered not only by sinful passions, but by an undue attachment to the lawful concerns of the present life.[19]

Worship reminded citizens of higher, spiritual things.

Furthermore, social worship helped shape public morality. As White explained, public worship "confirm[s] in us principles of integrity, of temperance, and of every virtue; which are the best preparation of honest industry, and pen the fairest prospect of its success."[20] Without the presence of public worship infidelity would flourish, with negative social consequences: "for let there cease all traces of the influence which religion asserts over the conscience of men . . . and immediately the magistrate will bear the sword in vain."[21]

This second point concerning the social usefulness of religion should also sound familiar to students of eighteenth-century Anglicanism. One of the key roles of the established church was to maintain the moral levels of the larger society, and White continues to see this role as a function of the new church.

But imbedded in White's description of the instructive quality of religion is a third theme, his belief that the common worship of the church has different messages for the different classes of society. Worship, for example, may elevate the poor: "For thus, the humblest walks of life become elevated above that extreme ignorance, which is the natural lot of man."[22] To reach

---

of Churches: Designed Chiefly for the Use of the Clergy (Burlington, VT: Smith and Harrington, 1836).

19. White, "Beauty of Holiness," pp. 5-6.
20. "Sermon at . . . St. James's," p. 20.
21. "Sermon at . . . St. James's," p. 30.
22. "Beauty of Holiness," p. 9.

these individuals the preacher must at times speak in a manner "uninteresting to fastidious ears" in order to "edify those who neither possess nor affect the literary stores of high culture and refinement."[23] White presumed that society was made up of varying levels of culture and attainment and that the role of the church was to appeal to all sorts and conditions, without confusing them or leveling them. Thus he explained that worship "lessen[s] the inequalities of mankind *without impairing the obligations of the different classes of them.*"[24] Although writing fifty years after the signing of the Declaration of Independence, White still assumed both a model of society with distinct classes and a vision of the church that saw its role as holding together this multileveled society. Just as had been in the case with the Church of England and the church of colonial Virginia, the Episcopal Church was called to bind together the society without amalgamating it.

This use of class language may seem foreign to twenty-first-century ears, but it was in keeping with the world of the late eighteenth century. As Gordon S. Wood has suggested in his seminal volume *The Radicalism of the American Revolution,* at the end of the eighteenth century many political patriots still envisioned a republicanism that included an emphasis upon a natural aristocracy, virtue, and decorum.[25] This republicanism, in Wood's schema, was an alternative to both the pretensions of monarchy and the leveling of democracy. In key ways this vision of a natural aristocracy was also White's vision for the Episcopal Church. And here themes of aesthetics and instruction came together. The worship of the church, he insisted, must reflect balance and propriety. To overemphasize adornment, for example, would be "as when in dress, superfluous finery is more conspicuous than the person who should be adorned by it."[26] Propriety and balance were part of the purpose of the church.

But as Wood goes on to argue, by the early nineteenth century the evolving national culture found less and less tolerance for this vision of the republican aristocrat. A more radical democratic impulse emphasizing an egalitarian, commercial middle-class order soon replaced the republican ideals of the Revolution.[27] This cultural shift was to militate against the religious vision of White. If an aristocratic republicanism found little place in the society, what role could it have in the church?

---

23. "Beauty of Holiness," pp. 9-10.
24. "Beauty of Holiness," p. 8 (emphasis added).
25. Wood, *Radicalism,* pp. 194-212.
26. White, "Beauty of Holiness," p. 16.
27. Wood, *Radicalism,* pp. 271-86.

The Contributions of John Henry Hobart

Throughout his ministry Hobart engaged himself in an elaborate campaign of reconceptualizing the idea of Anglicanism for better service in the new American environment. One difference between Hobart and White was age. Although a contemporary of White, Hobart (1775-1830) was a full generation younger and came of age in the early national period. A second difference was in theology. By both intellectual proclivity and familial connectedness Hobart can be viewed as a continuation of the eighteenth-century high church apologetic agenda seen in such figures as Samuel Seabury, Samuel Johnson, and Thomas Bradbury Chandler (the last gentleman also being Hobart's father-in-law). This high church position emphasized the divine nature of the institution of the church and the significance of its ministerial continuity as reflected in the succession of bishops from the apostles.

Hobart's contribution was to give to this high church theology a new intensity by an active identification of the fledgling Episcopal Church with the primitive church.[28] As he wrote,

> I . . . have the consolation of having faithfully borne my testimony to the principles of the Apostolic and primitive Church, to principles which the noble army of martyrs confessed in their writings, in their lives, in the agony of those cruel deaths to which their persecutors hunted them; to principles which in every age have ranked among their advocates some of the brightest ornaments of science, and intrepid champions of divine truth.[29]

The church was not the creation or invention of human beings but the creation of God, and Christians were responsible for being loyal to its ordinances.

Apostolic community was a sign of a true church, and it separated the Episcopal Church from the other American Protestant churches. But if it separated Episcopalians from Presbyterians, Methodists, and Baptists, it in turn united them with the larger Christian community of the Latin, Greek, English, Irish, Swedish, and Moravian churches. From the parochial American perspective Episcopalians might be a weak minority, with odd and peculiar views, but in actuality, Hobart insisted, they uniquely represented the catholic and apostolic faith.

This apostolic argument had two very important ramifications. The first

28. On the place of Hobart in shaping a distinctively American high church tradition, see Robert Bruce Mullin, *Episcopal Vision/American Reality: High Church Theology and Social Thought in Evangelical America* (New Haven: Yale University Press, 1986).

29. John Henry Hobart, *An Apology for Apostolic Order and Its Advocates,* 2d ed. (New York: Stanford and Swords, 1844), p. 16.

was that by defining the true church as one that was loyally continuous with apostolic teaching, order, and ordinances, it made the new Episcopal Church just as much a church as the Church of England. The cathedrals, deaneries, and trappings of the establishment were incidental. The real authority of the church was its theological heritage. American bishops might be elected, but their authority was from God and not from *vox populi*. Indeed Hobart in a number of places argued that the American church was superior to its mother church because the essentials were less hidden by trappings. As he wrote upon a return from England, the Episcopal Church was to be preferred to the Church of England. Both held the faith, ministry, and worship of the early church, but the American church "professes and maintains them in their primitive integrity, without being clogged or controlled by the secular influence or power which sadly obstruct the progress of the Church of England, and alloy her Apostolic and spiritual character."[30]

There was still a deeper psychological significance in this appeal to the early church. Anglicans had for centuries looked to the early church for an intellectual defense of its order, but Hobart looked to the primitive church also for another reason. In the pre-Constantinian centuries the church was small and surrounded by a large number of opponents. In the eyes of the world it was insignificant. Its power came not from its numbers but from what it stood for. In this sense American Episcopalians were like the primitive church, a small community in an alien society. Writings like those of Ignatius of Antioch and Cyprian of Carthage gave psychological solace to early-nineteenth-century American Episcopalians, because they could identify with them and their concern to maintain the faith in a social order so out of step with the spirit of the church. On the psychological level, Episcopalians felt themselves closer to the early church than to the established Church of England. Hobart's apostolic argument, therefore, was not just for doctrine but also for psychological understanding. The early pre-Constantinian church was a model of what the Episcopal Church was in the new republic.

The apostolic argument lies in the background of Hobart's consecration sermons, conveying his views of the nature of architecture and worship.[31] One thing that strikes the reader of these sermons is Hobart's interest in architectural place. For Hobart the consecrated house of worship was a place where the indi-

30. John Henry Hobart, *The United States of America Compared with Some European Countries, Particularly England* . . . (New York: T. & J. Swords, 1826), p. 18.
31. Hobart's four sermons that I examine here are "The Moral Efficacy and Positive Benefits of the Ordinances of the Gospel: A Sermon Preached at the Consecration of Trinity Church . . ." (New Haven: Oliver Steele, 1812), p. 22; "The Worship of the Church on Earth, A Resemblance of the Church in Heaven . . ." (Philadelphia: S. Potter and Co., 1823); and two others reprinted in volume two of *The Posthumous Works of the Late Right Reverend John Henry Hobart, D.D.* . . . , ed. William Berrian, 3 vols. (New York: Swords, Stanford, and Co., 1832-33).

vidual became particularly close to God. Read closely, Hobart appears quite early to have been sensitive to the fact that in cities like New York the presence of God was not always easy to discern. Churches were places where people could find God. It was not that God was absent from the city, but that its clamor and activity often distracted people. As he explained, even though a believer might intellectually recognize that God was everywhere, he or she needed something "definite, precise, visible, something marked by time and place, to aid his conceptions, to elevate his affections, to confirm his hopes, to fix and engage his faculties."[32] In still another place he wrote, "It is conformable to our nature, that the excitement and expression of the feeling of devotion should be aided by these external embellishments that delight the eye and gratify the taste and thus . . . enlighten the understanding and elevate the heart."[33] This was the point of church architecture.

At first glance this might sound like simply more of William White's defense of aesthetics in worship. But a closer analysis shows that for Hobart not just any aesthetic experience opened the heart, but that particular forms were more conducive to do so than others. In his study of refinement, Richard Bushman has suggested that the growing aesthetic concern for church architecture during the late eighteenth and nineteenth centuries was fueled by a variety of forces. One factor might be delineated "mansions shape meeting houses," or refinements in domestic architecture influence a more refined ecclesiastical architecture. Another factor was a desire to express social preeminence. High steeples and rounded windows witnessed to the social prominence of a congregation.[34] Both of these concerns may indeed lie behind the thought of William White.

But Hobart argued not only that architecture was a key part of worship but that some forms or styles were particularly conducive to a spirit of worship. As early as 1812, for example, he praised the religious power of Gothic architecture in elevating the heart. He was even more explicit in his remarks at the consecration of Saint Stephen's Church in Philadelphia. Whereas White saw no reason to mention the Gothic style of Trinity Church, Hobart praised not only the style but also the spirit it evoked.

> When . . . we view the splendid yet chaste ornaments of this sacred temple, our thoughts are carried back to those ages, when the talents of the architect employed the materials with which the wealth of the pious abundantly furnished him, in raising those consecrated structures. . . . And while we render the just tribute of praise to the taste and skill which planned and ex-

32. Hobart, "Consecration of a Church," in *Posthumous Works*, 2:35.
33. Hobart, "Worship of the Church," p. 14.
34. Bushman, *Refinement*, p. 179.

ecuted, and to the pious munificence that reared this noble sanctuary, we perceive in it that quality, the want of which would mar all other excellencies, a fitness in its architectural arrangements to the end of which it is designed; the worship of that High and Holy Being, to whom it is devoted, with the feelings of awful and reverential, yet lively and cheerful devotion.[35]

A preeminent purpose of architecture was to provide an environment conducive to worship, and few forms of architecture did this as effectively as Gothic.

The role and importance of worship was perhaps the dominant theme in Hobart's consecration sermons. The worship experience allowed for the surfacing of all sorts of holy affections that were usually stifled by everyday urban life. Thus the public worship of the church ought to be both affective and instructive. When one felt the presence of God one could proceed on the path of the development of the religious life, and worship (along with the design of the church) was geared to help the individual to do so. In explaining the meaning of worship, Hobart distinguished it from both learning and speculation. Worship, in contrast to both learning and speculation, was ultimately practical. It was an act and not merely an intellectual question.

But being *practical,* it had to be *practiced.* Worship required action. Participation in this worship action shaped and affected individuals. Often in sermons Hobart spoke of the "exercise" of religious worship, and just as the modern devotion to physical exercise rests upon its potential for transformation, so too Hobart believed that religious exercise changed people. In their participation in the forms and ordinances of the religious community they grew in religious understanding. He was proud of the fact that at Trinity Church as early as 1805 all of the festivals and fasts were regularly kept. As he wrote in a letter to a friend, "I am persuaded that a general observation of them would greatly tend to a revival of the genuine principles of our church and of that piety which is equally remote from any dangerous extremes of lukewarmness and enthusiasm."[36] In true worship one felt closer to God. In another sermon, for example, he defined the purpose of worship in the following way, "Let [the individual] *feel* especially that 'the Lord is in the place' where he thus worships, and his affections will be awed, his manner will be solemnized, his whole soul will be occupied in that homage which he offers to his God, glorious in holiness, fearful in praises."[37] The claim that worship created holy feelings and could even "awe the affections" would rarely have been heard in

---

35. Hobart, "Moral Efficacy," p. 22; Hobart, "Worship of the Church," p. 14.

36. The Rev. John Henry Hobart to the Rev. Joseph Jackson, 24 May 1805, Maryland Diocesan Archives.

37. Hobart, "Consecration of a Church," 2:37.

eighteenth-century Anglicanism and might have sounded strange to William White. Yet for Hobart true worship was instructive and affective.

In this reading of Hobart the apostolic vision undergirds his emphasis upon both architecture and worship. Just as in the early centuries of the Christian era a gulf existed between the church and the world, so too for Hobart a gulf existed between the world and vision of the Episcopal Church and those of the new republic. Unlike a more traditional society like Britain, where the church could rely upon the social order to instill and support religious values such as humility, submission, and reverence, in America the ecclesial community alone bore this burden. If persons were to be shaped in humility, submission, and reverence it would have to be by the church, and for Hobart this was to be through the ordinances of the community. The worship in the church was the place where one received this religious understanding.

If on the surface these sound like pious platitudes, they nonetheless give to Hobart's writings a thrust far different from White's. Well into the nineteenth century White continued to assume a traditional view of the nature of society and the church's role within it. Society was made up of various sorts and conditions, and the role of the church was to minister to these different classes, without merging them. Hobart had a very different view. His rhetoric, for example, contains virtually no mention or acknowledgment of class. The key point of worship for Hobart was that it brought together individuals in at least a rhetorically undifferentiated community. As he explained, "Before [God] the Universal Parent . . . the distinctions of life are leveled; and Christians appear . . . at his throne equally dependent on his power, equally amenable to his justice, and equally the subjects of his mercy."[38]

Indeed the great division was not one of class but between those on the inside (i.e., those loyal to the ordinances) and those outside the community. In turn, this allowed Hobart to reconceptualize certain religio-social categories that had been part of traditional Anglicanism. One is the concept of submission. In traditional Anglicanism, submission was both a religious and a social virtue. The passage from the Anglican Catechism quoted earlier suggested that submission to God was linked with a social submission in a hierarchical society. Hobart, however, translated this language of submission so as to emphasize its democratic dimension. Worship was a common submission towards God, linking all the faithful:

> For what purpose, and in what character, brethren, do we come to this sacred temple? . . . not, as the men of taste, to have the feelings delighted. . . . here we appear in a station to which are levelled all the human race; here we

38. Hobart, "Worship of the Church," p. 9.

appear in that undistinguished mass, where the high and the low, the rich and the poor meet together.[39]

Religious submission in true worship produced that unity and peace that religious and political elements of the culture strove vainly to achieve.

In this vein, Hobart also returned to the question of the distinctiveness of the Episcopal Church and its alleged superiority over other such other bodies as Presbyterians, Methodists, and Baptists. As he explained, it was simply that Episcopalians, in their humility, had submitted to God's ordinances (which included a continuation of the office of the episcopate) and had adopted them in their fullness, just as they had been passed down, without tailoring them. Other communities in their pride had jettisoned part of this heritage. They had assumed that if they could see no practical value in some part of the inherited order, they were free to change or discard it. But believers could never be in the position to know all of the reasons of God; they could only submit to God's ordinances. As Hobart explained, "If indeed [an individual] chooses to speculate, difficulties will gather around him, and confound his understanding and his hopes . . . [since] he knows . . . only the *surfaces* of things, only the *facts* of nature."[40] Episcopal exclusiveness was rooted not in pride but humility.

Modern readers must now feel that they have just been on a rhetorical roller coaster and that long-assumed attitudes and assumptions have been carefully put upon their heads. Indeed it is as if we have passed through the looking glass. Episcopalians, far from being an eccentric community, were really reflective of the universal church. The Episcopal Church's superiority lay not in an identification with the haughty and powerful established Church of England but in its fealty to the teachings of the persecuted early church. Its practices of worship, with the trappings of aristocracy and deference (special clerical vestments, kneeling during services, etc.), were in fact tools for creating a common humanity in worship. Finally, Episcopal exclusiveness vis-à-vis other religious groups reflected not pride but humility. Some might even expect to learn that the Mad Hatter was in apostolic succession. What is going on here?

Clearly this line of argument is not a neutral description of early-nineteenth-century Episcopal church life. Even sympathetic observers acknowledged that class issues continued to play a role in the antebellum Episcopal Church and that status and power continued to have their role in religious life.[41]

39. Hobart, "Consecration of a Church," 2:33-34.

40. Hobart, "Consecration of a Church," 2:32.

41. British observers often complained of the failure of the Episcopal Church to minister to the poor. See, for example, Samuel Wilberforce, *A History of the Protestant Episcopal Church in America* (London: J. Burns, 1844), pp. 431-34. For a contemporary American account of the contin-

Particularly in the South, the Episcopal Church because of the Revolution became much more socially homogeneous and very much a church of the elite.[42] Indeed, even in Hobart's own New York, ecclesiastical backbiting and disputation were far more the rule than this picture of a unified community.

This image of a community united in worship is at best a pious picture, but a pious picture with a purpose. What Hobart did in his apologetic was to provide rhetorical categories to maintain Episcopal distinctiveness in a republican context. Central to his agenda was the long-standing concern of other Anglican apologists: to defend the authority of the Episcopal system and the superiority of its worship practices. Earlier apologists had employed categories of class and establishment in this defense, but Hobart moved the debate over Anglican self-identity away from the older categories of class and establishment and into new categories of theology, history, and religious experience. In this way Episcopal distinctiveness could be defended more convincingly within the confines of the early American republic.

Such a line of argument was in many ways a fundamental reconceptualizing of the place of Anglicanism in the new society. In some sense it was a revolution. During the early years of the nineteenth century even other Episcopalians commented on the radicalism of Hobart and his supporters. His supporters were described as the zealous, younger clergy. Opponents claimed that it was a movement of young upstarts, disrespectful of older clergy and ways — they were "aspiring young men," insensitive to all who stood in their way.[43] Such language gives intriguing hints that Hobart's contemporaries were cognizant of his and his supporters' radical tendencies.

But let me end by reiterating my basic point. John Henry Hobart's vision was a radical break from the vision of Anglicanism found earlier. In his understanding of the nature of the church and the meaning of worship he offered a distinctive outlook. He offered a recasting of traditional Anglican categories more in line with republican sensibilities and emphasized a new role for both worship and architecture. In this way we may see him as claiming an American vernacular upon older Anglican traditions.

---

uing role of class in Episcopal church life, see Robert Bruce Mullin, ed., *Moneygripe's Apprentice: The Personal Narrative of Samuel Seabury III* (New Haven: Yale University Press, 1989), pp. 60-69.

42. See for example, Richard Rankin's study of study of religion and class in North Carolina, *Ambivalent Churchmen and Evangelical Churchwomen: The Religion of the Episcopal Elite in North Carolina, 1800-1860* (Columbia, SC: University of South Carolina Press, 1993).

43. See Cave Jones, *A Solemn Appeal to the Church . . .* (New York, 1811), p. 83; and [William Irving], *A Word in Season Touching the Present Misunderstanding in the Episcopal Church, By a Layman* (New York: D. & G. Bruce, 1811), pp. 5-6.

The Breadth of Orthodoxy:
On Phillips Brooks

Joseph Britton

Thou seemest human and divine,
The highest, holiest manhood, thou.
Our wills are ours, we know not how;
Our wills are ours, to make them thine.

Tennyson, "In Memoriam"

In the mid-nineteenth century, the Dean of Westminster A. P. Stanley observed in his *Lectures on the History of the Eastern Church* that "To be called 'orthodox' . . . implies, to a certain extent, deadness of feeling; at times rancorous animosity; narrowness, fixedness, perhaps even, hardness of intellect."[1] A similar sentiment was expressed some years later on the other side of the Atlantic in a polemical paper on "Orthodoxy" given by Phillips Brooks (1835-1893), who after a distinguished ministry in Philadelphia was for many years the great preacher at Boston's Trinity Church and, for the last eighteen months of his life, the much beloved Episcopal Bishop of Massachusetts.[2] His paper, delivered to the

---

1. Arthur Penrhyn Stanley, *Lectures on the History of the Eastern Church* (New York: Charles Scribner's Sons, 1868), p. 246.

2. The essential facts of Brooks's life are readily accessible in Alexander V. G. Allen, *Phillips Brooks, 1835-1893: Memories of His Life with Extracts from His Letters and Note-books* (New York: E. P. Dutton & Co., 1907), which is an abridged version of Allen's three-volume *Life and Letters of Phillips Brooks* (New York: E. P. Dutton & Co., 1901). For more-up-to-date biographies, see Raymond Wolf Albright, *Focus on Infinity: A Life of Phillips Brooks* (New York: Macmillan,

Clericus Club in Cambridge on June 2, 1890, gave vent to his impatience with the kind of narrow ecclesiasticism that he believed was behind criticism of his participation in certain non-Episcopal services.[3] In his presentation, he directly attacked the very idea of an authoritative orthodoxy, defining it simply as "truth as accepted and registered by authority."

Brooks's definition of orthodoxy implied, in his mind, two limitations: that only a portion of the full truth of God and humanity can be contained in any official formulation of the faith (since a new and fuller expression of truth must be found in each generation), and that whatever is authoritatively identified as truth may nevertheless be in error, since there is no infallible authority to which orthodoxy may ultimately appeal. The dangerous tendency of orthodoxy, Brooks argued, is to ignore these limitations, trying to foreclose what may be considered as truth in "a premature conceit of certainty," motivated by the innate human desire for safety and fixity. Brooks therefore criticized traditional orthodoxy as being "born of fear," with "no natural heritage either from hope or love."

Orthodoxy continues to be a word regarded with suspicion in much contemporary discourse, where the relativizing claims of competing cultural and philosophical perspectives argue against what is assumed to be the static and restrictive nature of a normative statement of truth such as that identified as "orthodox." Indeed, orthodoxy's etymological derivation as "rightness of opinion" seems to signify a tightly closed system that defies the modern valorization of the rights of free inquiry and individual autonomy, and even the Barthian "neo-orthodox" renewal of theology in the early twentieth century is now often

---

1961), and John F. Woolverton, *The Education of Phillips Brooks* (Urbana: University of Illinois Press, 1995). An analysis of Brooks's rhetorical style is given in David B. Chesebrough, *Phillips Brooks: Pulpit Eloquence* (Westport, CT: Greenwood Press, 2001); a study of his religious thought in its historical, cultural, and ecclesiastical contexts is offered in Gillis J. Harp, *Brahmin Prophet: Phillips Brooks and the Path of Liberal Protestantism* (Lanham, MD: Rowman and Littlefield, 2003). See also Robert B. Slocum's review article, "The Social Teaching of Phillips Brooks," ATR 84 (2002): 135-46.

3. Phillips Brooks, "Orthodoxy," in *Essays and Addresses,* ed. John Cotton Brooks (New York: E. P. Dutton & Co., 1894), pp. 183-97. The Clericus Club of Boston was a group of clergy of Brooks's own founding in 1870, modeled on an earlier organization in Philadelphia, which met monthly to share conversation and essays contributed by the members. The specific context for the paper on orthodoxy was the controversy following Brooks's participation in January of that year in the installation of Lyman Abbott as Henry Ward Beecher's successor at Plymouth (Congregational) Church in Brooklyn; Brooks was criticized as having implicitly acknowledged by his presence a non-episcopally ordained man to be a minister of Christ (Albright, *Focus on Infinity,* pp. 338-39). The Clericus continues to this day to meet monthly under the name of the "Phillips Brooks Clericus Club."

regarded as a heavy-handed appeal to fixed sources of revelation. Yet the word *orthodoxy* has also had a recent resurgence: led especially by the English theologians John Milbank, Catherine Pickstock, and Graham Ward, "radical orthodoxy" has sought to challenge the rationalist assumptions of modernity and its post-modern sequel, offering a destabilizing critique of the western philosophical tradition and thereby calling into question the nihilistic tendencies of the dissociation of the spiritual and rational.[4] At the same time, many current ecclesial and moral debates make more predictable appeals to the standards of orthodoxy, where the word is typically claimed to be congruent with other significant identifying traits such as "traditional" and "conservative" — one thinks of the controversial divergences over biblical interpretation in the Anglican Communion between certain literalist African theologies and their more liberal North American counterparts.

Given the claims that have recently been made for orthodoxy from both radical and conservative positions, one is led to inquire more carefully into its authentic role as a normative pattern of life and thought to which the community of the church adheres and from which it draws its identity. This pattern, whether expressed dogmatically, sacramentally, or homiletically, is presumably identifiable in the basic creedal and liturgical documents of the church, interpreted in continuity with a historical tradition. But is orthodoxy thus demarcated a clearly identifiable standard of catholicity against which other statements may be measured and verified? If so, then one is faced with the ineluctable task of articulating what constitutes that standard, which as Rowan Williams has shown in his essay on primitive Christian orthodoxy remains even there an "interwoven plurality of perspectives."[5] Or, as it is frequently invoked in ecclesial and moral debates, is orthodoxy's function primarily restrictive, in the sense that it keeps at bay inadmissible perspectives or behaviors that threaten to erode the divine-human relationship from within? Under the modern liberal critique dating back to the nineteenth century, such an essentialist conceptualization of orthodoxy has seemed increasingly indefensible or, at best, merely suggestive of an impractical nostalgia for a mythologized unity or uniformity that has never truly existed in the church. Has, then, orthodoxy lost its relevance for the contemporary church, embedded as the church now is in the variety of cultural and social perspectives that make up its global life? Such a degraded confidence in the uniqueness of God's revelation in favor of a mani-

---

4. John Milbank, Catherine Pickstock, and Graham Ward, eds., *Radical Orthodoxy* (London and New York: Routledge, 1999).

5. Rowan Williams, "Does It Make Sense to Speak of Pre-Nicene Orthodoxy?" in *The Making of Orthodoxy,* ed. Rowan Williams (Cambridge and New York: Cambridge University Press, 1989), pp. 1-23.

fold pluralism leads to the disturbing consequence of an apparent hollowing out of the content of the gospel, robbing it of any claim to an objective relationship to what Williams neatly summarizes as the formative Christian "events transacted in Jerusalem."

Because of the inconclusive and even unsatisfactory implications of each of these questions for a normative Christian identity, this essay engages in a renewed reflection on the nature of orthodoxy, in this case from an Anglican point of view. Rather than drawing on the usual Anglican sources in the early church or the classical English divines of the sixteenth and seventeenth centuries, however, the essay turns to the often under-appreciated resources of the nineteenth-century American experience, focusing specifically on a reading of certain homiletical and expository texts of Phillips Brooks. On the basis of his example, the essay suggests that the idea of orthodoxy can best be understood in relation to an appreciation of the elastic breadth of truth as it is discernible in the divine-human relationship itself, rather than in the fixed regulatory or restrictive terms with which orthodoxy is often regarded.

Brooks is a valuable source for a consideration of the breadth of orthodoxy because it was his particular genius to transcend any ecclesiastical party or category — he was claimed by broad churchmen and evangelicals alike and was equally admired by many high church partisans. As a consequence, Brooks's approach to Christian theology demonstrates a variegated understanding of orthodox belief that is singular because of the fact that he was someone who was both loyal to his own church and yet free of many of its limitations. Carefully distinguishing himself from any identifiable party affiliation within the church, Brooks said that he belonged to the "party of the future,"[6] a progressive stance that also encouraged his numerous civic, academic, and ecumenical engagements beyond the confines of his own denomination. All the while, he preached a dogmatically sophisticated yet popularly accessible Christian gospel, in which the theological content always supported yet remained discreetly concealed behind the practical application of Christian truth to human life. As the English observer J. Gregory noted, "His mission was to the thoughtful of all classes. . . . He spoke, we are told, to all alike as though in some way he had bridged the gulf that divides the people. He touched the common humanity."[7] In the breadth of his conceptualization of truth as well as the generosity of his interpretation of the divine destiny of human nature, he exemplified a rigorous yet comprehensive expression of an orthodoxy that extends beyond the limita-

---

6. Allen, *Phillips Brooks,* p. 267.

7. J. Gregory, *Phillips Brooks: A Study for Present-Day Preachers* (London: Arthur H. Stockwell, 1910), p. 85.

tions commonly associated with "right" belief and whose relevance to the religious concerns of our own day is not inconsequential.

1. The Limits of Orthodoxy

Despite the popularity and esteem that Brooks enjoyed during his lifetime, his sensitivities and vocabulary in many respects seem anachronistic to today's sensitivities, especially his confidence in the possibility of human progress, his championing of the "manliness" of religious faith, and the unashamed triumphalism of his Christian reading of history. Even Brooks's thoroughly Romantic personality can on the surface appear remote: he read widely in the classics, frequently expressed himself in verse (finding particular inspiration in the poetry of Alfred Lord Tennyson, especially "In Memoriam"), made the "grand tour" of Europe more than once, preached before Queen Victoria, and admired Abraham Lincoln as the greatest American example of a combined moral righteousness and practical sagacity. Although Brooks was descended from a strong Puritan background, his personality was shaped by America's Gilded Age, including a classical education at the Boston Latin School, four privileged years at Harvard, and finally three more years of formative study in the evangelical environment of the Virginia Theological Seminary before his ordination to the priesthood in 1860.

Brooks quickly established a reputation as a preacher of rare power and eloquence, and wherever he preached or taught, expectant crowds eagerly awaited his remarks, which he delivered at an extraordinarily rapid pace, yet always with extreme clarity and dignity. He was noted for exuding a true seriousness infused with a deep joy, and his energies and prodigious intellectual abilities were wholly focused on the task of preaching the Christian gospel. Numerous testimonies bear witness to the effectiveness of his homiletical skill and liberality of mind: in an editorial response to Brooks's funeral (during which all of Boston and Cambridge closed down to participate in the solemnities), M. C. Ayres wrote in the Boston *Daily Advertiser* that "It cannot be too clearly understood that one main cause of the unprecedented enthusiasm for Bishop Brooks was his breadth of Christian comprehensiveness."[8] It is precisely because of this distinctive comprehensiveness that Brooks's sermons remain germane to contemporary concerns regarding Christian identity, despite the fact that they are cloaked in the ethos of Victorian America.

---

8. M. C. Ayres, *Phillips Brooks in Boston: Five Years' Editorial Estimates* (Boston: George H. Ellis, 1893), p. 103.

Brooks's liberal theological stance, however, might initially seem to indicate a diametrical opposition to the implied constraints of an orthodox normativity. Indeed, in the 1890 paper given to the Boston Clericus, he proposed that orthodoxy should properly be regarded as only a "working hypothesis," in the sense that while it is an authoritatively recognized statement of truth, it still remains very much under investigation, continuously seeking verification in the evolving human experience. While Brooks was not trying here to clear the way for a personal denial of any basic tenet of creedal Christianity (he detested the "cheap notoriety and the disgusting partisanship" of controversy),[9] he was insisting upon the idea that orthodoxy is an imperfect and partial expression of the perfect and infinite truth of God, a perfection toward which human knowing is consistently moving but which is never fully realized. Over and against the easy yet potentially deadening assumption that orthodoxy is the transmission of a deposit of truth from one generation to another ("as a butcher freezes meat in order to carry it across the sea"), Brooks vigorously asserted the importance of individual, personal judgment as the underlying dynamic that carries theological inquiry forward.

Indeed, in an earlier essay presented to the Clericus in 1873 on "Heresy," Brooks had argued against regarding heresy simply as a form of intellectual error, stating that the discovery of truth relies upon a dialectical advance in human reflection, alternating between assertion and refutation.[10] Relying on examples from the epistles of the New Testament, Brooks asserted that heresy was instead a moral concept, to be understood as "a certain personal sin, consisting in the willful adherence to some view of truth which a man prefers, in rejection of that which God makes known to him." Heresy, he continues, is an overt disregard for demonstrable truth in favor of one's own self-interested purposes and desires; it is the morally corrupted "self-will of the intellect." Yet a defensible intellectual divergence is not in itself a part of this corruption, but only when it is implicated in what Brooks recalls Augustine as having identified as a search for "glory or power, or other secular advantages."

Because of Brooks's defense of the intellectual freedom of the individual, the doctrinal soundness of his "broad views" was in fact repeatedly called into question, particularly at the time of his election to the episcopate in April 1891, when a number of high-church bishops and dioceses made strenuous objection to his consecration. Concerns about the orthodoxy of his views were based

9. Phillips Brooks, letter to his brother, Arthur Brooks, 23 May 1873, cited in Allen, *Phillips Brooks*, p. 266.

10. Phillips Brooks, "Heresy," in *Essays and Addresses*, pp. 7-19. He presented this paper to the Clericus Club in October 1873.

largely upon Brooks's reputed indifference to the apostolic succession as the guarantor of authentic Christian ministry, as well as his supposed subversion of doctrine, particularly in regard to Christ's divinity and the Trinity.[11] Although the claims of doctrinal divergence were clearly exaggerated and anecdotal, it is entirely true that Brooks had repeatedly spoken out against the arrogance of the Episcopal Church's claim, based on its possession of apostolic orders of ministry, for a uniqueness among American Protestants. He made an alternative example of himself by speaking at a wide variety of Christian churches, as well as inviting their ministers to participate in services in his own church.

Moreover, in his sermons Brooks frequently decried the stranglehold that doctrinal formalism had exercised on Christian life in preceding decades (in particular the most rigorous forms of New England Puritanism and pietistic evangelicalism), aligning himself instead with the "new theology" that emerged in the late 1800s as a contrasting spirit of liberality.[12] Reacting against ideas commonly associated with the Puritan and evangelical traditions, such as the literal inspiration of scripture, the limitation of the church to the elect, the absolute centrality of the vicarious atonement, and the privileging of an emotive confession of faith over the development of character and will, Brooks embraced what he considered to be a new liberal movement that would prove to be as profound as the Protestant Reformation, characterized by a new understanding of "the nearness of the soul of God to the soul of man, and of the soul of man to God."[13]

In his embrace of the new theology, Brooks could be read as having subverted the ordinary meaning of orthodoxy as a standard of right belief, against

---

11. In reference to Brooks's consecration, George F. Seymour, Bishop of Springfield, summarized the objections to his theology: ". . . his theological position as to the incarnation seemed to be that of an *Arian* of some sort, as regards man's natural condition, that of a *Pelagian,* and as touching ecclesiastical polity, that of a *Congregationalist*" (George Seymour, *An Open Letter to the Rt. Rev. William C. Doane in Reference to the Consecration of the Rt. Rev. Dr. Brooks* [Springfield, IL: H. W. Rokker Printing House, 1892], pp. 9-10). More sympathetic commentators on Brooks's theology repeatedly stressed to the contrary the centrality of the Trinity and incarnation in his thought: see for example Gregory, *Phillips Brooks,* 138. Ironically, despite the controversy surrounding his ordination to the episcopate, Brooks is now memorialized in the Episcopal Church's calendar as one whose theology was both "conservative and orthodox" (*Lesser Feasts and Fasts,* 3rd ed. [New York: Church Hymnal Corporation, 1980], p. 124).

12. Brooks's association with the "new theology" places him most obviously in the tradition of English liberalism, represented especially by F. D. Maurice, whose theology Brooks read and with which he was frequently associated. See the chapter on Brooks's theology in Allen, *Life and Letters of Phillips Brooks,* 2:481-545.

13. Phillips Brooks, a sermon preached in 1884 and published in *Unity Church-Door Pulpit* (15 December 1885), cited in Allen, *Life and Letters of Phillips Brooks,* 2:502.

which other assertions of truth may be measured, in favor of a liberal reliance on human reason as the arbiter of divine revelation. Once he tempered the scope of orthodoxy's claims for determining the limits of theological inquiry, however, Brooks also acknowledged its uses, "meagre" as they might be: orthodoxy, he said, makes readily accessible great truths that are otherwise hard to apply or discern in the present life, and orthodoxy carries both the church and the individual across periods of "depressed and weakened vitality" when the Christian faith must rely on the insights into the relation between God and humanity discerned by previous generations.[14] Underlying this acknowledgment of orthodoxy's positive usefulness was Brooks's primary concern not for the preservation of received and accepted truths but for keeping open the ongoing possibility of a fuller and larger understanding of these truths as they gave meaning and purpose to human living. Orthodoxy, in other words, was in his view valuable to the extent that it could be conceived as supporting, rather than impeding, this basic religious quest for larger truths.

So despite Brooks's indictment of the negative influence that a calcified form of orthodoxy could impose on the discovery of truth, he nevertheless went on to reassert the importance of a "right" belief, so long as it was regarded in dynamic rather than static terms. Brooks thereby turned the table on orthodoxy conceived as the preservation of a magisterial deposit of received truth, converting it instead to the idea that orthodox faith continuously expanded as human beings discovered with ever-greater clarity the depth and richness of life in God. If one is to speak of orthodoxy in Brooks's terms, then, it must be as a process of both moral and intellectual discovery and progress rather than as limitation and preservation: instead of a minimal standard of what it is necessary to believe and to do as a Christian, orthodoxy interpreted in these terms speaks of the maximum that it is possible to believe and to do within the matrix of the divine-human relationship. Its function of giving definition to religious faith, in other words, presses toward the marginal limit, even while remaining attached to an anchoring center. Turning to a more careful consideration of this assertion will move beyond Brooks's apparent prefatory distrust of orthodoxy and more directly into the bountiful content of his sermons.[15]

14. Brooks, "Orthodoxy," in *Essays and Addresses,* pp. 193-94.
15. A number of volumes of Brooks's sermons were published at his own direction during his lifetime, and various collections were also published posthumously by various editors. The collected sermons fill some ten volumes. For a particularly rich introductory anthology, see Phillips Brooks, *Selected Sermons,* ed. William Scarlett (New York: E. P. Dutton & Co., 1949). Twelve of his best-known sermons have recently been reprinted in *The Consolations of God: Great Sermons of Phillips Brooks,* ed. Ellen Wilbur (Grand Rapids: William B. Eerdmans Publishing Co., 2003).

2. The Expansiveness of Truth

At the core of Brooks's understanding of orthodoxy is his particular concept of truth. Given his primary identity as a preacher, truth meant to him something that could not be expressed in the form of abstract propositions, but only as the presentation of the person of Jesus Christ as God's pragmatic and loving response to human need. Indeed, Brooks's theological reflection was consistently shaped by his consciousness of the homiletical requirements of preaching, and his great fear was that he should fall into the trap of defining doctrine from the pulpit rather than showing the man Jesus. In his well-known *Lectures on Preaching,* delivered at the Yale Divinity School in 1877 when he was forty-two years old, he reflected on the craft of the sermon specifically as the preaching of Christ. He told the students, "Beware of the tendency to preach about Christianity, and try to preach Christ."[16]

Brooks understood the individual's relationship to the truth of Christ to be one of personal development into the perfected humanity revealed in Jesus, and so he urged that this truth be continuously expressed through metaphors of evolution and movement, contrary to any formalistic notion of a static immutability of truth. So, for example, in one of his own sermons delivered in 1883 at Saint Mark's Church, London, Brooks cautioned that "the everlasting craving for a deposit of truth" threatens to make of the church "a reservoir instead of a river."[17] What is necessary instead is "a vital union by love and obedience with Him in whom truth and power eternally reside," a union that is a dynamic construction of human character in the likeness of Christ. Similarly, appealing to a favorite image of light, Brooks in a sermon on "The Light of the World" reflected on the "thousand things" that Christ means by ascribing the image of light to himself, all of which come down to "the essential richness and possibility of humanity and its essential belonging to Divinity." Brooks's conclusion is that the necessary truth for humanity is the truth of Christ, for "the more man becomes irradiated with Divinity, the more, not the less, truly he is man."[18]

Such dynamic images underscore the reality that for Brooks human perception of truth is always something partial, still in the process of realization as

16. Phillips Brooks, *On Preaching* (New York: The Seabury Press, 1964), p. 21. Originally published as *Lectures on Preaching* (New York: E. P. Dutton & Co., 1877), and more recently reprinted as *The Joy of Preaching,* ed. Warren W. Wiersbe (Grand Rapids: Kregel Publications, 1989).

17. Phillips Brooks, *Sermons Preached in English Churches* (New York: E. P. Dutton & Co., 1893), pp. 128-29. Cited in Chesebrough, *Phillips Brooks,* p. 8.

18. Brooks, *Selected Sermons,* pp. 282-83.

humans seek to be conformed to the likeness of Jesus. Paraphrasing a verse of Paul's first letter to the Corinthians, Brooks wrote in one of his notebooks during the year of his ordination, "Now I *know,* and I prize my knowledge as the gift of God and hold it sacred; but 'I know in part,' I wait till that which is in part shall be done away."[19] This conviction of the provisionality of truth might imply a net disregard in Brooks's thinking for the uniqueness of the revelation of God in Christ. In fact, however, his appreciation of the partiality of religious truth is grounded precisely in his belief that the meaning and purpose of human life is constantly to seek its perfection in the divine humanity of Christ, who fully reveals the kinship of human beings to God, as children to a father.[20] The partiality comes only from the imperfectness of human knowledge of and conformity to Christ, which nevertheless continues to define the heart of Christian living. Embarking on the Christian life, one enters into a spiritual culture that is the opportunity for the development of the person in imitation of the perfected humanity of Christ. Thus, as John Woolverton has observed in his study of Brooks's personal and theological formation, the doctrine of sanctification became the most important touchstone of Brooks's theology, with all the implications of an evolutive progress in the human embodiment and understanding of God's truth that the doctrine implies.[21]

The theme of human sanctification is one to which Brooks returned over and over in his preaching (he himself remarked that "I have only one sermon"),[22] constantly challenging his hearers to recognize in themselves the divine potential that is given in their very humanity. The greatest danger, in Brooks's estimation, is that human beings should miss the greatness of life as it was created for them by God. This aspiration to wholeness and fullness of life is reflected in many of the thematic titles given by Brooks to his sermons. In "Whole Views of Life," for example, he asserts that "Religion is the whole larger life of man,"[23] and again in "The Sacredness of Life" he voiced the idea that just as the life God gave Jesus to live was "vastly richer in character and destiny than he had dreamed of,"[24] so too is the life that is given to us by God. In a statement clearly evocative of Brooks's pragmatic understanding of truth as that which

19. Phillips Brooks, "Notebook," 1860, cited in Allen, *Phillips Brooks,* p. 111.

20. The importance of Jesus in revealing that "man is the child of God" is more carefully developed in Brooks's Bohlen Lectures given in 1879 at the Church of the Holy Trinity, Philadelphia, and published as *The Influence of Jesus* (New York: E. P. Dutton & Co., 1879).

21. Woolverton, *Education,* p. 80.

22. Quoted in M. A. De Wolfe Howe, *Phillips Brooks* (Boston: Small, Maynard & Co., 1906), p. 53.

23. Brooks, *Selected Sermons,* p. 59.

24. Brooks, *Selected Sermons,* p. 18.

promotes the expansion of the content of human living, he noted in this latter sermon that "the sacredness of life depends upon the preservation of clear ideas of the deepest purposes of life."

Yet while Brooks maintained a robust optimism for the capacity of each individual to realize this God-given potential, he nevertheless lamented in "The Seriousness of Life" that "The great mass of people are stunted and starved with superficialness."[25] Consequently, the church's mission may be thought of as the challenge to draw people more deeply into life by drawing them more deeply into Christ. Christian belief is not something to which one surrenders but something to which one aspires: life's true dimensions are shown only in Christ, so one must be constantly on guard lest one settle for some lesser conception. The church, then, becomes the location of the discovery of truth, for it is through the church that one comes to the human recognition of the lordship of Christ as the completion of human meaning.

The importance for an idea of orthodoxy of Brooks's conception of an expanding truth focused in the perfect humanity of Jesus can best be demonstrated by one of his own illustrations: the form of a circle. If traditional orthodoxy ("truth as accepted and registered by authority") defines a closed circle within which necessary and revealed truths can be circumscribed and contained, either dogmatically or liturgically, then a reorientation of truth to the more dynamic conception of the lived experience of personal relationship with Jesus focuses attention not on the limiting circumference of the circle but rather on Christ as the center from which truth moves out in all directions concentrically. In the sermon "The Opening of the Eyes," Brooks appealed directly to this image: "The centre once set, the circle builds itself. The manifestation of the Son of God, of Christ, gives all other blessings a place and meaning. . . ."[26] Truth, in other words, is something that perpetually radiates out from Christ, rather than something that is hermetically sealed within a definitive orthodoxy. As one commentator on Brooks's preaching noticed, "According to this, the circumference cannot be too widely drawn, if it is drawn from the living centre, that is from the centre which is Christ."[27] Truth is therefore grasped as an expanding and unlimited concept, reflecting the nature of God's own infinite love and concern for human nature; although orthodoxy partakes of truth, truth is always the larger category, so orthodoxy must be regarded as its subset. Yet as Brooks notes, given the proclivity of a defined orthodoxy to search for fixity and stability, the human tendency will always be "to draw a line of orthodoxy

---

25. Brooks, *Selected Sermons*, p. 95.
26. Phillips Brooks, "The Opening of the Eyes," cited in Woolverton, *Education*, p. 93.
27. Gregory, *Phillips Brooks*, p. 127.

inside the lines of truth."[28] If that happens without a corresponding regard for the larger reality of God's truth, religious belief is stunted, partaking of only a part of that truth to which it claims allegiance, rather than glorying in its full magnitude and potential.

To emphasize Brooks's expansive concept of the nature of truth is not to say, however, that he denigrated the importance of a normative doctrinal formulation of Christian faith. On the contrary, his preaching remained rigorously based on a dogmatic foundation, even if that basis was not always readily apparent at the surface of his rhetoric. As he himself taught in the *Lectures on Preaching*, "no preaching ever had any strong power that was not the preaching of doctrine."[29] Yet given his pragmatic homiletical predilections, Brooks consistently acted on the understanding that doctrine should always be shaped and interpreted by the exigency of applying it in the context of lived existence: "Doctrine means this, — truth considered with reference to its being taught."[30] He held that the ultimate goal of preaching is to bring persons to Christ, so that his salvific work may renew and perfect their characters, for "truth has always character beyond it as its ulterior purpose."[31]

In this respect, Brooks's homiletical method is not far from what Ellen Charry has called the "aretegenic" role of theology — a concept that may usefully be applied to his theological stance.[32] Charry regards the progenitive example of patristic theology as a "sapiential theology," devoted to developing knowledge of God and attachment to God. This sapiential orientation (which she believes was gradually lost in favor of a more scientific defense of the warrants for religious faith) was based on the conviction that human life can best flourish when it is lived by knowing and loving God; the consequences of such a life are a moral transformation of the believer through which the virtues of Christian living are both acquired and nourished. Charry uses the word *aretegenic* to describe the intention of such theology to be "conducive to virtue," since it was given over to the encouragement of the moral evolution of the believer.

Brooks's own deployment of such an aretegenic purpose is abundantly evident in his sermons. As an example, "The Symmetry of Life" fuses the development of character, a sense of moral duty, and obedience to God in a unified prescription for human living. Brooks takes as his text for this sermon Revelation 21:16 (the description of the dimensions of the mystical city Jerusalem,

---

28. Brooks, *On Preaching*, p. 24.
29. Brooks, *On Preaching*, p. 129.
30. Brooks, *On Preaching*, p. 45.
31. Brooks, *On Preaching*, p. 128.
32. Ellen T. Charry, *By the Renewing of Your Minds: The Pastoral Function of Christian Doctrine* (New York: Oxford University Press, 1997), pp. 4-5.

where "the Length and the Breadth and the Height of it are equal"), allegorizing the verse to mean that "the perfect life of man will be perfect on every side."[33] The length of human life is its "line of activity and thought and self-development," its breadth is the "diffusive tendency which is always drawing a man outward into sympathy with other men," and its height "is its reach upward towards God." As one commentator on such preaching as this remarked, "The keynote of [Brooks's] teaching may be summed up in one word — the word, LIFE. Faith must be tested by its bearing upon life and conduct. And what is true of faith is true of doctrine and dogma and theology."[34]

Yet while affirming the role of dogmatic orthodoxy, even in its homiletical form, Brooks also challenged it from within by insisting that it was comprehensible only in reference to the individual human person who was living into the perfected humanity of Jesus Christ. Orthodoxy cannot, in other words, be defined apart from its principal aretegenic function: orthodoxy is as much a moral as an intellectual concept, and it is defined as much by a rightness of spirit as by a freedom from error. In an early sermon delivered in 1864 to the Diocesan Convention in Pittsburgh, for instance, Brooks argued that the only way persons could be led to orthodox belief was by demonstrating how such truths were to be embodied in Christian duty and life.[35] No doctrine can be truly embraced except as it informs practical living, and, conversely, daily life must be shaped by the essential doctrinal convictions of God's providence and mercy. Thus "no idea, however abstract, shall be ever counted as satisfactorily received and grasped till it has opened to us its practical side and helped us somehow in our work."[36]

One might suspect that a classic hermeneutic circle has developed here in Brooks's account of the nature of doctrinal truth: doctrine is understood pragmatically to be formative of human character, while human character is also understood to be the tool for the interpretation of doctrine. Yet the circularity that characterizes Brooks's thought is not the endless repetition of moving from one point to another on the circumference of a hermeneutical circle, but rather the endless advance of moving outward from the center in Christ to ever broader circles, concentrically inscribed.

While Brooks was at work critiquing orthodoxy as a restrictive infringement on the freedom of human inquiry, therefore, he was also at work laying down a concept of truth that ultimately returned to reassert the importance of

33. Brooks, *Selected Sermons*, p. 195.
34. Gregory, *Phillips Brooks*, p. 153.
35. Brooks, sermon on the Prayer Book before the convention of the Diocese of Pennsylvania, 1864, cited in Allen, *Phillips Brooks*, p. 170.
36. Brooks, *On Preaching*, p. 88.

an objective, right belief as life's center of gravity, conceived as loyalty to the person of Jesus Christ. Traditional orthodoxy, he argued in his paper on the subject presented to the Clericus, would in the future be less the concern of humanity than this broader concept of truth: "truth will come to seem not a deposit, fixed and limited, but an infinite domain wherein the soul is bidden to range with insatiable desire, guarded only by the care of God above it and the spirit of God within it."[37] Read in light of the themes of sanctification that consistently mark his sermons, the essential element here again is that for Brooks truth must be regarded not in propositional terms but in the relational terms of a personal engagement with God, with all the limitless potential for discovery and growth that that implies.

Preaching on this theme in 1878 in a sermon entitled "The Mitigation of Theology," where he unusually addressed explicit theological questions by explaining his views on the "new theology," he noted that "Orthodoxy used to mean the intelligent and convinced reception of a large number of clearly defined propositions about God and Christ and man." In contrast, he said, the new meaning was "a sympathetic entrance into the spirit and genius of Christianity, and especially a cordial personal loyalty to Jesus. . . . The idea of personal sympathy and loyalty is everything."[38] While Brooks's evangelical roots are clearly evident in his call for personal relationship to Jesus, more consequential is his insistence that the requisite shift in emphasis in the new theology is not from the previous hard discipline of a restrictive orthodoxy to the supposed relative ease and sympathy of an individual relationship. Rather, the shift is toward a broader faith that is *more* difficult and *more* demanding — and therefore in the long run more deeply orthodox in the broadest understanding of that term: "the new faith demands a larger man and a profounder belief than that which went before." As Brooks summarized his understanding of this evolving religious insight in his address to the 1892 graduating class at the Massachusetts Institute of Technology, God is not leading the human race away from the old truths, but deeper into them.[39]

3. The Truth of Orthodoxy

We would do well here to return to the analysis of primitive Christian orthodoxy given in Rowan Williams's insightful essay, where in examining the ques-

---

37. Brooks, "Orthodoxy," p. 196.

38. Brooks, *Selected Sermons*, p. 273.

39. Brooks, Baccalaureate sermon at the Massachusetts Institute of Technology, 1892, cited in Albright, *Focus on Infinity*, p. 382.

tions of how and with reference to what the early Christians defined themselves, he argues that two tendencies must be simultaneously recognized. On
the one hand, the period had a relative chaos of competing interpretations and
expressions that defied any notion of a "mainstream" tradition but that set the
stage for the later imposition of an institutional, post-Nicene orthodoxy. Even
so, there was also embedded within the most basic forms of communicating
about Jesus a variation of perspective (such as the discrepancies within the gospel narratives themselves, or the epistolary witness of a diverse unity rather
than uniformity among the local churches), which continued to contribute to a
precarious evolution of "normative" Christianity, even under the hegemonic
influence of Rome. Williams concludes that to speak of orthodoxy as "a prevail-
ing sense of the norms of Christian identity," one must bear in mind a church
whose unity lies both "in a shared attention to the questioning story of a crucified and resurrected Lord, *and* an attention to how that story is being assimilated in diverse and distant communities, culturally and historically
strange. . . ."[40] In short, since the very nature of relational unity in the body of
Christ is not something that can easily be articulated and defined, orthodox interpretation of the reality behind that unity remains itself inherently and inescapably conditioned by the cultural and historical contexts of the variety of local Christian communities, even with all the untidiness and developmental
variation that that fact portends.

Viewed in light of Williams's critique of the idea of a primitive orthodoxy,
which at the very least recalls the complications of articulating the principles by
which any orthodoxy is to be defined, three aspects of Brooks's own concept of
truth come into sharper focus. First, his suspicion of orthodoxy as a universal
truth registered by authority derives from an unapologetic resistance to any
form of institutionalized ecclesiasticism, that is, any type of Christian life that
artificially substitutes a static form of ritualism or dogmatism for the social and
communal context of individual conviction and responsibility. Brooks sus-
pected that such institutional formalisms were in fact contrary to genuine faith
and symptomatic of an underlying unbelief,[41] for they "stand as splendid
screens between the Soul and the Love," becoming a "mere machinery" of religious behaviorism.[42] Even when inspired by an authoritative doctrinal orthodoxy, the substitution of religious symbolism for personal conviction — which
Brooks perceived to be the particular weakness of his own denomination, espe-

40. Williams, "Pre-Nicene Orthodoxy," p. 18.

41. Phillips Brooks, sermon for Thanksgiving Day 1874, cited in Allen, *Phillips Brooks,*
p. 303.

42. Phillips Brooks, sermon before the convention of the Diocese of Pennsylvania, 1869,
cited in Allen, *Phillips Brooks,* p. 221.

cially given its pretension to the episcopal claims of apostolic authority — was for Brooks a negation of the true personal piety of a Christian, which is "a deep possession in one's own soul of the faith and hope and resolution which he is to offer to his fellow-men for their new life."[43] Only the registration of the content of doctrine in the manner of life of the individual believer in community gives it true spiritual significance, rather than its reification into the forms of symbolic or propositional religion. What is at stake, therefore, is not only the transformation of the individual by an integrated faith and hope but also the transmission of that conviction within the body of Christ that is made possible only by the degree to which dogma has been transmuted into a culturally recognizable life of sanctity. Individual piety thus takes on a role as itself an authentic depository of orthodox normativity in the local church, to which the academic and ecclesiastical institutions of the church must attend.

A second central aspect of Brooks's concept of truth, related to his uneasiness with an artificial religious formalism, is his defense of religious tolerance as an attitude intrinsic to any authentic form of orthodoxy. Following F. D. Maurice, Brooks understood that a respect for a plurality of religious opinion was implied by the very idea of Christian belief, which must be based on the recognition of the vastness of God's truth as it is assimilated in what Williams reminds us are the "diverse and distant communities" of the Christian church. As Albright reads Brooks on this point, "Man becomes tolerant when he becomes aware that truth is larger than his own conceptions of it, and that what seem to be other men's errors must often be parts of the truth of which he has only a portion."[44] The invitation to growth and development that is offered to human beings through Christ assumes a continuously heterogeneous understanding of truth, as human beings experience and discover new insights — insights that will be conditioned by the variety of cultural and historical environments in which the faith is lived and embodied. To think otherwise would be to deny both the human capacity for thought and reflection and the historical contextuality in which faith must be enacted. As Brooks himself observed, "If you could make all men think alike it would be very much as if no man thought at all. . . ."[45] Orthodoxy thus paradoxically requires a pluralist dissent within its own precincts if it is to be a convincing expression of the fullness of God's truth — anything less would be a negation of the excess of divine freedom and creativity to which orthodoxy strives to give adequate expression.

Finally, Brooks associates an intellectual and moral vigor with Christian

---

43. Brooks, *On Preaching*, p. 38.
44. Albright, *Focus on Infinity*, p. 277.
45. Brooks, *On Preaching*, p. 23.

life, through which he implicitly denies that to assert the breadth of orthodoxy is only to inhabit a vast centrist terrain. In a statement whose vocabulary is now rather off-putting, Brooks confidently proclaimed that it is "a manly thing to be godly,"[46] drawing us into his cunning refutation of the common idea that religion is somehow a softening of the creative, intellectual, moral, and even physical capacities of the human person. Temperamentally, Brooks was very much at home with the Pauline language of a lively religious athleticism: Paul's repeated admonitions to fight the good fight or to finish the race easily resonated with Brooks's own physical strength, reputation for goodness, and intellectual vitality.

Yet Brooks's identification with such images went deeper as well, to the profound sense that human beings must be inspired by a vision of what is most noble and worthy of their best effort. In his sermon "Homage and Dedication," Brooks described what he took that vision to be: "The man most thoroughly alive, he who lives most, will be most reverent to God."[47] This reverence is emphatically not a compromised acceptance of a domesticated Christian faith, but rather what Brooks described in his *Lectures on Preaching* as "a continual climbing which opens continually wider prospects. It repeats the experience of Christ's disciples of whom their Lord was always making larger men and then giving them the larger truth of which their enlarged natures had become capable."[48]

Breadth, in other words, is not a dilution of the radical intellectual and moral demands of faith but a reinforced adherence to the "great truths" of Trinity, incarnation, atonement, and redemption — what Williams refers to as "a shared attention to the questioning story of a crucified and resurrected Lord." Brooks himself described what he meant by this quality of breadth:

> I do not mean liberality of thought, not tolerance of opinion, nor anything of that kind. I mean largeness of movement, the great utterance of great truths, the great enforcement of great duties, as distinct from the minute, and subtle, ingenious treatment of little topics, side issues of the soul's life, bits of anatomy, the bric-a-brac of theology.[49]

To appreciate the breadth of orthodoxy, then, is to recognize in such basic statements as the creedal affirmations a syllabus for an active engagement with the

---

46. Phillips Brooks, letter to his brother, William Brooks, 6 November 1858, cited in Allen, *Phillips Brooks*, p. 88. Brooks was at the time also working on a sermon entitled "Manliness of Faith."

47. Brooks, *Selected Sermons*, p. 324.

48. Brooks, *On Preaching*, pp. 70-71.

49. Brooks, *On Preaching*, p. 17.

divine excess rather than its foreshortened conclusion. To look to Brooks for a more rigorous systematic treatment of orthodoxy would perhaps be to overburden his governing identity as a preacher: his concern was for the conversion of his hearers and the encouragement of their growth into a wholeness of life rather than for strict theological exposition.

Yet while one may continue to ask of Brooks if there must not be some more identifiable parameters that distinguish authentically Christian statements (beyond his simple criterion that all truth is centered in Christ), one can nevertheless learn from his example that because orthodoxy treats the infinitely expansive subject of divine truth, it is by its very nature an idea characterized by a generosity of spirit and wideness of understanding, grounded in an abiding recognition that all truth is ultimately derived from God. It is this insight — that orthodoxy both conserves the primacy of the divine-human relationship as it has been historically disclosed to illuminate authentic purpose and meaning and opens the exploration of that truth to a boundless richness and diversity — that preserves orthodoxy's relevance in the contemporary global and laicized church. Orthodoxy as understood by Brooks is thus intrinsically more radical than conservative, yet at the same time it is also profoundly traditional in its loyalty to Jesus Christ as the expression of the full measure of God's love.

In mood (if not exactly in content), Brooks's understanding thereby parallels the ambition of today's "radically orthodox" theologians to recover a theology at once orthodox in "reaffirming a richer and more coherent Christianity" and radical in its return "to the Augustinian vision of all knowledge as divine illumination."[50] Their announced program of critiquing the dualisms of modern society that allowed secularity to assert a corrupting independence from divine transcendence was launched within a framework of human "participation" in the divine creativity. Rephrased in terms of an orthodoxy delineated in Brooks's own terms, this participatory foundation can be read as proposing truth as an expansive invitation into the divine excess, rather than as a restrictive limitation on evolution and discovery. As Brooks summarized this Christian aspiration in an evangelical sermon on "The Dignity and Greatness of Faith," to say "Jesus is Lord" is to "set foot in the region where man lives his completest life."[51]

Brooks's perspective should remind us that even beyond today's accepted "orthodoxies," there also lies a larger truth of God. Beyond the theological orthodoxy of the self-confident affirmations of the initiatory baptismal covenant,

---

50. Milbank, *et al.*, "Introduction. Suspending the Material: The Turn of Radical Orthodoxy," in *Radical Orthodoxy*, p. 2.

51. Brooks, *Selected Sermons*, p. 49.

for instance, lies the human dependence on the prevenient initiative of God for our spiritual regeneration and conversion; beyond the ecclesiological orthodoxy of historically ordained apostolic orders, the priority of service to the gospel remains the definitive characteristic of all Christian ministry; beyond the moral orthodoxy of an inclusive social ethic, the determinative pattern of sacrificial love continues to be manifested to us in the communal life of God; and beyond the canonical orthodoxy of local autonomy lies the communal interdependence of the church as the body of Christ. It is such a breadth of vision that was the bequest of Phillips Brooks to his church, and therefore it is especially appropriate that an essay celebrating his magnanimous spirit and comprehensive mind should be included in the present volume honoring the work of Professor J. Robert Wright. In choosing a passage to be read during the daily office on the anniversary of Brooks's death (January 23), Professor Wright himself appropriately turned to one of the *Lectures on Preaching,* where Brooks declares that "Definers and defenders of the faith are always needed, but it is bad for a church, when its ministers count it their work to define and defend the faith rather than to preach the Gospel."[52] It is within this same tradition of a lively orthodoxy whose breadth transcends any narrow ecclesial, cultural, or historical definition that Father Wright has profoundly contributed to the development of the church catholic and apostolic, whether in its scholarly, ecumenical, liturgical, spiritual — or priestly — life.

---

52. J. Robert Wright, ed., *They Still Speak: Readings for the Lesser Feasts* (New York: Church Hymnal Corporation, 1993), pp. 24-25.

Rearranging the Hierarchy of the Episcopal Church in the Second Decade of the Twentieth Century

Robert W. Prichard

J. Robert Wright has a keen interest in parish life in the Episcopal Church. Among his recent published works is a revised history of Saint Thomas Church, Fifth Avenue, in Manhattan.[1] While the subject of Wright's work was a single parish, it has nevertheless provided an interesting lens through which to look at change in the Episcopal Church on a far broader level.

The following essay examines a less important parish in a less prominent location — Clarke Parish, in the Shenandoah Valley of Virginia. Nevertheless, like the Wright work on Saint Thomas Church, it provides a lens through which to look at the changing character of parochial life in the Episcopal Church. In this case the focus is a relatively short period — the decade from 1910 to 1920. It was a period of rapid change, however, a period in which the form of organization in the parish changed significantly.

This essay focuses on a complex of changes involving the status of women, vestry organization, the relationship of African and European Americans, parish finances, and liturgical practice during the early twentieth century. It suggests that significant and interrelated changes took place in each area of Clarke Parish and that the change is related both to the national backdrop and to events taking place elsewhere in the Episcopal Church.

---

1. *Saint Thomas Church Fifth Avenue* (Grand Rapids: William B. Eerdmans Publishing Company, 2001).

Robert W. Prichard

The National Backdrop: A Time of Change

The second decade of the twentieth century was a time of sweeping change in the nation, a period in which Americans made major revisions in the hierarchical relationships of their society. During this time the social and economic relationships of the rural, agricultural nineteenth century gave way to new urban business patterns. Small-scale hierarchies for which the family was an important model yielded to larger, more complicated hierarchies. This shift took place both within the federal government and within the life of American churches.

The transition began, of course, long before 1910 and continued long after 1920. The decade, however, occupied a critical place in the transition. It was marked by America's entrance into a world war and by the shift in census data from a society the majority of whose members lived in rural areas to one whose majority resided in towns and cities. Three important events also occurred between 1910 and 1920: the segregation of the civil service, the adoption of the income tax as a source of government revenue, and the passage of women's suffrage.

These new elements replaced older methods of social organization that had been suited to the rural and small-town character of nineteenth-century America. That which had worked in the small communities of the nineteenth century did not function well in the cities of the twentieth century. In a stable, small-town setting, European Americans could exercise what they believed to be a proper level of control over their African American neighbors, but such controls were inadequate for dealing with the larger populations of African Americans in the American cities. Women living in small family-centered areas could influence the electoral process by advising fathers, husbands, and sons how to vote. Women who left their homes for jobs in the cities, however, had no such indirect means of influencing the political process. The major measure of wealth in rural communities might be land ownership, but the business conglomerates of the modern cities demanded currency. In the second decade of the twentieth century, the government adopted new legislation to deal with the new, more urban situation.

After the close of the Civil War, African Americans had gained the theoretical right but not the practical means to participate equally in American society. Most southern African Americans stayed in the same communities in which they had lived before emancipation. Economic ties to land owners and employers insured that most African Americans remained in subservient relationships with European Americans. As the century progressed, however, some African Americans gained the economic and educational tools to break out of such one-sided relationships, and others moved to communities — often northern cities — in which African Americans could live with little ongoing contact with European Americans. European Americans responded to this eroding of their authority by imposing Jim Crow legislation that regulated the relationships of African Americans and European Americans on a much larger scale. After southern states passed state segregation laws in the final two decades of the nineteenth century, the federal government followed suit in 1913. In that year Woodrow Wilson signed an executive order segregating the civil service.

In 1913 as well the passage of the sixteenth amendment signaled a new direction in government finance. In the nineteenth century the sale of government land had provided the major source of federal income. The Congress had experimented briefly with wartime income taxes in the nineteenth century, but the Supreme Court had ruled them unconstitutional. The amendment overcame this obstacle, authorizing Congress to levy income taxes. Congress immediately exercised that option.

The decade was also a period of rising enthusiasm for women's rights. American women were increasingly entering the market place. According to census figures only 3% of social, welfare, and religious workers and 25.4% of clerical workers were female in 1900. By 1920, however, women accounted for 65.5% of the workers in the first category and 45.7% of those in the second.[2] Women participating actively in American economic life saw little reason to accept exclusion from the political process. With the rising number of wage earners they had increasing economic resources with which to campaign for change. The long campaign for women's suffrage finally met with success in 1920 with the passage of the nineteenth amendment.

These three changes — the extension of segregation to a national level, the adoption of an income rather than a land-sales federal fiscal base, and the passage of women's suffrage — were three elements in a general shift in American society. Americans abandoned methods of organization more fitted to a rural, agricultural nation and adopted those more suitable for an urban nation. These changes provided the backdrop of the changes that took place on a local level at Clarke Parish.

Clarke Parish

In 1910 Clarke Parish was one of four parishes in Clarke County, Virginia. To the east lay Wickliffe Parish, the parent congregation from which Clarke had been founded in 1832. To the south lay Cunningham Chapel and Greenway Court parishes. Clarke Parish was composed of one congregation — Grace Church, in the town of Berryville. The parish had 171 communicants, drawn

---

2. Margery W. Davies, *Woman's Place Is at the Typewriter* (Philadelphia: Temple University Press, 1982), pp. 182-83.

from some 65 families, and a total budget of $2,421. There was one Sunday School with an enrollment of 25 students. The rector of the parish was Edward Wall (1851-1917). The son of a clergyman, he had been born at and graduated from Virginia Seminary. He came to Berryville in 1894 with twenty years' experience in parishes in Virginia and Maryland.

Both the parish register and the arrangement of pews in the Grace Church building bore witness to the fact that Wall's pastoral charge included both African and European Americans. The register in 1910 showed, for example, that Wall had baptized five European American and three African American infants and that he had presided at the weddings of one African American and five European American couples.[3] During worship services African Americans sat in a separate partitioned portion of a balcony at the rear of the nave.[4]

Clarke Parish comprehended three different economic and social groups. In economic terms, the three were (1) those who pledged to the operating budget, (2) those who supported the parish in other ways, and (3) those members of the parish who did not contribute financially. Each of these groups had its own major concern and its own place in the life of the parish.

At the top of the social ladder were the pledgers. They provided the majority of the funds for the operation of the parish and all of the members of the ten-man vestry. The vestry, presented as a slate to the annual meeting for approval, was a non-rotating body. Once elected, most served for life.

The major preoccupation of the pledgers in the second decade of the century was economic. The parish was in perpetual financial difficulty. An entry in the vestry minutes from January 1913 was typical:

> The Treasurer reported a deficiency to the first of January of $200, with pledges in hand payable April 1st of $450.00. On motion the Treasurer was requested to write to those who usually pay by Apl. 1st requesting them to anticipate, in part, at least their payments, so that the present deficit could be met.
>
> On motion the Treasurer was requested to call the attention of Mrs. E. H. Harriman to her failure to pay her pledge for the past year. On motion the Rector was authorized to appoint a Committee of five members of the Vestry, said Committee to be authorized to consider the financial condition of

---

3. *Journal of the 116th Annual Council of the Protestant Episcopal Church in the Diocese of Virginia Held in Christ Church, Winchester, Virginia, 17th, 18th and 19th of May, 1911* (Richmond: Whittet and Shepperson, 1911), p. 194.

4. Older parishioners in the 1980s still recalled the segregated seating arrangements in the balconies. Emma Weaks, an African American, explained that the partition was tall enough that she could hear but not see white balcony sitters.

the Church, and to take such action as they may deem best to get those not already pledged to pledge a definite amount each towards the expenses of the Church.[5]

As members of the vestry correctly understood, too few members of the congregation were contributing toward the support of the parish.

Early-nineteenth-century Episcopal congregations had been supported by pew rents. Under this arrangement, prominent members of the congregation paid annual fees for the use of seats in the church building. These rents were used to support the operating expenses of the parish. Benevolent enterprises and contributions to the diocese's budget were funded by special designated offerings. Those who were unwilling or unable to pay pew rents sat in the balcony or in the rear of the church in pews reserved for non-pew renters.

Near the middle of the nineteenth century some innovative Episcopal congregations began to eliminate pew rents. William Augustus Muhlenberg's Church of the Holy Communion in New York City became the first in 1846. This new *free sitting* system was gradually adopted by other congregations in the church. By 1910 only twenty percent of the sittings in Episcopal congregations were still rented.[6] In the diocese of Virginia, Clarke Parish was a part of the majority that offered only free pews.[7]

Pew rents were largely a thing of the past, but — the source of the financial troubles at Grace — no consistent giving policy had taken its place. Muhlenberg's experiment at the Church of the Holy Communion had been possible because of the financial support of his wealthy sister. Few parishes had such an option. For them the abolition of pew rents was a modification rather than a total reformation of giving patterns. Parishioners were no longer required to pay rents in order to sit in the pews in the nave of the church, but parish vestries and treasurers hoped that they would choose to do so. The announcement made by the vestry of Grace Church to the congregation in 1888 was typical:

Church expenses . . . are met by the pledges of the regular attendants upon the services of the Church. No fixed valuation is placed upon the pews. Per-

5. "Register's Book of Vestry, Grace Episcopal Church, 1892-1925," archives of Grace Church, Berryville, Virginia, p. 115.

6. *Journal of the General Convention of the Protestant Episcopal Church in the United States of America Held in the City of New York from October Eighth to October Twenty-fifth, Inclusive, in the Year of Our Lord 1913* (New York: The Sherwood Press, 1914), p. 398.

7. *Journal* (Diocese of Virginia, 1908), pp. 158-288. Cunningham Chapel Parish, 4 parishes in Richmond, 3 in Alexandria, and 1 each in Warrenton, Orange, and Fredericksburg were the only ones to retain pew rent in 1908.

sons who had pledged themselves for any amount for the expenses of the Parish, may have regular sittings or pews assigned them; but All pews are declared by the vestry to be FREE to strangers and visitors. . . . Persons wishing to have regular sittings will apply to the Senior warden; but these sittings cannot be assigned unless the applicant becomes a regular subscriber to the expenses of the Parish. . . .

Members of the congregation are urged to adopt the systematic plan of offerings for Missions. . . . The amount subscribed will be collected by duly authorized collectors once in three months. About three-fourths of the money so subscribed is devoted to Diocesan Missions.[8]

The formal elimination of pew rents had not changed two important features of parish giving in Clarke Parish. Parishioners continued to use separate methods of giving for parish upkeep and missions, and the vestry continued to associate regular giving to parish upkeep with designated seating.

In practical terms, those who had been pew holders became pledgers. European American non-pledgers were allowed to venture out of the balcony, so long as they were careful not to sit in contributors' pews, but they did not significantly increase their giving. They were no more willing to subscribe to the support of the parish than they had been to rent pews. Thus the abolition of the pew rent system had done little to broaden the base of financial support for the congregation. The same families continued to provide the majority of parish support. In the May 1913-April 1914 fiscal year, for example, there were only twenty-nine pledges of ten dollars or more. Over half — seventeen — came from individuals whose surnames had been represented on the vestry since 1900.[9] It was little wonder that the vestry persons felt that they were carrying a disproportionate share of parish expenses.

At nearby Wickliffe Parish, the financial situation was even more perilous. The annual report for 1918 noted only twenty communicants and a budget of only $312 for parish expenses. The following year the Wickliffe Parish closed. The few remaining parishioners transferred their membership to Grace or to one of the other area congregations.[10]

The pledging families carried the bulk of the parish budget at Grace. They did, however, receive benefits for their disproportionate financial support. They occupied the prominent seats in the church, provided the members for the con-

8. *Our Parish Work*, newsletter of Clarke Parish 1 (February 1888); Grace Church archives, Berryville, Virginia, p. 1.

9. "Grace Episcopal Church in Care of St. Baughman, Treasurer, 1909-1935," Grace Church archives, pp. 38-49.

10. *Journal* (Diocese of Virginia, 1919), pp. 155-56.

tinuing vestry, buried their dead in the parish yard rather than the town grave-yard, and exercised considerable control over the actions of the church's clergy-man. A later rector commented with some humor that he was like an employee of the landed class. He lamented that "landowners always and everywhere . . . underpay their help."[11]

Below the pledging families on the parish hierarchy were those European Americans who did not pledge but who contributed to the parish in other ways. The parish budget in this period gives some indication of this group. In 1913, for example, the pledging of the leading families provided only a portion of the parish income:

Parish Income in 1913[12]

		% of budget
Pledges	$747	60%
Other Contributions	$498	40%

The other contributions included $211 in loose plate offerings and $287 in enve-lope contributions, a category of giving about which more will be said later. While the parish records were not explicit, the general tenor of financial discus-sions at vestry meetings suggests strongly that the leading families were making some of the plate offering but none of the envelope contributions. Giving pat-terns of some older members in the 1970s supported this supposition. If it is ac-curate, persons in the second position in the parish hierarchy contributed be-tween twenty-three and forty percent of the budget.

While no envelope lists survive in the parish archives, it is possible to make some speculations about the identity of persons in this group of other contribu-tors. They probably included members of the parish women's organizations and their families. Reports in the Diocese of Virginia in the decade before 1913 give witness to the increasing popularity of such groups. Grace had three: a Parish Aid Society that contributed to parish projects, a Women's Auxiliary that raised funds for diocesan and national missionary projects, and a Junior Branch of the Auxil-iary, for younger women. In 1913 sixty women were active in these organizations, more than double the number (twenty-nine) of those who pledged over $10 that year. Not all of the women's group members, therefore, came from the pledging families. Some members of the choir were also from non-pledging families.[13]

Third in the parish hierarchy were those low-income European and Afri-

---

11. Louis Tucker, *Clerical Errors* (New York: Harper & Brothers, 1943), p. 344.
12. "Grace Episcopal Church in Care of St. Baughman," pp. 44-53.
13. *Journal* (Diocese of Virginia, 1914), p. 194.

can Americans who participated in the parish primarily through the pastoral offices and the church school. As has been noted, the rector of Grace Church routinely baptized, married, and buried African Americans. While no separate statistics were kept for low-income European Americans, the parish register gives some indication of their presence in the congregation as well. Most striking was the entry for September 5, 1920. Mr. and Mrs. John D. Richardson stood as godparents for eighteen persons who were baptized at a local school house.[14] The Richardsons, part owners of the National Biscuit Company, had a large farm on which they employed a number of those baptized. They had constructed the school building for the county to use for weekday classes and for the Episcopal Church to use for Sunday School.[15]

Sunday Schools in the Episcopal Church, as in other Protestant denominations, played a dual role. They were both educational institutions, intended to instruct the children of the parish, and missionary outposts, helping to educate those of modest income and limited education who might never be expected to become fully participating adults in the congregation. As the author of the "State of the Church" report at the General Convention of 1913 lamented, this second group may well have been larger than the former: "It has been asserted that 75 percent of the boys in Christian Sunday Schools disappear as active members of the Church."[16]

In the Diocese of Virginia two particular ethnic and social groups were singled out for particular attention in the Sunday Schools: African Americans and inhabitants of the Blue Ridge Mountains. In both cases this work in Virginia was coordinated by a diocesan archdeacon. In 1901 Bishop Francis M. Whittle (1823-1902) appointed John Moncure (?1857-1912) the Archdeacon for Colored Work.[17] He served in that capacity until his death in 1912.[18] He reported to the diocesan

---

14. "Parish Register, Grace Church, Clarke Parish, 1879-1927," Grace Church archives, pp. 122-25.

15. John D. Richardson, III, interview held in Berryville, Virginia, summer 1983.

16. *Journal* (General Convention, 1913), p. 400.

17. Before the Civil War, African Americans had occupied a place in the church roughly equivalent to that of children; they were ministered to as part of the extended family of European Americans. Many Episcopal clergy continued to look upon African Americans in their community in much the same way after the Civil War, but by the 1890s southern dioceses began to appoint archdeacons — special assistants to the bishop — to organize separate African American congregations. Virginia's John Moncure was neither the first nor the last of those. The bishop of South Carolina appointed William Walker as archdeacon in 1891, and the bishops of South Carolina and Southern Virginia followed suit with the appointment of Edmund N. Joyner in 1892 and James S. Russell in 1894. Arkansas's Daniel Ernest Johnson began his work in 1914, and Georgia's E. L. Braithwaite began in 1918.

18. *Journal* (Diocese of Virginia, 1913), p. 83.

councils of 1907 and 1908 in some detail. In 1907 he spoke of fifteen congregations and in 1908 of sixteen, but of these all but three — Meade Memorial and Good Shepherd in Alexandria and Saint Philip's in Richmond — were Sunday Schools attached to European American congregations.[19]

In 1904 Bishop Robert A. Gibson (1846-1919) appointed a second archdeacon, Frederick William Neve (1856-1948), with responsibility for missions in the Blue Ridge Mountains. Blessed with a longer life than Moncure, Neve was able to preside over work in the Blue Ridge that ultimately led to the founding of twenty-one schools.[20] He was already able to report to the 1911 diocesan council that sixteen schools were in operation.[21]

The Episcopalians in Clarke County were involved in bringing Sunday Schools to both African Americans and residents of the Blue Ridge. Efforts for the Blue Ridge were undertaken by parishioners of Wickliffe and Cunningham Chapel parishes, the two parishes in the county that bordered on the Blue Ridge. Parishioners of both parishes were also involved in the creation of Sunday Schools for African Americans, but after 1913 this work began to center in Berryville and Clarke Parish.

In most cases the leadership for these Sunday Schools was female. In the 1913 diocesan *Journal,* for example, the parochial report for Wickliffe Parish included the following heading: "Rev. R. C. Cowling — Rector, Miss Hannah F. Williams, Missionary Teacher."[22] Miss Williams was a native of Clarke County who had lived in Ohio; around 1900 she returned to Clarke County to live with her sister. As her title indicates, she became a missionary to the African Americans in her community. She organized a Sunday School that met first in the basement of her sister's home and then in a building specifically constructed for that purpose near Wickliffe Church. In 1913 members of Grace Church, led by Mrs. Annie C. Moore, began a similar effort in the town of Berryville.[23]

The work in the Blue Ridge was also largely the result of female initiative. Sometime before 1908 Mrs. Thomas Elsea had joined a neighbor in forming a church school of Wickliffe Parish in the Blue Ridge community of Pine Grove. To the south of Pine Grove Miss Bessie Kibby founded a day school and hired a

19. *Journal* (Diocese of Virginia, 1907), p. 290; *Journal* (Diocese of Virginia, 1908), p. 306.

20. Dexter Ralph Davison, Jr., "Frederick W. Neve: Mountain Mission Education in Virginia, 1888-1948," Ph.D. dissertation, University of Virginia, 1982, p. iii.

21. *Journal* (Diocese of Virginia, 1911), p. 119.

22. *Journal* (Diocese of Virginia, 1913), p. 211.

23. *The Clarke Parish Churches, 1819-1969* (Clarke County, VA: Episcopal Churches of Clarke Parish, 1969), p. 35.

deaconess to supervise it. Miss Kibby's school, Morgan's Mill Episcopal Mission School, was located in Cunningham Chapel Parish.[24]

This female leadership was not a local quirk. Indeed there was a widening awareness of the role of women in the church as in society at large. The Maine delegation to the General Convention of 1916 unsuccessfully introduced legislation calling for "full rights, responsibilities, and privileges" for female communicants. In the same year the Bishop of Hankow, an Episcopal missionary diocese in China that was represented in the General Convention, presented a petition from certain female lay workers in his diocese. The women requested that the church laws governing missionary dioceses be altered to allow female representation in diocesan conventions. The bishops denied the request.[25]

Other efforts were, however, more successful. In 1919 the Convention responded to a petition from the three Deaconesses' Training Schools by appointing a commission to adapt "the office of Deaconess to present tasks of the Church."[26] Some of the proposals of this commission — the establishing of a pension, the specifying of the role of the female deacon in canon law, and the authorizing of a form of ordination for female deacons — were passed at later conventions. Also in 1919 the Episcopal Church's National Council, the executive agency that administered the policies of the General Convention between its triennial sessions, added a representative from the Women's Auxiliary of the church's Board of Missions.[27]

Female Episcopalians were not yet able to claim full equality in diocesan and national affairs, but they were making progress. They were most successful in assuming responsibility and leadership in the one area in which they were least likely to be challenged — missionary outreach to the persons at the bottom of the parish hierarchy.

Parish Reorganization

In 1913 the structure of Clarke Parish began to change rather rapidly. The first move in this new sequence of events was the formation of a separate African American congregation. Archdeacon Moncure was an important actor in this drama. In 1912 he reported to the Virginia Diocesan Council that he had spent several days in Berryville. He had visited Wickliffe Church and spoken with

24. *The Clarke Parish Churches, 1819-1969*, p. 31.
25. *Journal* (General Convention, 1916), pp. 40-41.
26. *Journal* (General Convention, 1919), pp. 120, 139.
27. Margaret Marston Sherman, *True to Their Heritage* (New York: The National Council of the Episcopal Church, 1964), p. 15.

Miss Williams, apparently securing her approval for a plan to establish a ministry to African Americans in Berryville. Moncure then met in Berryville with Mrs. Annie C. Moore, a European American parishioner of Grace Church, and with Mrs. Fannie Massie, whom he described as "a colored woman, who had made her living by washing." Mrs. Moore initially planned simply to duplicate Miss Williams's Sunday School. Mrs. Massie disagreed; she felt that African American Episcopalians needed their own congregation and church building. The limited success of the Sunday School convinced Mrs. Moore of Mrs. Massie's wisdom. Archdeacon Moncure gave his consent as well, celebrating the Eucharist in a temporary location for the fledgling congregation.

Mrs. Massie and Mrs. Moore immediately set to work to secure a permanent building. Mrs. Massie donated the land and raised approximately $60 from African American and European American contributors. Mrs. Moore wrote an appeal for the *Southern Churchman,* asking that "men and women who had been nursed by a colored mammy upon whose headstones could be inscribed in all truth, 'Faithful unto death' . . . send a quarter, a dollar, or what they could to the rector of our town to build a church and help uplift the living in memory of the dead." A new building was soon in use.[28]

In 1913 Moncure felt that Clarke County was ready for an African American vicar. At his request Bishop Robert A. Gibson appointed J. T. Jeffrey (1887-1937), a Jamaican who had graduated in 1913 from Bishop Payne Divinity School, the Episcopal Church's seminary for African American men that had opened in Petersburg, Virginia, in 1878. In addition to working in Berryville, Jeffrey was also responsible for the African American Sunday Schools at Wickliffe and Cunningham Chapel Parish. When Wickliffe closed in 1918, Jeffrey arranged to bring Miss Williams's Sunday School building into Berryville by horse-drawn wagons. It became the parish hall for the new Berryville congregation, which took the name Saint Mary's.[29]

The decision to form Saint Mary's was a step toward greater self-determination for African Americans and also a step toward new forms of racial segregation. While leadership in Berryville had come from Mrs. Massie, an African American, that was not always the case in the diocese. Indeed, European Americans in the Diocese of Virginia had been pushing for new forms of segregation since the 1880s. In 1887 — the same time that southern states were enacting state Jim Crow laws to limit African American participation in predominantly European American society — a European American priest pro-

---

28. *Journal* (Diocese of Virginia, 1912), pp. 88-89; *The Spirit of Missions* 82 (April 1917): 261-62.

29. *Clarke Parish Churches*, pp. 35-36.

posed that African American representation in the diocesan council be limited to two priests and two lay persons.

A few African American clergy had been seated in the diocesan council since the Civil War, but with the founding of the Bishop Payne Divinity School in 1878 more African American men were entering the ordained ministry. By the 1880s Payne was producing three or four candidates for ordination a year. An increasingly successful pastoral ministry among African Americans accompanied this rise in the number of African American clergy. In 1886 one quarter of all couples married, and one sixth of all Sunday School students in the diocese, were African American. Some European Americans, like the priest who proposed limiting representation in 1887, were alarmed by this rise in African American activity in the church. The European American priest's proposal was tabled in 1887, but within three years the diocesan council adopted a similar proposal.[30]

The increase in African American ordinations that had worried European American Virginians in the 1880s continued into the early decades of the twentieth century. A comparison of the number of African American ordinations in the Episcopal Church by decades from 1870 to 1909 demonstrates the rising number of ordinations to the diaconate:

African American Ordinations to the Diaconate[31]

Decade	Number
1870-79	20
1880-89	45
1890-99	63
1900-1909	68

By the second decade of the century the European American deputies and bishops at the General Convention began to express some of the same segregationist attitudes toward African Americans that Southern Episcopalians had voiced in the 1880s. Two parties, both of whom favored forms of segregation, contended at the General Conventions from 1910 to 1916. They disagreed on the appropriate level for segregation.

Should African Americans be separated within their own dioceses, or should they be grouped into separate African American jurisdictions? Bishop Joseph B. Cheshire of North Carolina headed the group that favored the latter

30. *Journal* (Diocese of Virginia, 1887), pp. 56-57; *Journal* (Diocese of Virginia, 1890), pp. 102-3; Odell Greenleaf Harris, *The Bishop Payne Divinity School* (Alexandria, VA: Protestant Episcopal Theological Seminary, 1980), p. 36.

31. George F. Bragg, *History of the Afro-American Group of the Episcopal Church* (Baltimore: Church Advocate Press, 1922), pp. 267-79.

solution. The General Convention should establish, he believed, special jurisdictions with "racial" (i.e., African American) non-voting bishops, an action that would remove African Americans from participation in the dioceses in which they lived. Bishop Theodore Reese, the Bishop Coadjutor of Southern Ohio, headed a second group that favored making use of the office of suffragan bishop, which had been approved at the General Convention of 1910. A suffragan bishop was a permanent assistant to the diocesan bishop; if he outlived the diocesan bishop, he would become an assistant to the diocesan bishop's successor. Suffragan bishops also lacked a vote at the General Convention, though that situation later changed. Reese suggested election of African American suffragans who could direct African American work on a diocesan level. The Reese group won over the Cheshire group after debates at the General Conventions of 1913 and 1916. In 1918 two African American suffragan bishops — one for North Carolina and one for Arkansas — were elected.[32]

The suffragan approach had, however, only limited success. The assassination of suffragan advocate Bishop William Guerry of South Carolina by a European American priest opposed to the plan contributed to the abandoning of the approach by Southern dioceses. Even after 1918 the Archdeacon for Colored Work remained the senior church officer with a specific responsibility for African American congregations in most southern dioceses. The extended debate about the plan and its adoption, however, reveals something of the attitude toward African Americans of European American bishops and deputies at the General Convention. Though they disagreed about method, they strongly supported some form of segregation.

The formation of a separate African American congregation in Berryville in 1913 paralleled events in other Episcopal congregations across the country. Other southern congregations separated European Americans and African Americans. Episcopalians in California began Chinese and Japanese congregations, and dioceses that included northern industrial cities were opening special language congregations for European immigrants.

At Grace Church and other congregations this new policy toward minority groups contributed to a major change in the life of the European American parishioners who remained in the parent church. With minorities removed from participation in the parish, the European American leadership was more willing to share decision making and authority with the other parishioners; the remaining parishioners became, for their part, more willing to contribute to the financial support of the parish. In Berryville, the first step in this process — the recruiting of a wider number of contributors to the parish budget — took place in the fall of 1913.

32. *Journal* (General Convention, 1916), pp. 76, 96, 484-95.

At the November 11 meeting of the vestry a committee from the all-female Parish Aid Society asked to be heard. Aid Society members noted the financial difficulties facing the vestry and "tendered their services to aid in putting the finances of the Church upon a more business-like footing."[33] The vestry accepted the offer, appointing a committee to meet with the Aid Society. The committee was prepared to report at the December meeting. It suggested that "The Vestry adopt for the purpose of raising necessary funds for the congregation — including both general expenses and contributions for Missions[—]the "Duplex Envelope System" to go into effect April 1st next."[34]

The Duplex envelopes contained separate sections for giving to parish expenses and for giving to mission projects, thereby uniting in a single envelope two solicitations of income that had to that point been administered separately. The vestry adopted the recommendation with only two votes in the negative.

From the perspective of the later twentieth century it is difficult to appreciate the importance of this move. After eighty years of a separated budget process in which funds for parish expenses and missions were raised in different ways, the vestry had adopted a unified system of finance. Moreover, the vestrymen adopted the system without any reference to seating in the congregation. Finally the vestry had adopted a true alternative to the pew rent system.

That the decision in Clarke Parish was part of a more general trend was evident from the General Convention journals of the same period. Deputies and bishops also wrestled with what it meant to adopt uniform "business-like" methods of church finance. In 1913 they appointed a committee to study the question. This committee returned in 1916, suggesting a revision of the canon on church statistics and a new canon on business methods. Complaining that the existing system — in which individual dioceses chose what figures they would present to the national church — made it impossible to tell "within many millions of dollars, what the Church received or expended during the last calendar year," the committee convinced the General Convention to adopt a uniform fiscal year (January to December) and a standard set of financial forms.[35]

During the same sessions in which the church finances were discussed, members of the General Convention were developing another modern fiscal tool, the every-member canvass. The bishops and deputies at the previous convention (1913) had approved a "Nation-Wide Preaching Mission," in an attempt to bring all Episcopalians to pray for the worsening world situation.[36] The 1916

---

33. "Register's Book of Vestry," p. 117.
34. "Register's Book of Vestry," p. 119.
35. *Journal* (General Convention, 1916), pp. 536-39.
36. *Journal* (General Convention, 1916), pp. 540-43.

and 1919 General Conventions reappointed the committee responsible for the mission but changed its emphasis from prayer to fund-raising. The bishops and deputies designated the first Sunday in December 1919 as the date for "the Nation-Wide Campaign," an "Every-member Canvass to meet the needs of the Church."[37] Other American churches were making similar moves. In addition to denominational fund-raising efforts, an interdenominational organization known as the Interchurch World Movement planned to raise one billion dollars for world evangelism.[38]

Members of Clarke Parish were well informed of these developments at the General Convention. They participated in the Nation-Wide Preaching Mission in Advent 1915. In 1919 the vestry invited the Rev. William D. Smith, the rector of a nearby parish who had served as a General Convention deputy in 1913 and 1916, to explain the General Convention's new financial policy to the congregation. Grace Church adopted an every-member canvass and participated in the Nation-Wide Campaign.[39]

The total effect of these financial changes can perhaps best be gauged by examining elements of the budget from 1913 (May 1913-April 1914 fiscal year) and 1919. In 1913 the major sources of income for parish expenses were pledges, envelopes, and general (plate) offerings. The same was true in 1919, but the proportions of the budget from each category had greatly changed. This fact is particularly clear if one adjusts for inflation:

Clarke Parish Income, 1913-1919[40]

Source	1913	1919	Adj. 1919*	Change
Pledges	$747	$742	$428	-43%
Envelope	$287	$1397	$808	+182%
General	$211	$608	$551	+66%

*adjusted for inflation

A comparison of the pledging lists in 1913 and 1919 sheds further light on the shift in giving patterns. The major trend could be summarized in this way: the number of pledges over ten dollars had fallen from twenty-nine to fifteen,

37. *Journal* (General Convention, 1919), p. 560.

38. Sydney E. Ahlstrom, *A Religious History of the American People* (New Haven: Yale University Press, 1972), pp. 897-98.

39. "Register's Book of Vestry," pp. 125, 145.

40. "Grace Episcopal Church in Care of St. Baughman," pp. 97-107; inflation figure from *Historical Statistics of the United States 1789-1949* (Washington, DC: U.S. Government Printing Office, 1949), p. 231.

with a considerable percentage of those who ceased to pledge represented on the vestry. The remaining pledgers were able to increase their pledges enough to maintain the 1913-dollar value, but they could no longer keep up with inflation. The new envelope system, to which the non-pledging vestrymen were presumably contributing, had replaced the pledges as the major source of parish income.

In 1920 this new base of support proved equal to the demands of the Nation-Wide Campaign. In the first year of the campaign the total parish income doubled. While a major portion of this increase was given to the national campaign, there were increased funds for the parish expenses as well:

Clarke Parish Expenses in 1913 Dollars[41]

	1913	1919	1920
Parochial Expenses (including improvements, parochial charities, and pension)	$1579	$1418	$2087
Giving to Diocese and General Church	$568	$432	$2273
Total	$2147	$1850	$4360

A new base of support, adopted in the period from 1913 to 1919, was tested in the Nation-Wide Campaign and found to be a powerful source of income in Clarke Parish. Nationwide, the gross receipts of Episcopal parishes climbed from twenty-four to almost forty-two million between 1920 and 1925, a period in which the General Price Index actually decreased.[42]

Once this wider financial base was established, the vestry at Grace Church moved to make the parish governmental system more democratic. Before 1910 all decisions had been made by a self-perpetuating European American male vestry, drawn from the small circle of pledging families. On January 6, 1920, the congregational meeting at Grace Church adopted a resolution (made with vestry support) that created overlapping three-year terms for vestry members.[43] Members of the congregation were thus able to do more than simply endorse a single slate at annual meetings; they could make some real choices about their governing body.

Female and African American members of the parish were able to exercise leadership within certain spheres. For women this sphere was missionary

41. Virginia Diocesan *Journals* (1914, 1915, 1921).
42. *The Episcopal Church Annual 1981* (Wilton, CT: Morehouse-Barlow Company, 1981), p. 18; *Historical Statistics of the United States,* p. 231.
43. "Register's Book of Vestry," p. 151.

activity. Individual women created both Saint Mary's and the Sunday Schools from which it was formed. They conferred with the diocesan archdeacon and actively participated in the raising of funds. African American members of the parish now had their own African American vicar and their own vestry committee. They were able to play a more active role in decision making with this separate congregation.[44]

The shift in parish membership and budget also had liturgical consequences at Grace Church. The old financial and racial system had made it awkward to celebrate the Eucharist. Members of the parish were forced to deal with the division of the congregation into pew and balcony sitters. European American pew holders received communion while the balcony sitters were excluded. With the adoption of a new finance system and the creation of separate African American congregations, such problems no longer existed. The celebration of the Eucharist was a less complicated matter.

At Grace Church, rector Malcolm S. Taylor (1881-1961), arriving a year after the death of Edward Wall in 1917, instituted an early morning celebration of the Eucharist once a month. Elsewhere across the diocese similar innovations were taking place. In 1910, 132 parishes had celebrated the Eucharist 1515 times; in 1920, 155 parishes celebrated the Eucharist 2452 times, an increase of 38% in the frequency of parish celebrations.[45] Relatively few dioceses included statis-

---

44. By participating in the formation of Saint Mary's, African Americans had traded one form of segregation (inferior status within Grace Church) for another (separate but unequal congregations). The change was in keeping with the conventional wisdom of the day. Politicians suggested that the self-determination of individual racial groups was the solution to the political turmoil of Europe. Educator Booker T. Washington (1856-1915) spoke for many African Americans when he accepted segregation as a means of developing African American leadership and industry. Many Episcopalians were convinced that just as they had made their church more democratic with the 1919 decision to make the office of presiding bishop elective, so also they had democratized the church with the formation of separate ethnic congregations. The negative consequences of the decision soon became clear, however. With minorities removed from the mainstream of church life, European Americans made few additional concessions to non–European American church members. For European Americans, the racial problem had been solved. After the first flurry of interest in 1918, no further African American bishops were elected until after Episcopalians began to dismantle segregation in the 1950s. John Burgess of Massachusetts, consecrated in 1962, was the first African American bishop to serve in the U.S. since the election of Henry B. Delany and Edward Demby in 1918. In addition, almost no new African American parishes were established anywhere in the Episcopal Church after 1930 until formerly white parishes in changing neighborhoods were designated for African Americans in the 1960s. For an in-depth discussion see Gardiner Shattuck, Sr., *Episcopalians and Race* (Lexington: University Press of Kentucky, 2000).

45. *Journal* (Diocese of Virginia, 1911), p. 299; *Journal* (Diocese of Virginia, 1921), p. 301; *Journal* (Diocese of Chicago, 1911), pp. 110-12; *Journal* (Diocese of Chicago, 1921), pp. 112-15.

tics on the frequency of the Eucharist in their journals in 1920, but those that did also recorded an increased frequency of parish celebrations. The diocese of Chicago, a diocese with a very different liturgical tradition from low-church Virginia, registered a 21% increase in celebrations of the Eucharist in the same time span. These figures would suggest that a general increase in parish celebrations was taking place in the decade.

Architectural changes followed this increasing frequency of the Eucharist. With no one excluded from the nave, many congregations removed some or all of their balconies. An architectural committee of the General Convention appointed in 1919, which included noted gothic revivalist Ralph Adams Cram (1863-1942), popularized recessed gothic chancels as more fitting settings for the increasingly frequent celebrations of the Eucharist.[46]

At Grace Church members undertook a major building program in 1926 in which they removed the balcony and added a gothic chancel. The first closed-front altar was added at the time; previous altars had had open fronts and table legs. Parishioners also raised funds for a new altar window that depicted Jesus at the Last Supper in a scene that strongly resembled a parish celebration of the Eucharist at Grace Church. Saint Mary's Church mirrored these changes on a more modest scale.

An older member of Grace Church Parish remembers the twenties as the period in which pressed communion wafers replaced the loaf bread that had been used at celebrations of the Eucharist.[47] Perhaps the communion wafers were more convenient for the increasingly frequent celebrations of the Eucharist.

Rectors of Grace Church changed their manner of dress at the same time. The collection of portraits kept at Grace Church makes the point clearly. Every rector depicted before the First World War wore the secular dress of a gentleman of the period, but with one exception every clergyman after the war wore a clerical collar. The change may simply reflect a new trend in clerical dress. It is also suggestive, however, of a change in class identification. Perhaps the parish rectors no longer felt the need to identify themselves with the upper class members of the parish. Clerical dress may have allowed the rectors a means of identification as people distinct from but open to all in the parish. The presence of an African American vicar at Saint Mary's made this message all the more clear. The Episcopal priest was not simply a hireling of the upper class.

This investigation of change on a local level at Clarke Parish suggests a close connection between the adoption of new financial procedures in the parish, the adoption of a rotating vestry, the creation of a separate African Ameri-

---

46. *Journal* (General Convention, 1919), pp. 232, 314.
47. Lucille Smith, interview held in Berryville, Virginia, February 1981.

can parish, the rising women's rights movement, and more frequent celebrations of the Eucharist. A cursory examination of diocesan and General Convention journals and other indicators of parish life suggests, moreover, that this complex of changes was not limited to Clarke Parish but, rather, was illustrative of a significant change taking place nationally in the Episcopal Church. Small paternal hierarchies gave way to systems of organization that enhanced economic capability, preserved European American male prerogatives, and allowed women and minorities to exercise leadership within carefully defined limits. In the decade of the First World War, Episcopalians radically shifted the structure of their parish life.

Christ and Church in the Social Encyclicals of John Paul II

Victor Lee Austin

A Personal Introduction

It was Father Wright more than anyone else who encouraged me to pursue advanced post-seminary studies. His interests in ecclesiology and ecumenism fostered my own desire to study those subjects. At various times, he has been to me an academic and spiritual mentor, a colleague in the Anglican Society, and a guide through the hyper-politicized realms of the Episcopal Church. And he is a friend.

— Which is not to say that he will agree with what follows! For it seems to me that I have come to a more disinterested view of John Paul II than he has. And thus I have come, perhaps, to a more positive understanding of the pope's theology and to a rather unusual critique of its shortcomings. Father Wright will doubtless have things to say to me about this article. Yet it remains the truth that I would never have come to this point in my academic studies were it not for him.

The Phenomenon of John Paul II

History will judge John Paul II to be one of the most influential pontiffs. Everyone is acquainted with his internationalization of the papal office, through an unprecedented use of technology and travel and through a masterful use of his own native sporting and dramatic endowments.[1] His was one of the longest

1. The best biography remains George Weigel, *Witness to Hope: The Biography of Pope John Paul II* (New York: HarperCollins, 1999).

pontificates of any century, notably exceeding at his death in April 2005 that of Leo XIII (1878-1903). John Paul's encyclicals are the wordiest ever, and in total volume of words he probably published more than anyone except, perhaps, Leo XIII.[2]

Three of John Paul's encyclicals are explicitly social. First is *Laborem Exercens* (LE), issued on the ninetieth anniversary of Leo's *Rerum Novarum,* the 1891 encyclical often taken to be the inauguration of official modern Roman Catholic social thought. LE is an essay on the personal character of work, written in a discursive philosophical and religious style characteristic of this pope. Then in 1987 he issued *Sollicitudo Rei Socialis* (SRS), on questions of economic and social development. His third social encyclical was *Centesimus Annus* (CA), released in the centennial year of *Rerum Novarum.*

This last social encyclical is John Paul's most novel production. In it he professes to offer a hermeneutical "re-reading" of Leo's 1891 encyclical in the light of contemporary developments — one of the chapters is titled simply "The Year 1989," in reference to the year that communist and other repressive regimes fell in many places. Yet his hermeneutics leads him to embrace, for the first time in a papal encyclical, a form of capitalism that he calls "the free economy." In economic and cultural questions, this pope's overall legacy is a significant advance from his predecessors' skepticism about the market. John Paul had much less of the tit-for-tat condemnation of socialism and capitalism that one finds in his predecessors.[3]

But the proper concern for theologians is not only John Paul's particular social teachings but also his operative theological convictions. John Paul worked with a distinctive set of Christological emphases, emphases that were

2. In English translation, the standard reference for papal encyclicals is *The Papal Encyclicals (1740-1981)*, ed. Claudia Carlen, 5 vols. (Wilmington, NC: McGrath Publishing Company, 1981). Leo XIII takes a whole volume to himself. A similarly hefty volume is *The Encyclicals of John Paul II*, ed. and intro. J. Michael Miller (Huntington, IN: Our Sunday Visitor, 1996). It is, however, incomplete, lacking the post-1996 work of John Paul II.

3. The literature on John Paul's social teaching is vast. To list only commentaries on the single encyclical *Centesimus Annus* would take pages. For a collection of views from the neo-conservative side, see *Building the Free Society: Democracy, Capitalism, and Catholic Social Teaching*, ed. George Weigel and Robert Royal (Grand Rapids: William B. Eerdmans Publishing Company; and Washington, DC: Ethics and Public Policy Center, 1993); Richard John Neuhaus, *Doing Well and Doing Good: The Challenge to the Christian Capitalist* (New York: Doubleday, 1992). Some views from the left are included in *John Paul II and Moral Theology,* ed. Charles E. Curran and Richard A. McCormick, Readings in Moral Theology No. 10 (New York and Mahwah, NJ: Paulist Press, 1998); see particularly therein Donal Dorr, "Concern and Consolidation," pp. 291-309, and David Hollenbach, "Christian Social Ethics after the Cold War," pp. 352-75.

among his implicit convictions. Nowhere in his corpus did he expound a sys-tematic Christology.[4] In fact he never specifically stated that he worked from certain Christological convictions. His Christological views were, seemingly, simply assumed. Yet they have radical implications — to take, as one instance, the theme of this essay — for the understanding of ecclesiology.

The Pope's Christological Emphases

A close reading of John Paul's social encyclicals uncovers four operative Christological convictions:

1. Christ speaks God's word: Christ's divine revelatory function;
2. Christ has no political function;
3. In a divine anthropological solidarity, Christ is united with every human being;
4. The church brings Christ to Christ.

The categories form a logical progression, as each one raises a question to which the following category suggests an answer.

The First Three Convictions

The pope maintains the orthodox if unexceptional conviction that Christ has a divine revelatory function. Christ reveals God, and that revelation is a "word" that has been fully revealed in Christ Jesus and yet is unfolding in human his-tory (see SRS §1.2, where the pope cites the Vatican II document *Dei Verbum*).[5]

---

4. John Paul's principal Christological work is his series of weekly catechetical talks on the second paragraph of the Creed, given from 1986 to 1989 and collected in English in *Jesus, Son and Savior* (Boston: Pauline Books and Media, 1996). The short, weekly format prevents ex-tended systematic development, although the book nonetheless provides many clues and mark-ers for the pope's largely implicit Christology. Few scholars have made an effort to develop the pope's thought Christologically. One of those who has is John Saward, *Christ Is the Answer: The Christ-Centered Teaching of Pope John Paul II* (New York: Alba House, 1995). Saward uses Hans Urs von Balthasar's dramatic theology as the hermeneutical key for John Paul's Christology, to the extent that his exposition tends to be more about Balthasar than about the pope.

5. Citations such as "SRS §1.2" refer to the encyclical's section and paragraph (here the second paragraph of the first section of *Sollicitudo Rei Socialis*) in the English translation printed in Miller. While the section numbers correspond to the official Latin text, the para-graphs sometimes do not.

In addition, the pope clearly holds that Christ still speaks today and that his word gives the church a "newness" that allows it to address contemporary situations (see, e.g., CA §62.2, quoting Revelation 21:5). Indeed the pope sometimes says that Christ himself speaks a word directly to a problem of today's world (see SRS §33.4).

So Christ speaks God's word; but what is the word Christ speaks? For John Paul, it turns out never to be a word of judgment, for according to him, Christ does not have a political function. This development is surprising: what about the language of "Christ the King" and "the Kingdom of Christ"? What about the understanding that as "King of kings" Christ will ultimately judge all earthly judges and that in a sense he has already triumphed over every earthly ruler? The pope shuns all this language. When he is forced to use it — for instance, in preaching on Christ the King — he purges this language of its political meaning.[6] In fact, in the social encyclicals he never calls Christ a king. He assigns him no political function, neither of rule nor of judgment nor of ultimate authority over earthly rulers.

What then does John Paul make of Christ's three-fold office (*munus,* 'function') as prophet, priest, and king, given him by tradition? He holds that Christ's regal office amounts to self-mastery, a condition of personal holiness that makes Christ and his followers available for service to others.[7] That is the end of the pope's explication of Christ's regal office.

Why is judgment absent from John Paul's implicit Christology? Because (his third emphasis) Christ is united with every person. John Paul holds that Christ is located not in a position of judgment over human beings but is rather in a profound sense united with them. His key text for this point comes from the Vatican II "pastoral constitution" on the church in the modern world, *Gaudium et Spes* (GS): "By His incarnation the Son of God has united Himself in some fashion with every man."[8] This text is one of John Paul's favorites. His first encyclical makes it clear that he interprets the union of Christ with each human being as an unqualifiedly accomplished, real fact: "We are not dealing with the 'abstract' man, but the real, 'concrete,' 'historical' man. We are dealing with 'each' man, for each one is included in the mystery of Redemption and with each one

---

6. In his homilies on the feast of Christ the King, John Paul typically, as in his exposition of Matthew 25, turns the listener's attention from Christ the one who separates the sheep and the goats to Christ the one who was ministered to by the sheep. Solidarity trumps judgment. For an instance, see his homily delivered 21 November 1999, in *L'Osservatore Romano* (English weekly edition), 24 November 1999: 1, 3.

7. See his first encyclical, *Redemptor Hominis* (RH), §§19-21.

8. GS 2, in *The Documents of Vatican II*, ed. Walter M. Abbott and Joseph Gallagher (New York: America Press, 1966), pp. 220-21.

Christ has united himself forever through this mystery" (RH §13.3). He repeatedly insists that Christ has redeemed each person and is united with each person: "man — every man without any exception whatever — has been redeemed by Christ," and "with man — with each man without any exception whatever — Christ is in a way united, even when man is unaware of it" (RH §14.3).

That last statement shows that, for John Paul, Christ's anthropological solidarity does not depend on a person's having Christian faith. What Christ reveals is true for all people, regardless of their awareness of Christ: "Christ . . . guides him, even when he is unaware of it" (CA §62.3).[9] But in the end John Paul leaves a number of questions unanswered about the meaning of Christ's anthropological solidarity. It is clear that he does not conceive the union of Christ with each person to be a static matter; it does not allow an interpretation along the lines of a union of essences. The union is dynamic, not a static ontological affair. Furthermore, John Paul states that a spirituality of work involves helping all people to come closer to God, their Creator and Redeemer, through work; it also involves a deepened friendship with Christ by means of an acceptance and participation in his threefold mission (LE §24.2).

Thus the union with Christ, which John Paul insists is a given for all people and not merely for Christians, is not without a distance such that it is possible to draw closer and to deepen friendship with Christ. But who can draw closer? And how can a person be united with Christ radically, concretely, and historically and still be the object of the church's mission?

Implications for Ecclesiology

If Christ is united with every human being, what does John Paul say about the church's relationship to Christ and the church's role in Christ's mission?

John Paul holds that the church brings Christ to Christ.[10] This view is evi-

---

9. In his exposition of the union of Christ with every person, John Paul slightly modifies the teaching of Vatican II. The Vatican II "dogmatic constitution" on the church, *Lumen Gentium* (LG), speaks of the grace of Christ that elevates from within, so that through the activity of the faithful in the world, the spirit of Christ comes to permeate the world (LG §36). John Paul quotes LG §36 in LE §25.6, but he is silent about his own development of the teaching. Where LG speaks of the activity of the faithful, John Paul says that by means of work "man" — all people, not merely the faithful — "shares in the work of creation." Both passages signal the possibility of human action as the vehicle of divine influence upon the world. John Paul, however, goes beyond LG; his advance is predicated precisely upon the union of Christ with all people — in this case, with all people in their work.

10. The formulation "brings Christ to Christ" is not the pope's; I have phrased it in this way to highlight a paradox in the pope's thinking. It is of course true that the persons to whom

dent, for instance, in his depiction of Mary, who is a figure of the church, as one who "constantly remained beside Christ in his journey toward the human family and in its midst" and who "goes before the Church on the pilgrimage of faith" (CA §62.4). Of course, that sentence could be read as a simple historical statement: Mary was "beside" Christ as she carried him in her womb ("his journey toward the human family"); she was beside him in his life in the midst of humanity; she had a place of prominence in the early church (e.g., at Pentecost). But as a summary statement coming at the end of CA, it suggests that Christ continually both moves towards humanity and has a secured identification in the midst of humanity. Corresponding to this dual reality, the church follows the way of Christ by bringing the gospel of Christ to humanity, where, however, he is already found by virtue of his union with every human being.[11]

If the church is bringing Christ to Christ, then the church in serving the needs of humanity is at one and the same time serving humanity by bringing the gift of Christ to bear on a situation of need and serving Christ in his identification with humanity. The church in this sense consists in the followers of Christ on his way, who himself followed the way of humanity. One of John Paul's most pregnant formulations is "man is the way for the Church" (RH §14.3; cf. CA §§53-62).

John Paul describes Christ as the source or origin of the church. He holds that Jesus Christ is the "Founder" of the church, who sends the church forth in mission amidst the needy (CA §49.1).[12] Christ also, he believes, gives each pope his mission, which includes the "apostolic office" to intervene in social conflicts (CA §5.3). He further uses the words of Matthew 23:8 to describe Christ as the church's "one teacher," who, in the midst of the new things in every historical period, gives the church the responsibility "to show the way, to proclaim the truth and to communicate the life which is Christ (cf. Jn 14:6)" (CA §3.1). In

---

the church offers the evangelical gift, although they have been united with Christ in his anthropological solidarity, are not Christ *simpliciter*. Yet neither is that which the church brings Christ *simpliciter*. For John Paul, the missionary movement is irreducibly recursive, as the following discussion shows.

11. The nexus of Christ's anthropological solidarity and the church's resulting mission of somehow bringing Christ to Christ perdures in John Paul's thought in his 1995 encyclical *Evangelium Vitae* §81.1. There he states that *"the core"* of the gospel is "the proclamation of a living God who is close to us." He restates the point Christologically: "Jesus has a unique relationship with every person." Christ's relationship with each person, he immediately explains, "enables us" — i.e., the bearers of the gospel proclamation — "to see in every human face the face of Christ."

12. The pope teaches that each Christian should follow Christ in giving special primacy to charity for the poor, an imitation of Christ's attitude toward the poor, and the international outlook that results from such imitation (SRS §42.2; cf. CA §11.1).

these passages John Paul describes the action of Christ in a present, continuing sense. Christ is, as it were, not only the historical founder of the church twenty centuries ago but also, today, the one sending forth his church in witness. Christ is, to take another example, the on-going sole teacher of the church, and the church's mission, continually received, is at once to bear Christ and to witness to Christ. In bearing witness to Christ in the midst of social problems the church bears witness to human dignity: it is the same witness.

The pope returns repeatedly to the mystery of the church's role in Christ's mission, illuminating it from diverse sides. Adopting the language of Colossians 1:19, the pope says that the church, in its commitment to the development of peoples, is at the service of the divine plan to order all things to the fullness that dwells in Christ — a fullness that has been communicated to the church, the sacrament of God's own unity and of the unity of the human race (SRS §31.5). Elsewhere the pope writes of a possibility available to "the Christian and everyone who is called to follow Christ": the possibility of the toil of one's work being a sharing in Christ's suffering and death, i.e., Christ's own work of redemption (LE §27.3). The members of the church are able to collaborate in Christ's work.

One passage in CA shows the rich implications of the church as bringing Christ to Christ. Christ, the pope writes, has entrusted to the church the care and responsibility for the human person; on the basis of this trusteeship the church speaks on the social question. But the person for whom the church cares is *"each individual . . .* included in the mystery of the Redemption," through which "Christ has united himself with each one forever" (CA §53.1, citing RH §13). This circularity is key to understanding the function of Christ in John Paul's thought: Christ is at the origin of the church's mission, and at the same time he is at the object or the end of the church's mission. Christ entrusts the church to care for each human person, and each human person has already been united with Christ decisively and without end, "forever." This recursive or circular conception of the role of Christ *vis-à-vis* the church may be called bringing Christ to Christ.

The church, bearing Christ to Christ, experiences a "newness" that must be communicated to others in their concrete difficulties (CA §59.2). Faith, in other words, assists those who have it in finding solutions to concrete problems and in finding ways to make suffering humanly bearable — that is, so to condition suffering that the person undergoing it does not lose his or her human dignity. Members of the church can therefore be a source of new possibilities in particular economic, social, and cultural situations. Christ has set us free, John Paul writes, citing Galatians 5:1, to serve the process of liberation of the poor. Hence the church can live and work in solidarity, that is, in love and service of the neighbor (SRS §46.6), as disciples of Christ marked by the virtue of charity (SRS §40.1, citing John 13:35). The freedom of Christ is the newness that the church brings to the social question.[13]

Yet here too freedom is not a characteristic of the church only but has in a sense already been bestowed upon every human being by virtue of Christ's anthropological solidarity. As the church brings Christ to Christ, the church also brings freedom to those who have (or should have) freedom. To clarify, according to John Paul, an aspect of the dignity of the human person, which derives from Christ's anthropological solidarity, is that each person has rights of conscience: "The recognition of these rights represents the primary foundation of every authentically free political order" (CA §29.1). The rights of conscience include religious freedom, the right to seek the truth and to be bound only by the truth, and to live accordingly (CA §29.4). John Paul thus asserts both (a) the church's right, in any polity, to proclaim the gospel — including, as integral to the gospel, the church's social teaching and (b) the right of every person to religious freedom, including the right to hear the gospel and choose, if the choice be made, "to accept it and to be converted to Christ" (CA §29.4). The church, in other words, bears the gospel message of freedom with its inherent possibilities of newness, but those to whom this message is borne already have the capacity to exercise freedom and the corresponding right to exercise freedom, precisely because of Christ's anthropological solidarity.

Critique and Summary

John Paul's implicit Christology is a coherent set of emphases, each of which implicates the others. His work shows, at the minimum, that it is impossible to do ecclesiology without also doing a theological anthropology. How one understands the human being *per se* — before any faith-commitment — will be a determinant of what one's ecclesiology can be. Since John Paul understands the human being to exist as a re-creation, already united (in a sense left partially unclear) to Christ, his ecclesiology is forced to place the church in a recursive position *vis-à-vis* humanity. The church bears Christ, but it bears Christ to people who have already been united to Christ. It thus bears Christ while seeking

---

13. In a 1992 catechetical talk, John Paul stated: "Christ, then, is the divine answer which the Church gives to basic human problems: Christ, who is perfect man." He then quotes *Gaudium et Spes:* "Whoever follows Christ . . . becomes himself more of a man" (§41). Thus the anthropological solidarity of Christ, dynamically conceived, is the basis for the Church's offer of newness and hope in the face of social concerns. John Paul II, *The Church: Mystery, Sacrament, Community* (Boston: Pauline Books & Media, 1998), p. 181.

Christ. It points to Christ, and it points people, who are united to Christ, to Christ. Thus, in every sense possible, the human person is the way for the church.

If those are the facts, then all an ecclesiology can do is to state them as clearly as possible. But are they the facts? A critique of John Paul's ecclesiology might begin by inquiring into the nature of the church's mission. Why should the church bear Christ to those who are already united to Christ? One might answer that the church does so because Christ has told the church to do so and that thus, in its evangelical mission, the church is merely participating in obedience in Christ's own twofold identity as one who exists in the midst of humanity while ever moving towards humanity. But these are paradoxical formulations.

The older conception gave a clearer answer. The church brings Christ to the world because Christ is the King of glory, who will come again to judge the living and the dead. Can an ecclesiology be judged adequate to the givens of divine revelation if it studiously avoids speaking of Christ's political rule? In the tradition that John Paul has, it appears, silently rejected, it was held that the church is the governed political society that knows its true governor. As such, the church also knows that secular government is continuing only for a time and only for limited purposes, that in fact earthly rulers have already been conquered by the one who has ascended to his throne.[14]

John Paul's recasting of Christology and ecclesiology, as it appears implicitly in his social encyclicals and is confirmed in his other writings, is a suggestive theological departure. What it means for ecumenical and interfaith questions, time will tell. As to theology: if, as I suspect, the church cannot do without a political Christ, John Paul's development calls for a re-appropriation of the political tradition into the terms of the modern, or postmodern, world. It is not possible merely to reassert, for instance, Pius XI's theology of Christ the King.[15] Theologians will have to find a new way to understand Christ's political function. John Paul's work has made the problem clear.

---

14. The preeminent exposition of political theology at this time is Oliver O'Donovan, *The Desire of the Nations: Rediscovering the Roots of Political Theology* (Cambridge [UK] and New York: Cambridge University Press, 1996).

15. Pius XI established the feast of Christ the King and gave its rationale in his 1925 encyclical *Quas Primas*.

FROM ECCLESIALITY TO ECUMENISM

Odi et Amo: Loving and Hating Anglicanism

S. W. Sykes

Odi et amo: quare id faciam, fortasse requiris.
Nescio, set fieri sentio et excrucior.

I hate and I love: Why I do so you may well ask.
I do not know, but I feel it happen and am in agony.

Gaius Valerius Catullus, *Carmina*, 85[1]

"At what historical point can and should the study of Anglicanism begin?" So asked Bob Wright at the beginning of his "Essay on Terminology," contributed to *The Study of Anglicanism*.[2] He concluded:

> If the term is to be used descriptively, and not narrowly or prescriptively, it must finally go back conceptually/doctrinally to the New Testament and historically/geographically to the martyrdom of St Alban in the "patristic" period of "Anglican" church history.[3]

1. *Catullus* (Leiden: A. W. Sijthoff, 1966) and http://www.obscure.org/obscene-latin/carmina-catulli (accessed on June 11, 2005).

2. "Anglicanism, *Ecclesia Anglicana*, and Anglican: An Essay on Terminology," in *The Study of Anglicanism*, ed. S. W. Sykes and John Booty (London: SPCK; Philadelphia: Fortress Press, 1988), p. 424.

3. Sykes and Booty, *Study,* p. 428. The footnote to this statement generously refers to "a stimulating and provocative theological critique of this entire subject" in my *The Integrity of Anglicanism* (London: Mowbray, 1978).

Bob Wright has made a massive contribution to the modern debate about Anglicanism as scholar, teacher, and ecumenist. He has written a series of ground-breaking historical studies as well as maintaining a major tradition of Anglican self-interpretation developed in modern times by Stephen Neill, Henry McAdoo, and John Macquarrie. The reference work *The Anglican Tradition,* which he edited with Gillian Evans,[4] embodies the claim that to portray Anglicanism genuinely one must not begin with the sixteenth-century Reformation but with the "early church" — in fact, the extracts begin with Clement, Bishop of Rome (*c.* A.D. 96).

To *be* an Episcopalian or an Anglican is, of course, to be a Christian in a particular way. To *describe* that way is no easy matter, because there are both sub-species of Anglicans and also regional and local varieties. Much the same is true of most of the world-wide communions, though Anglican party theory and its notorious and ambiguous claim for "comprehensiveness" have tended to give formal shape to its diversity. All the more difficult, therefore, to *describe* Anglicanism without telling a story, and with all such stories we are in the construction industry. It is increasingly obvious to early modern historians that "classic Anglicanism" was an invention of the seventeenth century, and so to "describe" it was to create a construct.

The task of description receives another subjective knock from the realization that all such portraiture relates to the self-identity of the portraitist. To be personally involved in the truth claims of one's subject is no small matter. One wants at least to be able to give some reason that it is possible to be the kind of Christian one is, as a reasonably faithful member of that tradition. Rather than being a form of weakness, this absolutely unavoidable self-implication in the project of describing the specific tradition to which one belongs needs both open acknowledgment and occasional exhibition. In homage, therefore, to Bob Wright's major assistance in this task, and by way of contribution to a more self-critical description of Anglicanism, this paper is offered in the form of an answer to the question *Why am I (still) an Anglican?*

1.

I both love and hate being Anglican. As the author of a collection of papers entitled *Unashamed Anglicanism,*[5] I might be thought to find in my allegiance

---

4. G. R. Evans and J. Robert Wright, eds., *The Anglican Tradition: A Handbook of Sources* (Minneapolis: Fortress Press, 1991).

5. S. W. Sykes, *Unashamed Anglicanism* (London: Darton, Longman and Todd, 1995).

more unalloyed pleasure than in fact I do. Indeed the somewhat defiant title of the book has a rather particular social context. Regular visitors to England will know how deeply ingrained is the cultural habit of self-denigration. It may be, as some have asserted, that this trait is simply a disguise for that national pride for which we were once equally famous. Historians of nationalism used to say that the English invented nationalism, which was the direct consequence of being the largest and most unified national group on the European continent. We certainly invented "jingoism." For example, here is this music hall song from the end of the nineteenth century:

> We don't want to fight, but, by jingo, if we do,
> We've got the ships, we've got the men, we've got the money too;
> We've fought the Bear before, and while Britons shall be true,
> The Russians shall not have Constantinople.[6]

Despite victory in the two world wars, the loss of the British Empire and the attendant economic difficulties have had a massive impact on national self-confidence. It entirely fits the national mood when our golfers, cricketers, or rugby or football players regularly lose international games to those countries, often former colonies, to which we introduced the sport in the first place. There is a collective, world-weary pessimism, bordering on a cynicism, about our ability to do anything properly.

I am going to call this the "paradigm of decline," and it is clear that despite an altogether different history and cultural outlook, one can trace an analogous impact of the same paradigm on at least some of the churches in the United States. Important for my argument is the observation that churches are not separate and distinct from the life of the cultures in which they are set, and that sometimes things that happen in the culture are relevant to the way a church sees itself and formulates its own mission.

In England, or more generally in Britain, the paradigm of decline is relentlessly applied to the fate of the Church of England. Here one must speak of the growing impact of the media, especially of the media's habit of relentless assault upon the integrity of the leading institutions of the nation. The Church of England is only one of a series of targets, which include the monarchy, the political order, the business and financial worlds, and education. Each has in turn been singled out for extensive coverage as riddled with incompetence, immorality, and ruthless greed or ambition. The decline and predicted fall of the House of Windsor matches the paradigm of decline exactly. There is an instant

---

6. A music hall song of 1878, by G. W. Hunt.

and ready market for all the news that fits the paradigm; contrary indications have a hard time making themselves heard.

The Church of England is the largest church in England by a very considerable margin. In a recent survey 55% of respondents described themselves as members of the Church of England. If grossed up, this figure would represent some twenty-one million adults, at least nominal members, and to this number one should add, of course, children. The total population of England, the Isle of Man, and the Channel Islands is forty-eight million. But so negative and alarming has been the publicity given to the Church of England's own statistics of declining Sunday attendance that its statisticians have recently derived a new way of calculating the figures. From 2000, the benchmark year, it is claimed that at Christmas services there was an attendance of 2.85 million (half of whom were communicants) and at Easter 1.63 million; average Sunday attendance is put at 1.06 million of all ages, and average weekly attendance at 1.3 million.

These are not reassuring figures, and they represent a decline from any point in the previous century. Nor is the portrayal of the true context and impact of the contemporary Church of England merely a matter of numbers. A recent social historian, using an analysis of patterns of oral culture, announced the decline in the startling title of his book, *The Death of Christian Britain*.[7] The gap between the figures for baptised membership and active churchgoing presents ample opportunity for a variety of interpretations.

But it is the paradigm of decline, lodged firmly in the heads of the London-based elites who control the content of newspapers, that determines that the most pessimistic construction is placed on the worst set of figures. The claim is that the Church of England is in a terminal state of incompetence, bankrupt and riddled with sexual scandal. Throughout the very public debate about the ordination of women to the priesthood, a group of journalists specializing in religious affairs gave extra prominence to the predictions of those opponents who claimed that the Church of England would fall apart. There would be more than one thousand defections from the priesthood, it was suggested. In the event, there have been four hundred eighty-seven, of whom sixty-four subsequently returned. I constantly meet people who ask me how many have left, because that lower figure was given little media coverage since it does not fit the paradigm of decline.

The Episcopal Church lives in the context of a very different nation, with a different twentieth-century history and self-understanding. But it shares at least part of the experience of the Church of England, as it certainly participates

7. Callum G. Brown, *The Death of Christian Britain* (London and New York: Routledge, 2001).

in some of the pain of its popular reputation. If ever one were tempted to be an Episcopalian because of the esteem in which English culture, or the monarchy, or the Church of England was popularly held, one will now be on the lookout for excuses to change one's allegiance. Thus are the tables turned upon the Church of England, which John Henry Newman left in 1845 in part because it enjoyed the popularity he held to be incompatible with historic Christianity. Today to be an Anglican or Episcopalian requires some convictions about one's church. In *Unashamed Anglicanism* I wanted to write about my church in such a way as to make my own convictions clear, and not just convictions, but love and a sense of joy and liberation:

> to comfort all that mourn; to appoint unto them that mourn in Zion, to give them beauty for ashes, the oil of joy for mourning, the garment of praise for the spirit of heaviness; that they might be called trees of righteousness, the planting of the Lord, that he might be glorified. (Isa. 61:2-3)

2. "That He Might Be Glorified"

Someone self-professedly not ashamed of being an Anglican must first say two things: that the glory of the Lord (not of Anglicanism) is paramount, and that a careful distinction must be preserved between the gospel of salvation and the life and structures of the church. In the writings of William James there is a passage lampooning nineteenth-century Anglicanism in the following way:

> So massive and all-pervasive, so authoritative and on the whole so decent, in spite of the iniquity and farcicality of the whole thing. . . . Never were incompatibles so happily yoked together. Talk about the genius of Romanism. It is nothing to the genius of Anglicanism, for Catholicism still retains some haggard elements that ally it with the Palestinian desert, whereas Anglicanism remains obese and round and comfortable, and decent with this world's decencies, without one acute note in its whole life or history.[8]

There are sharp and critical things to say about the current state of our church, to which I will return at the end of this paper. But "that the Lord may be glorified" is an appropriate motto to place at the start of any treatment of the

---

8. From G. F. S. Gray, *The Anglican Communion: A Brief Sketch* (London: SPCK, 1958), p. 165.

positive aspects of the tradition we have received. I did not intend *Unashamed Anglicanism* to be an uncritical celebration of the advantages of our communion, nor a return to conservative confessionalism. But I do believe that the Lord had a hand in the planting of this tradition within the one, holy, catholic, and apostolic church and still has work for it to do. But what work? That is the point we should address.

Under four main headings I want to summarize what seems to be the ecumenical potential of Anglicanism. They are *characteristic* of the life of our communion, without necessarily being *distinctive.* Indeed it is not strong in our tradition to claim a great deal of distinctiveness for ourselves. We are glad, or should be glad, when features that are found in our tradition are also present in other churches. And Anglicanism as a whole is undeniably distinctive, even when made up of elements that are in themselves no more than characteristic, rather in the way in which Haydn's tune we call "Austria" is made up of phrases to be found in large numbers of other compositions.

A Quiet and Confident Catholicism

In *Unashamed Anglicanism* this phrase is defined as follows: "[a Catholicism] which does not posture, strive, or cry, which is serious about its prayer and self-discipline, which is energetic in its social witness, which understands secularity and accepts the obligation of honest evangelism, and which draws upon the intellectual and spiritual riches of the whole Catholic tradition."[9]

It is, of course, risky for any Anglican to begin with Catholicism without mentioning Evangelicalism or even Protestantism, a title or sub-title Anglicans were ready to accept for at least two centuries after the Reformation. But there are very strong grounds indeed for rejecting the common use of the term *catholic* to describe a party or tendency within the Anglican family.[10] If there is such a movement lending itself to a general descriptive label, then almost anything other than *catholic* would be preferable. The very point of the word *catholic* is, indeed, Christological and inclusive. The church and all members of it are catholic because they are in Christ. It was a German Lutheran theologian who described the incarnation as the *urkatholische Ereignis,* the foundational catholic event.[11] It is essentially for biblical reasons that Anglicans have found them-

---

9. Sykes, *Unashamed Anglicanism,* p. 122.

10. See the argument of T. A. Lacey, *Catholicity* (London: Mowbray, 1914), chap. 1.

11. Ernst Finke, cited in Avery Robert Dulles, *The Catholicity of the Church* (Oxford: Clarendon Press, 1985), p. 32.

selves receptive to the doctrine of incarnation, as an integral part of that Trinitarian theology confessed in the Nicene and Apostles' creeds.

At the head of this quiet and confident catholicism, I would put the reception of the Trinitarian faith of the whole church, as the rule by which the scriptures are ordinarily interpreted. There is, of course, much to discuss by way of critical objections to this tradition, and the controversies of the last thirty years were fierce. But the outcome at the moment can be said to be a renewed robustness of conviction about the capacity of Trinitarian theology to inform and shape the spiritual and practical life of the church, as well as its doctrine and ethical teaching. A recent radical report on the organization of the Church of England asserted: "The life of the Church, in a rich and yet mysterious way, is thus utterly Trinitarian in its ground, being and hope."[12] That would count, in my view, as a confident catholicism being put to work.

Part of the Christological inclusiveness of catholicism is its capacity to hold together a scriptural and evangelical emphasis with a sacramental life and catholic order. Indeed to tear them apart is to invite disaster. To denigrate the sacraments, or to be loftily indifferent to the unity of the church's ministry, is no part of a biblical faith. We are discovering with pleasure that we should read no less a theologian than John Calvin as teaching a consistency and interconnection between evangelical and sacramental religion.[13] In the last two decades developments in Anglican/Episcopalian-Lutheran relations on both sides of the Atlantic have demonstrated the vitality of what Archbishop Nathan Söderblom of Sweden once called "evangelical catholicity." And as for catholic order, it is prominent Roman Catholic and Orthodox theologians who are insisting that at no cost can the episcopate be separated from the life of the whole apostolic community. A quiet and confident catholicism will welcome the challenges from the Reformed Churches to explain how our ordained ministry relates to the preaching of the gospel and the developing structures of office in the life of the post-Pauline churches. In the process we shall be required to explain how the first element of the 1886/1888 Chicago-Lambeth Quadrilateral[14] (on the authority of scripture) is related to the fourth (on the episcopate). There is more, and creative, work to be done on this point.[15]

---

12. Church of England Archbishops' Commission on Organisation, *Working as One Body* (London: Church House Publishing, 1995), p. 2.

13. B. A. Gerrish, *Grace and Gratitude: The Eucharistic Theology of John Calvin* (Edinburgh: T&T Clark; Minneapolis: Fortress Press, 1993), pp. 158-59.

14. In 1886 the Episcopalians met in Chicago, and the international Anglican meeting was in 1888 at Lambeth.

15. This must surely take seriously the Scriptural foundations for a *theology* of the episcopate, not simply historical arguments about continuities.

S. W. Sykes

An Openness to a Plurality of Spiritual Traditions

The calendars of both ECUSA and the Church of England appropriately and convincingly contain the names of a number of rather prominent non-Anglicans. In *Common Worship*,[16] for example, we are encouraged to give thanks for Seraphim, Monk of Sarov (d. 1833), George Fox (d. 1691), Francis de Sales (d. 1622), Oscar Romero (d. 1980), Dietrich Bonhoeffer (d. 1945), John and Charles Wesley (d. 1791 and 1788, respectively), Thomas More and John Fisher (described as "Reformation Martyrs," d. 1535), John Bunyan (d. 1688), and Vincent de Paul (d. 1660). So far as I know, this modest indication of inclusiveness is unparalleled in any other church family. Fox, John Wesley, More, Fisher, and Bunyan are particularly striking indications of a readiness to regard even those who set themselves against the Anglican church of their time as worthy of commemoration and as offering us good examples to follow. In this way a certain generosity of judgment can be built into our common life, at least after the blessed forgetfulness of two centuries and more.

Together with this inclusiveness, one should also affirm the fact that Anglicans have every reason to learn from the spiritual insight and discipline of writers of many different ecclesial traditions. In our liturgical inheritance we have received a strong Benedictine formation. In the British isles, as well as in Ireland and elsewhere, we have every reason to be grateful for Saint Patrick, Saint Columba, and Saint Aidan, saints of the Celtic tradition. We have the example of outstanding women, Saint Hilda of Whitby, Saint Etheldreda of Ely, and Saint Margaret of Scotland (commemorated as Queen, Wife, and Mother). The Cistercian movement quickly took root in England, as did the Franciscan. And even the sixteenth-century quarrel with Rome had a positive outcome, in awakening an interest in and sympathy for the Orthodox churches of the East, as is clear from our commemoration of Saint Anthony of Egypt, Saint Athanasius, Saint John Chrysostom, and Saint Basil the Great.

Eclecticism has, of course, its negative side, as will be noted in due course. But no one, with the best will in the world, could possibly base a profound spiritual life upon merely Anglican writers. There is an Anglican spiritual tradition, but there is also an Anglican tradition of responding to and enjoying the variety of traditions, not excluding modern Protestant traditions, available in both East and West. But for us Anglicans it is a liberation that we are not obliged to prefer Western to Eastern saints or vice versa; nor are we bound to hold any saint incapable of error or excess. We can read their work in a teachable frame

---

16. *Common Worship: Services and Prayers for the Church of England* (London: Church House Publishing, 2000).

of mind and with gratitude, but we do not have to defend them on every point or to abandon our critical faculties.

We do well in this connection to remember George Herbert, who in *A Priest to the Temple* advanced the view that an Anglican country parson "hath read the Fathers also, and the Schoolmen, and the later writers, or a good proportion of all."[17] This generous breadth has surely an ecumenical future as well as a past.

Authority with Consent

A rather large proportion of *Unashamed Anglicanism* is occupied with a series of essays about authority in Anglicanism because of the discussion about the grounds for and organs of competent decision making in the Anglican Communion in the light of the proposal to ordain women to the priesthood and episcopate. In 1978 in *The Integrity of Anglicanism* I drew attention to the rather impressive formulation of so-called "dispersed authority" in one of the Reports of the 1948 Lambeth Conference.[18] This report had explicitly raised the question of whether Anglicanism has a sufficiently coherent form of authority to form the nucleus of a world-wide fellowship of churches or whether its famed "comprehensiveness" contained the seeds of its own destruction.

The first and original context of the Anglican discussion of authority had considered a plurality of doctrinal positions. With the increasing prominence of the intense debate about ending the male qualification for ordination, the issue was not so much comprehensiveness of theology as diversity of practice. Together with this theological argument went the argument that a single Anglican synod was incompetent to take what was called a "unilateral" decision on this matter. As a result, from 1981 onwards I was increasingly invited to prophesy on the subject of authority in Anglicanism.

In due course, it became obvious that one could not sensibly write on authority *in* the church without a basis in the theology *of* the church. In the meantime, however, it was possible to live out of the resources of an ecclesial instinct, deeply laid in the Anglicanism we had inherited and ingested, that urged the value of authority with consent. An Australian theologian, Keith C. Chittleborough, contributed an important and influential essay entitled "To-

17. George Herbert, "The Parsons Accessary Knowledge," *A Priest to the Temple,* in F. E. Hutchinson, ed., *The Works of George Herbert* (Oxford: Clarendon Press, 1941), p. 229.

18. Report IV, "The Anglican Communion," in *The Lambeth Conference 1948: The Encyclical Letter from the Bishops, together with Resolutions and Reports* (London: SPCK, 1948).

wards a Theology and Practice of the Bishop-in-Synod" to a collection produced in advance of the 1988 Lambeth Conference.[19] In it he pointed to the fact that the non-English pattern of synodical government expresses a truth, well formulated by Richard Hooker, that authority without consent is no better than tyranny and that the testing of consent is a reason for the inclusion of representative clergy and laity in synods. Behind Hooker lie the late medieval arguments against the Pope's claim to plenitude of power and the tradition now known as "conciliarism." Anglicanism may properly claim to have provided one provisional example of conciliar theory in practice.

The essays on authority in *Unashamed Anglicanism* largely defend this tradition. An episcopal church gives to bishops a measure of authority and, indeed, power. The episcopate sustains a connection with the church of the ages and with both the Orthodox and Roman Catholic Churches. But our way of relating bishops to the whole life of the church in an elected assembly offers both a forum for the eliciting of consent and a way of resisting the temptations of power abuse, familiar in the life of the church from biblical days onwards.

The modern church is in a state of massive confusion about the facts of power in the life of institutions, and it will remain so until and unless it acknowledges the relevance of sociological enquiry to its life. But it is at least arguable that there is an ecumenical future to the idea that the church lives neither democratically nor by despotism, but in a corporate or collective life, of which one example is that of a bishop-in-synod.

The arguments and decisions relating to the inclusion of women in the ordained ministry have tested this tradition of consent nearly to the breaking point in the last decades. It is instructive to read Dorothy Sayers' letter to C. S. Lewis, from July 1948, in response to his request that she write an article against the admission of women to priest's orders. She refused, and though regretting anything that might be an obstacle to good relations especially with the Eastern Orthodox, she added this theological comment: "If I were cornered and asked point-blank whether Christ himself is the representative of male humanity or of all humanity, I should be obliged to answer 'of all humanity'; and to cite the authority of St. Augustine for saying that woman is also made in the image of God."[20]

The form of Sayers' argument with its appeal to patristic tradition and, implicitly, to scripture is instructive. Doughty feminist though she was, she did

19. Keith C. Chittleborough, "Towards a Theology and Practice of the Bishop-in-Synod," in *Authority in the Anglican Communion: Essays Presented to Bishop John Howe*, ed. S. W. Sykes (Toronto: Anglican Book Centre, 1987).

20. Barbara Reynolds, ed., *The Letters of Dorothy L. Sayers*, vol. 3, *1944-1950: A Noble Daring* (Swavesey [UK]: Dorothy L. Sayers Society, 1999), p. 387.

not propose that the exclusion of women from ordained ministry was unjust. The application of civil rights argumentation to the question of who may be a candidate for ordination appears to carry with it a policy of "zero tolerance" once the supposed historic wrong has been righted. But it is undoubtedly possible to argue on scriptural and traditional grounds against the ordination of women, and this fact makes the issue of consent of great importance and difficulty. How are those who are unconvinced to be sustained within a church that has taken a decision to do so? And how are ordained women to be sustained in such a church?

Roman Catholics not infrequently remark that once a change (usually spoken of as a "development") has been decided upon in teaching or practice, it is enforced; those who resist are simply told they are wrong. Anglicans, such observers suggest by implication, lack both the structures of and the respect for competent authority to gain sufficient consent for their difficult decisions. A common example is the change in the Mass from Latin to English. The difference, however, is more apparent than real. Because of the context of universal education, both churches face large and literate lay publics, among whom argument has to be conducted in an open way. Mere authoritarianism has no future — indeed Anglicans and Episcopalians have had to discover that synodical authoritarianism is a possibility and that elected majorities can exercise their power in a tyrannous way as easily as can clerical elites. For Roman Catholic and Anglican churches there are real lessons to be learnt in the nurture of communities of discussion in which consent is openly and freely sought and dissent is sustained. Anglicans have currently some responsibility for minorities in both the Roman Catholic and Orthodox churches.

A Developing Baptismal Ecclesiology

One of the main arguments of *Unashamed Anglicanism* is directed towards establishing the need for an Anglican ecclesiology. Indeed I set about the deliberate destruction of a venerable Anglican shibboleth that "Anglicans have no special doctrines of their own," and I do so with a measure of blunt brutality.[21] We have for too long hidden behind a variety of defenses in refusing to articulate our understanding of the church. Our ecumenical partners find us intellectually elusive and a trifle arrogant. It is almost as if we *know* that our understanding of the church, the ministry, and the sacraments is true, without having to

21. S. W. Sykes, "Anglicanism and the Anglican Doctrine of the Church," first appeared in *Quadrilateral*, pp. 101-21.

submit to the inconvenience of explaining and justifying it. A great American theologian and somewhat closet Anglican, Hans Frei, of whom I am proud to claim to have been a friend, once revealed to me how intellectually damaging reliance on the reputation of the seventeenth-century Caroline divines had been to American Anglicans, as though one had merely to whisper the name Lancelot Andrewes to know at once that all vulgar traffic with modern theology could cease.[22]

But lest it be thought that I despise my own tradition (or a man who was once bishop of Ely), I cite a remarkable treatise on baptism written by another bishop of Ely a little after Andrewes' death:

> We are not baptized into this or that particular Opinion, nor received into a particular Church, but into the Belief of the Gospel, and into the Church of God in general, and therefore should love all the Disciples and Followers of our Lord, and embrace all of every Persuasion that live godily in Christ Jesus. . . . And therefore let us live with them all as our Confederates, as those that are tied together in the same Bonds, and united in the same Covenant, and engaged in the same Cause against the common Enemies, the devil, the World, and the Flesh; and let us never give these Enemies so much cause to rejoice, as an unhandsome word against any sincere Christian might administer.[23]

In a passage of this nature one hears not merely the love of generous inclusiveness, which we have noted earlier, but also a foundational element for a doctrine of the church.

In recent times Orthodox and Roman Catholic theologians have developed, in considerable detail, a theologically powerful eucharistic ecclesiology. There are serious grounds for asking what precise role baptism plays in these theological arguments. A strong case can be made out for starting with a theology of baptism, so that the existence of mutually recognized baptisms does not become an anomaly in an otherwise closed eucharistic fellowship. To use baptism as the basis for ecclesiology has the further advantage of forcing Anglicans

---

22. Bishop Lancelot Andrewes (1555-1626), successively bishop of Chichester, Ely, and Winchester, provided a strong statement on Anglican teaching together with replies to Roman Catholicism.

23. This constitutes the concluding paragraph of a sermon by Symon Patrick, later to be Bishop of Ely (1691-1706), on October 4, 1658, at the baptism of the infant son of a Presbyterian minister. Published as "Aqua Genitalis" or "A Discourse Concerning Baptism," in *The Works of Symon Patrick,* ed. Alexander Taylor, vol. 1 (Oxford: Oxford University Press, 1858); see "Editor's Preface," pp. ivff.

to give a more thorough and consistent account of episcopacy than might otherwise be necessary. It is not safe to be a bishop unless one realizes that there is no other status in the church than that of being baptised.

In addition, the development of ecclesiology in Anglicanism needs one further contribution, which does not figure in *Unashamed Anglicanism*. This is the distinction between a "thick" and a "thin" ecclesiology.[24] Because the church in its local form is its proper embodiment, a doctrine of the church ought to be developed that gives rich, many-sided, and critical expression to the reality of God's saving presence within a particular context. One might call that a "thick" doctrine of the church, deploying a term used by a social anthropologist, Clifford Geertz.[25]

Dependent upon such "thick" local ecclesiologies is the enterprise of a "thin" or universal doctrine of the church, which attempts to express what is or should be true of the church at all times and in all places. Too often the relationship has been thought of in the opposite way, that the local is a translation or expression of the universal. In fact the reverse is true. Not that a "thin" ecclesiology is untried or flimsy. Like certain forms of highly sophisticated modern metals, it is thin and exceptionally tough, proved in vast numbers of stresses. But it is dependent upon a vast array of "thick" ecclesiologies, available and relevant in many different contexts. The Chicago-Lambeth Quadrilateral,[26] for example, is a "thin" list of practices that, in the view of its authors, must characterize the church at all times everywhere. It is not a complete ecclesiology.

It is important and helpful to see Elizabethan Anglican ecclesiology, developed by such English writers as Richard Hooker or Richard Field, as "thick" in this sense. It is a whole-hearted attempt to speak of the embodied, saving presence of God in a particular culture. The contemporary churches of the Anglican communion also need thick ecclesiologies, not pale imitations or "translations" of Elizabethan Anglicanism, but full, rich, and relevant accounts of the embodiment of God's saving presence within a culture or locality. "Thick" ecclesiologies would relate to each other via "thin" ecclesiology. They would not be autonomous. The restless and assertive nationalisms of the contemporary church need a disciplined framework if the catholicity and unity of the church

24. This idea is derived from a recent discussion of theories of distributive justice developed by the American political philosopher Michael Walzer, in *Thick and Thin: Moral Argument at Home and Abroad* (Notre Dame and London: University of Notre Dame Press, 1994).

25. See *The Interpretation of Cultures: Selected Essays* (London: Fontana, 1993; original publication New York: Basic Books, 1973).

26. For the text, see J. Robert Wright, "Heritage and Vision: The Chicago-Lambeth Quadrilateral," in Quadrilateral, pp. 8-46.

are to be sustained. But I believe it to be liberating for Anglicans, in the vast variety of contexts in which such an understanding is now current, to know that the responsibility of developing a local understanding of the one, holy, catholic, and apostolic church is inalienably theirs.[27]

3.

I have listed four characteristics of the life of our communion that I believe to have ecumenical potential. Lest that exercise be thought to be unduly smug, let me finish with some warnings. Arthur Michael Ramsey (or was it Charles Gore?) is said once to have burst out to a friend that sometimes he hated the church, and I know what he meant.

I hate the triviality and superficiality into which our eclectic openness can fall. It is right that we believe that, in some mysterious way, the gross oppositions and tensions of historic Christianity belong together. But there is a real danger of taking nothing seriously enough to mind about contradictions. For example, because we doubt whether believing the doctrine of transubstantiation is necessary to salvation (and we may well remember that men and women were put to death for that doubt), the passionate devotion to the blessed sacrament that has inspired the love of countless saints and sinners is perhaps a little closed to us. And so perhaps is the passion with which a Luther or Calvin resisted the doctrines of a certain kind of sacramental realism and invested so much in the understanding of Christ's righteousness as applied freely to the life of a sinner. And so, on both counts, passion may elude us altogether and something else take its place, something for which William James's devastating word was "decency." If we are to take advantage of Anglicanism's blessed breadth and tolerance, it is vital to expose ourselves to and be swayed by the passions of the great spiritual writers and theologians. Otherwise the Anglican "mediocrity" can be deadly.

I also hate the proneness of Anglicanism to fashionable causes, in the absence of any profound engagement with its tradition. This is an era of great historical forgetfulness and of restless consumerism. The temptation for our church is to forget our orientation and responsibilities as belonging to the one, holy, catholic, and apostolic church and consciously or unconsciously to look for a niche in the religious marketplace, to adopt what look like successful strat-

---

27. This argument, without the use of the terms *thick* and *thin,* is deployed in the Virginia Report, chap. 4, published in *The Official Report of the Lambeth Conference 1998* (Harrisburg: Morehouse, 1999), pp. 43-49.

egies for church growth or to leap on the bandwagons of this or that lobbying group or cause.

And when I say things like that, I hate with almost equal fervor those who agree with me, because they too want to forget that there was a day when William Wilberforce and Thomas Clarkson lobbied against the slave trade. How do we discriminate between one cause and another? Or rather, how do we, like Wilberforce and Clarkson, acknowledge that the church is infinitely greater than its causes and that the gospel itself may be believed and proclaimed by those who are indifferent to or who oppose what you or I stand for?

What I hate so profoundly in modernity is the all-consuming ruthlessness of the campaigners, for whom politics is all. I cite Jeremy Taylor writing in strife-torn England of 1647. Schisms, wars and persecutions, and the dissolution of all friendships, he says,

> proceed not from this, that all men are not of one minde, for that is neither necessary nor possible, but that every Opinion is made an Article of Faith, every Article is a ground of a quarrel, every quarrel makes a faction, every faction is zealous, and all zeale pretends for God, and whatsoever is for God cannot be too much.[28]

Modern Anglicanism, for its very lack of spiritual passion, is prone to a self-righteous factionalism, in which neither generosity, affection, nor trust counts for anything.

It is not as though there is anything profound about the way a particular issue is analyzed. Indeed factionalism dispenses us from the challenges to profundity, because we speak only with those who agree with us; with the opposition we simply seek advantage by sound bites. The split between religious conservatives and liberals is one of the known consequences of secularization. It is by now a separation internal to most denominations. But a quiet and confident catholicism will be destroyed by it, because by definition that separation requires either the vilification or the canonization of the past. Anglicans are committed, and one hopes they may be passionately committed, to neither course.

---

28. From "Introduction," *A Discourse of the Liberty of Prophesying* (London: Macmillan, 1647), p. 5.

The New Ecumenism of the Possible

C. Christopher Epting

In Rocca di Pappa, Italy, on November 11-13, 2004, the Pontifical Council for Promoting Christian Unity gathered Roman Catholic bishops from around the world, representatives from twenty-seven other Christian communities, and leading ecumenists to celebrate the fortieth anniversary of the Second Vatican Council's Decree on Ecumenism. On that occasion Cardinal Walter Kasper, President of the Council, reminded the participants that perseverance, courage, patience, and hope are necessary as Christians continue to work and pray for unity. "We no longer have the ecumenical enthusiasm of the period immediately following the council," Kasper said, "but we cannot say — as some do — that ecumenism is going through the ice age or an ecumenical winter." These words enunciate a consistent theme in Kasper's teaching on the current state of the ecumenical movement — a recognition that the landscape has changed over the last twenty years or so and an unwillingness to give up hope or flag in zeal for church unity.

In "Vision of Christian Unity for the Next Generation," a May 17, 2003, address in England, at Saint Alban's Abbey, Kasper began by defining the present moment as one of ecumenical "crisis," "a situation where things are hanging in the balance, where they are on a knife-edge."[1] He challenged his audience to

---

An earlier version of this paper, entitled "Exercises in Spiritual Ecumenism," appeared in *The Ecumenical Review*, July 2003: 272-78.

1. Cardinal Walter Kasper, "Vision of Christian Unity for the Next Generation," *Origins* 12 June 2003: 71-76; here 72; repr. (abridged) "Ecumenism: The Way Ahead," *The Tablet* 24 May 2003: 32-34.

avoid two dangers: an ecumenism that is only an academic affair for professional theologians, and an ecumenical activism defined primarily by an endless series of meetings, conferences, and symposia. Instead he pointed to what he believes is a healthier ecumenism: "spiritual ecumenism and ecumenical spirituality" (p. 72).

This challenge built upon earlier remarks included in Cardinal Kasper's "Prolusio," opening remarks delivered at the Plenary of the Pontifical Council for Promoting Christian Unity in November of 2001. In his concluding section, "Ecumenical Praxis during the Transitional Period," he listed six challenges for the Council and therefore for the Roman Catholic Church. As the Presiding Bishop's Deputy for Ecumenical and Interfaith Relations for the Episcopal Church in the United States, I regard them as also challenges for the wider church, challenges to which the church needs to respond. They form the framework for this paper, which aims to point to ways forward in the present situation.

Reception

Cardinal Kasper's first challenge is for a wider reception of ecumenical dialogues and agreements already reached.[2] Ecumenical reception, which T. P. Rausch has defined as "the acceptance by one church of a theological consensus arrived at with another church, and ultimately the recognition of the other church's faith and ecclesial life as authentically Christian,"[3] is an extremely important aspect of ecumenical progress, and while the churches cannot artificially hasten the sometimes painfully slow process of reception by the communions, they must do all that they can to encourage it. The International Anglican–Roman Catholic Commission on Unity and Mission (IARCCUM), composed of Anglican and Roman Catholic bishops from around the world, gave hope of speeding up this process, but one result of the Anglican Communion's disagreement over the 2003 ordination as Episcopal bishop of New Hampshire of the Reverend Gene Robinson, a gay man living in an open committed relationship with another man, was that IARCCUM suspended its work.

A particularly unfortunate aspect of the hiatus in IARCCUM's work is the delay in the preparation and publication of a joint declaration summarizing and setting forth the substantial agreements reached over the years. Such agree-

---

2. Cardinal Walter Kasper, Prolusio to "Present Situation and Future of the Ecumenical Movement," *Information Service* (Rome: Pontifical Council for Promoting Christian Unity, 2002) n. 109 (2002/I-II): 11-20.

3. T. P. Rausch, "Reception Past and Present," *Theological Studies* 47 (1986): 497.

ments are the fruit of national and international dialogues, yet are largely un-known or ignored by the two communions themselves. It is critical that this joint statement be produced and publicized in such a way that it is actually studied and used by bishops' and clergy conferences, seminary and diocesan training programs, and congregations both large and small. An attractive and colorful printing style, a usable study guide, and even video and CD supplements will be essential for this material to get the kind of widespread usage and support it deserves.

Similarly, bilateral agreements of full communion between Lutherans and Anglicans, between Lutherans and churches of the Reformed tradition, and also between the Moravians and both Episcopalians and Lutherans must not be left to rise or fall on their own. They require constant affirmation and admonition by the organs of regular communication and coordination that the agreements set in place, organs such as the Lutheran-Episcopal Coordinating Committee. A focus on common mission, especially mission together in today's world, and on-going consultation about the various kinds of hindrances to implementation of the agreements will be essential if reception is to occur on the local level. Christians want to get on with the mission of the church!

Institutional Forms and Structures

A second challenge, according to Cardinal Kasper, is to find "institutional forms and structures for the present transitional period." Somewhat surprisingly, but happily, he suggests that at least in part such structures can be provided by councils of churches on the regional and national levels. While several such councils do exist, they would require considerable reform and renewal to make such a contribution. In the United States, for example, it is the height of folly to identify the National Council of Churches of Christ in the U.S.A. (NCCUSA) as such a council without the full and active participation of Roman Catholics, Evangelicals, and Pentecostal Christians, as almost everyone involved with that body would agree. Similarly, new movements such as Christian Churches Together in the U.S.A. (CCTUSA) and, on the international level, the Global Forum are a long way from being ready to inherit the honorable mantle of the National or World Council of Churches. However, they are responding to the proper impulse — one hopes it to be that of the Holy Spirit — to "broaden the ecumenical table" and include voices from those huge Christian communions that as yet do not participate, or participate only partially, in these national and international councils.

There is a legitimate fear that the prophetic witness of such organizations will be weakened in the attempt to include more communions. Will the church have anything at all to say to the world if it attempts to speak with one voice? It seems clear that if the churches do not have such a voice together, then they had best remain silent. Practically speaking, there will be many things that the churches can say together. It may well be that such entities as the NCCCUSA and CCTUSA will continue to exist side by side, at least for the present. But renewal and reform are necessary. It has long been said that if the National Council of Churches (NCC) or the World Council of Churches (WCC) did not exist, we would have to invent them. It is now time to (re)invent them both.

Ecumenical Dialogues

Kasper challenges the churches to continue their various bilateral and multilateral dialogues. As frustrating as they can sometimes be, as prone as they are to fall into the aforementioned "mere academic exercises" or "endless meetings," nothing can replace the slow, patient work of theologians, historians, laity, bishops, presbyters, and deacons as they gather — month by month and year by year — to remember the wounds of history, to understand one another better in the present, and, most important, to envision a future together in which full communion will be a reality, not only the goal.

Many of the easy questions facing such dialogues have been answered or at least addressed. Much progress has been made, as can be seen in some of the full communion agreements, in agreed statements such as *The Final Report* of the Anglican–Roman Catholic International Commission,[4] and at such a level of reception as documents — like the WCC's *Baptism, Eucharist and Ministry* — have received from various dialogues and from the communions.

Although the easy questions have been at least partially dealt with, the tough ones remain; in this situation, as Cardinal Kasper succinctly puts it, "false irenicism leads us nowhere." Even full communion relationships, such as the ELCA-Episcopal agreement as defined by the terms of *Called to Common Mission*,[5] have experienced resistance, perhaps because of the use of overly nuanced and even ambiguous language in the attempt to find common ground in the face of differences perhaps not sufficiently worked out even in the years of painstaking dialogue preceding the agreements.

---

4. Growth I, pp. 61-129.

5. *Anglican-Lutheran Agreements: Regional and International Agreements 1972-2002*, ed. Sven Oppegaard and Gregory Cameron, LWF Documentation No. 49 (Geneva: LWF and ACC, 2004), pp. 231-42.

Ordained Ministry

Perhaps chief among the difficult issues now to be confronted is that of the ordained ministry, specifically how the ministries of the various communions can be recognized and reconciled. This is the fourth of Kasper's challenges. While there is much value and much to be gained in taking into account with utmost seriousness the developments in understanding the ordained ministry as such developments unfolded in the history of the churches of the Reformation, the continuing witness of the Orthodox, Roman Catholic, and Anglican churches has been reinforced by contemporary scholarship such as that reflected in *Baptism, Eucharist and Ministry,* suggesting the essential nature of the historic episcopal succession and its place in the future.

Whether for the *esse* or the *bene esse* of the church (that is, its very being or its well-being), the practical fact is that no church unity can be envisioned without the vast majority of the world's Christians being part of it. Ecumenical breakthroughs such as the separating of "apostolic succession" — the faithfulness to apostolic teaching, which can be passed along in the church in a variety of ways — from the "historic succession" of bishops, which is understood to be a sign but not a guarantee of that faithfulness, provide new avenues for thinking about this previously church-dividing question.

To be sure, much renewal and reform of the old monarchial episcopate will have to be evidenced to quell Protestant fears of a dominating hierarchy unresponsive to the needs of the laity and capable of stifling the transforming power of the Holy Spirit or the truth of the Gospel. A "synodical episcopate" with a clear system of checks and balances and a democratic exercise of authority is a model attractive to many in Orthodox and Roman Catholic as well as Protestant circles. Movements in this direction can be seen in worldwide Anglican-Lutheran agreements such as the *Porvoo Common Statement* in Europe, *Called to Common Mission* in the United States, and the *Waterloo Declaration* in Canada. Extremely important work is going on in the United States in the Ministry Task Force of Churches Uniting in Christ (CUIC), successor to the Consultation on Church Union (COCU). This association of nine churches, enriched now by the addition of the Evangelical Lutheran Church in America and the Northern Province of the Moravian Church as "Partners in Mission and Dialogue," has struggled faithfully for over forty years to find a way to come together as an association of over twenty-two million Christians in the United States.

CUIC is seeking to achieve a breakthrough that would not only embrace and extend the historic episcopate but also incorporate the threefold pattern of ordained ministry — bishop, presbyter, and deacon — in the context of a baptismal ecclesiology that gives full place and dignity to the ministry of all the baptized, including those often simplistically called the laity. This process seeks to do justice to the legitimate concerns of American Protestantism while honoring the Episcopal Church's commitment to the historic succession of bishops, part of the Chicago-Lambeth Quadrilateral of 1886 and 1888.[6]

A related and equally thorny challenge in this fourth category is the future exercise of the "Petrine ministry" in the ecumenical future. It is vital to respond to Pope John Paul II's invitation in the encyclical *Ut Unum Sint* for a "fraternal dialogue" about the exercise of such a ministry.[7] While a number of communions have responded, this topic requires answers not only to Rome from individual communions but also among the various communions, as well as ongoing reflection within and among the communions. The question not only concerns the current and future occupants of the Holy See but also calls for serious consideration among all Christians, not least among the Eastern and Oriental Orthodox churches, which occupy such a central place in these discussions. Their ancient witness will be illuminating both for the Vatican and for Protestant churches, which need to learn more about the Eastern churches' autocephalous nature and about what it means at least theologically to be "first among equals."

Both the *Virginia Report*, written for consideration by the 1998 Lambeth Conference of Anglican bishops, and the more recent *Windsor Report*, commissioned in 2003 by the Archbishop of Canterbury on behalf of the Anglican Primates, recognize that as the Anglican Communion develops from a "federation" of national churches into a genuine worldwide communion, it may need a somewhat more centralized authority structure that allows some clarity on those issues that even the principle of subsidiarity deems appropriate for decision making on a global level. Similar impulses may arise as such worldwide entities as the Lutheran World Federation and the World Methodist Conference continue to develop and change.

When this issue is juxtaposed with many Roman Catholics' desire for more collegiality among bishops and more papal consultation with local bishops' conferences, is it not possible to postulate some middle ground? Could there not be somewhat more centralization of worldwide communions that have not known centralized authority and somewhat less centralization for the Latin church, which has known nothing else? It is my hope that both the *Virginia Report* and the *Windsor Report* will receive wide Anglican and ecumenical attention as the church seeks to discover what might appropriately be called legitimate "authority for the sake of mission."

6. BCP, pp. 876-77.
7. *Unum* §96.

Ecumenism *ad extra* and *ad intra*

Cardinal Kasper's fifth challenge for the ecumenical movement has two parts: "ecumenism *ad extra* through ecumenical encounters, dialogues and cooperation, and ecumenism *ad intra* through reform and renewal." Much of this paper is about the former. And, although Kasper did not identify this topic as one of the particular ecumenical encounters possible, I would like to raise the volatile topic of human sexuality. If there is today a potentially "church-dividing issue" — within and between the churches — it is the issue of human sexuality, specifically homosexuality and the place of gay and lesbian persons in the life and ministry of the church. The experience of the Episcopal Church in the United States, the Presbyterian Church (USA), the United Methodist Church, and many others certainly bears out this observation. All the churches would surely benefit from more ecumenical conversation and sharing about an issue with which they are all wrestling, often in relative isolation. Surely no ecumenical consensus can be reached about the blessing of same sex unions or the ordination of partnered gay and lesbian persons without such a conversation. It is long overdue in the ecumenical arena.

Other more familiar concerns of ecumenism *ad extra* include the Faith and Order movement, in its national and its international expressions. These ecumenical encounters, which have made enormous contributions over the years, must be supported in the future. To their credit, even in the face of dwindling financial support, both the NCCCUSA and the WCC continue to struggle to give Faith and Order a high priority. The churches must continue to support those efforts, especially if they do not continue to avoid issues such as human sexuality, which today threaten to be truly church-dividing.

While ecumenism *ad extra* is complex and difficult, ecumenism *ad intra*, reform and renewal of the churches themselves, may be even more so. Even before the 1952 Lund meeting of the Faith and Order Commission of the World Council of Churches, ecumenists have understood something of what has been called the "Christological method" in ecumenical dialogue,[8] an understanding that the closer churches are to Christ and the more faithful to the core values of the gospel, the closer they will draw to one another. This method requires conversion and reform, not only of individuals but also of the communions themselves. Such spiritual renewal takes many forms, including liturgical reform, charismatic renewal, a rediscovery of the discipline and practice of spiritual direction, the retreat movement, a deeper commitment to

8. Oliver S. Tomkins, "The Church in the Purpose of God," Faith and Order Commission Paper No. 3 (London: SCM Press, Parrett & Neves, 1950), pp. 97-98.

the church's role in working for justice and peace, ministry development, and the use of small cell groups of Christians for prayer, Bible study, and personal discipleship. A key element in many of these impulses is a return to more pristine forms of Christianity, found in the early centuries of the church's life, a period well within that which is sometimes known as the period of the undivided church.

Ecumenism *ad intra* would require that much more attention be given to such groups as the Consultation on Common Texts and a commitment to adopt such things as the *Revised Common Lectionary* and *Revised Common Lectionary: Prayers*.[9] The churches must also recognize, especially as they invite Pentecostals to be more present at the ecumenical table, that both Roman Catholic and Protestant churches have been enriched by the charismatic movement that swept through the churches in the 1970s and 1980s, bringing along its own brand of ecumenism and an attentiveness to the surprising work of the Spirit that many of the communions had chosen to overlook.

Many Christians have continued to deepen their spiritual lives by adopting a rule of life, participating in regular retreats, and even developing a relationship with a spiritual director or companion. Some of these relationships cross denominational lines and have served as important bridges. Prayer groups, Bible study groups, base communities, and communities for discipleship have had an internal impact on the life of the several churches while also having important ecumenical dimensions. Likewise, congregations, judicatories, and even some national church bodies are conducting experiments in corporate discernment in decision making rather than being forever wedded to the win-lose dynamic of the legislative model. These initiatives need to be encouraged at the highest levels.

Common explorations in what is often called ministry development also need to be encouraged. A rediscovery of the centrality of the sacrament of baptism has taken place in all the churches, as can be seen liturgically in a fuller celebration of the paschal mystery at the Easter vigil and in more and more churches celebrating baptism within Sunday morning worship. More important, this renewed emphasis on baptism is visible in "ministry in daily life" and as "the ministry of all the baptized," lay persons as well as deacons, presbyters, and bishops.

At the same time the renewal of the diaconate in many churches is now well into its fourth decade. While taking different shapes in the various communions, ordained deacons in the Roman Catholic, Orthodox, and Anglican

---

9. *Revised Common Lectionary: Episcopal Edition* (Wichita: St. Mark's Press, 2001); *Revised Common Lectionary: Prayers* (Minneapolis: Fortress Press, 2002).

churches, deacons and deaconesses in the Methodist Church, and deaconesses and diaconal ministers in the Evangelical Lutheran Church in America share common roots and offer common challenges to the church of today, even as the different traditions in various ways emphasize the qualities of servanthood, prophetic witness, and administration.[10] Similarly, a shortage of clergy available for congregations raises questions about the role of lay leadership and diaconal presence, as well as the more problematic issues of lay presidency at the eucharist or "ordination to place," which is being experimented with or discussed in a variety of settings. Surely ecumenical cooperation in addressing all these issues would be fruitful.

Finally, Christian formation and the making of disciples inevitably results in renewed Christians' asking hard questions of their societies and communities. In many cases, the struggle for civil and human rights had its genesis within the churches. While growing in imitation of Christ, many will experience a call to prophetic witness for justice and peace as they strive to respect the dignity of every human being. Such witness will challenge the various communions to be faithful to their mission of reconciliation and therefore to create a spiritual renewal of its own kind.

Spiritual Ecumenism

The last of Cardinal Kasper's six challenges follows from the call for church reform and renewal. In words resonant with the church's faith he reminds Christians that the movement toward church unity is God's wish, God's doing:

> the ecumenical movement has been and will continue to be an impulse and gift of the Holy Spirit. . . . So pre-eminence among all ecumenical activities belongs to spiritual ecumenism . . . [which] should be more strongly promoted, and relations with . . . ecumenically concerned monasteries, movements, brotherhoods and groups should be strengthened.

Religious communities of both men and women in the several traditions have long been in the forefront of ecumenical activity. As such communities have dwindled in size, they have found new forms of ministry, new ways to use their facilities, and new sources of income in responding to spiritual seekers. With the new popularity of retreats and conferences, those communities now

10. *The Diaconate as Ecumenical Opportunity: The Hanover Report* (London: ACC; Geneva: LWF, 1996).

have an opportunity to become places of ecumenical hospitality as well as spiritual renewal.

The charismatic movement has already been mentioned as having its own ecumenical dimension, which should be recaptured and reasserted today. Other movements, such as Cursillo, Marriage Encounter, the Catechumenal Process, and those providing leadership in corporate discernment, should claim this ecumenical moment as an opportunity for revitalization and reform in their own ranks. The Order of Saint Luke the Physician, the Brotherhood of Saint Andrew, and Daughters of the King are examples of groups committed to healing, evangelization, and prayer. They could develop their own ecumenical dimensions by including more partners as full members while also finding linkages with similar movements and groups in other communions.

Finally, liturgical observances such as walking an ecumenical Way of the Cross on Good Friday, holding common baptisms at the Easter Vigil, and hosting joint services of prayer and the word on the Eve of Pentecost are already possible at this current stage in the ecumenical journey. They should be happening in every community and around the world.

It appears that they are not happening at least in part because we as ecumenists are too busy with "merely academic exercises" or attending "endless meetings." I would like to challenge my colleagues in the leadership of the ecumenical movement — ecumenical officers, members of ecumenical commissions, seminary faculties, and participants in bilateral and multilateral dialogues — seriously to consider redirecting some time, energy, and material support to such efforts in "spiritual ecumenism."

No one is suggesting abandoning the dialogical process or settling for some kind of "cooperation" between the churches that has anything less than full communion as its goal. As Metropolitan John Zizioulas of Pergamon stated at the November 2004 gathering in Italy, Christian unity is not just a matter of helping Christians to respect and get along with each other; its aim is to heal the divisions in the body of Christ, the church: "Ecumenism must aim at church unity, not just the unity of Christians."

However, it is also true to say, as did Bishop Stephen Blaire, chairman of the NCCB Committee on Ecumenical and Interreligious Affairs, at the same gathering: "most ecumenism is practical. . . ." The task facing the churches, he said, "is not just a matter of solving theological problems first. You have to have that walking together and praying together, but you also have to look for the truth about the church."

A decade ago, one of my predecessors as ecumenical officer for the Episcopal Church in the United States edited a series of essays entitled *Ecumenism of* the Possible.[11] Some ecumenists are beginning to believe that the movement toward church unity could be greatly enhanced today if at least as much energy as now goes to our current efforts could be redirected toward responding to some of the six challenges so helpfully laid out by Cardinal Kasper. This might become the New Ecumenism of the Possible.

11. William A. Norgren, ed., *Ecumenism of the Possible: Witness, Theology and the Future Church* (Cincinnati: Forward Movement Publications, 1994).

We Ordain Them, They Don't: Must Differences on Gender and Sexuality Prevent Full Communion?

Ellen K. Wondra

For decades, the Anglican Communion and the Episcopal Church have been involved in serious, sustained ecumenical dialogue with many other churches. For much of that time, it has been possible to focus on certain clear theological and ecclesiological issues that have been divisive, the nature of the eucharist and the ordained ministry chief among them. For forty years at least, other issues have arisen that have not been church-dividing in the past but are at least divisive (if not church-dividing) today, whether within the Episcopal Church and the Anglican Communion or as part of the church's ecumenical relations. Chief among these are the ordination of women as well as men, the ordination of non-celibate gays and lesbians, and the blessing of same-sex unions. These issues share widely noted similarities as well as significant differences, to be sure, but what is significant for this essay is that they are all widely seen as divisive.

Whatever the similarities and differences, these issues are to some extent matters of justice, in that they have to do with the ecclesial status of groups that significant portions of the church have come to see as historically marginalized and oppressed on grounds no longer deemed applicable or adequate. These are also properly theological issues in that they have to do with how Christians understand humanity and human dignity, the ministry and teaching of Jesus Christ, and the character of the Christian life. They also have to do with how the church is to discern, embody, and proclaim God's saving work in the world.

And like all theological and ecclesiological issues, they arise not only in theory, but also in the lives of concrete persons. It is particular women and men who seek ordination and blessing. It is particular women and men who, as a corollary, are called upon to exercise unusual patience and forbearance and to sustain certain kinds of suffering. It is particular women and men whose lives are the subject of study, dialogue, and decisions. So it is particular women and men whose vocations and even faith are put to the test through the church's deliberations. In one regard, this is profoundly as it should be: Christianity is first and foremost about the Person of God and about God's incarnate Wisdom and Word Jesus Christ. The saving work of God in Christ through the Holy Spirit takes place primarily in the lives of persons, though aided in some sense by ideas and abstractions. In another regard, however, that some are asked to bear disproportionate burdens of suffering, patience, and forbearance is a further wounding, not just of particular persons but also of the Body of Christ, of which they are members incorporate.

Ecumenical movement is, of necessity, in part a matter of study, dialogue, and negotiation at a fairly generalized and abstract level, and it is at that level that I write this essay. But I do so in full recollection of the persons whose lives will be affected by such high-level considerations.

The stated ecumenical goal of the Anglican Communion and the Episcopal Church is the full, visible unity of the Christian church, understood as a "communion of communions" in which each of the churches offers its gifts and charisms to the others and receives their gifts and charisms in return, as members of the same Body of which Christ is the head. What is envisioned and prayed for is unity in diversity. This goal will require overcoming current divisions, by the grace of God and the work of the Holy Spirit, a difficult, long, and exciting process of investigating together what has been and perhaps still is divisive and even church-dividing, and discerning how these dividing disagreements may be resolved so that they contribute to the unity for which Christ prayed "so that the world may believe" (John 17:20-21).

The ordination of women as well as men by the Episcopal Church stands as a challenge to some of the Episcopal Church's ecumenical dialogues, including dialogues with the Reformed Episcopal Church and the Anglican Province of America, the Orthodox churches, the Roman Catholic Church, and some of the churches of the Union of Utrecht, all of which restrict ordination to men only. At the same time, the Episcopal Church's ordination of women as well as men has contributed positively to growth toward full communion and unity with many Protestant churches and some churches of the Union of Utrecht and has heartened and encouraged some members of the churches that continue to restrict ordination to men only. The ordination of non-celibate gays and lesbians and the blessing of same-sex unions pose even greater challenges, and to a wider array of ecumenical dialogue partners, even as these practices, too, hearten and encourage many within these churches. These practices constitute a new context for the ecumenical efforts of the Episcopal Church and the Anglican Communion.

My purpose in this essay is not to reopen (let alone resolve) the debates surrounding such ordinations and blessings. Rather, I intend to examine the implications of this practice for the Episcopal Church's ecumenical efforts and to indicate where there are possible precedents, avenues, and spaces for continuing dialogue with churches that disagree with either or both practices. In doing so, I will focus on certain facts, that is, things that churches have actually said and done, thereby locating the present dialogue within the "ecumenism of the possible." I will also consider particular, helpful reflections and ideas put forward by contemporary ecumenists.

Given that the desire in these dialogues is for full communion, I would put the current question in this form: *How may we move toward full communion in light of these differences that are for some churches divisive?* In addressing this question, I will consider the following points:

1. Dimensions of full communion as the Episcopal Church currently understands them. Here I will consider various definitions of full communion and the "unity by stages" of which it is a part,[1] identify their common elements, and identify what appear to be the primary sticking points for the present dialogues.
2. Possibilities for living with differences in doctrine and teaching. Here I will explore how the idea of a "hierarchy of truths" assists in assessing the nature and severity of differences that arise between churches.[2]
3. Possibilities in the area of recognition of ministries. Here I will examine a situation in which exceptions to the dimensions of full communion have been made precisely for the sake of that unity of which full communion is a stage.
4. Elements of the process of reception. Here I will focus on certain characteristics that pertain to the relation of ecumenical reception to reception of controversial new (or newly recognized) understandings and practices within at least one of the partner churches.

It is my hope that considering these areas will contribute to identifying or opening up some space in which ecumenical movement may proceed.

---

1. This idea has developed from its origins in the Anglican–Roman Catholic and Anglican-Lutheran dialogues; see below, p. 225.
2. Vatican Council II, *Unitatis Redintegratio (Decree on Ecumenism)* §11 (Vatican City, Rome: The Holy See, 1965); see below, pp. 226-28.

Movement into full communion under any circumstances is a process that entails various stages, decisions, actions, and practices that cannot all be accomplished at once. The various churches have, after all, lived separately for a period of time during which we have undergone continuing and "separated" reception of the Christian faith.[3] That is, each church has continued to receive the one faith that has been handed down, but it has done so apart from other churches and, in certain very significant ways, in contradistinction from them. This means that churches praying and pressing for unity are necessarily engaged in the process of reception, that is, "the acceptance by one church of a theological consensus arrived at with another church, and ultimately the recognition of the other church's faith and ecclesial life as authentically Christian."[4] Reception is properly carried out within the context of looking forward to full communion and the unity for which Christ prayed, "that the world may believe."

Full Communion and Stages of Unity

The goal of "full communion" has been described in a variety of ways by the Episcopal Church and the Anglican Communion. It is worth noting at the outset that how "full communion" is understood ecumenically is based significantly on an analysis of what has marked the full communion among members of the Anglican Communion. In other words, Anglicans have tended to begin with the realities of their relationships with each other in order to understand what it means to be in relationship with other, non-Anglican, churches.

The second Lambeth Conference, in 1878, described "the essential and evident unity in which the Church of England and the Churches in visible communion with her have always been bound together," beginning with a succinct but thorough statement of common faith, doctrine, discipline, and worship. The statement went on to recognize legitimate "variety of custom, discipline, and form of worship" that is the outgrowth of the Church's location in various nations and cultures. Further, the statement commended "principles of Church order," namely mutual respect of "the duly-certified action of every national or particular Church, and of each ecclesiastical Province," respect for the jurisdiction of bishops, and regulation of the functioning of clergy across

---

3. G. R. Evans, "The Genesis of the ARCIC Methodology," in *Communion et Réunion: Mélanges à Jean-Marie Roger Tillard,* ed. G. R. Evans and Michel Gourgues (Leuven: Leuven University Press, 1995), p. 136.

4. T. P. Rausch, "Reception Past and Present," *Theological Studies* 47 (1986): 497.

provincial boundaries.[5] In sum, for the Anglican Communion, full communion is constituted by

1. Mutual recognition of a shared faith that is catholic and apostolic grounded in the scriptures understood as "containing all things necessary to salvation,"
2. Mutual recognition of ministries as belonging to "Apostolic orders,"
3. Legitimate variety (or diversity) of "custom, discipline, and form of worship,"
4. Mutual recognition of jurisdiction, which implies a degree of autonomy within communion,
5. Mutual participation in mission and service,
6. Structures of consultation, communication, and co-ordination to preserve communion as well as for consideration of potentially divisive matters.

On this basis, member churches of the Anglican Communion have entered relationships of full communion with other churches. Three statements can serve as useful examples for this discussion.

The first, the Chicago-Lambeth Quadrilateral, identifies four things "as essential to the restoration of unity among the divided branches of Christendom": the holy scriptures as "the revealed Word of God," the Nicene Creed as "the sufficient statement of the Christian Faith," baptism and eucharist using the words and elements "ordained" by Christ, and the "Historic Episcopate, locally adapted."[6] Again, the constitutive elements are present here, at least by implication. (That is, for the sacraments to be duly administered, the ministers must be recognized as holding apostolic orders. Mission and service are corollaries of all four points. Consultation would seem to be a reasonable inference.)

The second statement, the 1931 Bonn Agreement between the Anglican Communion and the Old Catholic Churches (the churches of the Union of Utrecht), recognizes the "catholicity and independence" of each church and admits each other's members to the sacraments. It goes on to state that "Intercommunion does not require from either Communion the acceptance of all doctrinal opinion, sacramental devotion, or liturgical practice characteristic of the other but implies that each believes the other to hold all the essentials of the Christian faith."[7] Again, mutual recognition of ministries is implicit, here in the

---

5. Communion, pp. 217-18.
6. BCP, pp. 876-77.
7. The Office of Ecumenical and Interfaith Relations, *EIR Handbook* (2002).

second point. The statement presumes, I think, some continuing consultation. It should also be noted that the relationship established by the Bonn Agreement is one of full communion.[8]

The third (and most recent) definition of full communion is found in *Called to Common Mission,* the 1999/2000 agreement between the Episcopal Church and the Evangelical Lutheran Church of America. Each church "recognizes the other as a catholic and apostolic church holding the essentials of the Christian faith."[9] On the basis of this recognition full communion is established, while the churches retain diversity and autonomy. Full communion is defined as "a visible unity in the church's mission to proclaim the Word and administer the Sacraments." This visible unity entails mutual recognition of ministries (§§6-7). Again, the identified elements of full communion are present; they are made explicit throughout *Called to Common Mission.*

These three statements serve in various ways as models and standards for how the Episcopal Church approaches full communion. However, each of the statements contains significant, yet different, nuances. The Bonn Agreement, for example, explicitly recognizes that diversity in "doctrinal opinion, sacramental devotion, or liturgical practice" does not *necessarily* indicate disagreement in "the essentials of the Christian faith." *Called to Common Mission* makes provision for sharing "the Historic Episcopate, locally adapted" rather than requiring it as a condition for entering into full communion. All three statements recognize that there is agreement in faith, but none of them spells out in detail what that faith actually is. What is required, rather, is *recognition* that each holds the one faith without finding an agreed statement of content necessary.[10]

---

8. As the ecumenical movement developed, terms were clarified. The 1958 Lambeth Conference defined *intercommunion* and *full communion* in Resolution 14: "The Conference endorses the paragraph in the Report of the Committee on Church Unity and the Church Universal which refers to the use of the terms 'full communion' and 'intercommunion' and recommends accordingly that where between two Churches not of the same denominational or confessional family, there is unrestricted 'communio in sacris', including mutual recognition and acceptance of ministries, the appropriate term to use is 'full communion' and that where varying degrees of relation other than 'full communion' are established by agreement between two such Churches the appropriate term is 'intercommunion'" (http://www.am-cath.org/DTCHLIT.HTM). The Anglican Communion henceforth saw itself in a relation of full communion with the Old Catholic Churches.

9. CCM §2.

10. This is consistent with the claim of Pope Paul VI at Vatican Council II that there is a "distinction between a doctrinal formulation and the deposit of faith it is designed to express. Only when this truth is appreciated can *particular formulations* be understood as contingent rather than necessary" (Christopher Hill, quoted in Evans, "The Genesis of the ARCIC Methodology," p. 135).

Such recognition is necessary for the *reconciliation* of the churches. Reconciliation requires careful attention to the differences between the churches, wise assessment of whether the differences are simply that — differences — or if they are divisive, or even church-dividing. If differences are not church-dividing — that is, if they do not pertain to "the essentials of the Christian faith" or the order deemed necessary to these essentials — there is room to embrace, accept, understand, or resolve them. There is in all three statements at least a tacit recognition that diversity within the Body of Christ is not only a reality; it is also a necessary and positive contribution both to the fellowship of the church and to the church's mission.

There is also a recognition that communion among the churches will not be achieved all at once. Rather, what is looked for is what has been called "unity by stages." The 1988 Lambeth Conference Section on Ecumenical Relations identified the stages as fellowship in faith and mission, limited sharing of communion, full communion, and full, visible unity.[11] The Conference's Resolution 17 confirmed the idea of stages without committing the conference to the stages as described.[12]

In other words, while there are six elements considered to be constitutive of full communion, they allow considerable nuance. The possibility of nuance as well as the idea of "unity by stages" keeps open certain possibilities on the way to full communion. The current divisive issues pertaining to ordination and blessing seem, on the face of it, to touch on two of the six constitutive elements of full communion: mutual recognition of shared faith and mutual recognition of ministries. But differences in these two areas are not always so divisive as to pose impediments to full communion. In the next section, I will explore some of the ways that apparently divisive differences in faith and doctrine can be approached. Then I will turn to the matter of mutual recognition of ministries.

Differences and Mutual Recognition of Shared Faith

Intra-communion and ecumenical dialogues generally recognize in the earliest stages that there is much more on which churches agree than on which they

11. ACC, *The Truth Shall Make You Free: The Lambeth Conference 1988: The Reports, Resolutions, and Pastoral Letters from the Bishops* (London: Church House Publishing, 1988), p. 143. See also *Steps towards Unity: Documents on Ecumenical Relations Presented to ACC-6* (London: ACC, 1984). The 1988 report used the term *organic unity.* The 1998 Lambeth Conference used the term *full, visible unity.*

12. ACC, *The Truth Shall Make You Free*, pp. 215-16.

disagree. The areas of substantial agreement include what might be called the fundamentals or essentials of the Christian faith, meaning those things that are necessary to salvation, or those things on the basis of which we recognize each other as Christians.[13] Nevertheless, there are significant differences between divided churches, and these differences must be understood and assessed. Are these differences divisive, even church-dividing, or are they a legitimate expression of the diversity and richness of the Christian faith? Are all divisive differences of the same import? That is, which differences *must* be resolved (and how) in order for divided churches to enter more deeply into communion with each other?

To address this issue, Vatican Council II's *Decree on Ecumenism (Unitatis Redintegratio)* uses the idea of a "hierarchy of truths" to understand the interrelationships of the many elements of Christian faith, doctrine, and teaching:

> The way and method in which the Catholic faith is expressed should never become an obstacle to dialogue with our brethren. It is, of course, essential that the doctrine should be clearly presented in its entirety . . . in ecumenical dialogue, Catholic theologians standing fast by the teaching of the Church and investigating the divine mysteries with the separated brethren must proceed with love for the truth, with charity, and with humility. When comparing doctrines with one another, they should remember that in Catholic doctrine there exists a "hierarchy" of truths, since they vary in their relation to the fundamental Christian faith. Thus the way will be opened by which through fraternal rivalry all will be stirred to a deeper understanding and a clearer presentation of the unfathomable riches of Christ.[14]

The idea of a hierarchy of truths is intended to stand between two possibilities relative to the body of Christian doctrine: that all doctrines are of equal importance and therefore equally indispensable, on the one hand, or, on the other, that some doctrine is optional or dispensable because it is of lesser importance.[15] Instead, recognizing a hierarchy of truths makes it possible in theory to

---

13. Yves Congar states that substantial agreement "relates to a basic nucleus without which the message of salvation is not transmitted in its integrity, while accepting that neither doctrinal elaboration nor practice corresponds among the partner churches. The essentials are assured and there is the same shared intention of faith" (Yves Congar, *Diversity and Communion* [London: SCM Press, 1984], p. 140).

14. UR §11.

15. William Henn, "The Hierarchy of Truths and Christian Unity," *Ephemerides Theologicae Lovanienses* 66.1 (1990): 114.

identify the "fundamentals" or "essentials"[16] of Christian faith and then to identify the relationship that various doctrines have to these fundamentals.

But first there must be a differentiation "between propositional truths of doctrine and the realities which are known by means of the propositions."[17] The fundamental reality is the saving work of the Triune God in Christ through the Holy Spirit.[18] This reality is made known by divine self-revelation. The work of doctrine is to flesh out this reality so that it may be understood in faith and so shape the Christian community. The doctrines are not themselves this reality, and all statements of doctrine must be measured against the mysterious reality of the saving work of the Triune God.

Second, various differentiations can be made among doctrines. For example, some doctrines — e.g., the incarnation, the Trinity — may be judged to be of greater centrality than others — e.g., the universal primacy of the Petrine ministry. Or some may be seen to pertain to the goal of Christian faith — "the mystery of the Blessed Trinity, the Incarnation and Redemption, God's love and mercy toward sinful humanity, eternal life in the perfect kingdom of God, and others" — while others may be seen to pertain to the "means of salvation" that will no longer be needed once the goal is reached — "that there are seven sacraments, truths concerning the hierarchical structure of the church, the apostolic succession, and others."[19] Or some doctrines may be understood as implications of other, more central doctrines.[20] Yet other differentiations may be made between the truth of the matter and the way in which it is formulated historically. Some doctrines are formulated at points when the church feels itself under threat (such as the Nicene Creed or the Chalcedonian Formulation), others for less pressing reasons.[21] From another angle, doctrines are formulated in order to convey a truth in a particular socio-cultural context and might be for-

16. This approach is quite familiar in the Anglican tradition. For a summary and cogent critique see S. W. Sykes, "The Fundamentals of Christianity," in *The Study of Anglicanism*, ed. S. W. Sykes and John Booty (London and Philadelphia: SPCK and Fortress Press, 1988), pp. 231-45.

17. Joint Working Group between the Roman Catholic Church and the World Council of Churches, "The Notion of 'Hierarchy of Truths' — An Ecumenical Interpretation" (Vatican City, Rome: PCPCU, 1990), §17.

18. This is itself a propositional truth concerning known reality; there are many ways of putting this truth that can be judged as more or less adequate to that reality.

19. Archbishop Pangrazio, in introducing to the Council the idea of a hierarchy of truths. Quoted in Henn, "The Hierarchy of Truths and Christian Unity," p. 128.

20. For example, the Lutheran-Episcopal Dialogue in the United States was able to agree that the church is an implication of the gospel. This paved the way for CCM and its predecessor, Concordat.

21. Henn, "The Hierarchy of Truths and Christian Unity," p. 124.

mulated otherwise in another time and place. Further, differentiations can be made as to doctrines' or teachings' authoritative status.

Third, the intention and purpose of this approach are not to deem some doctrines or teachings or practices dispensable, but rather to understand and illuminate how they are related to each other and to the "discipline and worship" of the church. This investigation may indicate where particular churches have put more emphasis on one element of fundamental doctrine than have others (e.g., the Lutheran tradition on justification by faith). Such investigations may make it more evident where there is greater unity in faith than was previously recognized. And they may make it more evident what are areas of legitimate, even enriching diversity.

Or these investigations may indicate the possibility of a disagreement more fundamental than was first apparent (e.g., baptismal regeneration).[22] Or they may indicate that churches have reached opposite conclusions but by different paths. Either or both of these may be the case without concluding that a matter directly affects "a common confession concerning the triune God and the incarnate Son." In such cases, careful study and dialogue are necessary to resolve what may even so be very divisive.

The point is this: what is most fundamental is a shared faith. This shared faith will be expressed in differing ways because of context, heritage, and other factors. And it *may* be expressed in differing ways without being divisive as long as each church "believes the other to hold all the *essentials* of the Christian faith."[23] Such difference of expression may even touch on what has been held to be essential formulation of essential doctrine, as with the 1984 agreement between the Roman Catholic Church and the Syrian Orthodox Church (which does not accept the Chalcedonian Formulation). In such a case, it may be recognized that two churches express the same reality in quite different terms.[24] Further, there may be difference of "doctrinal opinion" within this shared faith. And there certainly may be "variety of custom, discipline, and form of worship."[25] Careful analysis of where differences lie and their degree of significance within a shared faith can assist churches in understanding whether their disagreements may or even must continue to divide them.[26]

22. George Vandervelde, "BEM and the 'Hierarchy of Truths': A Vatican Contribution to the Reception Process," *Journal of Ecumenical Studies* 25.1 (1988): 81.

23. "The Bonn Agreement," *EIR Handbook;* italics added.

24. See "Toward a Fully Unanimous Gospel Witness," common declaration by Pope John Paul II and Patriarch Zakka I of Antioch, 23 June 1984 (*Catholic International* 2:14 [15-31 July 1991]: 662-63).

25. Communion, p. 217.

26. William Henn, "The Hierarchy of Truths Twenty Years Later," *Theological Studies* 48

But how does this help in our current context?

It seems evident that none of the churches finds the relation of gender and ordination or sexual orientation and ordination or blessing to be a matter of the essentials of Christian faith on the same level as, for example, "the mystery of the Blessed Trinity, the Incarnation and Redemption, God's love and mercy toward sinful humanity, eternal life in the perfect kingdom of God,"[27] or the divine establishment and providence of the church. Rather, how churches judge these questions pertains to what is implied by these essentials. Even without reviewing all the arguments, it seems reasonable to say that for some, issues of gender and sexuality are primarily a matter of Christian anthropology, that is, of the constitution and character of the human. For others, they are a matter primarily of whether or not there is an operative and "commonly acknowledged criterion for the unity of faith," that is, the authority of scripture.[28] Both the doctrine of humanity and the doctrine of revelation are key elements of the Christian faith, but they are so because they are implied by what is more central or essential. That is, they do not stand as they are on their own, and they cannot stand without other doctrines, such as those of God, Christ, and salvation.

Assuming, then, that differences among the churches are not a matter of "essentials" but of what is implied by essentials, we may move to examine the current issues as they are located within the doctrines of humanity and of revelation. Here, we may conclude that a church may credibly teach that all persons are created in the image of God and that "that which is not assumed is not redeemed" *without* therefore concluding, for example, that women as well as men may be ordained. Or a church may credibly teach that scripture not only contains "all things necessary to salvation" but also provides authoritative ordering of corporate, ecclesial, and personal life *without* therefore concluding that only men may be ordained. Similar arguments in both directions may be made about the ordination of non-celibate homosexuals and the blessing of same-sex unions. (Of course there are other areas of doctrine that pertain to these matters; I have focused on these two as examples only.)

In other words, differences on the relationship of gender or sexual orientation and ordination or blessing may be judged to be differences of "doctrinal opinion" rather than of "shared faith" and therefore not to be of such a level of significance as to prohibit full communion. Further, these doctrinal differences

---

(1987): 439-71; Vandervelde, "BEM and the 'Hierarchy of Truths'"; Joint Working Group, "The Notion of 'Hierarchy of Truths.'"

27. Archbishop Pangrazio, as above. Some individual bishops have stated publicly that they do consider the relationship between ordination and sexual activity to be matters of shared faith, but in expressing their views they do not speak for the whole church.

28. Vandervelde, "BEM and the 'Hierarchy of Truths,'" p. 81.

may be legitimate rather than divisive. Two facts in the debate about the ordination of women would seem to indicate this is so. One is that the Eames Commission appointed by the Archbishop of Canterbury concluded that communion among the Provinces of the Anglican Communion could continue *as communion* even with controversial differences on gender and ordination[29] — as, indeed, it has done. The other is that bishops of churches that disagree on gender and ordination were able to embrace a detailed Declaration of Anglican Essentials and to sign the Atlanta Covenant at the Anglican Congress in December 2002.[30] That is, if gender and ordination is a matter of legitimate difference of "doctrinal opinion," then, in theory at least, mutual recognition of shared faith may be possible.

The factual basis is less clear for making a similar claim about the ordination of non-celibate gays and lesbians and the blessing of same-sex unions. The 2005 *Windsor Report* of the Lambeth Commission on Communion and the subsequent communiqué from the primates' meeting in February 2005 make it clear that issues surrounding sexual orientation are seen throughout the Anglican Communion as more divisive than those involving gender alone. But at this writing, none of the provinces of the Communion has acted officially on the Report's recommendations or on the communiqué, so a full assessment is not yet possible. Nor is it clear why sexual orientation ought to be considered an "essential" matter of doctrine on which churches must agree in order to be in communion. Even so, in reality differences on sexual orientation may indeed turn out to be church-dividing.

However, the current controversies in the area of human sexuality ought not to obscure the fundamental point of this section: it is entirely possible both in theology and in practice for churches to differ in various doctrinal areas while still remaining in or entering formal relationships of full communion. These relationships hinge on a shared faith, but they also recognize that how faith is expressed and enacted may legitimately vary, even at the level of doctrine. What is required is a careful, wise, and well-informed assessment of the roots of and reasons for differences on particular matters seen in relationship to the whole of the faith. Not all matters of doctrine carry the same weight.

29. Church of England, Commission on Communion and Women in the Episcopate (Eames Commission), *The Eames Commission: The Official Reports* (Toronto: Anglican Book Centre, 1994).

30. Jan Nunley, "Anglican Congress Seeks Convergence among Conservatives," Episcopal News Service (http://www.episcopalchurch.org/ens/2002-279.html), and other reports of the same meeting. It should be noted that at least one of the ECUSA bishop signatories himself ordains women; others do not.

Differences and Mutual Recognition of Ministries

Having established that a legitimate range of difference on doctrine may exist within the confession of a shared faith that is a prerequisite to full communion, it is now possible to turn to a key area where that full communion is expressed: mutual recognition of ministries. Disagreements on what constitutes "the same Apostolic orders" of ministry (Lambeth 1879) and whether such Apostolic orders ought properly to be a requirement for full communion have characterized the ecumenical work of the Episcopal Church and the Anglican Communion from the outset. Disagreements have focused on the validity of orders (Anglicans' and others'), the historic episcopate and *episkopē*, the diaconate, marriage and celibacy, the ordination of women as well as men, the ordination of non-celibate gays and lesbians, and no doubt others. These continue to demand careful and charitable discussion, as well as creative if at times controversial resolution. Only some of these disagreements have been barriers to full communion. In some cases, mutual recognition of ministries has been deemed possible without the consequence of full interchangeability of ministries. That is, the legitimacy and efficacy of certain ministries in one church have been recognized by another church without the second church's also according full equivalent status to such ministries.

The ELCA-Episcopal dialogue and agreements provide a helpful and timely example here. In the area of ministry and ordination, the *Concordat of Agreement* and *Called to Common Mission* deal most fully with the historic episcopate. In order to enter into full communion with the ELCA, the Episcopal Church took an unprecedented step in suspending its requirement that interchangeability of ministries occur only on the basis of ordination conferred by a bishop in the historic episcopate. Paragraph 16 of *Called to Common Mission* states in very precise terms that the Episcopal Church will "in this case only" suspend a particular part of the preface to the Ordinal in order "to permit the full interchangeability and reciprocity of all its pastors as priests or presbyters within The Episcopal Church, without any further ordination or re-ordination or supplemental ordination whatsoever, subject always to canonically or constitutionally approved invitation." This suspension was done "precisely in order to secure the future implementation of the ordinal's same principle in the sharing of ordained ministries. It is for this reason that The Episcopal Church can feel confident in taking this unprecedented step with regard to the Evangelical Lutheran Church in America."[31]

This proposal was controversial in both churches (albeit for quite differ-

31. CCM §16.

ent reasons), and it remains to be seen what the effect will be on the Episcopal Church's dialogues with other churches, especially the Roman Catholic and Orthodox Churches. The provision also has practical effects as the relationship of full communion unfolds: bishops of the ELCA who are not ordained in historic succession may not confirm or ordain in the Episcopal Church.[32] In other words, ELCA bishops' orders are not at this time fully interchangeable into the Episcopal Church.

Nevertheless, this provision recognizes that full communion becomes possible only with sustained exercise of Christian love toward an other from whom one has been separated. Such love entails generosity, hospitality, and a consistent commitment to the unity of the church. It also entails a high degree of flexibility even in areas considered to be in some sense essential to church unity, for the sake of that same unity. And it indicates that a certain theological and ethical stance is part of our obedience to the gospel: that the truth is to be spoken in love, or, as Henry Chadwick has put it, that we are "to allow charity to prevail over knowledge, which puffs up."[33] Further, the unity of the church for which Christ prayed is given a higher priority than church order, presumably because church order exists in service to fidelity and mission.

Not so well known, or so widely controversial, are *Called to Common Mission*'s provisions regarding the diaconate, an ordained ministry in the Episcopal Church but not in the ELCA. Paragraph 9 states that "Both churches acknowledge that the diaconate, including its place within the threefold ministerial office and its relationship with all other ministries, is in need of continuing exploration, renewal, and reform, which they pledge themselves to undertake in consultation with one another." At the same time, the Episcopal Church agrees that "Some functions of ordained deacons in The Episcopal Church and consecrated diaconal ministers and deaconesses in the Evangelical Lutheran Church in America can be shared insofar as they are called to be agents of the church in meeting needs, hopes, and concerns within church and society."[34] The ELCA recognizes that deacons in the Episcopal Church are ordained in that church[35] *without also* recognizing them as ordained ministers in the ELCA. Similarly, the Episcopal Church does not consider ELCA deacons and deaconesses to be ordained ministers in the Epis-

---

32. Clarified at the meeting of the Episcopal Church's Standing Commission on Ecumenical Relations, March 2003.

33. Henry Chadwick, "Anglican Ecclesiology and Its Challenges," in *Ecumenism of the Possible: Witness, Theology, and the Future Church*, ed. W. A. Norgren (Cincinnati: Forward Movement Publications, 1994), p. 8.

34. CCM §8.

35. CCM §§14, 21.

copal Church.[36] Consequently, the "orderly exchange" of ministries applies only to pastors and priests.[37]

Clearly, here is another major exception to the principle of interchangeability of ministries (and one arguably of greater practical consequence than the exception relative to bishops). The reservation in *Called to Common Mission* regarding the diaconate indicates that there still remain a significant theological question and ecclesial disparity in two areas. One of these is the threefold ordained ministry itself, both in regard to the diaconate and in regard to the theology of the other two orders. The second is the theology of ministry overall as it necessarily involves baptismal ministry as distinguishable but not separable from ordained ministry.

This disparity is not a minor matter: mutual interchangeability of ministries is generally held to be necessary to full communion. Interchangeability is based on substantial agreement on the theology and exercise of ministry. Yet in this case there is not *entire* agreement, nor is there *fully mutual* interchangeability. *Called to Common Mission* itself indicates that this situation exists: "Both churches acknowledge that the diaconate, including its place within the threefold ministerial office and its relationship with all other ministries, is in need of continuing exploration, renewal, and reform." In other words, because neither church has a settled or consistent understanding of diaconal ministry, neither is in a position, either theologically or ethically, to judge the other's understanding (or lack thereof). Furthermore, the two churches formally "pledge themselves to undertake in consultation with one another" further study of the diaconate.[38] There is, I suggest, a certain prioritizing of principles here: certainly, that of seeking and speaking the truth in love, but also, again, the priority of unity and mission over elements of the order that exists to serve them.

I give these two examples — and there are others[39] — because they pertain to a relationship that more generally coheres with the elements of full commu-

---

36. The provisions in the original Concordat were quite different but were changed in CCM in order to respond to certain Lutheran concerns.

37. See "The Orderly Exchange of Pastors and Priests under Called to Common Mission," http://arc.episcopalchurch.org/ministry/oepp/oepp.pdf.

38. A task force made up of representatives from ECUSA and ELCA ecumenical and ministry offices is meeting regularly to explore what shared diaconal ministry might entail.

39. Not exactly parallel but of significance are the provisions made in the Canons of the Episcopal Church for receiving ministers of other churches into the ministry of the Episcopal Church (The General Convention, *Constitution and Canons . . . of the Episcopal Church* [New York: Church Publishing Group, 2003], title III, canons 10-12). It should be noted that the two examples given in this essay do not pertain directly to gender.

nion identified above, and they show how careful modification of these elements can, in fact, further full communion. In addition, neither of these two examples is free of controversy, either within the two churches or between them, and that fact entails further consultation and continued exercise of the virtues of Christian love. At the same time, the two churches continue to live into their relationship of full communion, and it is at least a credible claim that the way these controversies are being handled may contribute to that relationship.[40]

In relation to the current discussion, my principal point is that, while mutual recognition and interchangeability of ministries is a central principle and goal of full communion, the practice of interchangeability admits to exceptions and variations *insofar as* they demonstrably serve this goal. This is a major contribution of *Called to Common Mission* to all Anglican ecumenical efforts. Further, exceptions and variations are possible when they touch upon things upon which neither church has a settled position (as with the diaconate, in this instance). These exceptions instantiate the ecumenical principle that one church may not require from another what it does not require from itself.[41]

This principle is directly relevant to present ecumenical discussions in that the practice of interchangeability of ministries is not universal throughout the Anglican Communion, specifically between those provinces that ordain women as well as men and those that ordain men only. Yet full communion still exists between these provinces. The situation is not ideal, of course, and a great deal of attention has been given to what it means and how it should be handled.[42] But it is recognized as a situation that legitimately accompanies the church's reception of a new aspect of its life.

---

40. Compare §49 of the report from the Section on Ecumenical Relations of the 1988 Lambeth Conference: "What is of ultimate Christian significance in the Anglican Communion is not that, where there is conflict, decisions are made in a particular way, but that they are made in the spirit of the prayer of Christ in John's Gospel (John 17), with a fearless regard for truth and holiness in Christ, and with a Christ-like, self-sacrificing, concern for the unity of all Christians in one God, and for their *visible* unity, so that the world might believe. The picture of a bitter and bickering Church, at odds with itself, contradicts and destroys the Gospel. However, conflict is bound to come, and the picture of a Church living with conflict in a Christ-like way, painfully struggling to find the truth in Christ, can itself be a witness to the Gospel of reconciliation" (*The Truth Shall Make You Free*, p. 135).

41. The roots of this principle lie in Acts 15:28: "For it has seemed good to the Holy Spirit and to us to impose on you no further burden than these essentials" (NRSV; Gk. ἐπάναγκες). The principle is stated in Vatican II's Decree on Ecumenism, *Unitatis Redintegratio* 18: "in order to restore communion and unity or preserve them, one must 'impose no burden beyond what is indispensable [*necessaria*].'"

42. See especially the reports of the Eames Commission. See also Patricia Wilson-Kastner, *et al.*, "A Theological Response to the 'Eames Report,'" ATR 74 (1992): 6-17.

Differences and Reception

As various ecumenical dialogues have proceeded from the study of differences to the identification of commonalities, and to convergence on and resolution of some differences, attention has been focused on how the various churches may receive these ecumenical advances and make them their own, and on what grounds. Reception is a lengthy and complicated process not given to easy formulation, but a brief discussion of it will, I think, aid these considerations.

In the ecumenical context, according to Henry Chadwick, "Reception . . . concerns the recognition by believers, who aspire only to obey the Gospel, of other believers with other customs who also aspire to obey."[43] The first thing to note is that reception does not concern only doctrinal agreements, as important as they are. More profoundly, ecumenical reception springs from our own reception of the Christian faith as a divine gift.[44] The grace of God and the work of the Holy Spirit enable believers to recognize the truth of the Christian faith and to respond to it in and through repentance, conversion, and formation in Christian belief and life, for the sake of service and witness. In this way, believers receive their faith. Through teaching and witness in the power of the Spirit, they also "hand on" the faith to others, as Saint Paul makes clear (esp. 1 Cor. 15:1, Gal. 1:9-12). This same process of reception is entailed when the people of God receive "particular ecclesiastical or conciliar decisions" and teachings within the church.[45] And the same process takes place as churches receive each other in a renewed and strengthened relationship of unity. Finally, this movement of gift and reception is present as the church presents itself to the world to be received, that is, in evangelism and mission.[46]

In other words, reception involves the whole of the Christian life. Ecumenical reception, as part of that life, entails more than agreement in doctrine; it also entails change of ecclesial life, which has developed through "separated reception." When two churches recognize in each other a shared faith, each must re-receive its own tradition (now cast in a different light by this new relationship of greater unity), *and* it must re-receive the apostolic faith (now seen

---

43. Chadwick, "Anglican Ecclesiology," p. 95. Cf. the definition by Thomas P. Rausch, S.J.: "the concept refers to the acceptance by one church of a theological consensus arrived at with another church, and ultimately the recognition of the other church's faith and ecclesial life as authentically Christian" (Rausch, "Reception Past and Present," p. 497).

44. J. D. Zizioulas, "The Theological Problem of 'Reception,'" *One in Christ* 21.3 (1985): 189.

45. Rausch, "Reception Past and Present," p. 497.

46. Zizioulas, "The Theological Problem," p. 189.

in a different, fuller way because of the new relationship) as it looks forward to full communion.[47] Both of these will require each church to make adjustments in its teachings and practices. In other words, reception has practical as well as theological implications, such as those elements involved in relationships of full communion.

The second thing to note is that reception is a process that takes place over time and that necessarily involves the whole people of God, not just duly constituted authorities. And it is to be expected that there will be disagreement and controversy. (The reception of the Council of Nicaea is a classic example.) A new relationship with another church (or a teaching, or a practice) must be carefully tested for its consonance with the apostolic faith and with the witness and service of the church in the world. When such a matter has been officially sanctioned, and when it has been "recognised by the faithful in the local churches as expressing the truth of the gospel,"[48] it may be said to have been received.

However, as Anglicans have long recognized, not everything that is taught or done *does* express the truth of the gospel; the church may err, even in matters of faith.[49] To say that a new relationship, a teaching, or a practice is "in the process of reception" is *not* to say that it will be received and become part of the *consensus fidelium*. Rather, its consonance with the apostolic faith is being discerned, and the outcome of that discernment is not yet known.

For example, the new relationship of full communion between the Episcopal Church and the ELCA is in the process of reception. Both churches have approved *Called to Common Mission;* various ministries, missions, and other activities have been undertaken jointly, and controversy continues within and between both churches. While there are certainly many signs that this new relationship is thriving, it is premature to conclude that it will be enduring. In other words, it is still being received.

Third, then, the primary arena in which reception takes place is not the necessary but somewhat out-of-the-ordinary context of official studies and dialogues. Rather, it is in and through the daily carrying on of worship, witness, and service by the churches. The fact that reception occurs in the course of ordinary life poses certain challenges, such as how churches relate to each other, how they make decisions that may affect their envisioned life together, and how they move toward unity on multiple fronts. It is unrealistic to expect churches

47. Zizioulas, "The Theological Problem," p. 193.

48. Inter-Anglican Theology and Doctrine Commission, *The Virginia Report,* in Lambeth Conference, *The Official Report of the Lambeth Conference 1998: July 18–August 9, 1998* (Harrisburg: Morehouse Publishing, 1999), p. 54.

49. The Articles of Religion, Article 19, BCP, p. 897.

to remain static until agreement on a particular matter of difference or controversy is resolved. And this is as it should be: the Christian faith, after all, is not a matter of propositions with which believers agree to greater and lesser degrees. It is a matter of how believers live their lives with each other in the midst of the changes and chances of human existence, and how that living together may itself be a vehicle for fidelity.

Finally, reception has an eschatological character: it is not yet clear what is coming into being, nor how the purposes of God will be fulfilled, either in history or beyond it. We are, therefore, called to live with uncertainty, controversy, and even the possibility of error. We are also called to live in trust and hope in the God who is making all things new, and whose Spirit will lead us into all truth.

It is widely recognized that a process of reception is taking place in regard to the relation of gender and ordination. Various assessments may be made of that process, but they must recognize that any judgment at this point is strictly provisional, as uncomfortable as such a recognition may be.[50] Nor is it entirely clear what are the criteria on the basis of which assessments may legitimately be made. Various recommendations have been made in the different churches and in differing ecumenical dialogues as to how to proceed with matters of unity in the midst of reception of what is a controversial matter. For example, within the Anglican Communion, the Eames Commission issued its first report in 1989, including certain recommended pastoral guidelines that were endorsed by the Anglican primates at their meeting in Cyprus in April-May 1989.[51] The Anglican-Orthodox Dialogue meeting in Dublin in 1984 noted that "the aim of our Dialogue is that we may eventually be visibly united in one Church. We offer this Report in the conviction that although this goal may presently seem to be far from being achieved, it is nevertheless one towards which God the Holy Spirit is insistently beckoning us."[52] It went on to conclude:

> We are not required to solve outstanding problems (such as the ordination of women) as a condition of continuing the dialogue. Nor are we trying to produce too quickly materials that might be used as the basis for early decisions to enter a new stage of relationships between our Churches. Instead,

---

50. *The Windsor Report* seems to suggest that the ordination of women as well as men *has* been received and so can serve as model for other controversial matters. However, many question the Lambeth Commission's assessment. See my address, "'The Highest Degree of Communion Possible': Initial Reflections on the Windsor Report 2004," ATR 87 (2005): 193-206.

51. See Eames Commission, pp. 99-102, for the primates' action.

52. Anglican-Orthodox Joint Dialogue Commission, *The Dublin Agreed Statement* (Crestwood, NY: St. Vladimir's Seminary Press, 1984), Preface, §1.

the Commission is more free to explore together and understand better the faith we hold and the ways in which we express it.[53]

Internationally and in the United States and Canada the Anglican–Roman Catholic dialogues have continued, with ARCIC issuing its third agreed statement on authority, *The Gift of Authority,* in 1998 and its agreed statement *Mary: Grace and Hope in Christ* in 2005.[54] In other words, the fact of this significant controversy has not halted ecumenical progress.

Until full visible unity is reached, all ecumenical relations are in the process of reception. While this is the case, each church must struggle with the extent to which its traditions and identity have been formed through "separated reception" over against each other. Repentance, conversion, and re-reception of the apostolic faith are no doubt needed — and they are not easy. Within this larger framework, we are also in a process of reception relative to the relation of gender and ordination, a process entailing the same struggles. Where these processes may take us, we cannot know at this time. "It does not yet appear what we shall be, but we know that when he appears we shall be like him, for we shall see him as he is" (1 John 3:2). In the meantime, it is within our ability to continue to search for unity with each other.

Conclusion

There is no question that today many churches desire to obey Christ's wish "that they may all be one, . . . so that the world may believe" (John 17:21). The Episcopal Church and the Anglican Communion have made it clear again and again that they are in this number, despite internal differences and divisions on gender and ordination, and even, perhaps, on sexual orientation and manner of life. The challenge before all involved is how we may most faithfully and effectively pursue this goal. In this paper I have examined some resources that I believe may assist the Episcopal Church in its ongoing movement toward communion with all Christians.

As I indicated at the outset, the Episcopal Church's stated goal of full communion has six characteristic elements,[55] two of which — mutual recogni-

---

53. *The Dublin Agreed Statement,* Conclusion, §4.

54. *Gift; Mary: Grace and Hope in Christ* (Harrisburg, PA: Morehouse Publishing, 2005).

55. Mutual recognition of shared catholic and apostolic faith, mutual recognition of apostolic ministries, legitimate diversity of "custom, discipline, and form of worship," mutual recognition of jurisdiction, mutual participation in mission and service, and structures of consultation, communication, and co-ordination.

tion of shared faith and mutual recognition of ministries — are apparently affected by differences on the ordination of women as well as men, and on the ordination of non-celibate homosexuals and the blessing of same sex unions. I have argued in this essay that the actual ecumenical practices of the Episcopal Church and the Anglican Communion indicate that these differences need not be seen as insurmountable even if there is no apparent prospect for their resolution.

On the face of it, differences on gender and ordination may appear to be a barrier to mutual recognition of a shared faith. However, examining this matter in light of the idea of a "hierarchy of truths," or of fundamentals or essentials, indicates that this is not a matter of essentials. Rather, it is a matter of the interpretation of doctrines that are themselves implied by what is essential. In other words, the relation of gender and ordination may be and has been judged to be a matter of "doctrinal opinion" rather than "shared faith." The case is both less clear and more hotly contested in relation to issues surrounding sexual orientation.

On the face of it, differences on gender and ordination may appear to be a barrier to mutual recognition of ministries. However, exceptions to mutual recognition and full interchangeability of ministries have been made for the sake of living into full communion. Further, such exceptions may be made when none of the churches has a settled position on the matter at hand.

Further, all churches are in a continuing process of reception of the apostolic faith, and reception of each other as churches is part of this process. Reception requires not only agreement but also change, and it must take place in the ongoing ordinary life of the church. Certain virtues — charity, patience, perseverance, and mutual encouragement — are required, as well as certain skills.

Throughout this paper, I have focused on possibilities made available by various practices. In conclusion, I also want to sound two notes of caution. First: It has been wisely said that "more theological consensus is needed to restore unity than to preserve unity."[56] As it progresses, every ecumenical dialogue is likely to uncover further, perhaps even more challenging, matters on which theological consensus is necessary. It is also the case that restoring unity faces particular challenges when churches have split from each other (as is the case here): there are residual wounds and resentments that must be addressed, as well as "separated reception," and it may be harder to develop and use the habits and dispositions that are required for ecumenical convergence.

---

56. Anton Houtepen, "Reception, Tradition, Communion," in Max Thurian, *Ecumenical Perspectives*, p. 148; quoted in Rausch, "Reception Past and Present," p. 500.

Second: moving toward full communion will probably entail more suffering by some than by others. In the two instances considered here, the ordination of women, and the ordination of non-celibate gays and lesbians and the blessing of same-sex unions, that suffering is borne primarily by persons who already bear the burden of overcoming the church's historical practices of exclusion and limitation. This reality is a matter of justice that cannot be ignored at any stage if genuine communion is to be attained. And it is a matter that calls not for the church's defensiveness but for its strongest compassion and wisest pastoral care. It must also be said that those who object strongly to new practices also stand to suffer in very real material as well as spiritual ways: acting on conscience may in fact mean sacrificing financial security in order to live faithfully. Again, the church is obligated by its faith to address and remedy such suffering as much as it is able to do.

A common goal for divided Christians is the unity for which Christ prayed "so that the world may believe." It is imperative that we pursue that goal, trusting in the grace of God and the power of the Holy Spirit. The realities of controversy and division on matters of gender and sexuality, while certainly serious, must not and need not be used as an excuse to abandon or slow our divinely empowered movement toward that goal.

A Ministry of a Universal Primate:
An Ecumenical Question

Mary Tanner

In 1982 at the plenary meeting of the Faith and Order Commission of the World Council of Churches in Lima, Peru, Professor J. Robert Wright, in whose honor this essay is written, made a lasting impression on me. The Commission was preparing the final revision of the document *Baptism, Eucharist and Ministry* (BEM), a report that was to prove the century's most important document of ecumenical convergence. The text had already gone through extensive discussion in the member churches, and revisions had been made in the light of responses received.[1] At the meeting in Lima more than 190 further suggestions were considered. Among those suggestions was one from Professor Wright inviting the Commission to consider whether the text ought not to include something on the matter of a ministry of a universal primate, "the Petrine ministry."[2]

Even to those most sympathetic to the idea this was a daring suggestion in the multilateral context of the World Council, particularly coming at such a late moment in the development of the document. There was, however, a considerable logic to this request. After all BEM already included a strong statement on the ministry of oversight *(episkopē)* exercised with "personal, collegial and communal" dimensions, implying that these were to be exercised at the different levels of the life of the church.[3] Taken to its logical conclusion this state-

---

1. *One Baptism, One Eucharist and a Mutually Recognised Ministry,* The Accra Text, Faith and Order Paper 73 (Geneva: WCC Publications, 1975).

2. *Towards Visible Unity: Commission on Faith and Order, Lima, 1982,* vol. 1: *Minutes and Addresses,* ed. Michael Kinnamon, Faith and Order Paper 112 (Geneva: WCC Publications, 1982), p. 82.

3. BEM, Ministry §§26, 27.

ment might be thought to point in the direction of a personal ministry of *episkopē* at a world level and to support the suggestion being made by Professor Wright.

In response to Professor Wright's suggestion, the Chairman of the Revision Committee, Professor Geoffrey Wainwright, commented that only one person had raised the matter, a matter however of such significance that the Commission itself must decide whether to take it up. The Moderator, Professor John Deschner, put the matter to the Commission. The minutes of the meeting record:

> While recognizing the vital importance of the issue of the Petrine ministry and the excellent work done on this issue in various bilateral conversations, the prevailing argument was that the subject had not previously been on the Faith and Order agenda and was of such significance that no hasty attempt should be made to incorporate a reference to the issue in the present document. The Moderator asked the editorial committee to reflect on the issue and possibly to propose a plan for future study.[4]

When at the end of the meeting the Commission voted that the revised text, *Baptism, Eucharist and Ministry,* was at "such a stage of maturity that it is now ready for transmission to the churches," there was no section on a ministry of universal primacy.[5] Nevertheless, the Moderator had signalled the intention of the Commission to study the matter in its future program. It was clear that Professor Wright, with characteristic insight, had identified a crucial issue for the ecumenical agenda in the future, an issue that would not go away.

Looking back at the Lima meeting, it is not surprising that the issue of universal primacy was raised. Not only was there a certain internal logic in the Lima Text that led in that direction, but some bilateral theological conversations were already turning attention to this question in their work, and not only those conversations that included a Roman Catholic partner. The presence after Vatican II of the Roman Catholic Church around the table made it essential that ecumenical conversations should include a study of the ministry of universal primacy. For the Roman Catholic Church communion with the bishop of Rome is one of the visible signs and bonds of communion. Visible unity entails a single ministry in communion with the see of Rome and its bishop. Moreover, Pope Paul VI had termed the papacy "the most serious obstacle on the path of ecumenism."[6] And

---

4. *Towards Visible Unity* §1.82.
5. *Towards Visible Unity* §1.83.
6. *Confessions in Dialogue: A Survey of Bilateral Conversations among World Confessional*

in 1974 the editors of *Confessions in Dialogue,* Nils Ehrenström and Günther Gassmann, had written this about the papacy:

> Several among the bilaterals are probing fresh approaches to this obstacle, attempting a critical-constructive reformulation of the problem in the wider setting of ecumenical understandings of the Church and its apostolic ministry. The prime question is no longer whether Christ instituted the papal office, but rather whether the worldwide Church in this global age does not need a visible symbol and servant of its universality, and, if so, whether a renewed papacy would be the appropriate embodiment of this universal ministry.[7]

Universal Primacy in Ecumenical Conversations before 1982

It was not simply the internal logic of the Lima Text that led a perceptive ecumenist like Professor Wright to ask the question he did, but also an acquaintance with the subject matter of the international bilateral dialogues of the decade before the Lima meeting. In 1976 the Anglican-Orthodox conversations, while not exploring the issue of universal primacy itself, had touched on the subject of infallibility. In a section on the authority of councils the report suggested that the two churches agreed that "infallibility is not the property of any particular institution or person in the Church."[8] It went on to remark that further work was needed on *infallible* and *indefectible* because of the way in which papal authority had previously been exercised.

The following year the Reformed–Roman Catholic dialogue hinted in a similar way at the agenda of the ministry of primacy in its treatment of the teaching authority of the church in its report, "The Presence of Christ in Church and World."[9] As in the Anglican-Orthodox report, "The Presence of Christ" raised the question of the ministry of the bishop of Rome in relation to the matter of infallibility, honestly documenting the difference between the Roman Catholic and the Reformed view of infallibility. Roman Catholics pointed out that in the Roman Catholic view infallibility belongs to the church. How-

---

Families, 1959-1974, ed. Nils Ehrenström and Günther Gassmann, 3rd ed., Faith and Order Paper 74 (Geneva: WCC Publications, 1975), p. 189.

7. *Confessions in Dialogue,* p. 189.

8. "Anglican-Orthodox Conversations, 'Moscow Statement 1976,'" in Growth I, pp. 41-49, here pp. 43-44.

9. "The Presence of Christ in Church and World" §§39-42, in Growth I, pp. 434-63, here pp. 443-44.

ever, they acknowledged that all too often infallibility has been attributed solely to the office of the pope. To clarify their position the Roman Catholic members quoted from *Lumen Gentium,* the document of Vatican II:

> The bishops taken in isolation do not enjoy the prerogative of infallibility; yet, even though dispersed throughout the world and conserving the bond and communion between them and with the successor of Peter, when in their authentic teaching concerning questions of faith and morals they declare with full agreement that it is necessary to support unhesitatingly such and such a point of doctrine, they then announce infallibly the teaching of Christ. This is all the more evident when, assembled in an ecumenical council, they teach and decide on questions of faith and morals for the whole Church; and their definitions must be adhered to in the obedience of faith (*Lumen Gentium*, 25).[10]

The Reformed, on the other hand, rejected any infallibility "which is accorded to men." Moreover, they said, "any claim to infallibility in the modern world represents an obstacle to the credibility of the proclamation." In the Reformed tradition, they explained, this rejection of infallibility does not detract from the weight given to the ancient ecumenical councils. What is infallible is "God's fidelity to his covenant, whereby he corrects and preserves his Church by the Spirit until the consummation of his reign."[11]

So in both of these bilateral conversations from the mid-seventies, the question of the ministry of the bishop of Rome surfaced within a more general discussion of the authority of the church. The reports reveal a gulf between the Roman Catholic position and that of the other three churches in the conversations, namely Orthodox, Anglican, and Reformed. What also comes across in these reports is the clarification that Roman Catholics hold the whole church to be infallible rather than the isolated ministry of the bishop of Rome.

Three Significant Conversations

Before the Lima meeting the three conversations that had dealt in greatest depth with the ministry of the bishop of Rome were those of the Roman Catholic Church with, respectively, Lutherans, Methodists, and Anglicans. In 1972 the Lutheran–Roman Catholic "Malta Report" included a section on "the question

10. "The Presence of Christ" §41, p. 443.
11. "The Presence of Christ" §42, pp. 443, 444.

of papal primacy," acknowledging that it was "a special problem for the relationship between Lutherans and Catholics." The Roman Catholic side said some important things about papal primacy — that the beginning of the doctrine was in the special position of Peter in the biblical witness, that a "new interpretive framework" was given by Vatican II's "doctrine of episcopal collegiality," that the primacy of jurisdiction was to be understood as a ministry of service and a bond of unity, that the office of papacy entailed "caring for legitimate diversity," and that the concrete shape of the office might vary "with changing historical circumstances."[12]

Lutherans in their conversations with Roman Catholics said similarly important things, including "that no local church should exist in isolation" and that they found the lack of a ministerial service of communion to be a problem. Then came a remarkable statement from the Lutheran participants: "The office of the papacy as a visible sign of the unity of the churches was therefore not excluded insofar as it is subordinated to the primacy of the gospel by theological reinterpretation and practical restructuring."[13] The question that remained controversial was:

> whether the primacy of the pope is necessary for the church, or whether it represents only a fundamentally possible function. It was nevertheless agreed that the question of altar fellowship and of a mutual recognition of ministerial offices should not be unconditionally dependent on a consensus on the question of primacy.[14]

In 1980 the Lutheran–Roman Catholic report "All Under One Christ" listed, as "honesty . . . compels," unresolved problems, including the primacy of jurisdiction and the infallibility of the Pope, promulgated in 1870.[15] In the 1981 report "The Ministry in the Church," Lutherans and Roman Catholics devoted more attention to the subject of the ministry of primacy.[16] In a section entitled "The Episcopal Ministry and Service for the Universal Unity of the Church," the subject was once more said to be a "problem" needing further and more detailed treatment.[17] The report again set out the Roman Catholic and Lutheran posi-

---

12. "Report of the Joint Lutheran–Roman Catholic Study Commission on 'The Gospel and the Church,' 1972 ('Malta Report')" [hereafter "Malta Report"] §66, in Growth I, pp. 168-89, here p. 184.

13. "Malta Report" §66, p. 184.

14. "Malta Report" §67, p. 184.

15. "All Under One Christ, 1980" §23, in Growth I, pp. 241-47, here p. 245.

16. "The Ministry in the Church, 1981," in Growth I, pp. 248-75.

17. "The Ministry in the Church" §3.5, pp. 269-71.

tions. The Roman Catholic position begins, it explained, with the ministry of the bishop in the local church and the collegiality of bishops gathered together. The communion between the bishops and, with them and through them, the communion of the local churches "has its point of reference in communion with the Church of Rome and the Bishop of Rome as holder of the chair of Peter," who presides over the *communio*. The report further clarified that the bishop of Rome has "the supreme pastoral office in the Church." His ministry "is to serve the unity of the universal church and legitimate diversity in the church," and "His ministry of unity is 'the perpetual and visible source and foundation of the unity of the bishops and of the multitude of the faithful.'"[18]

The report goes on to describe the pope's special ministry in relation to the unity of the faith: "through the power of the Holy Spirit he is preserved from error in teaching when he solemnly declares the faith of the church (infallibility)."[19] A lengthy paragraph follows in which the Roman Catholic members explain the different ways in which through two millennia the ministry of unity has been understood. It points out that Vatican I highlighted the service to unity with its two dogmas of papal jurisdiction and infallibility. However, the report openly acknowledges that Vatican I did not make clear the degree to which this service is embedded in the total life of the church.

"The Ministry in the Church" explains that Vatican II had the responsibility not only to confirm the teaching of Vatican I but also to anchor it in "an all-embracing ecclesial context." The paragraph concludes with a healing sentence:

> Aware as the Catholic church is that the papacy remains to this day for many Christians one of the greatest obstacles on the road to unity of the churches, it nevertheless hopes that as it is structurally renewed in the light of Holy Scripture and the tradition, it may more and more in the future provide an important service to unity.[20]

Lutherans also explained in "The Ministry in the Church" that they had become "aware of the interrelationship of the individual local and regional churches." With this awareness came the question of what "visible forms of church fellowship . . . represent a world-wide bond of faith." The model of conciliar fellowship was the model they most favored, for it allowed churches to be "part of a . . . binding fellowship without having to give up their legitimate

18. "The Ministry in the Church" §69, p. 269, citing LG §23.
19. "The Ministry in the Church" §70, pp. 269-70.
20. "The Ministry in the Church" §71, p. 270.

individual characteristics."[21] Lutherans explained that the Reformers had come to believe that "the papacy suppressed the gospel and was to this extent an obstacle to true Christian unity," a view confirmed in their view by the doctrinal decisions of Vatican I. A remarkable statement follows:

> Lutheran theologians today are among those who look not only to a future council or to the responsibility of theology, but also to a special Petrine office, when it is a question of service to the unity of the church at the universal level. . . .

While admitting that the question of how such a ministry could be exercised was still an issue, they continued:

> But in various dialogues, the *possibility* begins to emerge that the Petrine office of the Bishop of Rome also need not be excluded by Lutherans as a visible sign of the unity of the church as a whole, "insofar as [this office] is subordinated to the primacy of the gospel by theological reinterpretation and practical restructuring."[22]

The report is here simply re-affirming the words of the earlier "Malta Report." This is ecumenical theology at its best, when both sides of the conversation are able to think self-critically, to think daring new thoughts, and to record them openly and honestly. Roman Catholics admitted to the need for the renewal and restructuring of the papal office, and Lutherans admitted that in certain circumstances the office of the bishop of Rome, as a visible sign of unity, might be acceptable. No doubt this report had been not a little influenced by the important work on papal primacy done by the regional bilateral conversation between Roman Catholics and Lutherans in the United States, published in 1980.[23]

It is perhaps surprising for some to discover that one of the earliest conversations to reflect on the Petrine ministry was that between the Roman Catholic Church and the Methodists. Only the year before the meeting in Lima this dialogue published the "Honolulu Report."[24] Once more the subject arose in a

---

21. "The Ministry in the Church" §72, p. 270.

22. "The Ministry in the Church" §73 (brackets in document), citing LG 22, p. 271.

23. *Papal Primacy and the Universal Church*, ed. Paul C. Empie and T. Austin Murphy (Minneapolis: Augsburg Publishing House, 1974); *Teaching Authority and Infallibility in the Church*, ed. Paul C. Empie, T. Austin Murphy, and Joseph A. Burgess (Minneapolis: Augsburg Publishing House, 1980).

24. "Honolulu Report, 1981," in Growth I, pp. 367-87.

section on authority in the church. The report noted that, as in other conversations, "special difficulties" persisted "in the matter of papal claims and the character of dogmatic definitions." But even here the situation was not seen as incapable of change:

> we believe that emotions surrounding such relatively modern terms as infallibility and irreformability can be diminished if they are looked at in the light of our shared doctrine concerning the Holy Spirit. The papal authority, no less than any other within the Church, is a manifestation of the continuing presence of the Spirit of Love in the Church or it is nothing. . . . It was declared at Vatican I to be "for the building up and not the casting down on [sic] the church" — whether of the local Church or the communion of local Churches.[25]

The report went on to acknowledge that this primary aspect of the papal ministry was often missed because of the emotions aroused by such terms as *infallibility* and *universal and immediate jurisdiction*. It pointed out that these were terms that belonged to the thinking of the 1870s and had to be understood in light of the debates of that time. As had the Lutheran dialogue, the dialogue partners thought that Vatican II had adjusted some of the imbalance of Vatican I. The terms *infallibility* and *immediate jurisdiction* had to be understood, they said, not as glorifying a single office but as related to "the total responsibility of the teaching and disciplinary office in the Church."[26]

But for all the re-thinking of the terms in a wider context, the report said honestly that it was unlikely that Methodists would in the foreseeable future feel comfortable with them. Then came a very important and promising statement:

> Methodist awareness of the papacy has enlarged and greatly altered in recent times, and the general idea of a universal service of unity within the Church, a primacy of charity mirroring the presence and work in the Church of the Spirit who is love, may well be a basis for increased understanding and convergence.[27]

The reports from the conversations in the mid-1970s of the Roman Catholic Church with Lutherans and with Methodists are remarkable in the open-

---

25. "Honolulu Report" §35, p. 377.
26. "Honolulu Report" §36, p. 377.
27. "Honolulu Report" §37, p. 378.

ness of their treatment of papal primacy. Both conversations recognized the problem that the ministry of the bishop of Rome posed for them, particularly in relation to immediate jurisdiction and infallibility. But neither dialogue gave the impression that it was coming to the end of the line on such matters. Quite the reverse. They expressed a welcome for the broader interpretation of Vatican II, with its setting of the ministry of the bishop of Rome in the context of the whole church charged with the task of exercising authority. What is remarkable is the way in which both of these conversations seem to suggest that the ministry of universal primacy in some reshaped way might, in the future, be acceptable to a wider ecumenical fellowship. The great generosity shown by both sides in reaching this position augurs well for the future.

It was the Anglican–Roman Catholic conversations that before the Lima meeting had devoted most time to the question of the Petrine ministry.[28] In describing the exercise of authority in the church the final report of the Anglican–Roman Catholic International Commission (ARCIC) begins with the bishop in the local church exercising jurisdiction, then moves to the coming together of bishops in councils at the regional level, to the emergence of prominent sees with their jurisdiction, and eventually to the see of Rome with universal jurisdiction. At each level of the church's life the ministry of primacy and conciliarity belong together. The description is an ideal one and does not correspond to the current reality in either communion. The description moves from the local to the universal and gives no sense of a church that acts from the top down, from pope to bishops to priests, to laity. According to this description, subsidiarity is the principle that characterizes the life of the church — nothing is done at a higher level than is necessary. The exercise of authority is in the service of the fellowship of the church. It is an attractive picture of what the exercise of authority should be like.

Time and time again the ARCIC report acknowledges the past failures of the church to reflect the authority of Christ; it is particularly strong in its statement of the failures of the ministry of the bishop of Rome:

> Sometimes functions assumed by the see of Rome were not necessarily linked to the primacy: sometimes the conduct of the occupant of this see has been unworthy of his office: sometimes the image of this office has been obscured by interpretations placed upon it: and sometimes external pressures have made its proper exercise almost impossible. Yet the primacy, rightly understood, implies that the bishop of Rome exercises his oversight in order to guard and promote the faithfulness of all the churches to Christ

28. *Final Report.*

and one another. Communion with him is intended as a safeguard of the catholicity of each local church, and as a sign of the communion of all the churches.[29]

In their Preface to the first statement on authority the co-chairmen of the Commission raised the possibility of a common recognition of Roman primacy in the future: "The prospect should be met with faith, not fear."[30] In 1981, just before the Lima meeting, ARCIC published a second statement on authority, in which it turned to the particular claims that had developed in relation to the ministry of the bishop of Rome, including what sort of teaching authority belonged to the bishop of Rome. They avoided the term *infallibility* and asked whether there is a special ministerial gift of discerning the truth of teaching, bestowed at crucial times on one person to enable that person to speak authoritatively in the name of the church in order to preserve the people of God in truth.

The report emphasized the teaching authority of councils and a universal primate working together, and reception of teaching by the people of God as the ultimate vindication that a matter of faith has been preserved from error. Nevertheless, at the end of its exploration of the exercise of authority, the report acknowledged the existence of two different positions: that of Roman Catholics, who argue that if certain conditions are fulfilled a judgment is preserved from error, and that of Anglicans, who hold that if a statement is not manifestly in line with biblical faith and orthodox tradition, they would want to put it to the test of study and discussion.

It is very hard indeed, even for the most careful reader, to see precisely what the area of disagreement is between the two positions. The hopeful note at the end of the report suggests that

> Contemporary discussions of conciliarity and primacy in both communions indicate that we are not dealing with positions destined to remain static. We suggest that some difficulties will not be wholly resolved until a practical initiative has been taken and our two Churches have lived together more visibly in one *koinonia*.[31]

So in the decade before the meeting of the Faith and Order Commission in Lima in 1982, a number of bilateral conversations had already treated the

29. "Authority in the Church I (Venice Statement) 1976" §III.12, in Growth I, pp. 88-118, here pp. 93-94.

30. "Authority in the Church I" Preface, p. 89.

31. "Authority in the Church I" §33, p. 115.

ministry of universal primacy within the context of statements on the exercise of authority in the church. In particular the Lutheran and Anglican conversations with the Roman Catholic Church were open to the possibility of some form of universal ministry in the service of unity, even though the particular claims of infallibility and universal jurisdiction that had come through history to be associated with the ministry of the bishop of Rome were not acceptable, at least in the way they had been interpreted by Vatican I.

Some Convergence Emerges

But the conversations also reveal some reconciliation of positions. The various reports emphasized infallibility as belonging to the whole church and a willingness on the part of Roman Catholics to reconsider and renew the practice of the ministry of universal primacy, together with a remarkable recognition of the distortions of the office at some points in the past. Indeed, the process of reinterpretation was shown to have already begun in the work of Vatican II, particularly in the setting of primacy within the collegial life of the church. On the other side, churches that had rejected the ministry of the bishop of Rome were becoming open to the possibility of in the future being in communion with a renewed and reformed universal primacy.

The unthinkable had thus been thought by churches on both sides of the Reformation divide. Further work was needed, but it was not thought that positions were so polarized that there could be no movement in the future. In view of this climate it was understandable that Professor Wright should have put his question to the Faith and Order Commission about including a reference to the Petrine ministry in the Lima Text.

In the twenty years following the Lima meeting a number of the bilateral conversations have reflected on the ministry of universal primacy. The Anglican-Orthodox conversations in a rather pointed way talk about the fundamental agreement between the Anglican understanding of primacy and the Orthodox understanding of seniority, as if, some might think, to make an alliance against the Roman view. The ministry of seniority on the universal level, they say, is "to strengthen unity and to give brotherly help to the bishops of the local churches in the exercise of their common ministry which exists to safeguard scriptural truth . . . , to promote right teaching and living, and to further the church's mission to the world."[32]

---

32. "Agreed Statement, Anglican-Orthodox Dialogue 1976-84, Dublin, Ireland, 19 August 1984" §25, in Growth II, pp. 81-104, here p. 89.

The bishop who has seniority, the Anglican-Orthodox report says pointedly, does not have the right to intervene arbitrarily in affairs of a diocese other than his own. He must respect the local bishop, act collegially, and take account of discernment entrusted to the whole people, both clergy and laity. The report goes on to assert that Christian unity needs to take account of the see of Rome. However, it notes, universal jurisdiction is a claim contrary to the early church. Nor can there be claims to infallibility, for that belongs to God alone, and to refer it to a human being even in restricted circumstances can bring misunderstanding. A statement, either of any individual bishop or of an episcopal assembly, cannot be guaranteed, since the ecumenicity of a council is manifested through its acceptance by the body of the church.

The Dublin Report claims that Anglicans and Orthodox agree about all of this. Here Anglicans and Orthodox are not only stating their joint agreement about primacy but also, it appears, pointing to a shared disagreement with the Roman Catholic Church. What they say here is very much in line with the Roman Catholic-Orthodox "Valamo Report" of 1988, which concludes by suggesting that "the primacy of the bishop of Rome [is] . . . a question which constitutes a serious divergence among us and which will be discussed in the future."[33] In a similar way the Old Catholic–Eastern Orthodox report on the church accords a position of honor to the bishop of Rome, who, the delegates say, possesses a presidency of honor, but the report is quick to point out that in terms of episcopal authority he does not differ from other bishops. Moreover, it says, it is unacceptable to regard the bishop of Rome as infallible when he defines doctrine *ex cathedra*.[34]

Once more in these years the Roman Catholic conversation with the Reformed referred to the Petrine ministry. The report of that dialogue, "Towards a Common Understanding of the Church," is remarkable for the honesty with which it sets out the way the Reformed regard the ministry of the Roman Catholic Church and *vice versa*. It is reconciling in the way the partners re-read history together, claiming as much convergence as they presently can but also honestly recording the remaining different perspectives. The promising thing is the way they set out the convergence they have discovered on the way the authority of Christ is exercised in the church. For instance, they agree that the ministry is essentially collegial and that there is need for *episkopē* on the regional and on the universal levels, and they claim to have begun to come to terms with the

---

33. Eastern Orthodox–Roman Catholic Dialogue, "The Sacrament of Order in the Sacramental Structure of the Church, New Valamo, Finland, 26 June 1988" §55, in Growth II, pp. 671-79, here p. 679.

34. Old Catholic–Eastern Orthodox Dialogue, "Ecclesiology, Chambésy, Geneva, Switzerland, 7 October 1983," in Growth II, pp. 248-49, here p. 249.

particularly difficult issue of the structure of ministry required for communion in the universal church. In a program for future work they determine to examine "What significance is there for the church today in the role assigned to Peter in several central New Testament passages — and in the way in which that role was interpreted in the ancient church?"[35]

Two further, perhaps unexpected, bilateral conversations in the years following Lima make passing reference to the ministry of the bishop of Rome. In the Pentecostal–Roman Catholic report of 1984, "Perspectives on Koinonia," the Roman Catholic members described how the bishops keep local churches in communion with one another: "The bishop of Rome . . . presides over the whole Catholic communion."[36] Pentecostals stated their problem with the assertion of LG 22 that "'the Roman Pontiff has full, supreme and universal power over the church' . . . which 'he can always exercise . . . freely.'"[37] The conversation of the Disciples of Christ with the Roman Catholics in 1992 simply noted that the primacy of the bishop of Rome and the belief that it is founded in the will of Christ for the church should be explored in the future.

A New Phase of Roman Catholic Conversations with Lutherans, Methodists, and Anglicans

While new and surprising conversations are beginning to acknowledge the significance of the ministry of universal primacy for their future relationships, in the years following Lima most advance was made in the Roman Catholic conversations with Lutherans, Methodists, and Anglicans. A significant statement came in the Lutheran–Roman Catholic conversations. In outlining tasks for the future, the 1993 report "Church and Justification" stated the Roman Catholic position that "the primatial function of the bishop of Rome is an essential element of the church" and that "each local church must be related to the primacy of the church of Rome and its bishop in order to be in the full communion of churches." Therefore the subject must be dealt with. Catholics, moreover, it went on, must be open to self-criticism: "the doctrine of primacy must be further developed, and primatial practice must be shaped accordingly." The two sides agreed that future work on the "ministry of leadership for the universal church" needed to be taken up "within the framework of communion ecclesiology."[38]

35. Reformed–Roman Catholic Dialogue, "Towards a Common Understanding of the Church, Second Phase, 1984-1990" §144, in Growth II, pp. 789-818, here pp. 812-13.
36. "Perspectives on Koinonia" §82, in Growth II, pp. 735-52, here p. 747.
37. "Perspectives on Koinonia" §87, p. 748.
38. "Church and Justification, 1993" §106, in Growth II, pp. 485-565, here pp. 511-12.

A marked advance in convergence came in the 1986 Methodist–Roman Catholic report "Towards a Statement on the Church," in its substantial section on the Petrine Office. This report begins with an impressive exploration of the ministry of Peter in the New Testament and the development of the role of the Roman see in the early church, leading to the conclusion that

> . . . the primacy of the bishop of Rome is not established from the scriptures in isolation from the living tradition. When an institution cannot be established from scripture alone, Methodists . . . consider it on its intrinsic merits, as indeed do Roman Catholics; but Methodists give less doctrinal weight than Roman Catholics to long and widespread tradition.
>
> The Roman Catholic members are agreed that being in communion with the see of Rome has served as the touchstone of belonging to the church in its fullest sense. This commission is agreed that not being in communion with the bishop of Rome does not necessarily disqualify a Christian community from belonging to the church of God. . . . Likewise, Methodist members are agreed that Catholic acceptance of the Roman primacy is not an impediment to churchly character.[39]

It was clear to the members of this dialogue that for two churches committed to visible unity there was a fresh urgency about the matter: "Methodists accept that whatever is properly required for the unity of the whole of Christ's church must by that very fact be God's will for his church." Then comes the remarkable statement: "A universal primacy might well serve as focus of and ministry for the unity of the whole church."[40] The report goes on to examine the two matters of jurisdiction and infallibility.

On jurisdiction the Roman Catholic members of the conversations agreed that the relation of the authority of the Pope and the authority of the local bishop remained unfinished: "It would not be inconceivable that at some future date in a restored unity, Roman Catholic and Methodist bishops might be linked in one episcopal college and that the whole body would recognize some kind of effective leadership and primacy in the bishop of Rome."[41] When the report came to struggle with the matter of infallibility, it put the Roman Catholic position perhaps more clearly than in any other bilateral report so far referred to, explaining that under the guidance of the Holy Spirit the episcopal college discerns the faith of Christians, always with reference to the supreme

---

39. "Towards a Statement on the Church" §§55-56, in Growth II, pp. 583-96, here p. 593.
40. "Towards a Statement on the Church" §58, p. 593.
41. "Towards a Statement on the Church" §62, p. 594.

norm of the scriptures. Moreover, they say, quoting LG 25, "To definitions of a council 'the assent of the church can never be wanting, on account of the action of the Holy Spirit, by which the universal flock of Christ is kept and makes progress in the oneness of faith.' "[42]

Papal infallibility, the report shows, is according to Roman Catholic understanding "another embodiment of the infallibility with which the church has been endowed." Only in "carefully defined and limited circumstances" does the pope exercise this ministry. In such cases "the assent of the faithful cannot be lacking."[43] Then comes a very important clarification:

> When the pope teaches infallibly, infallibility is, properly speaking, not attributed to the pope, nor to the teaching, but rather to this particular act of teaching. It means that he has been prevented by God from teaching error on matters relating to salvation. It does not mean that a particular teaching has been presented in the best possible way, nor does it mean that every time he teaches he does so infallibly.[44]

Methodists registered remaining hesitations. For them, even this careful statement of infallibility, in which the infallibility of the church is primary, "seems to imply a discernment of truth which exceeds the capacity of sinful human beings."[45] Methodists believe that the final judgment of whether something is guaranteed from error depends on the assent of the whole people. Nevertheless, the fact that Roman Catholics were giving an increasing amount of attention to the understanding of reception was seen as a welcome development. The report suggested that "An approach towards convergence in thinking about infallibility may perhaps be reached by considering the Methodist doctrine of assurance."[46] On any reckoning this discussion was a remarkable exploration of the Petrine ministry, an exploration that seems to bring these two communions much closer together in understanding the ministry of the bishop of Rome within the teaching authority of the whole church.

The report that moves beyond making comparative statements on the matter of universal primacy towards being a consensus statement is the work of ARCIC, *The Gift of Authority: Authority III*, published in 1999. Building upon the two earlier reports on authority coming from the period before the Lima meeting, this third report set the ministry of the bishop of Rome within the

---

42. "Towards a Statement on the Church" §66, p. 595.
43. "Towards a Statement on the Church" §§69-70, p. 595.
44. "Towards a Statement on the Church" §71, p. 595.
45. "Towards a Statement on the Church" §72, p. 595.
46. "Towards a Statement on the Church" §74, p. 596.

collegiality of all the bishops. When the bishop of Rome speaks, the document says, he "proclaims the faith of the local churches" as that has been represented in the college by those who represent local churches. "It is thus the wholly reliable teaching of the whole Church that is operative in the judgement of the universal primate" when "in certain circumstances" he "discern[s] and make[s] explicit."[47] What is not clear is whether this discernment is simply like any good chairperson saying "this is what I hear you saying" or whether this discernment and making explicit is in fact the personal judgment of the bishop of Rome.

What is striking in this report is that the word *infallible* is never used of the ministry of the bishop of Rome. Infallible teaching is emphatically attributed to the whole church. *Gift* also emphasizes that when the bishop of Rome so discerns and makes explicit, his discernment is received by the people. Assent is inevitable in this case because the bishop of Rome is only playing back what the College of Bishops has discerned to be the mind of the local churches. In other words reception has already been a part of the discernment process and precedes rather than follows a pronouncement. This explanation surely puts a new light on the matter of the reliability of papal teaching.

What is remarkable in *Gift* is the number of challenges it gives to both communions, challenges to reform and renew their own lives. The most daring challenge to both communions is to re-receive the ministry of the bishop of Rome, a ministry of primacy "exercised in collegiality and synodality — a ministry of *servus servorum Dei*," a primacy that would uphold diversity and encourage mission.[48] The portrait is an attractive one:

> We envisage a primacy that will even now help to uphold the legitimate diversity of traditions, strengthening and safeguarding them in fidelity to the Gospel. . . .
>
> Such a universal primate will exercise leadership in the world and also in both communions, addressing them in a prophetic way. . . . A universal primacy of this style will welcome and protect theological enquiry and other forms of the search for truth, so that their results may enrich and strengthen both human wisdom and the Church's faith. Such a universal primacy might gather the churches in various ways for consultation and discussion.[49]

The report's major and startling suggestions are "that Anglicans be open to and desire a recovery and re-reception under certain clear conditions of the

---

47. *Gift* §47.
48. Cf. *Gift* §60.
49. *Gift* §§60, 61.

exercise of universal primacy by the Bishop of Rome" and "that Roman Catholics be open to and desire a re-reception of the exercise of primacy by the Bishop of Rome and the offering of such a ministry to the whole Church of God."[50] Moreover, it is suggested that such a primacy could be both offered and received even before the establishment of full communion.

The Emergence of Greater Understanding of a Ministry of Universal Primacy

The twenty or so years since the Lima meeting with the request of Professor Wright have thus seen a number of bilateral theological conversations treating the subject of the ministry of universal primacy. Certain things emerge. The first is a widespread recognition that this topic is an important one for all churches committed to visible unity, particularly because for Roman Catholics full visible unity entails communion with the bishop of Rome. But there is also a growing awareness that this topic is important not only for this reason but also because of a growing recognition of the importance and potential for unity and mission that a personal ministry of unity at the world level could have. The reports show a willingness shared by the Roman Catholic Church and other churches to listen to each other's experiences and perceptions.

Roman Catholics openly acknowledge the times of distortion of the office and the failure of occupants of the see of Rome to live up to their calling. Representatives of other churches speak honestly about their fears and the problems they have with the way the ministry has been exercised. In explaining the ministry of the bishop of Rome, Roman Catholics accept the development of the office throughout history and openly acknowledge that the claims of Vatican I, which were made very much within a particular historical setting, have now been helpfully re-assessed by Vatican II. Many reports quote from Vatican II's statement *Lumen Gentium* to support this claim.

Hard Issues of Jurisdiction and Infallibility

Nevertheless, while there is clearly a willingness to consider a personal ministry of unity at the world level, the issues of jurisdiction and infallibility, with the two particular Marian dogmas, remain hard for those outside the Roman Catholic Church. But even here positions are not polarized and are open to creative

50. *Gift* §62.

thinking and exploration. There is a definite move in the Lutheran, Methodist, and Anglican documents to talk of the infallibility of the whole church and to view the ministry of the bishop of Rome within that framework. Primacy is always exercised in collegiality and conciliarity and not exercised apart from these wider dimensions of the church's life. Here the doctrine of reception is also helping to open up the discussion as the various dialogues acknowledge that reception by the whole people of God belongs within the process of the infallible teaching of the whole church, with the universal primate playing a crucial role in that teaching.

It is still necessary to have a discussion about when the process of reception takes place. Even if progress has been made on infallible teaching, it seems that more needs to be done, perhaps even that the discussion would best continue with new language rather than the polemical language of the past. The Methodist dialogue, for example, talks of the need to explore the characteristic Methodist doctrine of assurance. It might be helpful for others to have a discussion of the teaching authority of the church and the role of the bishop of Rome couched in fresh terminology that leaves behind the polemical term of *infallibility*. Such an approach would prevent the gut reactions that always meet the use of polemical language from past controversy.

No report yet seems to have faced the question of universal jurisdiction with much clarity. There might be something to be gained if Anglicans were to look at the primatial ministry of the Archbishops of Canterbury and York at the provincial level, a ministry that affords to these archbishops the possibility under certain circumstances of exercising ordinary jurisdiction in the dioceses of their provinces. As Colin Podmore has written, Anglicans opposed to jurisdiction attached to a universal primacy have to show why jurisdiction is appropriate at provincial level but not at a universal level.[51] There is more to be said, and so far the best treatment of jurisdiction comes in the discussions with the Lutherans. Only *Gift*, the Anglican–Roman Catholic report, has gone as far as challenging both communions to re-receive the ministry of the bishop of Rome now and ahead of the establishment of full communion.

Whatever advances these reports seem to have made, it needs to be pointed out that they are reports of small dialogue teams who have come to know and trust one another. Two questions still remain: how far they represent the world communions, and whether what they say about a ministry of universal primacy will be received by the communions concerned.

---

51. Colin Podmore, "Primacy in the Anglican Tradition," in *Community — Unity — Communion: Essays in Honour of Mary Tanner*, ed. Colin Podmore (London: Church House Publishing, 1998), pp. 277-93.

A Remarkable Papal Encyclical

The other major contribution since Lima on the question of universal primacy came in 1995 in the publication of the remarkable papal encyclical *Ut Unum Sint*. In this encyclical Pope John Paul II asked forgiveness for his own office's responsibility for the "painful recollections" that have made the papacy a difficulty for most other Christians.[52] The Pope talked of his ministry, emphasizing that it is the ministry of the servant of the servants of God. He invited leaders of other traditions to engage with him "in a patient and fraternal dialogue on this subject . . . leaving useless controversies behind" and to help him rethink his ministry in the service of unity, which he says is "an immense task . . . which I cannot carry out by myself."[53] This is a generous invitation to which some churches have already responded. It will be interesting to see the Holy Father's response to the responses and whether it opens the way to a re-reception of the Petrine ministry by other churches and by the Roman Catholic Church itself.

The State of the Multilateral Conversation

The twenty years following on the Lima meeting have seen some bilateral conversations making significant statements on the ministry of universal primacy, and the bishop of Rome himself has encouraged Christians from all traditions to help him in better understanding his ministry in the service of the unity of the church. How then has the multilateral discussion within the Faith and Order Commission responded to the intention expressed in Lima by its then Moderator to study the matter in its future agenda?

In the years following Lima the Faith and Order Commission devoted attention to monitoring the responses to BEM as well as to developing new studies on the apostolic faith and church and world. All of this work fed into the Fifth World Conference on Faith and Order in 1993, under the title "Towards *koinonia* in Faith, Life and Witness." The preparatory study document for that meeting noted that the question of primatial ministry should be addressed. The report of the participants in Section 3 of the Conference declared the necessity of discussing the topic in the future:

> At this stage in our journey into koinonia, the issue of the necessity or desirability of a primatial office and its nature can be only briefly touched

52. *Unum* §88.
53. *Unum* §96.

upon. Churches from different traditions adopt very different positions with regard to such an office. Before taking up this matter, some will have to deal with the prior question of personal episkope as a focus of unity. Others have already reached a measure of agreement which allows them to discuss it. This issue should be on the agenda in any future ecumenical study of ecclesiology.[54]

Following the World Conference the major study of the Commission was on ecclesiology. In 1998 the Commission published *The Nature and Purpose of the Church: A Stage on the Way to a Common Statement*.[55] Only a short passage touches on the ministry of primacy, in the section dealing with the first of the triad — "personal, collegial, communal":

> N.B. Primacy, wherever it exists, is an expression of the "personal" mode of ministry. It is a service of presidency to be exercised in a spirit of love and truth. Primacy is inseparable from both the collegial and communal dimensions of the Church's life. It strengthens the unity of the Church and enables it to speak with one voice.[56]

A following section on conciliarity and primacy agrees that wherever local or regional churches come together to take counsel and make decisions there is need for someone to summon and preside over a gathering, to help with the process of discerning and articulating consensus:

> The one who presides is always to be at the service of those among whom he/she presides . . . in love and truth. It is the duty of the president to respect the integrity of local churches, to give voice to the voiceless and to uphold unity in diversity.[57]

An accompanying commentary says simply that there is much work to be done between those who believe conciliarity and primacy to be necessary at the world level and those who do not.

It is clear that this statement on ecclesiology says more than BEM in the area of primacy. Nevertheless, it would not be surprising if Professor Wright

---

54. *On the Way to Fuller Koinonia*, ed. Thomas F. Best and Günther Gassmann, Faith and Order Paper 166 (Geneva: WCC Publications, 1994), p. 251.

55. *The Nature and Purpose of the Church: A Stage on the Way to a Common Statement*, Faith and Order Paper 181 (Geneva: WCC Publications, 1998).

56. *Nature and Purpose of the Church* §103, p. 51.

57. *Nature and Purpose of the Church* §109, p. 54.

were not a little disappointed that in the years since Lima more has not been accomplished in the multilateral context on the ministry of universal primacy. What is said in *The Nature and Purpose of the Church* is very general indeed and is not based on any detailed study by the Faith and Order Commission of the matter of universal primacy. There is surely now an important role for Faith and Order to take up the question asked by Professor Wright, building on the work on *episkopē*/episcopacy and reflecting on the contributions of the bilateral dialogues in this area.[58]

A Relevant Question Still

One important aspect of the web of ecumenical theological conversations is that the insights of the bilateral conversations have come to influence the work of the multilateral dialogues and *vice versa*. If the multilateral conversation does not bring together the insights of the bilaterals, there is a very real danger that one bilateral will make progress in a way that in the long run could be harmful to the one ecumenical movement. BEM has done much to keep a consistency between the various bilaterals on the themes of baptism, eucharist, and ministry. There is need for a similar convergence document on authority, one that includes within it a treatment of the Petrine ministry. The prime question in this area is, as Ehrenström and Gassmann put it in 1974, "whether the worldwide Church in this global age does not need a visible symbol and servant of its universality, and, if so, whether a renewed papacy would be the appropriate embodiment of this universal ministry."[59] This is a relevant question in a world that desperately needs a ministry of reconciliation in each and every place.

58. *"Episkopē" and Episcopacy and the Quest for Visible Unity*, ed. Peter C. Bouteneff and Alan D. Falconer, Faith and Order Paper 183 (Geneva: WCC Publications, 1999).
59. Ehrenström and Gassmann, *Confessions in Dialogue*, p. 189.

Anglican-Orthodox Relations:
A Long-Term Overview

E. Rozanne Elder

Because J. Robert Wright once attended the annual International Medieval Studies Congress at Western Michigan University, Kalamazoo, I found myself involved in the fascinating and frustrating world of ecumenism. A few years after I had participated in the Anglican-Orthodox dialogue in the United States, he invited me to present a summary chronicle of this relationship. What follows is an abbreviated version of that summary.

Relations between the Anglican Communion and the Orthodox churches began in the seventeenth century and fall into three successive but overlapping eras, which I have chosen to call the Age of Illusion (the early sixteenth to the mid-nineteenth centuries), the Age of Optimism (the mid-nineteenth to mid-twentieth centuries), and the Age of Disillusionment (from *c.* 1965 onwards).[1]

The Age of Illusion

At the Reformation the church of the first five Christian centuries was as familiar to Anglican divines as — and far more congenial than — the English church of the tumultuous early sixteenth century. A deep love of the patristic tradition, rekindled during the bitter disputes of the Reformation, provided

---

1. A thorough study of contacts between Orthodox Christians and the Carolines and nonjurors has recently been published but was not available to me when this was written: Judith Pinnington, *Anglicans and Orthodox: Unity and Subversions 1559-1725* (Leominster: Gracewing, 2003) [available in the U.S. through Morehouse Publishing].

theologians with ancient warrant for rejecting late medieval scholasticism and its methodology, and many of its theological conclusions. Some substituted the scholastic theologies of Lutheranism or, more often, Calvinism, but most looked back to what they saw as the unanimous consent of the undivided church and modeled the reformed Catholic church of England on fifth-century ecclesiological and theological patterns, oblivious to the historical, political, ecclesiastical, and theological experiences of the Eastern church over the intervening millennium.

Traditionalist divines might see in Constantinople a model for non-papal Catholicism, but those influenced by "Puritan" ideas saw in contemporary Orthodox churches something suspiciously redolent of the "popery" England had cast off. The privileged at their prayers in college or private chapels might continue to make the sign of the cross, practice private confession, and celebrate the feasts and fasts of The Book of Common Prayer, but to merchant Englishmen in direct contact with Orthodox through the Levant Company or the Muscovy Company, these habits smacked of "popery" and "works righteousness," a vainglorious denial of the all-sufficiency of God's irresistible and unmerited grace. Conversely, wrote the consul of the Levant Company in 1678,

> It will not be difficult to conjecture under what notion the Eastern apprehends the Western Reformed Churches, for they, taking notice that the English neither keep Fasts, nor practise Confession, nor ordinarily make the Sign of the Cross . . . , are not only scandalized thereat, but . . . wondering what sort of Heresy or Sect is sprung up in the world, so different from the Religion of all the Prophets; at which undecent practice, the Roman Clergy taking advantage to disparage the Protestants, represent them to the Greeks under the notion of Calvinists. . . . And in reality, were it not that the English Nation by the orderly use of their Liturgy and discipline of their Church, observing the Lord's Day and the Grand Festivals, did vindicate themselves of these aspersions, it were impossible to persuade the Oriental Countries that those which we call Reformed were Christians, or at least retain anything of Ancient and Apostolical Institution.[2]

Orthodox resentment of Rome had been fanned by Roman intransigence at the Council of Ferrara-Florence (1438-1445), Jesuit proselytizing in Orthodox

---

2. Paul Ricaut, *The Present State of the Greek and Armenian Churches, Anno Christi 1678* (published 1679 at the command of Charles II), Preface. The author had been Consul of the Levant Company from 1667 to 1679. Cited from Paul E. More and Frank L. Cross, *Anglicanism: The Thought and Practice of the Church of England* (London: SPCK, 1962), p. 75.

lands, and the creation in the waning years of the sixteenth century of a "Uniate" Church, which was liturgically byzantine but ecclesiologically papal.[3] Pressure to accept late medieval Latin doctrinal definitions had led Orthodox to define their own theological positions; relying on the Church Fathers, they articulated with new precision Eastern teaching on the church, scripture, and tradition, "that which has been handed down by Christ himself and by the apostles and by the holy ecumenical councils."[4] Long isolated under Turkish suzerainty, early modern Orthodox engaged with a world very different from the one they had known.

In 1611, an Englishman visiting Alexandria met its youthful patriarch, Cyril Loukaris, whom he described as "a man of approved virtue and learning, a friend to the reformed religion."[5] Through his agency, a correspondence of some quarter century developed between Loukaris and two archbishops of Canterbury, George Abbot and William Laud. As a generous and symbolic gesture representing the development of the relationship between these representatives of the two churches, in 1631 Loukaris, by then patriarch of Constantinople, presented King Charles I of England with the *Codex Alexandrinus* and Archbishop Laud with an Arabic manuscript of the Pentateuch. Neither king nor archbishop realized that the open-minded Loukaris had taken an interest in more reforms than England's and would shortly be anathematized by many of his own clergy as "the wicked new iconoclast,"[6] "a Lutheran,"[7] a heretic espousing "a Calvinistic faith . . . [to which] our church has never yielded . . . and never will."[8] Nor was

3. At the Councils of Brest Litovsk (Poland) in 1595 and 1596.

4. *Confession of Dositheus* 11; τὰ δογματικὰ καὶ συμβολικὰ μνημεία τῆς ὀρθοδόξου καθολικῆς ἐκκλησίας [*Ta dogmatika kai symbolika mnēmeia tēs Orthodoxou Katholikēs Ekklēsias*], ed. Ioannes N. Karmires, 2 vols., 2nd ed. (Athens and Graz: Akademische Druck- u. Verlaganstalt, 1960-68), p. 835, cited by Jaroslav Pelikan, *The Christian Tradition: A History of the Development of Doctrine*, vol. 2: *The Spirit of Eastern Christendom (600-1700)* [hereafter *Spirit*] (Chicago and London: University of Chicago Press, 1974), p. 287.

5. *Relation of a Journey Begun Anno Domini 1610* (London, 1631), p. 115, cited by Colin Davey, "Anglicans and Eastern Christendom, 1534-1984" (typescript), p. 1.

6. Synod of Constantinople (1638), in τὰ δογματικὰ καὶ συμβολικὰ μνημεία, p. 654, cited by Pelikan, *Spirit*, p. 285.

7. Patriarch Cyril Lucaris, *Epistle* 92, in *Bibliographie hellénique ou Description raisonée des ouvrages publiés par des Grecs au dix-septième siècle*, ed. E. L. J. Legrand, 5 vols. (Paris: [A. Picard et Fils], 1894-96; [J. Maisonneuve], 1903), 4:279, cited by Pelikan, *Spirit*, p. 284.

8. Synod of Jassy, Moldavia (1643), in *De ecclesiae occidentalis atque orientalis perpetua consensione*, ed. Leone Allacci (Cologne, 1648), pp. 1084-85, cited by Pelikan, *Spirit*, p. 285. The Patriarch's case may not have been helped by recollections of a translation of the *Augsburg Confession*, slightly adapted to Orthodox sensitivities, once sent to the patriarch of Constantinople by Melanchthon. Though refusing to enter into theological debate, the Orthodox singled out for special condemnation Loukaris's *Eastern Confession of the Christian Faith* and "its espousal

the patriarch to know that not long after his death in 1633 archbishop and king would follow one another to the scaffold, in no small part because they too had seriously misjudged the religious sensitivities of their subjects.

Archbishop Loukaris also received encouragement from a certain Antonio de Dominis, an erstwhile Roman Catholic archbishop recently, if transiently, turned Anglican. Dominis criticized the Church of Rome as "in regard of temporal estate over-glorious" and commended England:

> the land of Goshen where the light of the Gospel shineth most clearly, . . . where I have liberty to write in defence of truth freely and safely, as in a place where the cause of Christ triumpheth under a most godly and most wise King, a true defender of the true, ancient and Catholic Faith.[9]

In 1617 Loukaris had sent Metrophanes Kritopoulos, a monk of Mount Athos, to study at Oxford.[10] Thirteen years later Kritopoulos returned home, eventually to become patriarch of Alexandria, wondering "if after all there is some hope of our coming together one day." He pinned his hopes on the reformed churches' realization of their need for the Fathers, the tradition, and the full sacramental life of the church.[11] Subsequent events make it appear that his close view of the Church of England had not engendered opinions as sanguine as those attributed to his archbishop, Cyril Loukaris, by Paul Ricaut of the Levant Company, who was the British consul at Smyrna. Himself convinced of the affinities between the Greek and English churches, and of the shortcomings of Roman Catholicism and Calvinism, Ricaut was also

> persuaded that this Cyrillus, having . . . observed that purity of our doctrine and the excellency of our discipline which flourished in the beginning of the Reign of King Charles the Martyr, and viewed our Churches trimmed and adorned in a modest medium, between the wanton and superstitious dress of Rome and the slovenly and insipid Government of

---

of 'Holy Scripture devoid of the exegeses of the holy fathers of the church' and the divinely inspired traditions and conciliar decrees" (Synod of Jassy, p. 1082, from Pelikan, *Spirit*, p. 285). Pinnington points out that "Caroline Anglicans and their Nonjuring successors encountered Orthodoxy at a particularly 'broken' stage of its pilgrimage," when some Eastern Christians were importing Latin spirituality and ecclesiology and others were resisting all things Western" (*Anglicans and Orthodox*, p. 215).

9. More and Cross, *Anglicanism*, p. 74.

10. For the biography of this monk, see Colin Davey, *Pioneer for Unity: Metrophanes Kritopoulos (1589-1639)* (London: British Council of Churches, 1987).

11. Davey, "Anglicans and Eastern Christendom, 1534-1984," p. 6.

Geneva, entertained a high opinion of our happy Reformation; intending thence perhaps to draw a pattern, whereby to amend and correct the defaults of the Greek Church, retrenching the length of their Services and the multitude of their Ceremonies, and also by that exemplar to reduce their Festivals to a moderate number, to create a right apprehension of the state of souls after separation, and wholly to take away certain conceits both superstitious and savouring of Gentilism, and confirm his Church in a reverend opinion of the Holy Sacrament of the Eucharist, without launching so far into the explication of that Mystery, as of late they have done. . . .[12]

At the restoration of the English monarchy in 1660, many members of the restored episcopacy, critical of Reformation Protestantism and chary of Roman papalism, aimed "at nothing else but that the primitive faith may be revived. . . . in Christianity there can be no concerning truth which is not ancient; and whatsoever is truly new, is certainly false."[13] This attitude reopened the doorway to the East. At the request of the Anglican chaplain at Constantinople, in 1672 the patriarch dispatched to England *A Synodical Answer to the Question, What are the Sentiments of the Oriental Church of the Greek Orthodox, Sent to the Lovers of the Greek Church in Britain.*

At the "Glorious Revolution" of 1688 the English Parliament replaced its Roman Catholic monarch, James II, with his daughter Mary and her Dutch Calvinist husband, William of Orange.[14] Nine bishops and some four hundred priests, few of whom had any reason to love the exiled king, could not in conscience bring themselves to take the Oaths of Allegiance and Supremacy to a new monarch while the old still lived. Replaced in their benefices by clerics of less tender conscience, these "nonjurors" looked east for a catholic, apostolic church home. Through Czar Peter the Great they requested recognition by the Orthodox Church. In a clandestine correspondence that extended from 1716 to 1725, this "Catholick remnant" of Britain negotiated terms on which they might be received into the Orthodox Church while retaining their own liturgy — a combination of The Book of Common Prayer and primitive liturgies[15] — and

12. Ricaut, *The Present State,* Preface, cited from More and Cross, *Anglicanism,* pp. 75-76.

13. John Pearson, Dedication to *Exposition of the Creed* (London, 1659), a standard work of the period, cited by Ted A. Campbell, *John Wesley and Christian Antiquity: Religious Vision and Cultural Change* (Nashville: Kingswood Books, 1991), p. 13.

14. High churchman Samuel Johnson described King William nearly a century later as "one of the most worthless scoundrels that ever existed" (David L. Edwards, *Christian England,* 3 vols. [London: Collins, 1983], 2:470).

15. Florovsky says the nonjurors probably expected this liturgy to be "'the best proof and recommendation' of the Non-jurors' 'doctrinal orthodoxy'" (George Florovsky, "The Orthodox

the traditional western theologies on *filioque,* the eucharist, saints, and icons. "We desire . . . to unite with you, O ye religious remnant of the Britons," came the answer, ". . . that both of us may have one Church, to the glory of God; and that those who for a long time have lost the Orthodox oriental and unspotted Faith may again recover it . . . and may be one with us of the Eastern Church."[16]

Cyril Loukaris had cast a long shadow, however, and the Orthodox were "gravely suspicious of anything that sounded like Protestant ideas."[17] The patriarchs of Constantinople, Alexandria, Antioch, and Jerusalem would accept no less than full submission to Orthodoxy and therefore abjuration of the faith the nonjurors had left the Church of England to defend.

The nonjurors' activities, discovered in the reign of George I, made them not only an embarrassment to the Church of England but also a diplomatic liability. Their imperial Russian champion undisguisedly supported the Stuart pretenders to the British throne and had designs on Hanoverian territory on the continent. The archbishop of Canterbury therefore squelched further negotiations by writing to inform the patriarch of Jerusalem that

> Certain schismatical Priests of our Church have written to you under the fictitious titles of Archbishop and Bishops of the Anglican Church, and have sought your Communion with them; who, having neither place nor Church in these realms, have bent their efforts to deceive you who are ignorant of their schism. . . . Of these men I pray and beseech your Reverence to beware.[18]

A cautious suspicion, followed by oblivion, overtook Anglican-Orthodox relations.

As enlightened Deism spread through the eighteenth-century church, mainstream Anglican reliance on the Church Fathers faded. By the time John

---

Churches and the Ecumenical Movement Prior to 1910," in *A History of the Ecumenical Movement, 1517-1948,* ed. Ruth Rouse and Stephen C. Neill, 2nd ed. [London: SPCK, 1967], pp. 171-215, here p. 191, cited by Leon Litvack, *John Mason Neale and the Quest for Sobornost* [Oxford: Clarendon Press; New York: Oxford University Press, 1994], p. 38).

16. Cited by Litvack, *John Mason Neale,* p. 39. For the nonjurors' proposals and the Orthodox patriarchs' reply, see George Williams, ed., *The Orthodox Church of the East in the Eighteenth Century, Being the Correspondence between the Eastern Patriarchs and the Nonjuring Bishops. With an Introduction on Various Projects of Reunion between the Eastern Church and the Anglican Communion* (London: Rivingtons, 1868), pp. 4-11, 15-67.

17. H. W. Langford, "The Non-Jurors and the Eastern Orthodox," *Eastern Churches Review,* 1/2 (Autumn 1966): 125, cited by Litvack, *John Mason Neale,* p. 40, n. 9.

18. Williams, *The Orthodox Church of the East,* pp. 4, lvii, lviii, cited by Litvack, *John Mason Neale,* pp. 39-40.

Wesley arrived at Oxford in 1720, the libraries bristled with editions of patristic works, learned scriptural commentaries, histories of the early church, and polemical tracts claiming the support of authoritative antiquity.[19] But to most churchgoers during the Age of Enlightenment the disciplines of "Christian Antiquity" had become unfamiliar, and the transcendent yet immanent God of the Fathers was widely viewed as impersonal causation.[20] Wesley's personal appropriation of patristic teaching led him not Eastward but into Pietism. His "Methodist" movement was marked by an affective individualism as unknown in the East as it was unwelcome in the established church. On neither Methodists nor Anglican Evangelicals did the living tradition of the East have any influence. At the end of the Age of Illusion, Charles J. Abbey and John H. Overton explain, the "Eastern Church, after attracting a faint curiosity through the overtures of the later Nonjurors, was as wholly unknown and unthought of as though it had been an insignificant sect in the furthest wilds of Muscovy."[21]

The Age of Optimism I: Personal Relations

In the mid-nineteenth century, the affective "Evangelical Revival" began to be balanced by the more formal "Catholic Revival," with its "unequivocal assertion of the identity of Anglicanism with the continuing life of the universal Church. . . ."[22] *Semper, ubique, ab omnibus,* and *quinquesaecularism* became part of the Anglican vocabulary. John Henry Newman posited the branch theory of Catholicism, according to which in the Church Militant three ancient traditions — Roman Catholic, Greek Catholic, and English Catholic — were

19. Campbell states that "At least sixty-nine editions and translations of ante-Nicene Christian works were published in the seventeenth and eighteenth centuries, most coming from presses in London or Oxford" (Campbell, *John Wesley and Christian Antiquity,* pp. 9-10). Campbell's figures are drawn from Stanley Lawrence Greenslade, *The English Reformers and the Fathers of the Church* (Oxford: Clarendon Press, 1960), pp. 9-10; William P. Haugaard, "Renaissance Patristic Scholarship and Theology in Sixteenth-Century England," *Sixteenth Century Journal* 10 (1979): 37-60; Norman Sykes, *William Wake, Archbishop of Canterbury, 1657-1737,* 2 vols. (Cambridge [UK]: Cambridge University Press, 1957), 1:63, *et al.*

20. See William C. Placher, *The Domestication of Transcendence* (Louisville: Westminster John Knox Press, 1996), *passim.*

21. Charles J. Abbey and John H. Overton, *The English Church in the Eighteenth Century,* 2 vols. (London: Longmans, Green, and Co., 1878), 1:157-62, cited by Peter Benedict Nockles, *The Oxford Movement in Context* (Cambridge [UK] and New York: Cambridge University Press, 1994), p. 161.

22. E. C. Miller, *Toward a Fuller Vision: Orthodoxy and Anglican Experience* (Wilton, CT: Morehouse Barlow, 1984), p. 61.

bound by invisible yet indivisible ties in one Church Catholic. While Newman focused his attention on Rome, others cast their gaze on the equally venerable, equally catholic, and historically less controversial churches of the East.

Edward Bouverie Pusey, the intellectual leader of the Oxford Movement, in 1840 wrote with all the confidence of imperial Britain when he asked:

> We cannot have communion with Rome; why should we not with the *Orthodox* Greek Church? . . . Certainly one should have thought that those who have not conformed with Rome would, practically, be glad to be strengthened by intercourse with us, and countenanced by us.[23]

In the following year, 1841, the archbishop of Canterbury consecrated a bishop with jurisdiction over Anglicans and Lutherans in Jerusalem. "This was the third blow, which finally shattered my faith in the Anglican Church," Newman later wrote.[24] Four years later he abandoned the Church of England. His branch theory had been grafted onto the tradition, however, and it led an "earnest-minded and devout" young Englishman — William Palmer of Magdalene College, Oxford — to visit Russia to study Orthodox theology and liturgy, led by Newman's words:

> Deeply convinced of the great truth that our Lord had instituted, and still acknowledges and protects, a visible Church — one, individual, and integral . . . considered at present to exist in three main branches, or rather in a triple presence the Latin, the Greek and the Anglican, these three being one and the same Church, distinguishable from each other by secondary, fortuitous, and local, though important characteristics. . . .[25]

Palmer considered it his right as an English Catholic to receive the sacraments in Russia. The Russians, firmly believing the one holy, catholic, and apostolic church to be coterminous with the Orthodox Church, regarded Palmer's Church of England as a mixture of Lutheranism and Calvinism and would permit him to receive the sacraments only if he submitted "absolutely and without restriction to all the doctrine, discipline and ritual of the Orthodox (Eastern)

---

23. Henry Parry Liddon, *The Life of Edward Bouverie Pusey, D.D.,* 4 vols. (London and New York: Longmans, Green, and Co., 1893-97), 3:148-49, cited by Litvack, *John Mason Neale,* p. 43.

24. John Henry Newman, *Apologia pro Vita Sua,* ed. Ernest Rhys, Everyman's Library (London: J. M. Dent and Sons; New York: E. P. Dutton & Co., 1927), p. 143.

25. William Palmer, *Notes of a Visit to the Russian Church in the Years 1840, 1841,* ed. John Henry Newman (London: Kegan Paul, Trench, 1882).

Church."[26] The Russians considered the request frivolous, Rome the appropriate partner for Anglicans, and Palmer a very atypical Anglican.

Future events were influenced not by Palmer's actions but by his personal contacts. He convinced the Chief Procurator of the Holy Governing Synod to send a chaplain, Eugene Ivanovich Popov, to the Russian embassy in London. There Popov studied Anglican theology, reported on the ecclesiastical scene, and became close friends with many leaders of the Victorian church.[27] Palmer also carried on a ten-year correspondence with Alexei Stepanovich Khomiakov (1804-60), layman, poet, theologian, and, in the words of Metropolitan Anthony Bloom, "one of the most passionate polemicists against Catholicism and Protestantism at the same time. . . ."[28] To Khomiakov, a chastened Palmer declared:

> I am perfectly sure of the existence in the Anglican Church of an element of faith and doctrine not only *like,* but *identical* with, the faith and doctrine of the Eastern Church: so that though union with the present Anglican Church, which is made up of conflicting and undeveloped tendencies, partly orthodox and partly heretical [read *calvinistic*], is out of the question, union with the orthodox element of the Anglican Church, whenever it shall have asserted its own exclusive ascendency, and expelled its heretical antagonist, will be perfectly natural and easy, and scarcely need any negotiation or conference, except for merely subordinate matters of discipline and ritual.[29]

26. Palmer, *Notes,* p. 415, cited by Litvack, *John Mason Neale,* p. 46.

27. Popov lived in London for thirty-two years, enjoyed a close friendship with John Mason Neale, and had ties with both Newman and Pusey and with other Tractarians, university dons, and clergy. L. Brodsky notes that "Popov managed to raise the status of the Russian priest in the eyes of the English and held high the banner of Russian Orthodoxy" (L. Brodsky, ed., "Materials concerning the Question of the Anglican Church," *Khristianskoe chtenie* [April 1904], pp. 596-97, cited by Litvack, *John Mason Neale,* p. 51).

28. Anthony Bloom, "Holiness and Prayer," in Anthony Bloom, *God and Man* (London: Darton, Longman and Todd; Crestwood: St. Vladimir's Seminary Press, 1983), pp. 73-119, here p. 87.

29. Letter of 4 June 1845. The correspondence is published in W. J. Birkbeck *et al., Russia and the English Church During the last Fifty Years* (London: Rivington, Percival and Co., 1895); this quotation occurs on p. 24. See also Athelstan Riley, ed., *Birkbeck and the Russian Church* (London: SPCK; New York: Macmillan Co., 1917). Of Birkbeck, Arthur Michael Ramsey wrote that he "will ever have a place of special honour in the story of Russian and English Church relations. A scholarly layman of ardent devotion and an accomplished Russian linguist, he strove throughout his life to make the Church of England known in Russia and to stir English Churchmen to a concern for the Russian Church" (Preface to H. M. Waddams, ed., *Anglo-Russian Theological Conference, Moscow, July 1956* [London: The Faith Press; New York: Morehouse-Gorham, 1957], p. viii).

Khomiakov, wrote Nicolas Zernov,

> longed to see the Anglican and the Orthodox Churches restored to inter-communion: yet he returned over and over again to his logical position, that if the Church is one and the Eastern Christians are part of it, those who are not in communion with them are outside her fold, and that therefore William Palmer was not a member of the Church, and ought first of all to be baptized.[30]

While informal ecumenism foundered, the rich hymnody of the East was becoming familiar to Victorian Anglicans through the translations of John Mason Neale, who in 1847 also published the first volume of his *History of the Holy Eastern Church: The Patriarchate of Alexandria.* "In treating with the East," he wrote,

> we come with no pretensions of superiority, with no claims to domination; we come, free from many of the stumbling-blocks which Latin Christianity presents to their eyes — purgatory, indulgences, the denial of the cup to the laity, azymes, and in two of the liturgies out of the three branches of our communion, the Scotch and the American, we approximate very closely, we are identical, on all essential points, with those of S. Chrysostom and S. Basil.[31]

Yet other clerics collaborated in translating the works of the ante- and post-Nicene Fathers into English in series that made patristic teaching commonplace among Anglicans and that continue to be reprinted and used today.

The Age of Optimism II: Official Contacts

Official relations between the Anglican Communion and the Orthodox Churches date to this same period. Dialogues among Anglicans and Orthodox theologians in 1879 produced a list of differences between them, in three categories: (1) What should be revised *(filioque)*, (2) what should be discussed (the number of sacraments, the Eucharist, transubstantiation, priesthood, the sec-

---

30. Nicolas Zernov, "Alexei Stepanovich Khomiakov," *Sobornost* 10 (June 1937): 10-11, cited by Litvack, *John Mason Neale,* p. 50.

31. J. M. Neale, *Essays on Liturgiology and Church History,* 2d ed. (London: Saunders, Otley, 1867), p. 281; originally published 1855 in *The Christian Remembrancer.*

ond marriage of clergy, the invocation of saints, prayers for the dead, icons and the seventh ecumenical council), and (3) what could be maintained (the marriage of bishops).[32]

In 1888, the nonacentenary of the conversion of Russia, Anglican bishops from around the globe meeting together at Lambeth sent greetings to Kiev and approved four criteria for serious discussions aimed at the reunion of Christendom. The "Chicago-Lambeth Quadrilateral" affirmed

a. The Holy Scriptures of the Old and New Testaments, as "containing all things necessary to salvation," and as being the rule and ultimate standard of faith.

b. The Apostles' Creed, as the Baptismal Symbol; and the Nicene Creed, as the sufficient statement of the Christian faith.

c. The two Sacraments ordained by Christ himself — Baptism and the Supper of the Lord — ministered with unfailing use of Christ's words of Institution, and of the elements ordained by Him.

d. The Historic Episcopate, locally adapted in the methods of its administration to the varying needs of the nations and peoples called of God into the Unity of His Church.[33]

An Orthodox observer at Lambeth commented to the Bishop of Ely: "When I return to Greece I will say that the Church of England is not like other Protestant bodies. . . . I will say that it is a sound Catholic Church very like our own. I trust that by friendly discussion union between the two Churches may be brought about."[34]

Nineteenth-century actions by the remaining "third branch" of Catholic Christendom also contributed to growing Anglican fascination with the East. In 1870 Rome promulgated the dogma of papal infallibility and then asserted the bishop of Rome's universal ordinary jurisdiction throughout Christendom. Four years later, Anglicans and Orthodox, at a conference with Lutherans and Old Catholics, had no difficulty in agreeing in opposition to what they consid-

---

32. George Williams, *A Collection of Documents Relating Chiefly to the Visit of Alexander Archbishop of Syros and Tenos to England in 1870* (London: Rivingtons, 1872), cited by Methodios Fouyas, *Orthodoxy, Roman Catholicism and Anglicanism* (London, New York, and Toronto: Oxford University Press, 1972; rept. Brookline, MA: Holy Cross Orthodox Press, 1984), p. 39.

33. BCP, pp. 877-78.

34. The Greek Archbishop of Syra and Tenos. Cited from *The Six Lambeth Conferences, 1867-1920*, compiled by Randall Davidson (London: SPCK, 1929), p. 167, n. 3, cited by William H. van de Pol (*Anglicanism in Ecumenical Perspective*, Duquesne Studies Theological Series 4 [Pittsburgh: Duquesne University Press, 1965], p. 165).

ered a novel and extravagant challenge to the doctrine of episcopacy developed by Ignatius, Cyprian, and other Fathers of the primitive church.

When in 1896 the papal bull *Apostolicae Curae* pronounced Anglican orders "absolutely null and utterly void," Anglicans immediately looked East to a church of undoubted apostolic origin for affirmation that the sacred orders they had preserved at great cost through the Reformation, the Civil War, and the Commonwealth were indeed valid. Constantinople declared, cautiously, in 1922 that Anglican orders "have the same validity as those of the Roman, Old Catholic and Armenian Churches,"[35] an opinion echoed by the churches of Jerusalem, Cyprus,[36] Alexandria,[37] and Romania.[38] Heartened, Lambeth bishops broadened the dialogue, sponsored the translation of "books and documents setting forth the relative positions" of the two churches, and asked the English church to consult "personally or by correspondence" with the eastern churches "with a view to . . . securing a clearer understanding and . . . establishing closer relations between the Churches of the East and the Anglican Communion."[39]

Subsequent Lambeth Conferences authorized a permanent committee to "take cognisance of all that concerns our relations with the churches of the Orthodox East"[40] and set down communion-wide pastoral guidelines for Anglican hospitality to Orthodox in diaspora, "when they are deprived of the ministrations of a priest of their own Communion."[41]

The Russian church was removed from this developing dialogue by the October Revolution. Within a few years, however, the flood of Russian *émigrés* brought the living tradition of the East to the attention of Western Christians. An on-going forum for sharing scholarship, worship, and friendship was founded in England in the Fellowship of SS Alban and Sergius. Books and arti-

---

35. *Ekklesiastiki Aletheia* 42 (1922): 327, 343; George K. A. Bell, *Documents on Christian Unity,* First Series, 1920-24 (London: Oxford University Press, 1924), pp. 93-96, cited by Fouyas, *Orthodoxy, Roman Catholicism and Anglicanism,* p. 100, n. 1.

36. *Nea Sion* 18 (1923): 127-28; *Ekklesiastiki Aletheia* 43 (1923): 96; Bell, *Documents on Christian Unity,* pp. 97-98, cited by Fouyas, *Orthodoxy, Roman Catholicism and Anglicanism,* p. 100, n. 2.

37. *The Christian East: A Quarterly Review Devoted to the Study of the Eastern Churches* 12 (1931): 1-3; Bell, *Documents on Christian Unity,* Third Series, 1930-1948 (London: Oxford University Press, 1948), p. 38, cited by Fouyas, *Orthodoxy, Roman Catholicism and Anglicanism,* p. 100, n. 4.

38. *Orthodoxia* 11 (1936): 282-84; Bell, *Documents on Christian Unity,* Third Series, p. 49, cited by Fouyas, *Orthodoxy, Roman Catholicism and Anglicanism,* p. 100, n. 5.

39. Lambeth 1897, Resolution 36. Resolutions are cited from *Resolutions of the Twelve Lambeth Conferences, 1867-1988,* ed. Roger Coleman (Toronto: Anglican Book Centre, 1992).

40. Lambeth 1908, Resolution 61.

41. Lambeth 1908, Resolution 62.

cles by such Orthodox theologians as Georges Florovsky, Anthony Bloom, and John Meyendorff introduced many to the rich spirituality hitherto hidden in the East.

In 1920 the Lambeth Conference received the first official delegation of the Œcumenical Patriarchate. While attaching "the greatest importance" to the visit, the assembled bishops advocated deeper acquaintance before action. "[O]ur progress will be no less sure because it is slow,"[42] they warned:

> The spiritual leadership of the Catholic Church in days to come, for which the world is manifestly waiting, depends upon the readiness with which each group [of Christian churches] is prepared to make sacrifices for the sake of a common fellowship, a common ministry, and a common service to the world.[43]

Consequently, they discouraged "general schemes of intercommunion or exchange of pulpits" before thorough theological discussion and agreement had taken place.[44]

The Terms of Intercommunion Suggested between the Church of England and the Churches in Communion with Her and the Eastern Orthodox Church, published the following year by the Archbishop of Canterbury's Eastern Churches Committee[45] in consultation with the patriarch's delegates,[46] balanced theological agreement with caution and marked out issues of concern to Orthodox (the division of confirmation/chrismation from baptism, and retention of the *filioque* unilaterally and uncanonically inserted in the creed), and to Anglicans (the authority of the Seventh Ecumenical Council's declarations on icons). Ominously, it was noted, "There was disagreement on the doctrine of the Church."[47]

The document illustrated growing awareness of the historical conditioning of vocabulary and of theological concerns within the two churches. Anglican willingness to consider the Eucharist as sacrifice was balanced by Orthodox readiness not to insist on the vocabulary of μετουσίωσις, in Anglican opinion a

---

42. Lambeth 1920, p. 147.
43. Lambeth 1920, Resolution 9.
44. Lambeth 1920, Resolution 12.
45. Reapproved and reauthorized by Lambeth 1920, Resolution 19, "as helping greatly to forward the cause of reunion with the Orthodox Church."
46. See Bell, *Documents of Christian Unity,* First Series, pp. 77-89.
47. Church of England, Eastern Churches Committee, *Terms of Intercommunion Suggested between the Church of England and the Churches in Communion with Her and the Eastern Orthodox Church* (London: SPCK, 1921).

term equivalent to *transubstantiation* and unacceptable to Anglicans, who had always refused to define how Christ is present in the Eucharist. Arthur Michael Ramsey, noting that the theologians had addressed traditional categories of differences at Bucharest in 1935 and produced "Agreements on Scripture and Tradition, Holy Eucharist, Holy Mysteries and Justification," also pointed out:

> a more correct title to [their] statement would be "justification and sanctification": the statement: Man partakes of the redeeming grace through faith and good works would be better stated: Man partakes of the redeeming grace through faith which issues in good works.

Reflecting a few years later on misunderstandings to which Russian and English Christians were prone, the astute and prayerful Ramsey underscored one of the difficulties inherent in all dialogue between long-separated Christians. "What is the border-line between dogma and theological opinion?" he inquired. Differences of language, spiritual formation, and theological training complicate discussion, he pointed out, but "there are also differences which arise from the two Churches asking different questions as a result of totally different historical experiences."[48]

Anglicans admitted that what held their communion together was not uniformity of doctrine but shared common prayer, and they increasingly realized that broad differences of theological opinion made them a sometimes perplexing dialogue partner. Christians who share the English heritage, a 1938 doctrinal commission of the Church of England pointed out,

> are the heirs of the Reformation as well as of the Catholic tradition; and they hold together in a single fellowship of worship and witness those whose chief attachment is to each of these, and also those whose attitude to the distinctively Christian tradition is most deeply affected by the tradition of a free and liberal culture which is historically the bequest of the Greek spirit.[49]

On their side, the Orthodox began to realize that the doctrine and devotion of all Anglicans were not identical with those of some Anglicans, and that in pews around the world knelt a number of people who would be uncomfortable with,

---

48. Ramsey, Preface, p. x.

49. *Doctrine in the Church of England* (1938), p. 25, cited from G. R. Evans and J. Robert Wright, *The Anglican Tradition: A Handbook of Sources* (London: SPCK; Minneapolis: Fortress Press, 1991), pp. 401-2.

if not downright hostile to, the veneration of icons, the invocation of the saints, and prayers for the dead.

Over the iron curtain that divided East from West politically after World War II, Anglican and Russian Christians initiated "the first exchange of thought held for many years between the theologians of two Churches long separated."[50] Anglican bishops from around the world "heartily" welcomed this,

> ... convinced that the contribution of the Orthodox tradition is essential to the full life and witness of the Universal Church and that a deepened understanding and fellowship between our two Communions has much to give to the healing of the nations, and especially to the growth of mutual understanding between East and West in the world today.[51]

In North America — as in other one-time British colonies — meanwhile, Episcopalians and Orthodox in many places lived side by side and contrasted their similarities with Protestant diversities. At a meeting of bishops, theologians of various traditions, and representatives of two ecumenical organizations, the World Council of Churches and the National Council of Churches of Christ, in the autumn of 1960 Archbishop Iakavos of the Greek Orthodox Church of North and South America cordially but unequivocally brushed aside the NCCC "conciliar" approach to ecumenism as "merely a romantic connection" and singled out Presiding Bishop Arthur Lichtenberger of the Episcopal Church: "Orthodox and Episcopalians must get together *soon*," Iakavos declared. "The time is here to get down to business on unity." After eighty years of official conversations, he went on, "here there are no sharp problems and no problems are pending."[52] Both churches taught the doctrine defined and proclaimed by the early ecumenical councils; both looked to the Fathers of the church more than to medieval theologians; both held that Christ is truly present in the eucharist without attempting to define just how he might be present.

The U.S. Anglican-Orthodox Theological Consultation assumed wide-ranging doctrinal agreement. By 1964, members reported full agreement on eucharistic theology, the nature of Christ's sacramental presence, the role of the Holy Spirit, and the doctrine of sacrifice, and they could "regard as superfluous

50. Ramsey, Preface, pp. x-xi.
51. Lambeth 1948, Resolution 66.
52. Minutes of the meeting at Seabury House, Greenwich, CT, 5-6 October 1960. I am grateful to the Reverend William A. Norgren and the Ecumenical Office at the Episcopal Church Center, New York, for sharing these Minutes with me.

any further discussion of the Eucharist by this Consultation except as it may illuminate related doctrines." They concentrated their attention on pastoral matters. Orthodox unable to attend their own churches in the vast, mostly Protestant, country were urged to attend the Episcopal Church; Episcopalians in mixed marriages were not to be required to promise to raise their children as Orthodox. The orderliness of Orthodox divorce procedures was contrasted with the episcopal discretionary approach Episcopalians had hastily concocted after they had allowed remarriage after divorce. More than once the consultation reprimanded clergy in both churches who proselytized members of the other church or who in their "individualism and excessive zeal" proselytized or presented full communion as a goal already achieved.

Archbishop Ramsey summed up Anglican-Orthodox relations when he wrote of a conference at Bucharest in 1965:

> With the Holy Orthodox church Anglicans feel some special bonds, and we believe that in strengthening those bonds we may serve the total cause of Christian unity in a special way. The Anglican Communion is a family of autokephalous Churches, sharing the same faith, the same sacramental order, the same doctrine, and (with some local variations) the same liturgy . . . it is our claim to be, like the Holy Orthodox Church, Catholic without being papalist.

The archbishop also reminded Anglicans and Orthodox that, despite differences born of different historical experiences, the two churches shared a common faith and the common conviction that Christian men and women, created in the image and likeness of God, were called to be holy as God is holy and that the church existed to nourish that holiness and witness to that faith:

> We cannot forget that the unity of Christians is inseparable from the sanctification of Christians. Already the Holy Paraclete dwells in the souls of the Orthodox and the souls of the Anglicans, and as souls are restored in holiness, the unity of the Church is restored. The holiness of Christians is manifested in prayer, and prayer is itself a mighty part of the work of unity. So too is the holiness of Christians manifested in works of love, brotherhood, peace and justice, to heal the terrible wounds of the human race. Christians will find that the unity of the Church grows in truth and holiness while they give themselves to serve mankind and to heal the broken unity of the human race.[53]

53. Cited from the September 1965 Anglican-Orthodox Consultation Minutes.

Ecumenists might do worse than to ponder his words against an unconscious desire to remake their ecumenical partners in their own ecclesiastical image, rather than in the image of the Image of the invisible God.

The Age of Disillusionment

Not long after that moment of insight, a chill wind blew over the American dialogue. By the 1970s, it turned into a howling blizzard nationally, and internationally temperatures plummeted. The Age of Disillusionment had begun.

Why? The easy answer, often alleged, is the change in mentality and canons by which in 1976 the American and Canadian Anglican Churches permitted women in some dioceses to be ordained to the diaconate and the priesthood. Anglican bishops at Lambeth in 1978 themselves scrambled on how to deal with this divisive issue, aware that a still more contentious act, the ordination of women to the episcopate, might soon follow,[54] and that these actions might shatter both Anglican solidarity and ecumenical discourse:

> We recognise that our accepting this variety of doctrine and practice in the Anglican Communion may disappoint the Roman Catholic, Orthodox, and Old Catholic Churches, but we wish to make it clear
> (A) that the holding together of diversity within a unity of faith and worship is part of the Anglican heritage;
> (B) that those who have taken part in ordinations of women to the priesthood believe that these ordinations have been into the historic ministry of the Church as the Anglican Communion has received it; and
> (C) that we hope the dialogue between these other Churches and the member Churches of our Communion will continue because we believe that we still have understanding of the truth of God and his will to learn from them as together we all move towards a fuller catholicity and deeper fellowship in the Holy Spirit.[55]

54. 1978 Lambeth, Resolution 22 on Women in the Episcopate: "While recognising that a member Church of the Anglican Communion may wish to consecrate a woman to the episcopate, and accepting that such member Church must act in accordance with its own constitution, the Conference recommends that no decision to consecrate be taken without consultation with the episcopate through the primates and overwhelming support in any member Church and in the diocese concerned, lest the bishop's office should become a cause of disunity instead of a focus of unity."

55. Lambeth 1918, Resolution 21.

Orthodox reaction to these events can be gauged from the reaction of Archbishop Methodios Fouyas of Thyateira and Great Britain. As recently as 1972 he had written:

> When the Anglican Church and its tradition is more fully understood by the Orthodox, I am sure it will be recognized that Anglicanism represents a genuine spirit of Orthodoxy so developed as to be understood by modern thought. Anglicanism is not a Protestant Church, but a reformed Catholic Church, which maintains its unity with the tradition of the ancient undivided Church.[56]

After the ordination of women, he reconsidered this opinion: "The situation between the Orthodox and the Anglicans is growing worse, due to the instability of the contemporary Anglican Church with respect to the catholic elements of the Church of Christ."[57]

In fact, however, the chill predated the ordination of women. A rival had entered the apparently exclusive courtship between Anglicans and Orthodox. At the Second Vatican Council (1962-64), the Church of Rome committed herself irrevocably to ecumenism, not on the perceived Counter-Reformation grounds of "come home, submit to Rome" but with an openness to genuine dialogue. For nearly a millennium, Constantinople and Rome had been out of communion, and England and Rome for half a millennium. Both Constantinople and Canterbury had sundered relations with Rome, not with one another, and it suddenly seemed intuitively clear that reconciliation should begin where schism had begun. An Anglican–Roman Catholic International Consultation began its work in 1967. A Joint International Commission for Theological Dialogue between the Roman Catholic Church and the Orthodox Church was established in December 1979. The age of what Fr. Colin Davey has called the Anglican-Orthodox "alliance against Rome"[58] was over. As the published statements of both dialogues make clear, very different historical and doctrinal fences were being mended.

Rome was not the only rival to Orthodox-Anglican courtship. Orthodox chilliness in the United States was coeval with Orthodox realization that the Episcopal Church had committed itself to the Consultation on Church Union, a group of nine churches in the Reformed and Methodist traditions, none of whom — except the Episcopal Church — claimed, and most of whom did not

---

56. Fouyas, *Orthodoxy, Roman Catholicism and Anglicanism*, p. 88.
57. Fouyas, *Orthodoxy, Roman Catholicism and Anglicanism*, p. viii.
58. Davey, "Anglicans and Eastern Christendom," p. 9.

want, episcopacy in the historical succession, and all of whom taught — at least officially — the sufficiency of scripture without reliance on the Fathers. Like a kaleidoscope suddenly turned ninety degrees, the patterned image of Anglicanism as a church basing its doctrine and discipline on scripture, reason, and patristic tradition splintered into random fragments. If Episcopalians could take seriously the series of proposals that issued from COCU,[59] then, Orthodox concluded, Anglican ecclesiology was not what they had been led to believe it to be.[60] There must indeed be deep-seated "disagreement on the doctrine of the Church."[61]

Close familiarity revealed what occasional meetings had not. "Comprehensiveness demands agreement on fundamentals, while tolerating disagreement on matters in which Christians may differ without feeling the necessity of breaking communion," argued the Committee on Anglican-Orthodox Relations of the 1968 Lambeth Conference. "In the mind of an Anglican, comprehensiveness is not compromise. Nor is it to bargain one truth for another. . . . Rather it implies that the apprehension of truth is a growing thing; we only gradually succeed in knowing the truth."[62] The development of doctrine was not a theory congenial to many Orthodox. On the other side, as Victorian courtliness has given way to post-modern candor, Anglican writers, even those who hope for union with the East, have muttered of "the danger of sclerosis"[63] and contrasted Anglicans' involvement in and openness to history, "in a way which seems scandalous to many Orthodox," with Orthodox "withdrawal from history, standing apart from its vicissitudes in a way which seems scandalous to many Anglicans. . . ."[64]

Agreed statements issued at Moscow in 1977 and Dublin in 1984 by the International Anglican-Orthodox Theological Dialogue yet again reviewed the long-studied fundamental agreements and disagreements of the two churches. They differed from nineteenth- and early-twentieth-century studies only in

59. Now known as Churches Uniting in Christ (CUIC).

60. In fact, the CUIC discussions have gone on from 1960 to the present with no positive action taking place and with only cautious encouragement from successive General Conventions. See GC 1988, Resolution A038a; GC 1991, Resolution B043; GC 1994, Resolution A029s. On contemporary Anglican ecclesiology, see Henry Chadwick, "Anglican Ecclesiology and Its Challenges," in *Ecumenism of the Possible: Witness, Theology and the Future Church*, ed. William A. Norgren (Cincinnati: Forward Movement Publications, 1994), pp. 3-12.

61. See above, n. 46.

62. *The Lambeth Conference Report 1968*, p. 140, cited by A. M. Allchin, *The Kingdom of Love and Knowledge: The Encounter Between Orthodoxy and the West* (London: Darton, Longman and Todd, 1979), pp. 154-55.

63. Allchin, *Kingdom*, p. 147.

64. Allchin, *Kingdom*, p. 147.

their inclusion of new subjects of disagreement and in laying a foundation for international, regional, and local conversations.

Meanwhile, the goal of what was once called "intercommunion" and institutional consolidation has been replaced among Anglicans by hopes for a unity envisaged by the Ecumenical Committee of the 1988 Lambeth Conference of Anglican Bishops as a gradual growing together that evolves in four stages:

1. fellowship in faith (expressed in teaching and in practice) and mission,
2. limited sharing of communion once Churches have sufficient agreement in faith and are committed to proceed ultimately to full communion,
3. Full communion, allowing for interchange of ordained ministers and members while remaining distinct ecclesiastical bodies; and only then,
4. Organic unity.[65]

The Episcopal Church, after four hundred years' experience of a religiously pluralist society, has chosen to aim its ecumenical efforts at achieving "one eucharistic fellowship . . . a communion of Communions"[66] rather than "organic unity." In this they echo the late Orthodox theologian, Alexander Schmemann, who reminded the American dialogue in 1968: "Our study of the church should not be of church as a structure, but of its content. What is being given [is] the gift of the Holy Spirit."[67]

The International Dialogue continues to meet, although the ordination of women to the priesthood and episcopacy and, more recently, the ordination of an acknowledged homosexual to the episcopacy have made hope of full communion in our lifetime seem bleak. Can we hope that, having been brutally disabused of our illusions, we can now regard one another and ourselves without illusion and still engage in candid, respectful friendship, foster ecclesiastical cooperation, and pray and work for the unity for which Christ prayed?

Illusion did not provide a firm foundation. Personal contacts and ecclesiastical pronouncements have not forced the Spirit, who "bloweth where he listeth" (John 3:8 AV) — the Elizabethan way of saying that Christ's Church will be one as and when God wills, not when we pull it off. We can delay or advance the visible unity of the Body of Christ; we cannot achieve or thwart it.

Did Bishop Germanos of Thyateira accurately represent the Orthodox

65. *The Truth Shall Make You Free,* The Lambeth Report 1988: Ecumenical Relations, §83.

66. "Declaration on Unity" adopted by General Convention 1979, affirmed by General Convention 1988. Fr. Wright had a leading hand in this resolution.

67. Minutes of the 1968 Anglican-Orthodox Theological Consulatation, unpaginated.

position when in 1927, after declaring that the Orthodox Church "concedes to theologians freedom of thought as regards things which are not essential," he asked:

> ... what are the elements of Christian teaching which are to be regarded as essential? The Orthodox Church holds the view that it is not necessary that these should be discussed and determined at the present time, since they have been already determined in the old symbols and decisions of the seven Ecumenical Synods. Consequently, the teaching of the ancient undivided Church of the first eight centuries, free from every question which did not have a direct relation to these things which were to be believed, must to-day also constitute the basis of the reunion of the Churches.[68]

Did Archbishop Arthur Michael Ramsey accurately represent the Anglican position when, in 1956, he described affinities linking Anglicans and Orthodox?

> From the end of the sixteenth century Anglicans have looked towards the Holy Orthodox Church as to a Church which, like their own, rejects the supremacy of Rome, appeals to Holy Scripture and to the ancient Fathers, and claims continuity with the ancient Church in its hierarchy and its sacramental life. The progress of mutual knowledge between the Churches was inevitably slow, as a result of centuries of separation and radically different historical experiences. To the West, Eastern Orthodoxy seemed strange, as it knew neither medieval Papalism nor the convulsions of the Reformation; to the East, the Church of England seemed no less strange as an off-shoot of the Western Papal Church. But within both Churches there has come about a feeling that the other is significant for the reunion of Christendom just because it goes behind some of the familiar modern categories in its claim to a primitive catholicity different alike from Rome and from the Reformation.[69]

If these statements continue to be true for the speakers' churches, then surely we can look forward to a new age, one in which the great church of the East, now more closely in contact with the western churches, may think itself

68. H. N. Bate, ed., *Faith and Order. Proceedings of the World Conference, Lausanne 1927* (London: SCM, 1927), pp. 20-21, cited by Michael Kinnamon and Brian E. Cope, eds., *The Ecumenical Movement: An Anthology of Key Texts and Voices* (Geneva: WCC Pubs.; Grand Rapids: William B. Eerdmans Publishing Co., 1997), pp. 14-15.

69. Ramsey, Preface, pp. vii-viii.

able to reappraise the links between doctrine and discipline, and one in which the Anglican Communion, after a period of sometimes unconsidered modernism, may re-appropriate its own long and rich tradition and reclaim patristic and medieval as well as modern exegeses in proclaiming Christ's gospel to the world.

Lutheranism and Orthodoxy:
An Exploration of Complementarity

William G. Rusch

Over more years than perhaps should be recalled, I have valued my friendship with J. Robert Wright. His considerable gifts as a scholar and ecumenist have contributed much to my own ecumenical thinking and commitment. His deep faith and alliance to the church of Christ have been models for us all to emulate. Thus I am indebted to the editors of this Festschrift for the opportunity to honor him.

It seems to me that among Professor Wright's ecumenical interests two may claim some special place in view of the significant time and energy that he has devoted to them. They are Lutheranism and Orthodoxy. His major role in the development of Episcopal-Lutheran relations in the United States and his profound dedication to Anglican-Orthodox relations are well known and applauded.[1]

In this brief essay, I wish to explore the relationship of these two interests of Professor Wright to each other. I shall consider the relationship from my own perspective as a Lutheran and leave to some person of the Orthodox tradition the future task of addressing the relationship from the Orthodox point of view.

In selecting this topic, I am not entering unplowed territory, for since the sixteenth century there has been Lutheran attention to the Orthodox churches.[2] Yet in the present moment when so much of American Lutheranism

---

1. In regard to Orthodoxy and the patristic church, Professor Wright is an example of a long-standing interest in Anglicanism in both of these subjects and an embodiment of the high quality of scholarship devoted to them. See, e.g., Arthur Pierce Middleton, *Fathers and Anglicans: The Limits of Orthodoxy* (Leominster: Gracewing, 2001).

2. See for example Georges Florovsky, "The Greek Version of the Augsburg Confession,"

seems struggling to find, or preserve, its identity and there appears to be so much stress on the "Protestant" character of Luther and Lutheranism, it may be helpful to recall a larger and more complex portrait than some are willing to acknowledge today.[3]

Lutheran and Orthodox Self-Understanding

Lutheranism sees its origins in a reforming movement within the western church. Its adherents have described it both as a corrective of the church catholic and as constitutive of something new in the history of the church. Both groups would acknowledge that Lutheranism is confessional, in the sense that a certain corpus of writings, the Confessions, offers its understanding of the Christian faith. These Confessions set forth the gospel as an unconditional promise of God's grace given in Christ Jesus. They have been seen as a proposal of dogma to the entire church, a proposal summed up in the teaching of justification by grace through faith.[4]

Thus for Lutherans the church and its unity are bound to the gospel's being purely preached and the holy sacraments administered according to the gospel. It follows then that agreement in the faith, or *consentire de doctrina evangelii,* is required for the unity of the church. This agreement must be stated and formulated in a binding manner for church unity.[5]

Orthodoxy perceives its origins in the one holy, catholic, and apostolic church. In the articulation of this understanding of its origins and nature, doc-

---

Lutheran World 6 (1959): 153-55, and "An Early Ecumenical Correspondence," in *World Lutheranism of Today* (Oxford: B. H. Blackwell; Rock Island, IL: Augustiana Book Concern, 1950), pp. 98-111; reprinted as "Patriarch Jeremiah II and the Lutheran Divines," in Georges Florovsky, *Christianity and Culture,* The Collected Works of Georges Florovsky vol. 2 (Belmont, MA: Nordland Publishing Co., 1974), pp. 143-55.

3. E.g., David S. Yeago, "The Catholic Luther," in *The Catholicity of the Reformation,* ed. Carl E. Braaten and Robert W. Jenson (Grand Rapids, MI: William B. Eerdmans Publishing Company, 1996), pp. 13-34.

4. See *Die Bekenntnisschriften der evangelisch-lutherischen Kirche* (Göttingen: Vandenhoeck & Ruprecht, 1959); *The Book of Concord: The Confessions of the Evangelical Lutheran Church,* ed. Robert Kolb and Timothy J. Wengert, trans. Charles Arand (Minneapolis: Fortress Press, 2000).

5. More recent interpretations of Lutheranism include Edmund Schlink, *The Theology of the Lutheran Confessions,* trans. Paul F. Koehneke and Herbert J. A. Bouman (Philadelphia: Fortress Press, 1961); Eric W. Gritsch and Robert W. Jenson, *Lutheranism: The Theological Movement and Its Confessional Writings* (Philadelphia: Fortress Press, 1976). Gritsch and Jenson see the Confessions as a proposal of dogma to the church catholic in terms of justification by grace through faith.

uments do not play the same role as they do in Lutheranism. The Orthodox churches see themselves as the preserver and witness of both the faith and the tradition of the one undivided church, the church of the Fathers. In Orthodox understanding the unity of this church is grounded in its foundation by Christ and in communion of the Holy Trinity and in the sacraments. This unity is expressed through apostolic succession, including the episcopate and the sacramental priesthood, the patristic tradition, and the ecumenical councils. Orthodoxy has no experience comparable to the Reformation in the West.[6]

In view of these different perceptions of identity, is there any point of contact between these two Christian traditions besides that of contrast? At first glance it would appear that the possibilities are not promising. Yet the search for a common element need not be fruitless.

It should be clear at the initial stages of this inquiry that the quest for a complement should not be viewed as an attempt at blurring the distinctiveness of each tradition. The pursuit of a common point should be seen within a context that acknowledges both Lutheranism and Orthodoxy as representatives of the legitimate diversity within the one Christian tradition.[7] This view is more compatible with Lutheran understandings of Lutheranism than with Orthodox perceptions of Orthodoxy. Nevertheless, the fact that on both the international and the national level Orthodoxy has entered into dialogue with Lutheranism at least implies an Orthodox recognition that both traditions have some claim to being "church," claims that are worthy of exploration and discussion.[8]

The thesis put forth here is rather simple and direct: Lutheranism and Orthodoxy should enjoy a relationship that is based on a common appreciation, indebtedness, and recognition of authority in the patristic tradition of

---

6. The texts of the first seven ecumenical councils, which carry great weight for Orthodoxy, can be found in *Decrees of the Ecumenical Councils,* ed. Norman Tanner, 2 vols. (London: Sheed & Ward; Washington, DC: Georgetown University Press, 1990), pp. 1-156. For Orthodox statements on the unity of the church and the ecumenical movement, see *The Orthodox Church in the Ecumenical Movement,* ed. Constantin G. Patelos (Geneva: WCC, 1978).

7. *Tradition* is used here in the sense of the definition of the Fourth World Conference on Faith and Order. See *The Fourth World Conference on Faith and Order, Montreal 1963,* ed. P. C. Rodger and Lukas Vischer (New York: Association Press, 1964), p. 52: ". . . the Tradition of the Gospel (the *paradosis* of the *kerygma*) testified in scripture, transmitted in and by the Church through the power of the Holy Spirit. Tradition taken in this sense is actualized in the preaching of the Word, in the administration of the Sacraments and worship, in Christian teaching and theology, and in mission and witness to Christ by the lives of the members of the Church. What is transmitted in the process of tradition is the Christian faith, not only as a sum of tenets, but as a living reality transmitted through the operation of the Holy Spirit."

8. Growth II, pp. 219-29; *Salvation in Christ: A Lutheran-Orthodox Dialogue,* ed. John Meyendorff and Robert Tobias (Minneapolis: Augsburg Publishing House, 1992).

the church of the first five centuries. What an official acknowledgment of such a relationship would mean in terms of satisfying the Lutheran commitment to a consensus in doctrine and the Orthodox conditions for a full ecclesial relation between the two traditions lies outside the scope of this short presentation.

The notion of any positive evaluation by Lutheranism of the church of the first several centuries might strike some persons as strange. Indeed one of the charges that Martin Luther and his followers had to answer was that they were innovators who were departing from the catholic tradition. This was the thrust both of the *Catholica et quasi ex temporalis responsio* and of the *Confutatio* issuing from the Diet of Augsburg in August of 1530.[9] Both texts are examples of a larger polemic to discredit the Lutheran Reformers for leaving the historic faith of the church catholic.

One way to probe Lutheranism's attitude to the patristic church is briefly and selectively to examine both Luther and the Lutheran Confessions. Martin Luther wrote much and said much more, as the famous Weimar *Ausgabe* of his works demonstrates in over a hundred volumes. The edition of the Lutheran Confessions in their original languages is 1228 pages. Thus this survey examines only two writings of Luther and selected passages of the Confessions.

In 1522 Luther composed his "Sincere Admonition to All Christians." The work originated in the context of the disturbances at Wittenberg while Luther was in seclusion at the Wartburg Castle after the Diet of Worms. It provides an insight into Luther's views in the light of the upheaval being caused by Andreas Karlstadt and Gabriel Zwilling. Luther penned some sentences that have been frequently quoted:

> In the first place, I ask that men make no reference to my name; let them call themselves Christians, not Lutherans. What is Luther? After all, the teaching is not mine. Neither was I crucified for anyone. . . . Not so, my dear friends; let us abolish all party names and call ourselves Christians, after him whose teaching we hold. . . . I hold, together with the universal church, the one universal teaching of Christ, who is our only master.[10]

---

9. See *Die Konfutation des Augsburgischen Bekenntnisses, ihre erste Gestalt und ihre Geschichte,* ed. Johannes Ficker (Leipzig: Johann Ambrosius Barth, 1891); *Die Confutatio der Confessio Augustana vom 3. August 1530,* ed. Herbert Immenkötter (Münster Westfalen: Aschendorff, 1981).

10. Martin Luther, "Sincere Admonition to All Christians," in *The Christian in Society II,* ed. Walter I. Brandt, Luther's Works vol. 45 (Philadelphia: Muhlenberg Press, 1962), pp. 70-71.

This was not an isolated opinion of Luther. He repeated it a few months later in his treatise "Receiving Both Kinds in the Sacrament":

> True, by any consideration of body or soul you should never say: I am Lutheran, or Papist. For neither of them died for you, or is your master. Christ alone died for you, he alone is your master, and you should confess yourself a Christian.[11]

Luther repeated this position a few months later; he repeatedly declared that he was not establishing a new church. Whenever the suspicion arose that he and his followers were doing so, they reacted with strong feelings, declaring that they were part of the one universal church of Christ that had existed throughout the centuries. The Lutheran Reformation had one main thrust: the continuity of the one church, specifically the one patristic and medieval church across the centuries.[12]

This judgment was held not only by the early Luther but also by the older Luther of 1539, the year he composed "On the Councils and the Church." Written at a time when he had given up any hope for a free Christian council, the work examines the historical significance of the apostolic council at Jerusalem and the first four ecumenical councils — Nicaea, Constantinople, Ephesus, and Chalcedon — and argues that the authority of such councils is limited to reaffirming the ancient faith of the apostles. Some of Luther's conclusions on the councils in this work are strikingly modern.[13]

Scholarship today recognizes that the acts of the councils were handed down in various forms and that forgeries were inserted into some of them. Commenting on one of the articles of the Nicene Council, Luther comments:

> But I cannot escape the suspicion that a fraud was committed and that the dear holy fathers never did set up such an article. Surely they would have spared the emperor Constantine this, he who had liberated them from the

---

11. Martin Luther, "Receiving Both Kinds in the Sacrament," in *Word and Sacrament II,* ed. Abdel Ross Wentz, Luther's Works vol. 36 (Philadelphia: Muhlenberg Press, 1959), p. 265.

12. Two reflections of this insight in secondary literature dealing with both Luther and Lutheranism can be found in Arthur Carl Piepkorn, "Why Lutherans Should Engage in Conversation with Roman Catholics," in *The Church: Selected Writings of Arthur Carl Piepkorn,* ed. Michael P. Plekon and William S. Wiecher (Delhi, New York: ALPB Books, 1993), pp. 99-104; and in David S. Yeago, "The Catholic Luther," pp. 13-34.

13. Martin Luther, "On the Councils and the Church," in *Luther's Works: Church and Ministry III,* ed. Eric W. Gritsch, Luther's Works vol. 41 (Philadelphia: Fortress Press, 1966), pp. 9-177.

tyrants, not with St. Anthony's monkery, but with war and sword. It looks as though the other loose bishops pasted it on or smuggled it into the records later.[14]

While recognizing the limits of councils — they cannot make new doctrine, they have disagreed among themselves, they have erred — Luther had a keen sense of appreciation for what the councils achieved for the life of the patristic church. Although he makes some errors on detail, his account of these councils is refreshing and positive. He states that he has studied the early church with care — more so than his opponents — and the entire work reflects the honesty of this statement.[15] Given the highly polemical nature of the time, he must be granted high marks. He cannot be judged for lacking all the tools of a contemporary patristic scholar. But he has a positive and critical evaluation of the councils of the early church: he is willing to build on them and certainly not to repudiate or ignore them.[16]

Although pessimistic about holding a council in 1539 to solve the problems of the church of his day, Luther wrote,

> "Well," you say, "it is futile to hope for such a council." I myself think so too. But if one wants to talk about it and asks and wishes for a council, one would have to wish for a council like that, or forget about it completely, desire none, and say nothing at all. For the first council in Nicaea, and the second one in Constantinople, were councils like that — whose examples could indeed be easily followed.[17]

Yet Luther tended to see councils as exercising emergency functions in the church, not as something that could go on forever. The Nicene council he compares to a group of people hurrying over to assist a neighbor whose house is on fire and who is unable to extinguish it. For Luther a genuine council should do what the four early councils did: they should confess and defend the ancient faith. Luther also had some words of caution. He applied them directly to the councils:

> In summary, put them all together, both fathers and councils, and you still will not be able to cull from them all the teachings of the Christian faith,

14. Luther, "On the Councils and the Church," p. 41.
15. Luther, "On the Councils and the Church," p. 48.
16. Luther, "On the Councils and the Church," pp. 133-34.
17. Luther, "On the Councils and the Church," p. 141.

even if you culled forever. If it had not been for Holy Scripture, the church, had it depended on the councils and fathers, would not have lasted long. And in proof of this: where do the fathers and councils get what they teach or deal with? Do you think that they first invented it in their own day, or that the Holy Spirit always inspired them with something new? . . . Or were there no Christians before the councils and fathers came up?[18]

If you have all the councils you are still no Christian because of them; they give you too little. If you also have all the fathers, they too give you too little. You must still go to Holy Scripture, where you find everything in abundance, or to the catechism, where it is summarized, and where far more is found than in all the councils and fathers.[19]

Thus one would say that Luther approved the early church but considered that it was not to be followed slavishly but, like the church of any age, to be judged by the gospel. Luther applied the same standard of judgment to individual church Fathers. Writing of Saint Cyprian (martyred in A.D. 258), he notes Cyprian's error on re-baptism but concludes with affectionate commendation of Cyprian:

But we are well content with St. Cyprian, for in him Christ comforts us poor sinners mightily, showing that his great saints are after all still human — like St. Cyprian, this excellent man and dear martyr, who blundered in more serious matters, about which we lack the time to speak now.[20]

Of course Luther saw Augustine of Hippo as the greatest of the Fathers, writing at one point: "For when St. Augustine is eliminated from the ranks of the fathers, the others are not worth much." Luther could overstate his case! He continues, "Moreover, it would be senseless and intolerable not to consider St. Augustine one of the best fathers, since he is revered as the best by all of Christendom."[21] One of Luther's favorite quotations from Augustine, which he reproduces in "On the Councils and the Church," comes from Augustine's preface to "On the Trinity":

My dear man, do not follow my writing as you do Holy Scripture. Instead, whatever you find in Holy Scripture that you would not have believed before,

---

18. Luther, "On the Councils and the Church," p. 52.
19. Luther, "On the Councils and the Church," p. 136.
20. Luther, "On the Councils and the Church," p. 44.
21. Luther, "On the Councils and the Church," p. 27.

believe without doubt. But in my writings you should regard nothing as certain that you were uncertain about before, unless I have proved its truth.[22]

There was the hermeneutical key with which Luther was willing to read the entire corpus of the faithful interpreters of the scripture. They are brothers in Christ to be heard with respect.

Luther recognized that figures in the medieval church also emphasized the authority of scripture. He calls particular attention to the fact that the twelfth-century Bernard of Clairvaux insisted on the priority of scripture over patristic writing:

> He adds that he regards the holy fathers highly, but does not heed all their sayings, explaining why in the following parable: he would rather drink from the spring itself than from the brook, as do all men, who once they have a chance to drink from the spring forget about the brook, unless they use the brook to lead them to the spring. Thus Scripture too must remain master and judge, for when we follow the brooks too far, they lead us too far away from the spring, and lose both their taste and nourishment, until they lose themselves in the salty sea, as happened under the papacy.[23]

This insistence on relying on scripture in preference to the church Fathers is a recurring point.[24]

The Lutheran Confessions

The index in *Die Bekenntnisschriften* contains numerous references to the Fathers: e.g., Ambrose, Athanasius, Augustine, Basil, John Chrysostom, Cyprian, Cyril of Alexandria, Dionysius the Areopagite, Eusebius of Caesarea, Gregory the Great, Gregory of Nazianzus, Jerome, Hilary of Poitiers, Irenaeus, John of Damascus, Justin Martyr, Leo the Great, Origen, and Tertullian.[25]

---

22. Luther, "On the Councils and the Church," p. 25.

23. Luther, "On the Councils and the Church," p. 20.

24. There is a considerable body of secondary literature devoted to Luther's evaluation and use of the patristic tradition and the way he related that tradition to the authority of scripture. See, e.g., Wolfgang A. Bienert, "The Patristic Background of Luther's Theology," trans. Carolyn Schneider, *Lutheran Quarterly* 9 (1995): 263-79; Bernhard Lohse, *Evangelium in der Geschichte*, vol. 2, *Studien zur Theologie der Kirchenväter und ihrer Rezeption in der Reformation*, ed. Gabriele Borger, *et al.* (Göttingen: Vandenhoeck & Ruprecht, 1998), esp. pp. 191-284.

25. *Die Bekenntnisschriften*, pp. 1145-55.

In the Augsburg Confession quotations from the church Fathers occupy the most prominent place next to scripture. The usual placement of these quotations after the scripture texts gives the impression that the authors of the Confessions consciously accorded them an inferior position.[26] Numerous emphatic statements indicate how decisively the authors of the Confessions placed the church Fathers under the norm of scripture: "There is also a great variety among the Fathers. They were human beings who could err and be deceived"; "The writings of the holy Fathers bear witness that at times even they built stubble upon the foundation but that this did not overturn their faith."[27] It will not do, the Confessions insist, to make articles of faith out of the holy Fathers' words or works. Even the words of Augustine are not to be accepted "lacking support from Scripture."[28] With a single statement of the apostle Peter thousands of quotations from the church Fathers may be opposed.[29]

Nevertheless, the writers of the Lutheran Confessions wished to express their unanimity with the church of the past fifteen centuries, doing so by means of copious patristic quotations, as by the "Catalog of Testimonies" of both scripture and of orthodox antiquity added to the *Book of Concord,* the final edition of the Lutheran Confessions.[30] But like Luther, these writers consistently made the Fathers subject to the norm of scripture. Why then did the Lutheran Reformers bother to quote the church Fathers at all? Why not quote only scripture? They cited the Fathers because of the Fathers' consensus in the exposition of scripture; again and again the Reformers introduced patristic quotations with phrases emphasizing that consensus: "similarly," "the same," "not only . . . but also."[31]

While the Lutheran Confessions by no means place the church Fathers on the same level as holy scripture, they give the Fathers' exposition of scripture an authority close to their own: "For the name of spiritual father belongs only to those who govern and guide us by the Word of God."[32] Further, the patristic quotations demonstrate that the doctrine of the Confessions offers nothing new: "So that no one may quibble that we have contrived a new interpretation of Paul, this entire approach is supported by the testimonies of the Fathers."[33]

---

26. Augsburg Confession, Article XX, in *The Book of Concord,* p. 55.

27. Apology of the Augsburg Confession, Articles XXVII.95, VII.20, in *The Book of Concord,* pp. 276, 177.

28. Smalcald Articles, II.14, in *The Book of Concord,* p. 304.

29. Cf. Apology of the Augsburg Confession, Article XXII.70, p. 199.

30. "Catalogus Testimoniorum," in *Die Bekenntnisschriften,* pp. 1101-35.

31. One can consult the biographical index in *The Book of Concord,* pp. 677-93, under the names of various Fathers, to document this point.

32. Large Catechism, I.158, in *The Book of Concord,* p. 408.

33. Augsburg Confession, Article XX.12, p. 55.

The rejection of the new does not preserve ecclesiastical traditions but rather rejects an arbitrary exegesis. It is especially a caution arising from some distrust regarding the possibility of the arbitrariness of ecclesiastical traditions. The Reformers cite the church Fathers not for their own sake but for the sake of the church's understanding of scripture. The Fathers become a warning, serving both as examples through their false exegesis and as aids to correct exegesis. Even by means of questionable or false exegesis they open the horizon for manifold exegetical possibilities.

If the patristic quotations serve a clarifying purpose for the interpretation of scripture by acting through warning and assistance — by means of correct and false exegesis — to uncover the richness of the exegetical possibilities, it is obviously not of decisive importance which Father says this or that, but whether he speaks the truth. In spite of certain gradations of esteem enjoyed by individual Fathers, they all remain equally subject to scripture. Thus the Reformers' treatment of the Fathers in the Confessions exactly mirrors Luther's.

The inclusion of the three ancient ecumenical creeds in *The Book of Concord* is a case in point.[34] These three creeds, the Apostles', Nicene, and Athanasian, constitute the first section of *The Book of Concord*. In the German edition they are captioned "The Three Chief Symbols or Creeds of the Christian Faith, which are commonly used in the church," but in the Latin "The Three Catholic or Ecumenical Symbols." The Formula of Concord, the last-composed Lutheran confession, applies the adjectives "unanimous, universal, Christian" to these three creeds and declares them to be the confession of the orthodox and true church of Christ.[35] These titles served not only to classify the three creeds and to indicate their use in the church at the time but also by implication to suggest their venerable position in the history of the church.

By including these creeds in *The Book of Concord,* the Lutherans of the sixteenth century testified to their acceptance of the ancient doctrines of the church, doctrines concerning Christ and the Trinity. They approved these doctrines and thus accepted the creeds that stated them. But the Formula of Concord says that they are only a testimony to and an explanation of faith. In accord with this view articles of the Creeds that prompted controversy in any period reveal how the people who lived at that same time understood and ex-

34. *The Book of Concord*, pp. 19-25, where one finds the Apostles' Creed, the Nicene Creed, and the Athanasian Creed, which are described in *Die Bekenntnisschriften*, p. 19, as "Die drei Haupt-Symbola" or "Tria Symbola catholica sive oecumenica."

35. *The Book of Concord*, p. 486. In the original languages the text reads "einhelligen, allgemeinen, christlichen" or "unanimae, catholicae, Christianae," *Die Bekenntnisschriften*, p. 768.

pounded scripture, and how they rejected and condemned doctrine contrary to scripture.[36]

Philipp Melanchthon, friend of Luther and author of the Augsburg Confession, repeatedly made a similar distinction in his writings.[37] He insisted that scripture be obeyed and the ancient creeds be accepted. Therefore to see Lutherans' endorsement of the creeds as only a means of escaping persecution, as some scholars have suggested, is to miss the point. The Lutheran Reformers wished to underscore their identity with the church of the patristic era, but only as long as it was a church living in obedience to the scripture.

This idea permeates the Lutheran confessional writings, as a quick glance at the Augsburg Confession shows. Article I begins by stating its reliance on Nicaea and rejection of anti-Nicaean heresies:

> In the first place, it is with one accord taught and held, following the decree of the Council of Nicea. . . . Rejected, therefore, are all the heresies that are opposed to this article such as Manichaeans, . . . the Valentinians, the Arians, the Eunomians; also the Samosatenians. . . .[38]

Article II, on original sin, rejects the views of the Pelagians.[39] Article VII, on the church, declares: "It is also taught that at all times there must be and remain one holy, Christian church."[40] Here again is that linkage with the church of every age. Article VIII, also on the church, rejects the views of the Donatists, as does Article XII, on repentance, which condemns the Novatians.[41]

The case becomes clear. Lutheranism is neither hostile to nor indifferent towards the early church. In fact it has a healthy and critical appreciation of it, going to great efforts to demonstrate its relationship with Christians of the early centuries. In fact it was Lutheran theologians such as Johann Gerhard and Johann Hülsemann in the seventeenth century who introduced and spread the use of the term *patrology.*[42]

Whether Lutheranism has always correctly seen this continuity between

---

36. Formula of Concord, Epitome — Introduction.8 in *The Book of Concord,* p. 487.

37. E. P. Meijering, *Melanchthon and Patristic Thought: The Doctrines of Christ and Grace, the Trinity, and the Creation* (Leiden: E. J. Brill, 1983), esp. pp. 109-37; Heinz Scheible, *Melanchthon: Eine Biographie* (Munich: C. H. Beck, 1997), pp. 137-38.

38. *The Book of Concord,* pp. 36-37.

39. *The Book of Concord,* pp. 36-39.

40. *The Book of Concord,* p. 42.

41. *The Book of Concord,* pp. 42-43, 44-47.

42. Otto Bardenhewer, *Patrology: The Lives and Works of the Fathers of the Church,* trans. Thomas J. Shahan (Freiburg im Breisgau and St. Louis: B. Herder, 1908), p. 9.

itself and the Christian tradition as expressed by patristic authors and thus its potential complementarity with Orthodoxy cannot be explored here. Ecumenical dialogue between Lutherans and the Orthodox is still in a preliminary stage of its development, although with encouraging results.[43] Clearly the Lutheran Reformers believed that in their faith and teaching this continuity was present. As they looked at the patristic church and its theologians, these Lutheran Reformers applied only one standard of judgment: was that early church faithful to the scriptures, to the gospel?

But this position is actually nothing other than what the Fathers of the patristic church themselves wished to do. There is no title that the Fathers would have coveted more for themselves than that of biblical theologians.

It is here precisely that there is a constellation of interests that J. Robert Wright represents so well for many of us: a commitment to the patristic tradition of the undivided church as witnessed to, lived out, and shared among the traditions of Anglicans, Lutherans, and Orthodox. We are all indebted to him as an ecumenist and church historian as he urges us to explore both that complementarity among and that commitment for Anglicans, Lutherans, Orthodox, and other Christians who seek the visible unity of Christ's church.

---

43. Growth II, pp. 219-29; and *Salvation in Christ.*

Consistency and Difference in Anglican-Lutheran Relations:
Porvoo, Waterloo, and *Called to Common Mission*

Michael Root

J. Robert Wright's contributions to the life of the ecumenical movement have been many, but none is more significant than his path-breaking work in Anglican-Lutheran relations. Full communion between the Episcopal Church U.S.A. (ECUSA) and the Evangelical Lutheran Church in America (ELCA) simply would not have come to pass without Bob Wright's unflagging commitment, a commitment tested many times during the more than a decade and a half that transpired between the initial appointment of the third round of Lutheran-Episcopal dialogue in the U.S. and the final action of the General Convention of the Episcopal Church in 2000. Lutherans, Anglicans, and all those committed to the visible unity of the church are in Bob's debt.

The new relation between Lutherans and Episcopalians in the United States is not an isolated phenomenon. Lutherans and Anglicans in many parts of the world have entered into closer relations over the last fifteen years. In three areas — Northern Europe, Canada, and the United States — relations have been established that can be labeled *full communion*. All three of these new relations have similar roots; each can be seen as a regional adaptation of a similar model. But are the differences nevertheless significant? Do the differences indicate differing understandings of the perennially neuralgic issue of episcopacy, of the nature of church unity, or of the most fruitful ecumenical path forward?

Sections of this essay are adapted from "Porvoo in the Context of the Worldwide Anglican-Lutheran Dialogue," in *Apostolicity and Unity: Essays on the Porvoo Common Statement,* ed. Ola Tjørhom (Grand Rapids: William B. Eerdmans Publishing Company, 2002), pp. 15-33.

This essay will compare the three new relations with these questions in mind.[1] The issues are not trivial. They affect not only potential Lutheran-Anglican relations in other parts of the world but also the way Lutherans and Anglicans understand the nexus of issues at the intersection of ecumenical possibilities with ecclesiology and the doctrine of ministry. How those issues are understood and addressed will shape the sort of ecumenical future that lies immediately before us.

The New Relations between Lutheran and Anglican Churches

The three new relations should be seen as part of a single movement. All were part of a single theological and ecclesiastical development and include most of the same elements, even if the related ecumenical texts display some disagreement about the precise significance of this constellation of elements. All three agreements meet many definitions of *full communion,* but each of the agreements has its own approach to the concept of *full communion.*

The various international and national Anglican-Lutheran dialogues of the 1970s and 1980s, together with the Ministry section of the Faith and Order Commission of the World Council of Churches' text on *Baptism, Eucharist and Ministry* (BEM), set the stage for decisive work on the doctrine of episcopacy by the Anglican-Lutheran International Continuation Committee, *The Niagara Report* of 1988.[2] The Northern European and American statements were developed in the wake of *Niagara.*[3]

The Northern European *Porvoo Common Statement (Porvoo),* involving the British and Irish Anglican churches and the Nordic and Baltic Lutheran churches, was completed in 1992 and adopted in 1994 and 1995 by all the Anglican churches involved and by six of the eight Lutheran churches involved.[4]

---

1. In 1994, I published an essay comparing only the U.S. proposal and the Northern European action (Michael Root, "The Concordat and the Northern European Porvoo Common Statement: Different Paths to the Same Goal," in *A Commentary on "Concordat of Agreement,"* ed. James E. Griffiss and Daniel F. Martensen [Minneapolis: Augsburg Publishing House, 1994], pp. 138-51). While I would still support what I then wrote, the revision of the U.S. proposal, the publication and ratification of the Canadian proposal, and the ongoing discussions between British and Irish Anglicans on the one hand and, on the other, German and French Lutheran and Reformed have cast a new light on the similarities and differences among these proposals.

2. This historical background is traced in Michael Root, "Anglican-Lutheran Relations: Their Present State, History, and Challenge," *Midstream* 32 (1993): 39-55.

3. The connections among the texts are partly a matter of personnel. Drafters of *Niagara* were also involved in drafting the U.S. and Northern European proposals.

4. The *Porvoo Common Statement* (hereafter simply *Porvoo*) can be found in *Together in*

Although the American *Concordat of Agreement* was proposed in 1991, a year before *Porvoo,* it had a far more circuitous path to adoption.[5] In 1997, a slightly revised version of the *Concordat* easily passed the General Convention of the Episcopal Church but failed by less than one percent to receive the necessary two-thirds majority of the Churchwide Assembly of the ELCA. A more thoroughly revised proposal, renamed *Called to Common Mission* (CCM), was adopted by both churches in 1999 and 2000.[6]

Porvoo and the *Concordat* were developed with very little mutual consultation. Each proposal was already close to completion before the drafters involved had any detailed knowledge of the proposal being developed in the other part of the world. The Canadian drafting team had the advantage of a full knowledge of both proposals when it produced its own text in 1997, *Called to Full Communion: The Waterloo Declaration.* A revised version of this proposal was adopted by both the Anglican Church of Canada and the Evangelical Lutheran Church in Canada in 2001.[7]

The three proposals take quite different textual forms. *Porvoo* is a text of about twenty-five pages and seeks to lay out a general theological argument for its proposal. Within this text is the much shorter — less than two pages — "Porvoo Declaration," which constitutes the action actually taken by the churches.

The American *Concordat* did not itself contain a theological explanation or argument for its proposal. The theological basis for the proposal was elaborated in a book-length text, *Toward Full Communion.* This text was originally bound with the *Concordat,* but the *Concordat* soon became separated from this theological argument. The *Concordat* itself, on which the churches voted, was far more detailed and juridical than the brief "Porvoo Declaration."

The Canadian *Waterloo Declaration* was also brief, only slightly longer than the "Porvoo Declaration," with a short explanatory Introduction preced-

---

Mission and Ministry. The Porvoo Common Statement with Essays on Church and Ministry in Northern Europe (London: Church House Publishing, 1993), pp. 1-33. The two Lutheran churches involved but not affirming *Porvoo* are the Latvian and Danish churches.

5. The original *Concordat of Agreement* can be found in *"Toward Full Communion" and "Concordat of Agreement": Lutheran-Episcopal Dialogue, Series III,* ed. William A. Norgren and William G. Rusch (Minneapolis: Augsburg Publishing House; Cincinnati: Forward Movement Publications, 1991), pp. 95-110.

6. ELCA, *Called to Common Mission: A Lutheran Proposal for a Revision of the Concordat of Agreement* (Chicago: ELCA, 1999).

7. The original proposal, together with an "Official Commentary" written in 1998, can be found in *A Companion to The Waterloo Declaration: Commentary and Essays on Lutheran-Anglican Relations in Canada,* pp. 11-28. The final version, with its "Official Commentary," can be found at http://anglican.ca/ministry/inchurch/waterloo_revised_annotated.html.

ing a series of mutual acknowledgements, affirmations, a declaration, and commitments. An "Official Commentary" was distributed with the "Declaration" and provided a theological elaboration of its contents.

For the sake of theological contrast, two other, more limited European agreements need to be mentioned. Each is an agreement between Anglican churches on the one hand and Lutheran and Reformed churches acting together on the other. *The Meissen Agreement* between the Church of England and the Evangelical Church in Germany (EKD) was signed in 1991.[8] A similar agreement was reached between the British and Irish Anglican churches and the French Lutheran and Reformed churches in the *Reuilly Common Statement* produced in 1999.[9] These two agreements are much alike, in that they involve extensive mutual recognition of sacraments, faith, and ministries but do not include a provision for a mutual interchangeability or reconciliation of ministries because of continuing disagreements on episcopacy and episcopal succession. In this respect, they are much like the interim agreements reached between the Lutheran and Anglican churches in the U.S. in 1982 and in Canada in 1989.

Common Theological Framework

The three agreements share a common theological outlook on the one issue that has stood in the way of closer Lutheran-Anglican relations: episcopacy. Each adopts the theological approach to this question elaborated in *Niagara*.

Decisive for *Niagara's* approach is the thoroughgoing placement of the issue of episcopal succession in the wider context of the continuity of the church in its total mission. As it explains, the identity of the church is tied to its continuity with the apostolic mission to all nations. "Apostolic succession" is above all continuity in this mission and is a characteristic of a church as a whole rather than simply of its ministry or doctrine. Continuity in doctrine (e.g., the continued use of the early church's creeds) or in ministry (e.g., episcopal succession) is bound up with and is to serve this larger continuity in mission.

According to *Niagara*, the ultimate basis of the church's continuity is not

8. See *The Meissen Agreement: Texts,* Council for Christian Unity Occasional Paper, no. 2 (London: Council for Christian Unity, General Synod, Church of England, 1992). When originally proposed in 1988, *Meissen* involved not only the two churches named above but also the Federation of Evangelical Churches in the German Democratic Republic. German reunification permitted these churches to re-enter the EKD.

9. See *Called to Witness and Service: Conversations Between the British and Irish Anglican Churches and the French Lutheran and Reformed Churches. The Reuilly Common Statement with Essays on Church, Eucharist and Ministry* (London: Church House Publishing, 1999), pp. 1-46.

its own faithfulness but the faithfulness of God to his promise to be with the church (*Niagara* §28). The church is thankful for the means God uses to hold the church in faithfulness — e.g., canons, creeds, and structures of ministry — but recognizes that all such means are open to human abuse:

> God has persevered with the church even when the Scriptures have been mutilated, ignored, traduced or idolized; even when baptism has been administered promiscuously or received frivolously; even when the Lord's Supper has become routine or been neglected; even when the loss of the connection between Gospel and dogma has led to inquisition and authoritarianism on the one hand, rejection and apostasy on the other hand. (*Niagara* §30)

The text then adds: "In the context of our study of *episcope* we have been led to trust God's faithfulness also when bishops in historic succession have been unfaithful in an effluvium of evil" (*Niagara* §30).

It is in the context of this theology of continuity that *Niagara* takes up episcopacy. Lutherans and Anglicans have always agreed, it points out, that there exists a divinely instituted ministry to serve the mission of the gospel. Anglicans in their theological reflection and Lutherans in their practical experience have recognized that some form of oversight is a necessity: "Ministries of pastoral leadership, coordination and oversight have continuously been part of the church's witness to the gospel. Indeed we may say that the mission of the church required the coherence of its witness in every aspect of its life, and that this coherence required supervision" (*Niagara* §20). It is this ministry of oversight that is the heart of episcopal ministry (*Niagara* §54). As minister of oversight, the bishop is vitally related to both the unity and continuity of the church:

> The symbolic position occupied by the bishop had two dimensions, the spatial and the temporal. The connections between the local and the universal, the present and the past, are both aspects of the one *koinonia* or communion. On the one hand, the bishop "is responsible for preserving and promoting the integrity of the *koinonia* in order to further the church's response to the Lordship of Christ and its commitment to mission" (Anglican–Roman Catholic International Commission, *The Final Report*, Authority I, 5), a *koinonia* that "is realized not only in the local Christian communities, but also in the communion of these communities with one another" (*ibid.*, 8). On the other hand the bishop as confessor of the faith links the church with its foundation in the prophetic and apostolic scriptures (Eph. 2:20). (*Niagara* §52)

Fellowship in a ministry of oversight in continuity with the early ages of the church is thus seen as highly desirable for unity and continuity in the church's apostolic mission. Nevertheless, *Niagara* also recognizes that "the New Testament does not entitle us to assert that such supervision was carried out by a uniform structure of government inherited directly from or transmitted by the apostles" (*Niagara* §20). Episcopal succession cannot be presented as essential to the New Testament identity of the church in the sense that, for example, baptism or the eucharist is essential: "Study of the life of the early Christian communities reflected in the pages of the New Testament should make it unthinkable for us to isolate ordination at the hands of someone in linear succession to the apostles as the sole criterion of faithfulness to the apostolic commission" (*Niagara* §20). *Niagara* also gives theological (in distinction from simply historical) grounds for this conclusion:

> It is the oversight or presiding ministry that constitutes the heart of the episcopal office, and that oversight is never to be viewed apart from the continuity of apostolic faith. The fact of bishops does not by itself guarantee the continuity of apostolic faith. A material rupture in the succession of presiding ministers does not by itself guarantee a loss of continuity in apostolic faith. (*Niagara* §54)

Niagara explicitly avoids giving a single unambiguous judgment of what such a rupture does mean. It notes that in both the English and the Lutheran churches efforts were made, conditioned by the different ecclesiastical situations in different lands, to maintain forms of continuity with the ancient church and secure dependable means of oversight (*Niagara* §§55-56). In neither case was continuity in episcopal succession realized in a way that all would recognize as canonical.[10] The discussion concludes: "A similar problem faces both Anglicans and Lutherans, namely that the succession in the presiding ministry of their respective churches no longer incontestably links those churches to the *koinonia* of the wider church" (*Niagara* §58).

As a result of broad agreement in the gospel, of a renewed recognition of complex realities that constitute the apostolic succession of both churches, of significant agreement on the role of the ministry of oversight for the unity and continuity of the church, and of a joint confession of the failures of both churches in their faithfulness to the faithfulness of God, the two teams in the di-

---

10. "In the English Reformation, it may be argued, the episcopal succession was secured in an uncanonical fashion in that no currently sitting diocesan bishops could be found who were willing to consecrate Matthew Parker" (*Niagara* §55).

alogue conclude that "neither tradition can, in good conscience, reject the apostolic nature of the other," that "the ordained ministry is no longer an issue which need divide our two churches," and that "the continued isolation, one from another, of those who exercise this office of *episcope* in our two churches is no longer tolerable and must be overcome" (*Niagara* §59). *Niagara* thus recommends that the two churches take concrete steps to bring themselves into full communion with each other and into a more faithful relation to the mission of the gospel in their exercise of the ministry of oversight. In the future, each church should install or consecrate bishops with the laying on of hands by at least three other bishops, in accord with the canons of the council of Nicaea. At least one of these bishops should be from the other tradition. Anglicans are asked to "recognize the full authenticity of the existing ministries of the Lutheran churches" and to make the related canonical revisions. This reconciliation of ministries should "avoid any suggestion of reordination, mutual recommissioning of ministries, crypto-validation, or any other ambiguity" (*Niagara* §115).

Differences among the Three Relations

Against the common background of this theological understanding, the three relations take differing forms. To a degree, these differences are a function of historical and ecclesial context. The question is to what degree they also represent significant theological differences. If the differences are theological, are they a function of contradictory theological judgments, raising questions of the agreements' theological compatibility?[11] The differences among the three relations have three foci: the nature of the final ecumenical goal implied in each agreement, the nature of the mutual ministerial recognition achieved at the beginning of the new relation, and the way in which episcopacy is or is not a condition of communion in the three proposals.

The Ecumenical Goal

In 1983, an international Anglican-Lutheran Joint Working Group meeting in Cold Ash, England, laid out an extensive definition of "full communion" as the

---

11. This question was explicitly asked by the 1998 Lambeth Conference, *The Official Report of the Lambeth Conference 1998: Transformation and Renewal, July 18–August 9, 1998, Lambeth Palace; Canterbury, England* (Harrisburg: Morehouse Publishing, 1998) (hereafter Lambeth 1998), p. 220.

goal of Anglican-Lutheran relations. In a relation of full communion, the Cold Ash Report stated, each church "maintains its own autonomy and recognizes the catholicity and apostolicity of the other." While it concludes that "there should be recognized organs of regular consultation and communication, including episcopal collegiality," there is no mention of the need for a movement toward a truly shared ministry of oversight that would eliminate overlapping episcopal jurisdictions.[12] Cold Ash thus envisages the continued existence of distinct churches on the same territory as compatible with full communion.

The U.S. *Concordat* and its revision explicitly adopted the Cold Ash definition of full communion (*Concordat,* Preface; CCM, Introduction). This adoption corresponded to more general ecumenical policies already adopted by both churches. In 1979, the Episcopal Church adopted a "Declaration on Unity," which stated that "the visible unity we seek will be one eucharistic fellowship, . . . a communion of Communions, based upon acknowledgement of catholicity and apostolicity."[13] A 1978 report from the Episcopal Diocesan Ecumenical Officers made clear that this statement was meant to reject a model of unity that required "organizational or governmental merger; we do not envisage joining in one church body."[14] In 1991, the ELCA adopted an ecumenical policy statement that contained a listing of elements of full communion very similar to those in the Cold Ash Report.[15] The understanding of the ecumenical goal in the *Concordat* and CCM thus reflects the prior understandings of these two churches.

This understanding has come in for significant criticism in some Anglican circles.[16] The Cold Ash understanding of full communion drew criticism even before its embodiment in actual proposals.[17] The "Agros Report" of the Ecumenical Advisory Group of the Anglican Communion, written in preparation for the 1998 Lambeth Conference, denied that full communion as achieved

---

12. The Cold Ash Report can be found in Growth II, pp. 2-10, here pp. 6-7.

13. In *Ecumenical Bulletin* (Episcopal Church) no. 95, May/June, July/August 1989: A-6.

14. Communion, p. 31.

15. *Ecumenism: The Vision of the ELCA,* English text with Spanish, German, and French translations (Minneapolis: Augsburg Publishing House, 1994), p. 14.

16. A June 1995 response to the *Concordat* by the Faith and Order Advisory Group of the Church of England devoted five of its eight pages to this topic.

17. See Mary Tanner, "The Goal of Unity in Theological Dialogues Involving Anglicans," in *Einheit der Kirche: Neue Entwicklungen und Perspektiven,* ed. Günther Gassmann and Peder Nørgaard-Højen (Frankfurt am Main: Verlag Otto Lembeck, 1988), pp. 72-74; and the report of the first meeting of the Anglican-Lutheran International Continuation Committee, October 1986, in *Anglican-Lutheran International Continuation Committee, The Niagara Report: Report of the Anglican-Lutheran Consultation on Episcope, Niagara Falls, September 1987* (Cincinnati: Forward Movement Publications, 1988), p. 61.

in the *Concordat* could truly be the ecumenical goal: "Beyond the full communion aimed at in the *Concordat* lies the road to fuller communion."[18] While the 1998 Lambeth Conference was less explicit, it referred to "overlapping jurisdictions" as an anomaly.[19]

Some Anglican interpreters have seen in *Porvoo* a more congenial ecumenical vision. *Porvoo* does not define or use the term "full communion." While it contains a section entitled "The Nature of Communion and the Goal of Unity," the description given is silent on whether the continued existence of distinct churches in the same territory is or is not compatible with true unity. *Porvoo* could be silent on this question because, unlike the *Concordat,* it does not involve geographically overlapping churches. It does, however, include a mutual commitment "to welcome diaspora congregations into the life of the indigenous churches" (*Porvoo,* §58b[iv]). Such diaspora congregations are the primary example of overlapping jurisdictions among the *Porvoo* churches. The Lambeth Conference sees in this commitment the intention "that episcopal oversight will come to be shared, as a further stage towards the resolution of the anomaly of overlapping jurisdictions."[20]

Porvoo is certainly open to this reading, but it is not clear that it requires such a reading. "Welcoming diaspora congregations" could be justified and understood along different lines.[21] It is also striking that these readings of *Porvoo* come entirely from Anglican sources. Lutherans have most often been unwilling to see the sort of integrated or organic unity required for the elimination of overlapping jurisdictions as a necessary element in the ecumenical goal. The Lutheran World Federation has consistently espoused a vision of unity within which overlapping jurisdictions are not seen as incompatible with unity.[22] Two

18. Anglican Communion Ecumenical Advisory Group, "The Agros Report: A Report of the Ecumenical Advisory Group of the Anglican Communion," 1996, para. 123, photocopy.

19. Lambeth 1998, p. 407.

20. Lambeth 1998, p. 220.

21. The section on this provision in a "Commentary on The Porvoo Declaration," produced by a meeting of church lawyers from the *Porvoo* churches held in London on 16-17 January 1998, chaired by Bishop of Oslo Andreas Aarflot, stated that "The incorporation of diaspora congregations into the structure of the indigenous church so that they become parishes of that church is not required (although that possibility is not excluded). Each church should identify ways of allowing the clergy and people of diaspora congregations to become involved in its life that are appropriate to its particular context. The clergy of such congregations should thereby be placed in a relationship (though not necessarily a legal relationship) with the local bishop." (I have this text only in typescript and do not know if it was ever published.) This provision again does not exclude the reading of *Porvoo* discussed above, but it does not imply it either.

22. See especially LWF, Seventh Assembly, "The Unity We Seek," Assembly Statement in

of the *Porvoo* Lutheran churches are also members of the Leuenberg Church Fellowship (Lutheran, Reformed, and United churches, mostly in Europe), which is also more open to overlapping jurisdictions. Because the *Porvoo* churches are all located in different countries, the issue of overlapping jurisdictions can be (and, I would argue, has been) left ambiguous.

As in many other respects, the Canadian *Waterloo Declaration* adopts aspects of both of its predecessors. Like the U.S. proposal, *Waterloo* uses the term *full communion* to describe what is being established and offers its own definition of full communion (Introduction, §7). According to this definition, recognizable as a paraphrase of the Cold Ash definition, the churches remain distinct, each maintaining its own autonomy. In the Canadian context, such distinctness and autonomy imply overlapping jurisdictions. The Lambeth Conference thus understandably grouped *Waterloo* with the *Concordat* when it mentioned a perceived difference in approaches to unity in the Anglican-Lutheran actions.[23]

The Official Commentary to the *Waterloo Declaration* (not produced until after the 1998 Lambeth Conference), however, ends with the statement:

> Full communion between Lutherans and Anglicans in Canada marks but one step towards the eventual visible unity of the whole Church catholic. We have entered a new stage on our journey together; there may yet be stages that we can only imagine dimly at this point. (Official Commentary, Conclusion)

Does this statement imply that Lutheran-Anglican communion in Canada is but one step in a worldwide process that will bring other churches to the same place, or that full communion itself is but one stage in a process that might lead on to greater unity?

Alyson Barnett-Cowan, Director of Faith, Worship and Ministry of the Anglican Church in Canada, reports that the Joint Working Group that produced *Waterloo* used an understanding of unity by stages in which full communion did not represent the final stage. Beyond full communion lies organic union, which "would be a structural union, the establishment of a united church with one set of structures and one episcopacy." The Joint Working Group, however, "believes that this is premature as a proximate goal for Anglicans and Lutherans in Canada."[24] As with *Porvoo*, the text of *Waterloo* is consis-

---

Budapest 1984: In Christ — Hope for the World, Proceedings of the Seventh Assembly, LWF Report no. 19 (Geneva: WCC Publications, 1985), p. 175.

23. Lambeth 1998, p. 220.

24. Alyson Barnett-Cowan, "Full Communion: Where Does This Phrase Come From,

tent with this reading, even if it does not require it. The reading of the Joint Working Group that produced the text is important but not in itself decisive. The question is the reading of the churches that adopted the text. Nevertheless, the option outlined by Barnett-Cowan as that of the Joint Working Group is yet another alternative, one that places *Waterloo* closer to *Porvoo* than to the U.S. texts.

Close observers of the ecumenical world will recognize in these differences a manifestation of a much larger debate about the nature of the ecumenical goal that has gone on since the beginning of the modern ecumenical movement.[25] While some specific issues about the role of the bishop as a sign of unity are involved, the wider question touches on a variety of more comprehensive ecclesiological topics. Answers to this wider question are shaped by the specific histories of the churches in different parts of the world. To insist on the removal of overlapping jurisdictions as an explicitly mentioned ecumenical goal is one thing in England, with its established church historically taking in the majority of the population and without extensive experience in the bureaucratic tangles of church mergers, and another in the United States, with its thorough ecclesiastical fragmentation and its close acquaintance with the headaches that go with "organic unity."

Even if the removal of overlapping jurisdictions must be a part of our final ecumenical goal, is that goal best approached through what in the U.S. would be a very long series of organizational mergers, each absorbing great amounts of time, energy, and money? The various Anglican-Lutheran texts have taken different approaches, but this difference should be seen less as a contradiction than as varying ways forward toward a goal no one can define in detail. Discussions of "the unity we seek" will need to continue in the dialogues, within the worldwide Lutheran and Anglican communions, and in the wider ecumenical movement. Differences need to be taken seriously, but the open-ended attitude of the Canadian Joint Working Group seems to represent the most constructive and realistic option.[26]

---

and What Does It Mean?" in *A Companion to The Waterloo Declaration: Commentary and Essays on Lutheran-Anglican Relations in Canada,* ed. Richard G. Leggett (Toronto: Anglican Book Centre, 1999), p. 54.

25. See Harding Meyer, *That All May Be One: Perceptions and Models of Ecumenicity,* trans. William G. Rusch (Grand Rapids: William B. Eerdmans Publishing Company, 1999).

26. In a lecture given at the Centro pro Unione in Rome on 20 November 1994, John Vikström, Archbishop of Turku and Primate of the Church of Finland, also gave such an open-ended reading to *Porvoo*. To my knowledge, this lecture was not published.

Mutual Recognition of Ministries

The Northern European, Canadian, and American relations all involve an immediate mutual recognition of ministries, implying a mutual availability of ordained clergy, and also a commitment to a shared episcopacy, including mutual participation in the laying on of hands for bishops. They differ, however, in their approach to existing Lutheran bishops not consecrated in succession.

Decisive for *Porvoo* is the recognition that all the Nordic and Baltic Lutheran churches, including the Danish, Norwegian, and Icelandic churches, where a succession of consecrations was broken in the sixteenth century, are essentially episcopal (see especially *Porvoo*, §§8, 34, 49). The question *Porvoo* asks is whether the *single* break in the succession of consecrations, suffered in a time of turmoil during which the bishops had radically failed in their calling, means that in a comprehensive judgment about these churches and their ministries one should conclude that they simply lack a true episcopal ministry, especially if they are demonstrating their willingness to re-enter an unbroken line of consecrations by adopting *Porvoo*. *Porvoo*'s conclusion is that a straightforward denial that these churches are "episcopal" would rest on an overly narrow emphasis on an unbroken line of consecrations that ignores the wider reality of both the life and mission of these churches and their real and historically continuous episcopal ministries. Episcopal succession cannot be reduced to an unbroken succession of consecrations, *Porvoo* says. In adopting *Porvoo*, the Norwegian and Icelandic churches have accepted an additional sign of episcopal continuity (§58b[vi]), but they have not "adopted the historic episcopate" as something new in their lives. Thus, *Porvoo* implies a mutual recognition by all the churches of the episcopal ministries each exercises and, within organizational and practical limits, an interchangeability of episcopal ministry (§58b[v]).

The situation is quite different in the U.S. American Lutheranism has a short history of episcopacy. Unlike *Porvoo*, both the *Concordat* and CCM did call for the Lutheran participant to accept the historic episcopate for the first time. The Episcopal Church was called to recognize the authenticity of the ordained ministry in all forms *claimed* by the ELCA. Since the ELCA does not claim the historic episcopate, its present bishops would be recognized simply as "pastors/priests exercising a ministry of oversight *(episkope)* within its synods" (CCM, §15). Thus, while *Porvoo* involves an immediate interchangeability of bishops as bishops, CCM does not. According to CCM, the ELCA and the Episcopal Church will grow into a fully interchangeable episcopal ministry over time (CCM, §14).

This rather detailed difference has various consequences. While *Porvoo* says that mutual participation in episcopal consecrations will occur "normally"

(§58b[vi]), implying the possibility of exceptions, CCM states (§12) that such mutual participation will occur "regularly," officially defined as constituting the rule to be followed without exceptions.[27] To a degree, this difference reflects the greater geographical proximity of the U.S. churches, but it also reflects a difference in what the Lutheran partner is undertaking in the two cases.

More significantly, because CCM involves no recognition of the ELCA as already episcopal, ECUSA, unlike the British and Irish Anglican churches in *Porvoo*, has suspended in relation to the ELCA its requirement that all clergy be episcopally ordained (§16). Only thus could clergy be interchangeable, a requirement if the mutual recognition of ministries was to be in deed and not just in word. Such a step is unprecedented for Anglicans.[28]

Because the American Lutheran and Anglican churches start farther apart in the practice of episcopacy than their Northern European counterparts, each partner has had to take larger steps to meet the other. This difference between CCM and *Porvoo* casts the Canadian "Waterloo Declaration" in a particularly interesting light. The history and present situation of the Canadian churches are more like those of the American churches than like those of the Northern European ones. As in America, the title *bishop* has been adopted only recently by Canadian Lutherans. Nevertheless, in relation to the difference just sketched, *Waterloo* is closer to *Porvoo* than to CCM. A full recognition and interchangeability of ministries, including a recognition and interchangeability of bishops as bishops, occurred at the beginning of the new relation (*Waterloo*, B3, D1).

Waterloo takes the argument of *Niagara* a significant step further than did either *Porvoo* or CCM. Three elements lay the foundation for this extension: (1) a recognition by each church of the other as apostolic, (2) a recognition of the intent during the Reformation of even the non-episcopal, German Lutheran churches to continue a ministry of oversight, and thus the episcopal function, even when ordinations were conducted by presbyters,[29] and (3) a clear willingness of the Canadian Lutheran church to enter episcopal succession and, unlike the ELCA, to recognize the installation of a bishop as an ordination (*Waterloo*, Introduction 9, D2).[30] On this basis, the churches each recog-

---

27. The original *Concordat* had said that such mutual participation would take place "on an invariable basis" (§3). The language of CCM is rhetorically softer but has the same result.

28. The Faith and Order Advisory Group of the Church of England criticized this aspect of the U.S. proposal.

29. "The succession of a presiding ministry was preserved, given that the reformers had themselves been episcopally ordained, and the authority of the bishop passed to the presbyters acting collegially" (*Waterloo*, Official Commentary B3).

30. The *Concordat* included such an action by the ELCA (§7); it was the focus of widespread Lutheran criticism. CCM dropped this provision.

nize the ordained ministries of the other, including a mutual recognition of episcopal ministries as episcopal. On the one hand, *Waterloo* makes apostolicity of ministry a function of the apostolicity of the church and its total mission even more thoroughly than do the other agreements. On the other hand, it identifies the substance of episcopal ministry (of which succession is a sign) more thoroughly with episcopal function, which may be authentically present apart from the sign of a succession of episcopal consecrations.

In *Porvoo*, a broader continuity in episcopal ministry bore the absence of the specific sign of a succession of consecrations. CCM treated continuity in apostolic mission and ministry as the basis for a mutual recognition of existing ministries but did not require it to bring ELCA bishops within the historic episcopate so that episcopal ministries would be immediately interchangeable. In *Waterloo*, the three elements listed above led to the conclusion that the Canadian Lutheran bishops were bishops in a sense that allowed immediate interchangeability. As did *Porvoo*, *Waterloo* saw sharing in a succession of consecrations as a consequence of the mutual recognition of episcopal ministries rather than as something that had to be in place before such recognition (*Waterloo*, Official Commentary D2).

As a result, *Waterloo*, like *Porvoo* and unlike CCM, did not find it necessary to require that Anglicans suspend the traditional restriction that only episcopally ordained ministers could function among them as priests. *Waterloo* can thus avoid the complexities introduced into CCM by its non-recognition of present episcopal ministries. Nevertheless, in at least one respect, *Waterloo* is similar to CCM: the presence of bishops of one church at the ordinations of bishops in the other is not to occur merely "normally." An earlier draft had said such interconsecration would occur "regularly," but this word was omitted "to indicate unambiguously the unfailing commitment to invite bishops of both churches to participate in each other's installations/ordinations" (*Waterloo*, Official Commentary D2).

Waterloo and CCM make contrasting demands upon their participants. While CCM demanded of the American churches significant shifts of practice (the Episcopal suspension of the restriction related to episcopally ordained clergy, the Lutheran explicit adoption of the historic episcopate as a *novum*), *Waterloo* demands significant theological judgments that not all Lutherans or Anglicans might be willing to make (the Anglican recognition of Lutheran bishops as episcopal in an interchangeable sense without claims to either a personal or a local succession; the Lutheran commitment to installation in the episcopal office as an ordination). The Episcopal Church's criticism of *Porvoo*'s recognition of episcopacy outside a succession of consecrations[31] and criticism

---

31. SCER, ECUSA, "Response to the Porvoo Declaration," 25-28 January 1995, typescript.

within the ELCA of the Canadian proposal to understand episcopal installations as ordinations are reliable indications that the Canadian proposal would not have proved acceptable in the U.S. *Waterloo* and CCM offer differing ways, rooted in part in different judgments about the nature of episcopal continuity, of applying the theological argument of *Niagara* to a situation quite different from the Northern Europe of *Porvoo*.

Episcopacy as a Condition of Communion

The debate between Anglicans and Lutherans over episcopacy has not concerned simply the desirability of episcopacy in some specific form but also the theological role of a shared episcopacy in establishing fellowship. The issue was clearly stated in the 1972 "Pullach Report" of the first Anglican-Lutheran International Conversation.[32] The Anglican participants stated that they "cannot foresee full integration of ministries (full communion) apart from the historic episcopate" (§87). The Lutherans, however, insisted that "the historic episcopate should not become a necessary condition for interchurch relations or church union" (§89). All three agreements needed to overcome this apparent impasse. The assertion has been made that a significant difference exists in the way in which "the historic episcopate" is or is not a condition of communion in the different relations.[33] There is in fact a difference here among the actions, but it is almost entirely a function of the just-discussed difference in the nature of the mutual recognition of episcopacy. The importance of any difference among the actions in relation to episcopacy as a condition of communion should not be exaggerated.

The questions involved in episcopacy and the conditions of communion are complex, involving historical issues (the interpretation of the famous *satis est* clause of Article VII of the Augsburg Confession), theological issues (under what conditions are non-essential conditions acceptable?), and conceptual issues (what does it precisely mean to say that x is a condition of y?). Matters are made worse by the vagueness of the term "the historic episcopate." Does it refer simply to succession?[34] Does it somehow imply a threefold ordering of ministry, and thus an ordained diaconate? This essay can take up only the question of

---

32. Anglican-Lutheran International Conversation, "The Pullach Report (1972)," in *Growth I*, pp. 13-34.

33. See, most clearly, André Birmelé, *La communion ecclésiale: Progrès oecuménique et enjeux méthodologiques* (Paris: Les Éditions du Cerf, 2000), p. 307.

34. *Niagara* defined *historic episcopate* only in terms of succession (§3).

potential differences among the agreements in relation to the historic episcopate as a condition of communion.[35]

The question of conditionality is most clear in the texts issuing from the U.S. dialogue, where it was debated the most intensely. Crucial for the agreement was that each church fully recognized the pastoral and priestly ministries of the other without any sort of further rite of ordination by a bishop or additional confessional subscription. An understanding of ordination that would make ordination by a bishop in succession simply essential to authentic ministry was thus excluded.[36] An earlier American Lutheran study of "The Historic Episcopate" had focused on this question as decisive, and resolution of this question was decisive for the proposal.[37] In the *Concordat* and CCM, authentic ministry is thus not made conditional upon episcopal ordination.[38]

In both the *Concordat* and CCM, however, the Episcopal Church (1) makes its recognition and acceptance of the interchangeability of ELCA bishops conditional upon all bishops' being in fact in episcopal succession

---

35. See my own argument on the question of conditionality, Michael Root, "Conditions of Communion: Bishops, the Concordat, and the Augsburg Confession," in *Inhabiting Unity: Theological Perspectives on the Proposed Lutheran-Episcopal Concordat*, ed. Ephraim Radner and R. R. Reno (Grand Rapids: William B. Eerdmans Publishing Company, 1995), pp. 52-70.

36. A complex question is the degree to which this recognition was dependent upon the commitment of the ELCA to enter episcopal succession in the future. The original *Concordat* seemed to imply such a condition when it stated that the mutual recognitions were "in light of" the commitments of the two churches made in the text (§§4, 9), although the extended explanatory document "Toward Full Communion" (§76) stressed the simultaneity of the ELCA's commitment to enter episcopal succession in the future with the Episcopal Church's recognition of ELCA ministries. Because CCM removed the "in light of" phrases (see §7), it gives no impression of these recognitions' being conditional. Since the recognition is included in the same document as the commitment and the document was voted on as a whole in each church, the recognitions could have been acceptable to some only because of the commitments. The only way to remove such a possibility would be to separate the recognitions and the commitments as two independent issues to be settled independently.

37. "When the 'historic episcopate' faithfully proclaims the gospel and administers the sacraments, it may be accepted as a symbol of the church's unity and continuity throughout the centuries provided that it is not viewed as a necessity for the validity of the church's ministry" (Lutheran Council in the USA Division of Theological Studies, *The Historic Episcopate* [New York: Lutheran Council in the U.S.A., 1984], p. 7).

38. *Porvoo* is not clear on this question. Since it involves a mutual recognition of the episcopacy in each church and explicitly excludes non-episcopally ordained clergy from its provision for mutual interchangeability (§58b[v]), it leaves open the possibility that the Church of England might still refuse to recognize non-episcopally ordained clergy. The mutual recognition of clergy in *Reuilly* removes this possibility, but the lack of interchangeability in *Reuilly* means that the Church of England is still significantly more restrictive on these questions than ECUSA.

(§§14, 15) and (2) views the new relation as acceptable only because it includes fellowship in an episcopal ministry in succession (§9). CCM devotes a paragraph to the "expectations" each church brings to this relation of full communion, which include for the ELCA "an immediate recognition by the Episcopal Church of presently existing ordained ministers within the ELCA" and for the Episcopal Church "a commitment by the ELCA to receive and adapt an episcopate that will be shared" (§9). Each church has its conditions that must be met as a part of the new relation.

A close examination of *Porvoo* and *Waterloo* reveals that their difference from the U.S. action is not as great as has been asserted. As was noted above, the difference is not that the U.S. Anglicans make the presence of the historic episcopate a condition of an interchangeable ministry, while the Canadians and British do not. All are committed to the historic episcopate as a condition. The difference is that the Canadians and the British see this condition as fulfilled in their Lutheran partner, and the Americans do not. As Christopher Hill, a consultant to the commission that produced *Porvoo,* stated: "Anglicans will now be able to discern an authentic historic continuity of episcopal ministry in *all* the Nordic and Baltic Lutheran churches."[39] Similarly, Alyson Barnett-Cowan of the Anglican Church of Canada has said: "The Canadian dialogue has focused ways of describing the episcopate that can lead Anglicans into accepting Lutheran bishops as being already sufficiently within the bounds of apostolic succession."[40] The differences among the texts lie in the conditions under which the different Anglican churches are able to recognize the presence of the historic episcopate, not whether the historic episcopate must be present for an interchangeable ministry.

In this light, the second condition mentioned above can also be understood, that a condition of the new relation established is that it include sharing in an episcopal succession of consecrations. As has been noted, the U.S. proposal is clear on this question. *Porvoo* and *Waterloo* have appeared to some to avoid such conditionality, citing as evidence *Porvoo* §53: "The mutual acknowledgement of our churches and ministries is theologically prior to the use of the sign of the laying on of hands in the historic succession." *Waterloo* includes a virtually identical sentence.[41] Günther Gassmann has identified this

39. Christopher Hill, "Introduction," in *Together in Mission and Ministry: The Porvoo Common Statement with Essays on Church and Ministry in Northern Europe* (London: Church House Publishing, 1993), p. 52.

40. Alyson Barnett-Cowan, "Anglican-Lutheran Relations in Canada," *Ecumenical Trends* 25 (1996): 50.

41. "This mutual acknowledgement of our churches and ministries precedes the use of the sign of the laying on of hands in the historic succession" (Official Commentary, D2).

sentence as perhaps the most important in *Porvoo*,[42] and others have made similar statements.[43]

This sentence says less than one might think on first reading. It reflects the readiness of both the British and Canadian Anglican churches to recognize the presence of the historic episcopate even where there has been a break in the succession of consecrations. Thus, they are willing to recognize the presence of such bishops even before a sharing in such a succession. What is *not* implied is that such a sharing in a succession of episcopal consecrations has ceased for the Anglicans to be a necessary aspect of (and thus a condition of) the new relation established. The Anglican interpretation of *Porvoo* §52 makes this point clear. The paragraph states: "Faithfulness to the apostolic calling of the whole Church is carried by more than one means of continuity." Thus, a church that preserved a continuity of episcopal consecrations "is free to acknowledge an authentic episcopal ministry in a church that has preserved continuity in the episcopal office by an occasional priestly/presbyteral ordination at the time of the Reformation," such as the Danish, Norwegian, and Icelandic Lutheran churches. These Lutheran churches are "free to enter a relationship of mutual participation in episcopal ordinations with a church which has retained the historical episcopal succession and to embrace this sign [of a succession of consecrations], without denying its past apostolic continuity."

The question has been raised in various circles whether this paragraph implies that the respective Lutheran churches are free, within the structure of *Porvoo*, to take up or not to take up this sign of a succession of episcopal consecrations.[44] Anglicans have given a forceful "no" to this question. Mary Tanner has stated:

> The historic episcopal succession is not for *Porvoo* an optional extra. . . .
> The use of the phrase "free to embrace" is not used in the sense of free to decide whether to embrace the sign or not. It is rather a strong use of the

42. Günther Gassmann, "Das Porvoo-Dokument als Grundlage Anglikanisch-Lutherischer Kirchengemeinschaft im Nördlichen Europa," *Ökumenische Rundschau* 44 (1995): 178.

43. Olav Fyske Tveit, "What and Who Define Our Profile? A Short Presentation of Reflections in the Church of Norway on Compatibility of the Agreements with the Anglican and Reformed Churches — with Particular Reference to the Historic Episcopate," in *The Ecumenical Profile of Lutheran Churches Relating Simultaneously to Churches of Episcopal and Non-Episcopal Traditions, Presentations and Relevant Documents from a Consultation in Geneva, 24-25 August 2000* (Geneva: LWF, 2001), p. 21.

44. On this question, see Tveit, "What and Who Define Our Profile?" p. 22, and William Henn, "Apostolic Continuity of the Church and Apostolic Succession," in *Apostolic Continuity of the Church and Apostolic Succession, Louvain Studies* 21/22 (1996): 188.

word "free." As the text itself says, these churches should embrace the sign. The agreement liberates them and they can do no other.[45]

That a willingness to share in the sign of a succession of episcopal conse-crations is a condition of the Anglican acceptability of *Porvoo* is made clear by the limitations of the Anglican conversations with the German and French Lu-theran and Reformed churches. The dialogues with these churches have pro-duced texts conceptually, often even verbally, identical with *Porvoo* on many is-sues. The decisive difference is the inability to reach agreement on a common participation in episcopal succession. As a result, *Reuilly* achieves a mutual rec-ognition of ministries "as possessing not only the inward call of the Spirit but also Christ's commission through the Church" (*Reuilly,* §46a[v]) but stops short of any mutual interchangeability of clergy.[46] Because of a lack of agree-ment on a common participation in episcopal ministry, the Anglicans are not willing to enter into the sort of communion or visible unity with the French and German Lutheran and Reformed churches that they are willing to enter into with the Nordic and Baltic Lutherans. The obvious conclusion is that had the Norwegian and Icelandic churches been unwilling to accept the sign of a succession of episcopal consecrations, they would be in the same situation as the French and German churches. A willingness to accept this sign is a condi-tion of communion for *Porvoo* as it is for the *Concordat* and CCM.

We do not have a similar recent test case to judge whether the Canadian Anglicans would be willing to accept full communion with a church unwilling to share in a succession of episcopal consecrations as one aspect of full com-munion. The 1998 Lambeth Conference, however, explicitly reaffirmed the

45. Mary Tanner, "The Anglican Position on Apostolic Continuity and Apostolic Succes-sion in the Porvoo Common Statement," in *Apostolic Continuity of the Church and Apostolic Succession, Louvain Studies* 21/22 (1996): 122-24.

46. The recognition in *Reuilly* does mean that here the recognition has been achieved in-dependently of an agreement on episcopacy that would make full communion or visible unity possible. It is thus clear here that recognition is not dependent on an acceptance of a sharing in episcopal succession, as it is not in the U.S. and Canadian actions (where recognition and recon-ciliation are achieved in the same step) or in the ongoing German discussions, where the mutual recognition of ministries is phrased in a significantly weaker fashion, raising the question whether a full mutual recognition is intended ("we acknowledge one another's ordained minis-tries as given by God and instruments of his grace" [*Meissen*, §17A(iii)]). This wording seems to echo that of the Lambeth Appeal of 1920, which clearly did not intend a full recognition of non-episcopal ministries ("we thankfully acknowledge that these [non-episcopal] ministries have been manifestly blessed and owned by the Holy Spirit as effective means of grace," Lambeth Conference 1920, "An Appeal to All Christian People," in *The Six Lambeth Conferences: 1867-1920,* compiled by Randall Davidson [London: SPCK, 1929], Appendix, 28).

Chicago-Lambeth Quadrilateral, with its inclusion of "the historic episcopate" as an element Anglicans expect to be a part of full, visible unity or communion.[47] It would be surprising if any Anglican church were willing to abandon that commitment.

In summary, *Porvoo*, *Waterloo*, and CCM are not significantly different in terms of the conditions of communion. Rather, because they are different in regard to the conditions needed to recognize the existence of the historic episcopate, they differ in their judgments on what aspects of those conditions have already been met in their respective Lutheran partners and what aspects need to be met by some new, additional action by those partners.

More needs to be said on the question of ministry, episcopacy, and conditions of communion. Both Lutherans and Anglicans approach possible relations of full communion or visible unity with expectations about the recognition and mutual availability of clergy, expectations that can be called conditions. To reject the notion of "conditions" out of hand is to insist that ecumenism can move forward without change.

Conclusion

These new Anglican-Lutheran relations have been among the most important ecumenical developments of the end of the twentieth century. They rest on a common theological basis with roots beyond the Anglican-Lutheran dialogues, reaching into the multilateral discussions surrounding BEM. The differences among them, while certainly significant, do not point to any incoherence among the actions. The differences in relation to the ecumenical goal are part of a much wider debate, which will probably continue as long as the goal itself is not reached. The most significant difference among the actions relates to how far the argument of *Niagara* and *Porvoo* can be extended to churches without the specific history of the Northern European churches. On this question, *Waterloo* and CCM offer different options, reflecting different ecclesiastical contexts and different theological judgments, resulting in different practical and theological demands on the churches. Further work is needed on these issues.

That further work on these matters lies before us is not surprising and should not occasion ecumenical disappointment. Rather, we should give thanks for how far we have come, and significant thanks are certainly owed to Bob Wright.

47. Lambeth 1998, p. 404.

The Gift of Authority:
Mountain or Milestone?

Jon Nilson

As a Roman Catholic friend and collaborator of the Rev. Dr. J. Robert Wright, I want to honor him on this occasion by assessing the prospects of the text of the Anglican–Roman Catholic International Commission (ARCIC), *The Gift of Authority*. The cause of Anglican–Roman Catholic unity is important to both of us. This topic is also appropriate for this occasion because Fr. Wright published one of the first Anglican evaluations of this text.[1] In his essay he asked "is authority really a gift?" as a way of exhorting his fellow Anglicans to approach this controversial agreement with an open mind.

Fr. Wright's accomplishments span a number of fields: church history, theology, liturgy, editorial direction, pastoral care, and consulting. Less gifted and dedicated individuals could maintain such a high level of activity and success only at the cost of neglecting their students. But along with many others, I can attest to Fr. Wright's dedication to his teaching vocation. His generosity to his students at the General Theological Seminary, both inside and outside of the classroom, will show forth in their priestly ministries for decades to come.

Fr. Wright's commitments and contributions to ecumenism on the national and international levels are well known within the Anglican Communion and among its ecumenical partners. What is perhaps not well known is the extent of the sacrifices he has made in order to make those contributions.

Let us, as Cicero said, pass over in silence the long days spent sitting around meeting tables in conference centers and retreat houses, where pains-

---

1. J. Robert Wright, "'The Gift of Authority': Contents and Questions," *The Anglican* 28.4 (1999): 4.

taking discussions, Spartan accommodations, and institutional food are the realities of a "working weekend" in the church. The hours and days that Fr. Wright could have legitimately called his own but that he has given to the cause of church unity are innumerable.

Seasoned ecumenists like Fr. Wright cannot be hungry for academic glory. In the first place, they cannot turn their labors into magisterial, field-defining books that lead to lecture invitations and endowed chairs. The ecumenical scene and situation change too quickly for that. Second, much ecumenical work is carried out in unpublished discussions and position papers, which can take years to come to fruition. The results finally appear in collaboratively crafted documents or "agreed statements," the products of painstakingly sought and carefully wrought consensus. Authorship is ascribed to a committee, not to an individual, no matter how important a single individual's contribution may have been. To recall only the most important ecumenical texts to which Fr. Wright has contributed — *Baptism, Eucharist and Ministry* (1982), under the auspices of Faith and Order of the World Council of Churches; *Salvation and the Church* (1986), from ARCIC; *Towards Full Communion* and *Concordat of Agreement* (1991), the texts culminating in *Called to Common Mission* (1999) between the Evangelical Lutheran Church of America and the Episcopal Church — is to glimpse something of Fr. Wright's dedication.

But the full measure of Fr. Wright's commitment is taken only with the realization that those who give themselves to the cause of church unity will not live to see and rejoice in its success. Ecumenists like Fr. Wright resemble the nameless artists and artisans who poured their genius and sweat into the great cathedrals like Rouen and Chartres, knowing they would never live to witness the last stone put into place. Yet Fr. Wright has continued to work for church unity in obedience to Jesus' call for unity among his followers, in love for the church of Christ that can never show God's saving love to the world in its present divided state, and in love for a world that can be drawn more effectively to the gospel's saving truth only by a united church.

Initial Roman Catholic Responses to *The Gift of Authority*

When the quest for full, visible unity between the Anglican Communion and the Roman Catholic Church was initiated by Archbishop Michael Ramsey and Pope Paul VI in 1966, it was obvious that authority would be one of the central and most difficult issues to be resolved. It was not surprising, then, that half of the first ARCIC's *The Final Report* (1981) was devoted to authority. The official responses to *The Final Report* lauded the progress made by ARCIC and urged it to continue its work. Thus, in spring 1999, ARCIC released *Gift* after "five years of dialogue, of patient listening, study, and prayer together."[2]

The Commission's hopes for this document are noteworthy:

> The statement will, we hope, prompt further theological reflection; its conclusions present a challenge to our two Churches, not least in regard to the crucial issue of universal primacy. Authority is about how the Church teaches, acts, and reaches doctrinal decisions in faithfulness to the Gospel, so real agreement about authority cannot be theoretical. If this statement is to contribute to the reconciliation of the Anglican Communion and the Catholic Church and is accepted, it will require a response in life and in deed.[3]

To review the Roman Catholic responses to *Gift* since its appearance five and one half years ago is an easy task. They are, unfortunately, all too few — at least so far. The longest and most substantial is the semi-official commentary by William Henn, which was released by the Pontifical Council for Promoting Christian Unity along with the ARCIC text.[4] In the month of the text's release, Francis Sullivan, a member of the Anglican–Roman Catholic Consultation in the United States (ARCUSA), and Edward Yarnold, a former member of ARCIC, introduced *Gift* to the educated non-specialist readers of *The Tablet.* One month later in the same periodical Hans Küng offered a stinging and (in my view) somewhat unfair assessment of it. For *America* magazine, George Tavard, formerly a member of ARCIC and a member of ARCUSA since its inception nearly forty years ago, set *Gift* in the context of the previous ARCIC texts on authority, which had appeared in "The Final Report." Sara Butler, a member of the Commission that produced *Gift,* described it for the readers of *Ecumenical Trends.* I offered an analysis of the document in the Spring 2000 issue of *One in Christ.*

Henn is surely right in his claim: "Within the ecumenical landscape, it is fair to say that no other community has come so far along with Roman Catholics in common agreement about the primacy of the Bishop of Rome."[5] No wonder that *Gift* alarmed a number of Anglicans, who spoke up early and loud to say, "This text does not speak for us!" They repudiated it long before the An-

---

2. *Gift,* Preface. The text has been published in a number of places, e.g., *One in Christ* 35 (1999): 243-66.

3. *Gift,* Preface.

4. William Henn, "A Commentary on *The Gift of Authority* of the Anglican–Roman Catholic International Commission," http://www.usccb.org/seia/commentary.htm.

5. Henn, "Commentary," §17.

glican Communion Council called for an Anglican study of *Gift* to lay the groundwork for a formal response by the Lambeth Conference.

However, before the process of reception could be solidly established, Gene Robinson, an openly gay priest living with his partner, was elected, approved, and consecrated Bishop of New Hampshire. Reactions to this event were vociferous and alarming, since they seemed to presage the breakup of the worldwide Anglican Communion.

How could Anglican unity be preserved in the face of divisions as deep and angry as these were proving to be? It became the task of a commission appointed by the Archbishop of Canterbury to find out. This commission presented its analyses and proposals in the *Windsor Report* (October 2004), which is to be studied, discussed, and acted upon over many months.

What, then, can still be said of *Gift?* Has the Anglican crisis turned it into a once promising but now useless dead letter? By no means. Of course, we Roman Catholics will follow Anglican discussions with great interest. But we have our own work to do with respect to *Gift.* As ARCIC's co-chairmen have said, ". . . its conclusions present a challenge to our two churches, not least in regard to the crucial issue of universal primacy."

Gift of Authority: A Prophetic Challenge to the Roman Catholic Church

Among other interpretations, *Gift* can and should be read as a stern call to conscience for the Roman Catholic Church. Indeed the scope and depth of this call may partly explain why Catholics, by and large, have still to come to terms with it. It is, I maintain, a call to conscience for two reasons: first, it accuses the Roman Catholic Church of major responsibility for the continuing Anglican–Roman Catholic division; second, it summons the Roman Catholic Church not only to do whatever it can to heal those divisions and make reconciliation possible but also — and thereby — to become truer to its own identity, that is, to become more visibly the church of Christ that is portrayed in the texts of Vatican II.

As is noted above, ecumenical texts are written by committees. The authors aim at consensus — and even unanimity — among themselves to win the widest possible support for the agreements articulated in the documents. So the language of these texts is rarely eloquent and soaring. Instead, the wording plods along slowly and deliberately. The less the boat is rocked, the more will people stay on board. So *Gift* has to be read closely to discern its accusation and summons to the Roman Catholic Church.

First, the accusation. When *Gift* was released, Bishop John Baycroft, an Anglican member of ARCIC, told reporters that if the Roman Catholic Church "truly believes universal primacy is a gift for the whole church, then they have no right to exercise it in a way which prevents the whole church from receiving it."[6] This statement is a clue to the Commission's mind. It points to exercises of authority in which the Roman Catholic Church is manifestly keeping the rest of the church from receiving that universal primacy that it claims as a gift for the whole church.

For example, *Gift* observes that ". . . debates and decisions about the ordination of women have led to questions about the sources and structures of authority and how they function for Anglicans and Roman Catholics" (§3). Certainly the ordination of women has provoked debates within the Anglican Communion, but these seem mild in contrast to the debates and discussions provoked by John Paul II's statement in *Ordinatio Sacerdotalis* (1994) that the church has "no authority whatsoever" to ordain women, as well as by the "Responsum ad dubium" of the Congregation for the Doctrine of the Faith one year later, which maintained that the teaching of *Ordinatio sacerdotalis* was infallible.[7]

Section 5 of *Gift* declares that "The exercise of authority can be oppressive and destructive. It may, indeed, often be so . . . even in churches when they uncritically adopt certain patterns of authority." In its Dogmatic Constitution on the Church, *Lumen Gentium,* Vatican II carried forward a task left unfinished by Vatican I in 1870 by locating papal authority firmly within the context of episcopal authority: "Together with its head, and never without this head, the episcopal order is the subject of supreme and full power over the whole Church" (LG §22). Since the promulgation of the Constitution in 1964, the Roman Catholic theological literature on this topic has become vast.

Yet authority continued to become more and more centralized in the Church, specifically in the Roman Curia and in the office of the Bishop of Rome. This assessment is not the complaint of a few disgruntled liberals but, according to reliable news reports, the view of many of the church's leading bishops, who gathered for a month-long Synod in October 2001.

A textbook example of damning with faint praise is the note in §40 of *Gift* that the "tradition of synodality has not ceased" in the Roman Catholic Church. After a list of examples to back up this none-too-stunning claim, the

6. Bob Harvey, "Embrace Pope's Teachings, Anglicans Urged: Commission Seeks Greater Unity between Faiths [sic]," *The Ottawa Citizen,* 13 May 1999, sec. A10.

7. For the response of one group of Roman Catholic theologians to the Congregation, see "Tradition and the Ordination of Women," *Proceedings of the Catholic Theological Society of America* 52 (1997): 197-204.

text says, "All these synodal institutions provide the possibility of a growing awareness by both local bishops and the Bishop of Rome of ways of working together in a stronger communion." Only the *possibility?* And not the possibility of actually working together but merely of an awareness that *could* lead to working together? These bland words constitute a serious accusation, coming as they do nearly forty years after the Council painted a portrait of a different sort of exercise of authority in the church.

Gift's §57 can be read as an "examination of conscience" for bishops, especially for the bishop of Rome. The text is framed as a list of questions that somewhat obscure the accusations, but the charges are real. Why, for instance, is there a need to ask whether "enough provision [has] been made to ensure consultation between the Bishop of Rome and the local churches prior to the making of important decisions" unless there are good grounds for thinking that not enough provision has in fact been made? Why ask whether "the structures and procedures of the Roman Curia adequately respect the exercise of *episcope* at other levels" unless there is *prima facie* evidence that they do not?

In §47 comes the greatest understatement in the document, concerning the ministry of the bishop of Rome: "This particular service has been the source of difficulties and misunderstandings among the churches." No comment needed here. As Archbishop John Quinn has argued[8] and as Fr. Wright has so often reminded us Roman Catholics, unity has a painful price. *Gift* maintains that we have not yet begun to pay it — or even to acknowledge our obligations here.

Notes on the Painful Price of Unity

ARCIC's members are convinced that Anglicans are "open to and desire a recovery and re-reception under certain clear conditions of the exercise of universal primacy by the Bishop of Rome" (*Gift* §62). They do not, however, specify what these certain clear conditions might be. At the very least, they would have to be conditions that securely establish in the life of the church collegiality and synodality, characteristics of the Anglican ethos and ideals of the Roman Catholic Church.

Gift is not calling merely for assurances and promises but also for safeguards. Provision of such safeguards would require major structural reform in

8. John R. Quinn, *The Reform of the Papacy: The Costly Call to Christian Unity* (New York: Crossroad, 1999).

the Roman Catholic Church. Principles and procedures insuring collegiality and synodality would have to become part and parcel of the church's Canon Law. But Canon Law, past and present, in the Roman Catholic Church has drawn upon European models. These models lack effective ways to structure and limit the exercise of discretionary authority. Even in the new Code of Canon Law, promulgated in 1983 to bring the Church's law into accord with the Second Vatican Council, a pre-conciliar legal ethos and spirit remains. Thus the Code does little to protect the rights of subordinates in situations where their superiors have abused and misused their power.[9]

Beyond the need for structural and canonical reform in the Church is the more elusive but essential challenge of changing the Church's mentality or culture, which has reigned for nearly two hundred years. Every level of the Church's life must be renewed. The consultation entailed in collegiality has to become a matter of instinct in the Church, not just an ideal that is realized only now and then. Synodality must become almost a synonym for church life, not just a strange piece of theological or ecumenical jargon.

But a culture cannot be transformed or discarded merely by good will and pure intentions. Nor can a transformation like this be mandated from the top down, although it can be strongly encouraged and modeled. Nor can it be plotted on a timetable, as Fr. Wright and the other architects of *Called to Common Mission* foresaw.[10]

Consequently, *Gift* poses a major challenge to the Roman Catholic Church. The challenge is memorably stated in Bishop Baycroft's words, quoted above: ". . . they have no right to exercise it in a way which prevents the whole Church from receiving it." Is the challenge of reform so monumental, so mountainous, that it will never be met — and, therefore, that the vision of *Gift* will remain just a fond dream?

If "real agreement about authority cannot be theoretical" and *Gift* "will require a response in life and in deed," as ARCIC's co-chairmen say in the Preface, there is ample reason to be gloomy about the prospects for a positive and genuine reception of the text by the Roman Catholic Church in the short term. Yet, in a longer view, there are reasons for thinking that *The Gift of Authority* may be a turning point, a milestone on the road to Christian unity.

---

9. For a fuller discussion of this point, see Jon Nilson, "*The Gift of Authority:* An American, Roman Catholic Appreciation," *One in Christ* 36.2 (2000): 141-42.

10. Recall that "Called to Common Mission" does not create full communion; rather, it puts the Evangelical Lutheran Church of America and the Episcopal Church inescapably on the road to it and alerts both churches to discern the *kairos* when full communion has become a reality.

Signs of Hope for the Anglican–Roman Catholic Future

The first hopeful sign is that the leadership of the Anglican Communion and the Roman Catholic Church have resolved to end the drift and stagnation that have characterized the relationship for so long. In spring 2000, three and one-half years of preparation culminated in a week-long meeting at Mississauga, Ontario, outside Toronto. Led by Archbishop George Carey and by Cardinal Edward Idris Cassidy, then head of the Vatican's Pontifical Council for the Promotion of Christian Unity (PCPCU), Anglicans and Roman Catholics confirmed their commitment to unity by establishing a Joint Unity Commission. The Commission held its first meeting in November 2001.

This group, among other tasks, oversees and coordinates the various Anglican–Roman Catholic efforts towards unity. It is also charged with oversight of a "Joint Declaration of Agreement," which will "set out: our shared goal of visible unity; an acknowledgment of the consensus in faith that we have reached, and a fresh commitment to share together in common life and witness"[11] — and, it said, once completed, this Declaration would be celebrated around the world. Regular consultation and follow-up have been slated as well. All in all, the communiqués from this meeting declare, "No more business as usual!"

Second, in 2001, Cardinal Walter Kasper succeeded Cardinal Cassidy as head of the Pontifical Council. Diplomacy, not theology, was Cassidy's background and *forte*. Vatican watchers felt that this situation left the PCPCU at a disadvantage when its work was vetted by the Congregation for the Doctrine of the Faith, then headed by Cardinal Joseph Ratzinger, as is required by the current curial *modus operandi*. But Kasper's reputation as a theologian is fully the equal of Ratzinger's. Moreover, when Kasper was Bishop of Stuttgart, he tangled with the Curia. He knows first hand the pastoral costs of an overly centralized authority structure in the church.

Third, *Gift's* treatment of primacy is a significant contribution to the dialogue urged by Pope John Paul II in his 1995 encyclical *Ut Unum Sint*. There he said, "I insistently pray the Holy Spirit to shine his light upon us, enlightening all the pastors and theologians of our churches, that we may seek — together, of course — the forms in which this ministry may accomplish a service of love recognized by all concerned" (§95). Then came his history-making invitation to a "patient and fraternal dialogue" (§96) to discern ways of exercising the ministry of the primacy, so that it may become truly a service of unity — and may be

---

11. "Communion in Mission: Statement from Mississauga Meeting, May 2000." See www.anglicancommunion.org/ecumenical/dialogues/rc/iarccum/acns2137.cfm.

perceived as such. *Gift,* then, stood high on the agenda of John Paul II and on the agenda of Catholics who agree with him that the quest for unity is central, not marginal, to the church's life. Since his election, Benedict XVI too has forcefully reiterated the same convictions.

Fourth, a month-long meeting in Rome of the Church's Synod of Bishops in October 2001 was devoted to the role and ministry of the bishop. Accurate coverage of these gatherings is sometimes hard to obtain, yet reliable reports agree that fully twenty percent of the speeches at the Synod called for invigorating collegiality and synodality. When we recall the persistent observations (and complaints!) about Roman control of the Synod's deliberations, this percentage becomes all the more noteworthy. The voices for reform are growing not only numerous but also more prominent in the church.

Fifth and last, but definitely not least, is the fact that *Gift*'s understanding of primacy mirrors the vision of Vatican II itself. To demonstrate this claim adequately would require another complete essay. Yet many statements in *Gift* have their counterparts in the documents of Vatican II, especially its Dogmatic Constitution on the Church, *Lumen Gentium,* e.g.: "The exercise of teaching authority in the church, especially in situations of challenge, requires the participation, in their distinctive ways, of the whole body of believers, not only those charged with the ministry of memory" (*Gift* §43).

Gift enters the history of the church at a time when a certain conviction is becoming more and more widely shared: reforming the exercise of authority is imperative not only as a condition for the full, visible unity of the churches but also as a necessity for the Roman Catholic Church to fulfill its mission to be a "sacrament of intimate union with God, and of the unity of all humanity" (LG §1; translation amended). The church, as Vatican II taught, is a communion, a life shared, and this communion must be enacted at every level of its life. How, then, can the Roman Catholic Church be true to its Lord, until and unless it is reunited with its "ever beloved sister," as Pope Paul VI called the Anglican Communion?[12]

When that day of reconciliation dawns at last, its arrival will have been hastened by the dedication and talent of J. Robert Wright, a man of the church — the whole church of Christ.

---

12. "Remarks at Canonization of Forty Martyrs" (25 October 1970), in *Called to Full Unity: Documents on Anglican–Roman Catholic Relations, 1966-1983,* ed. Joseph W. Witmer and J. Robert Wright (Washington, DC: USCC, 1986), p. 54.

Sisters and Strangers

George Tavard

The instruction *Dominus Jesus,* which was issued in Rome by the Congregation for the Doctrine of the Faith on August 6, 2000, brought up a question of interest to the friends of J. Robert Wright and to all who have appreciated and admired his unequaled contribution to the eventual restoration of organic unity between the sees of Canterbury and of Rome. This question — "What is a Christian church?" — relates to the meaning and use of the expression *Sister-churches.*

In *Dominus Jesus* the context of this question is a broader concern with the dialogues between Christians and the followers of other religions, a subject that is, though more indirectly, related to J. Robert Wright's career. The remarks that are made on the nature of the church and on the meaning of terms like *church* and *community* appear as a kind of appendix, an afterthought unrelated to the central topic of the document. It is true that the interreligious dialogue gains a great deal of clarity from being approached in the light of ecumenical dialogues, to which Professor Wright has devoted so much of his theological acumen. The reverse process of thought, however, in which consideration of the great religions of the world helps to determine the status of Christian churches, is not really helpful. The placement of the remarks on Christian churches and ecclesial communities toward the end of *Dominus Jesus* (nn. 16-17) did in fact raise excessive anxieties in ecumenical circles, partly because it was chiefly they that caught the attention of the media.

This placement conveys the impression that ecumenism is seen in Rome as a variety of the encounter of the Roman Catholic Church with the great religions of the world, a conception that would be gravely erroneous. The dialogue among those who confess the Holy Trinity and the name of Christ as the only Savior is certainly closer to the heart of the Christian faith than the recent conversations of Christians with some of the traditional religions of Asia. Giving priority to the dialogue of religions would be completely at odds with the line that was adopted at Vatican Council II. It would have been wiser, in order to avoid the misunderstandings that soon emerged, to separate the two perspectives. The following pages will take for granted the ecumenical rather than the interreligious priority.

Which Churches Are Sisters?

When read in Latin, *Dominus Jesus* sounds quite harmless and even conventional, at least if one has not already read some of the versions in modern languages. While the curial Latin under John Paul II was not so distinguished as it was under Paul VI, it still kept an innate propensity to abstraction that made it more speculative and therefore more theoretical and less abrasive than modern vernaculars, the grammatical concreteness of these being multiplied today by the daily experience of catching instant news and exacerbated by the visualization of far-away lands and events.

In any case it should have been obvious to the writers of *Dominus Jesus* that interreligious dialogue does not provide a congenial context for a Christian discussion of the meaning and scope of the expression *Sister-churches*. The insertion of such a discussion in *Dominus Jesus* shows a degree of insensitivity not only to the feelings of sincere Christian believers but also to a basic theological principle. If indeed there exist a number of communities that call themselves Christians (whether churches or ecclesial communities in the technical sense), they all belong within the one Christian baptism and the one Christian faith. In this context, whether all Christian communities constitute Sister-churches is a legitimate question, but one that is irrelevant to the interreligious dialogue. Raising the problem in *Dominus Jesus* could only have been intended as a reminder of the "Note on the expression Sister-Churches" that was addressed on June 30, 2000, to the Presidents of the National Conferences of Bishops, along with a covering letter from Cardinal Ratzinger. These documents were not public. The letter even specified that the Note would not be printed in the official *Acta Apostolicae Sedis* (AAS). They were nevertheless eventually leaked to the press, and they are now in the public domain.[1]

---

1. The letter and Note, along with the other Vatican documents discussed below, are available at the Vatican website, http://www.vatican.va.

The point of the Note was to restrict ecclesial sisterhood to the relations between the Roman Catholic and the Orthodox Churches and accordingly to avoid the formula in regard to the churches of the West that, in various forms and to different degrees, have inherited the Protestant Reformation. The Note made a brief survey of the history of the expression, which was in its patristic origin related to interdiocesan relations and to the patriarchal pentarchy. The appellation was used from time to time in both East and West, until in 1965 it took central place in the decision of Paul VI and Athenagoras of Constantinople to forget the excommunications of 1054 and bring the Orthodox and Roman Catholic Churches closer together in true sisterhood.

But the Note ignored the fact that Paul VI had also used the expression in regard to the Anglican Communion. *Unitatis Redintegratio,* the decree on ecumenism of Vatican II, had stated: "Among those in which Catholic traditions and structures continue to subsist the Anglican Communion holds a special place [*locum specialem*]" (UR 13).[2] Paul VI had gone still further on the occasion of the canonization of the English martyrs on October 25, 1970:

> . . . when — God willing — the unity of the faith and of Christian life is restored . . . there will be no seeking to lessen the legitimate prestige and the worthy patrimony of piety and usage proper to the Anglican Church, when the Roman Catholic Church, this humble servant of the servants of God, is able to embrace her ever-beloved Sister in the one authentic communion of the family of Christ, a communion of origin and of faith, a communion of priesthood and of rule, a communion of the saints in the freedom of love of the Spirit of Jesus.[3]

One can certainly argue that this text presents church-sisterhood as a thing of the future, to be manifested in the final reunion of the churches. While this perspective may have been in the mind of Paul VI, it need not mean that sisterhood among churches is not also a present reality. Indeed it must already be present, though imperfectly, if it is seen on the model of traditional eschatology, in which the future, though not yet here, is anticipated in the present. Past, present, and future were in fact already inextricably linked in the way Paul VI referred to the Orthodox Church, as when he said (and the Note quotes this statement): "Now, after a long period of division and mutual misunderstand-

---

2. Austin P. Flannery, ed., *The Documents of Vatican II* (New York: Pillar Books, 1975), p. 463.

3. "Remarks at Canonization of Forty Martyrs" (25 October 1970), in *Called to Full Unity: Documents on Anglican–Roman Catholic Relations, 1966-1983,* ed. Joseph W. Witmer and J. Robert Wright (Washington, DC: USCC, 1986), p. 54.

ing, the Lord, in spite of the obstacles which arose between us in the past, gives us the possibility of rediscovering ourselves as Sister-Churches."[4] Furthermore, Paul VI pointed to the legitimate and effective basis of this rediscovery when he asked: "Since this mystery of divine love is at work in every local Church, is not this the reason for the traditional expression, Sister-Churches, which the Churches of various places used for one another?"[5] In other words, according to the Instruction a Sister-church is one in which another church recognizes the mystery of divine love at work.

This conception of Sister-churches relates to the lately debated question of local or particular churches. In an ecclesiology of communion, neither is the local church a department of the universal church nor is the universal church the sum total of local churches. Rather, the very same presence of Christ among the disciples is experienced in its reality and its totality at the two levels of the universal and the local.

Another important question looms behind the discussion of church-sisterhood. In the decree *Unitatis Redintegratio,* Vatican Council II declared that ecumenical dialogues required the participants to behave *par cum pari* as they discussed the doctrines and practices of their traditions.[6] This principle of equality is necessary to dialogue, at least as dialogue was understood in Paul VI's first encyclical, *Ecclesiam Suam* (August 6, 1964), and as it was described by the Vatican Council on the backdrop of inter-Christian dialogue and cooperation. *Par cum pari,* however, can hardly rule the minds of the dialogue partners if a similar parity does not also rule the mutual relations of church leaders and thereby the churches themselves as partners along the way of salvation. As it presides over the ecumenical dialogues and the relations between the spiritual leaders of the churches, the principle of acting *par cum pari* becomes an eloquent manifestation of sisterhood among churches that, though having suffered estrangement after behaving like sisters, are now engaged in the recovery of their pristine sisterhood through a patient and far-reaching process of reconciliation.

The example of Paul VI was in fact followed by John Paul II. As he closed the Great Jubilee of the year 2000 with the apostolic letter *Novo Millennio Ineunte* (January 6, 2001), John Paul II referred to "our brothers and sisters of the Anglican Communion and of the Ecclesial Communities issued from the Reformation" (§48).[7] This formulation itself may well be assailed on historical grounds, since it seems to assume that there was a sharp distinction between

---

4. Paul VI, Brief *Anno ineunte,* 17 July 1967, AAS 59, 852, Note, n. 7.

5. Paul VI, Brief *Anno ineunte,* 17 July 1967, AAS 59, 852, Note, n. 7.

6. UR 9.

7. http://www.vatican.va/holy_father/john_paul_ii/apost_letters/documents/hf_jp-ii_apl_20010106_novo-millennio-ineunte_en.html.

the Anglican and the continental reformations, the outcome of which would have been a communion in England and only ecclesial communities on the Continent. The exact differences are of course open to historical and theological discussion. Whatever they were, however, they were sufficient to justify the language of Vatican II about "a special place."

In contemporary ecclesiological reflection a communion *(koinōnia)* is undoubtedly a church or a group of churches that shares one *typos.*[8] And "the Universal Church," in the judgment of the Congregation for the Doctrine of the Faith, "is the body of the Churches; and for this reason it is legitimate to apply the notion of Communion analogically to the union of the particular Churches among themselves, and to understand the universal Church as the Communion of the Churches."[9] Given this notion of communion one may logically conclude that John Paul II's language strongly affirmed the ecclesiality of the Anglican Communion, though not that of the Lutheran or Calvinist churches.

This use of the designation *Ecclesial Communities,* however, is in fact not in keeping with the intent of the Decree on Ecumenism, chapter 3, where the expression appears for the first time. In the mind of the writers of this chapter (of whom I was one), the expression was intended to respect the position of the Christian communities that do not call themselves churches, such as the Society of Friends and the Salvation Army, which were represented by official observers at the Council. It did not belong to the Council, as we thought, to decide which associations of Christians were churches and which were not, and the Council displayed no wish so to decide, even though its constant usage assumed that a church, in the catholic sense of the term, was centered on the reality of the Eucharist, while an ecclesial community might not be.

Further, since 1991 the Lutheran World Federation has identified itself as "a Communion of Churches."[10] This instance should be sufficient to show that the distinction between churches and ecclesial communities cannot be as simple as *Novo millennio ineunte* seems to assume. It would be difficult to maintain that congregations in which "the Word is preached in its purity and the holy sacraments are administered according to the Gospel"[11] are merely communities, even if also ecclesial, rather than churches.

8. See Cardinal Jan Willebrands' address in Cambridge, England, on 18 January 1980, in ARC DOC I, pp. 32-41, here pp. 38-41.

9. Congregatio de doctrina fidei, *Litterae . . . de aliquibus aspectibus ecclesiae prout est communio,* 28 May 1992, n. 8; Vatican website.

10. *The Church as Communion. LWF Documentation,* n. 42/1997, 2nd printing (Geneva: LWF, 1998), p. 216.

11. *Augsburg Confession* VII; *The Augsburg Confession. Anniversary Edition* (Philadelphia: Fortress Press, 1980), p. 12.

In any case, the question of church-sisterhood is related to the theological investigation of the church as communion that has been going on for some years. This was one of the six "models of the Church" identified by the future cardinal Avery Dulles in 1974.[12] Furthermore, as I explained in 2000,[13] church-sisterhood should be seen as a dimension of the mark of catholicity that is confessed to be one of the essential qualities of the church. One may even wonder if it is not somehow connected with one of the current problems of the Roman Catholic administrative system: what is the ecclesial status of National Conferences of Bishops, and what is the level of their participation in the collegiality of the church? Each Roman Catholic diocese is certainly a Sister-church of all the other dioceses. When their bishops gather as National Conferences they manifest the sisterhood of their particular churches, a sisterhood that is undoubtedly an expression of their collegiality. The principle is unimpeachable, though it may take time, reflection, and some degree of conversion to decide to what extent their decisions taken as a conference are binding on each bishop of the conference.

That church-sisterhood can be experienced and presumably subsist even in cases of misunderstanding and conflict was painfully and for that reason all the more eloquently witnessed to on February 9, 1897, when the archbishops of Canterbury and of York responded to Leo XIII, who had just declared their orders invalid. In *Saepius Officio* they called the Church of Rome "a sister Church of Christ" (§II) and Pope Leo their "brother" (§XX).[14] If this response indeed witnesses to the resilience of church-sisterhood in the Anglican experience, is it then totally impossible in the judgment of the Congregation for the Doctrine of the Faith for Roman Catholics in communion with the see of Rome to discern the mystery of divine love at work in the preaching of the Word and the administration of the sacraments that take place in the Anglican Communion?

The Interreligious Dialogue

The dominant question of *Dominus Jesus* concerns the present dialogues with non-Christians, the changing nature of the mission *ad gentes,* and some recent

---

12. Avery Dulles, *Models of the Church* (Garden City: Doubleday, 1974); see Dennis M. Doyle, *Communion Ecclesiology* (Maryknoll, NY: Orbis Books, 2000).

13. "Sister-churches in the Twenty-first Century?" in Lawrence Cross and Edward Morgan, eds., *Orientale Lumen, Australasia–Oceania, 2000. Proceedings, July 9-12, 2000* (Melbourne: Australian Catholic University, 2000), pp. 1-22.

14. *Anglican Orders. Essays on the Centenary of* Apostolicae Curae, *1896-1996,* ed. R. William Franklin (New York: Morehouse Publishing, 1996), pp. 138, 149.

studies in missiology. The central question is not new. It flared up in the fifth century when the Roman Senate debated whether to remove the statue of the goddess Victory from the Senate chambers. In Milan, Saint Ambrose pressured the Emperor to have it removed. In Rome, Senator Symmachus vainly opposed the removal. He argued of course from the old Roman tradition, but he also stated a philosophical or theological principle: "Surely, such a great mystery is not to be reached along one way only!" Ambrose's view of course was that the only way is the way of Jesus Christ.[15]

The question has now taken on new colors, the contemporary context being naturally unforeseen at the time of Ambrose and Symmachus. The question today emerges in part from the recent interreligious dialogues and in part from the widespread impression that the future of religion lies in interreligious dialogue. In this case the ecumenical dialogue, among Christians, takes second place in the preoccupations and concerns of what may well be a growing number of theologians.

The occasions and reasons for this shift in priorities are numerous. I will mention several of them: (1) in academic scholarship and university programs, a move from Comparative Religion to the study of religions for their intrinsic human value; (2) in Protestant intellectual circles, a reaction against Karl Barth's theology and its application by Hendrik Kraemer to the missionary situation;[16] (3) in the WCC, the growing importance of the younger churches and their natural concern for dialogue with the traditional religions of their lands, along with the personal conceptions of the present General Secretary as he expresses them in one of his books;[17] (4) in world culture, the philosophical interest in Zen, the popularity of the Dalai Lama and the appearance of Buddhist-Tibetan centers in Western countries, and the emergence of new religious movements that are in part focused on a unification of religions, as in the doctrines of the Unification Church; (5) in the Roman Catholic Church after Vatican II, the changing nature of the missionary enterprise, in keeping with the decree *Ad Gentes;* (6) in New Testament studies, the recent emphasis on "the God of Jesus," a topic that invites comparison with the God of Mohammed and the God or gods of Hinduism and of traditional ethnic religions, as well as with Buddhism as a non-theistic religion.

Whatever its reasons, the shift of attention to the world religions raises a major question that touches on the very essence of the church: Is it possible in

15. See the debate between Ambrose and Symmachus, in NPNF 10, pp. 411-22.

16. Hendrik Kraemer, *The Christian Message in a Non-Christian World,* 3rd ed. (London: J. Clarke and Co., 1956).

17. Konrad Raiser, *Ecumenism in Transition. A Paradigm Shift in the Ecumenical Movement?* (Geneva: WCC Publications, 1991).

interreligious dialogue to affirm, or at least to bear witness to one's belief in, the centrality of Jesus Christ as the ultimate revealer of God and the only Savior, and at the same time to engage in an open dialogue with a listening and welcoming attitude toward the convictions of our partners, convictions that by the nature of the case exclude the centrality of Jesus Christ as either Revealer or Savior? It is inevitable that the theologians engaged in interreligious dialogue should wish to emulate the *par cum pari* situation of ecumenical dialogues, even though the Council did not directly face the perspective of a dialogue between religions. This new question amounts to asking whether *par cum pari* applies to persons only, or whether it implies the religions themselves as they become partners in dialogue.

If I understand *Dominus Jesus* correctly, the Congregation for the Doctrine of the Faith fully endorses the parity of persons in dialogue but not that of religions or doctrines. In other words, the religions with which one enters into dialogue should not be considered equivalent to the Christian religion as regards revelation or salvation, whatever high levels of culture they may have nurtured over the centuries. The problem does not concern what is often called the equality or inequality of the religions, a formulation that makes little sense because it introduces quantitative measurements in what should be purely spiritual, the truth value of religious convictions and attitudes. What is at stake is the validity of the Judeo-Christian prophetic movement that Jews and Christians in their diverse ways identify with divine revelation.

In a broader perspective, the question leads to the fundamental distinction between the religions of the Book and the religions of the Indian subcontinent. The former are convinced that God has revealed himself historically through his Word by the medium of specific prophets, even if they do not identify the same prophets as the ultimate media of the revelation. The latter are convinced that the Ultimate, whatever the divine names, may be reached from within by anyone with proper spiritual guidance. This bifurcation in the religious dimension of humankind has naturally led each line to draw the logical implication that all other insights into invisible reality are deficient.

It follows that Christian believers must see the natural law and the constructions of the many and varied human cultures as radically subordinate to the Word, spoken first, then written, then transmitted and understood through a tradition that is providentially guided. Since however a search for common ground is essential to any dialogue, it is proper to raise the question "What common ground is there between the Christian faith and the convictions of the great religions of the world?"

The problem should be faced at several levels. A first level is that of myth and mythology. Each religion constitutes a system of life and thought that has inspired and is therefore expressed in myths. One can compare the great myths of Hinduism, Buddhism, Jainism, Sikhism, and Zoroastrianism, or some elements of these myths, with the biblical story, which may itself be considered one of the great myths of humanity. Thus it is not uncommon to compare the story of creation in Genesis with the creation-myths of Mesopotamia. This sort of study reveals interesting similarities and contrasts; it raises questions of historical influences back and forth and possibly of the existence and origin of psychological archetypes with a religious dimension. It opens up artistic perspectives and philosophical theories. But I do not think that it reaches the ultimate question of the nature of the religions. Nonetheless, one may discover a great deal of common ground in the intent and in the structure (the insights of Structuralism should not be ignored) — if not in the content — of the great religious myths of humanity.

A second level, closely related to the first, is that of liturgical ritual. All religions practice some type of worship, which can be common or private. Some religions have even gone to great lengths in defining and teaching corporate and personal rituals, forms of prayer, and methods of meditation, and in opening contemplative perspectives. One may compare their practice and understanding of pilgrimage, their use of images, incense, fire, water, and offerings to the Deity, their position for prayer, their sacraments or quasi-sacraments, and so on. One may find much common ground in their understanding of worship and its purpose.

A third level is that of the interior experiences that inspired the founders and shapers of the great religions, many of these experiences having been recorded and illustrated by mystics, notably by the Sufis of Islam, by the authors of the Upanishads, and by many a Buddhist holy person in both the Hinayana and the Mahayana. From a Christian point of view one can argue that authentic impressions of the Word and of the Spirit do take place outside of Christendom. The ensuing insights must have close connections with those of Christian mystics. And they can be related to the doctrine of the Trinity, though the exact scope and value of these connections are difficult to assess.

A fourth level is that of ethics and behavior. In all religions the personal experience of belief and prayer is expected to show fruits in good works, in whatever way the corresponding culture may identify good works. Works are seen to be good in light of a legal system, of commands and prohibitions that are beyond questioning and the observance of which is believed to be essential to the common welfare. Laws can be compared. Comparison, however, ought to lead further. Thus a careful analysis of polygamic societies and religions shows that the differences between monogamy and polygamy are not adequately accounted for by reference to acknowledgement or ignorance of the natural law.

333

The affirmation that there is a natural law is itself a philosophical option that is not accepted in all advanced intellectual cultures. Beyond the philosophical problem, ethical behavior relates to varying orientations and diverse levels of culture that require careful analysis, especially as regards the status and role of women in a given society and the basic understanding of womanhood in which they are grounded.

A fifth level is precisely that of the essence of each religion, if at least one question can be answered: "To what aspect, if any, of the experience and the knowledge of God does a specific religion point?" The unity and the uniqueness of God are insistently affirmed in Islam. The eternity and ultimacy of the Divine are profoundly expressed in Hinduism, through the infinite multiplicity of their symbols in myth and in art and through numerous attempts to describe the divine attributes and to understand them philosophically and theologically.

One is thus led to make distinctions between popular religion with its assumptions and practices and the same religion as lived by its saints and interpreted by its scholars; between religions of nature (the many forms of Animism in Asia, Africa, and the Americas; Wicca) and religions of prophetic revelation; between monotheistic (the religions of the Book, Zoroastrianism, Sikhism, Bahaï), monistic (Hinduism in its many forms) and non-theistic religions (Buddhism, Jainism); between the Christian religion in its classical forms (Orthodox, Roman Catholic, Anglican, Lutheran, and Calvinist) and the reinterpretations of the Christ-event that have been proposed by newer religious movements, such as the Latter-Day Saints (Mormons), Christian Science (of Mary Baker Eddy), the Holy Spirit Association for the Unification of World Christianity (the Reverend Moon); between these communities, which have achieved a degree of social responsibility and respectability, and numerous sects and cults that have emerged from the cultural and spiritual confusion of the modern world, whether they claim to bring new revelations and the intuitions of new prophets or explore the assumed promises of the age of Aquarius (New Age).

It is hardly surprising that, like some respected theologians, several organs of the Holy See should be puzzled at the complexities of the contemporary religious phenomena and should fear lest further confusion be fostered by encouraging dialogues with their adepts.

To try to determine which theologians the Congregation for the Doctrine of the Faith had in mind in composing *Dominus Jesus* would hardly be a useful exercise if the Holy See itself had not, so to speak, let the cat out of the bag. On June 24, 1998, the Congregation issued a "notification concerning the writings of [the late] Anthony de Mello," an Indian Jesuit who is known chiefly for his retreats and his writings on spirituality, in which, the notification says, he revealed "the influence of Buddhist and Taoist spiritual currents." The Congregation detected in these writings "a progressive distancing from the essential elements of the Christian faith." Again, on January 21, 2001, the Congregation issued a "notification on the book *Toward a Theology of Religious Pluralism*" by Jacques Dupuis, a living Belgian Jesuit who spent many years in India. In his book the Congregation found

> notable ambiguities and difficulties on important doctrinal points, which could lead a reader to erroneous or harmful opinions. The points concern the interpretation of the sole and universal salvific mediation of Christ, the unicity and completeness of Christ's revelation, the universal salvific action of the Holy Spirit, the orientation of all people to the Church, and the value and significance of the salvific function of other religions.[18]

In order to remedy these defects the Congregation ordered "the doctrinal content indicated in the *Notification*" to be included in further editions or translations of the book. Fr. Dupuis agreed to do so.

This notification makes it evident that what prompted the writing of *Dominus Jesus* was concern about possible deviations leading to oblivion or qualification of the centrality of Jesus Christ, the Word made flesh, as the unique way of salvation for all humans, a danger that can emerge from immersion in a religious culture other than that of Judeo-Christianity. The ensuing warnings, when they come, ought to be received with understanding but also *cum grano salis,* with discernment, because they are not always formulated with a deep knowledge or understanding of the actual situation.

These dimensions of the interreligious scene lead to the question "What can Christians learn from the religions?" Such a query can only be answered specifically, in relation to each one of the religions and religious movements. It is nevertheless possible to posit the principle that the religions can teach Christians a great deal regarding the human experience of the invisible dimensions of creation, the analogy of being that ties the material, the animal, and the human levels of creation in what one may call a spiritual cosmology, and the orientation to the divine that is inherent in the human mind and unveils the anthroposophic dimension of human experience.

Dominus Jesus is in fact open to all these aspects of interreligious dialogues, as long as one stops short of suggesting that part of God's self-disclosure is missing in the Christian revelation. Meanwhile, the document points to two

18. Both of these notifications may be found on the Vatican website.

dangers that threaten any dialogue between cultures, philosophies, theologies, or religions: ambiguity and indifferentism. There is ambiguity in the notion that all or many of the non-Christian religions are ways of salvation. That their members are covered by God's salvific intention and the divine plan of salvation is not in question. What is in question is whether they are saved by their beliefs and their way of life as such, apart from the inseparable redemptive actions of the Word and the Holy Spirit.

Some theologians have been led to suggest that while there is only one New Testament there may be several Old Testaments, each in its own way having a propaedeutic function in relation to the Christian faith, or that the only Savior who is the Word of God made flesh has been manifested by the Holy Spirit in various forms in the great non-Christian religions, or even that God has sent many prophets to many different peoples. Indeed the connections that may be found, historically or thematically, between the various religions and the Trinitarian pattern of creation and redemption are a proper matter of research.

No theory, however, can be legitimate to Christian believers if the hypotheses proposed in it contradict the central tenets of the Christian faith. In *Dominus Jesus* these tenets are succinctly subsumed under the affirmation of "the salvific unicity and universality of Jesus Christ and the Church."[19] The principle remains true even when the unicity of the church is expressed in an excessively Bellarminian way.

When contrasted with previous statements of Paul VI and others of John Paul II himself, *Dominus Jesus,* with its amalgam of problems raised by interreligious conversations with questions of inter-Christian dialogue, conveys the impression that the various organs of the Holy See have determined priorities and chosen orientations that may be internally consistent but are not in harmony with one another and that, by the same token, do not promote a good image of the Roman primacy in its exercise. The Holy See could use the services of a coordination officer, just to keep track of what is going on in the dicasteries, and of a first-rate Public Relations officer, who would be able to foresee the impact of potential documents on the outside world and their eventual reception by the media.

Beyond this immediate need there lies the huge problem of the part that reception by the People of God plays in determining the authoritative value of a pontifical document. Pope John's apostolic constitution *Veterum sapientia* (1962) had, by virtue of its source, all the trappings of authority when it came

19. This phrase is the subtitle of *Dominus Jesus.*

out. And yet when it was read it became evident that it was an exercise in nostalgia for the Latin language that carried no authority whatsoever for the present and the future.

Although the process of making known the thought of the Holy See is far from perfect, the responsibility for the enormous confusion that followed the publication of *Dominus Jesus* is not one-sided. The immediately shocked and mostly hostile reactions of the press did not favor the serenity that ought to mark the relations of the Apostolic See both with the Roman Catholic laity and with the Christian world at large. Those who wish their churches to be or to become sisters have to learn not to behave like strangers. That another reaction was entirely possible was shown by the officers of the World Methodist Council. On September 7, 2000, the headquarters of the Council in North Carolina issued a statement that was infinitely more constructive than most other reactions in the Protestant organizations. This statement correctly caught the essential purpose of the text, and it turned the more questionable allusion to the problem of church-sisterhood into a motive for deeper dialogue:

> The World Methodist Council welcomes the reaffirmation of Jesus Christ as the one Savior of the world made by the Vatican in the recent *Dominus Jesus*. In its continuing dialogue with the Roman Catholic Church the World Methodist Council looks forward to further exploration on the question of how each partner can come to a fuller recognition of the churchly character of the other.

Contributors

The Rev. Dr. Victor Lee Austin, theologian-in-residence, Saint Thomas Church Fifth Avenue, New York

The Rev. Dr. Walter R. Bouman, the late Edward C. Fendt Professor Emeritus of Systematic Theology, Trinity Lutheran Seminary, Columbus, Ohio

The Very Rev. Dr. Joseph Britton, Dean of the Berkeley Divinity School, Yale University

Dr. Marsha L. Dutton, Professor of English, Ohio University, Athens, Ohio

Dr. E. Rozanne Elder, Professor of History, Western Michigan University; Director, Institute of Cistercian Studies; Editorial Director, Cistercian Publications

The Rt. Rev. C. Christopher Epting, the Presiding Bishop's Deputy for Ecumenical and Interfaith Relations for the Episcopal Church, formerly bishop of Iowa

Dr. John V. Fleming, Lewis W. Fairchild '24 Professor of English, Princeton University, Princeton, New Jersey

The Rev. Dr. R. William Franklin, Associate Director of the American Academy in Rome, Associate Priest and Visiting Fellow of the Anglican Centre in Rome

The Rev. Patrick Terrell Gray, Curate, The Church of the Advent, Boston; Th.D. candidate, The General Theological Seminary, New York

The Rev. Dr. Petra Heldt, Director, Ecumenical Theological Research Fraternity in Israel; Professor, Jerusalem University College

The Rev. Dr. Joanne McWilliam, Emerita Professor of Religious Studies, University of Toronto

Dr. Robert Bruce Mullin, Professor of Church History, The General Theological Seminary, New York

Dr. Jon Nilson, Associate Professor of Theology, Loyola University, Chicago

The Rev. Dr. Richard A. Norris, Jr., late Professor Emeritus of Church History, Union Theological Seminary, New York

The Rev. Dr. Robert W. Prichard, The Arthur Lee Kinsolving Professor of Christianity in America, Virginia Theological Seminary, Alexandria, Virginia

The Rev. Dr. Michael Root, Dean and Professor of Systematic Theology, Lutheran Theological Southern Seminary, Columbia, South Carolina

The Rev. Dr. William G. Rusch, Executive Director, Foundation for a Conference on Faith and Order in North America, New York, NY

The Rt. Rev. Stephen W. Sykes, Principal of St. John's College, Durham (UK), Emeritus Professor of Theology, University of Durham (UK), and formerly bishop of Ely

Dr. Mary Tanner, *former* General Secretary of the Council for Christian Unity of the General Synod of the Church of England

The Rev. Dr. George Tavard, A.A., Professor Emeritus of Theology, Methodist Theological School in Ohio, Delaware, Ohio

The Rev. Dr. Ellen K. Wondra, Professor of Theology and Ethics, Seabury-Western Theological Seminary, Evanston, Illinois

Index

Act of Supremacy, 3

African American, anti-slavery, William Wilberforce and Thomas Clarkson, 207; bishops: non-voting and suffragan, 175; Cheshire, Bp. Joseph B. and segregation, 174; Civil War, 164; clergy, 174; congregation: separate, 172, 174-75; Diocese of Virginia, representation in, 173-74; Europeans and, 163-64, 166, 169-70; Grace Church, 166, 169-70, 175; Guerry, Bp. William, 175; Jeffrey, J. T., vicar, first African American, 173, 180; Jim Crow, 165, 173; Ordination, 174; Payne Divinity School, 173; Sunday school: women and, 171, 173, 175; women, 169, and leadership, 178

Anglican, bishops: authority of, 124; British and Canadian Churches, 312-14; unity, goal of, 220

Anglican Communion, 99; African theologies and American counterparts, 146; Consultative Council, 118; laity in, 116; modern, 207, 219-21, 230, 234, 237-39; tolerance in, 206

Anglican-Lutheran, Joint Working Group, Cold Ash, England, 302; Partners in Mission Dialogue, 212; rela-

tions: definitions of, 297; theological basis, 315

Anglican–Old Catholic Churches, Bonn Agreement, 223

Anglican Orders, 117, 273; and ordination of women, 121, 320; validity of, 231

Anglican-Orthodox, dialogue in the USA, 262; doctrine, devotion, and theology, 275-76; relations and differences, 272-73

Anglicanism, authority, 201-3; church life, 202; "conciliarism" and laity, 202; distinctive doctrine, 101; ecclesiology: Baptism, as basis for, 204-5; essence of Anglicanism, 101; historical, 118; identity of, 268; life: characteristics: catholicity, 198-99, inclusivity, 116, 200; modern, 207; synodality in, 126; tolerance in, 206; parts: constituent, 129; theological synthesis of, in Julian, 115

Antiochenes, 56, 63, 67

Apostolic Office, 187

Apostolic Orders, Lambeth (1879), 231

Apostolic Succession, 212, 299; *Niagara Report*, 302; *Porvoo*, 307-9

ARCIC (Anglican–Roman Catholic International Commission), 118

Arian controversy, 62

Aristotle, 69
Augsburg Confession, communion and episcopacy, 310
Augustine, 68-69; divine nature, 59; doctrine, 105; grace, 59, 61; incarnation, 57; *On the Trinity,* 59; Origen, 58; *Treatise on the Gospel of John,* 60; union, Christological, 57-58, 60-61
Authority, centralized, 213; episcopal, 252; and medieval life, 72; of pope, 254

Baptism, confession as condition of, 19; consequences and meaning of, 26; teaching patterns, 21-23; triadic form, 23-24, 26; Baptismal, action, 27; confession of faith, 14, 25; formulas, 24
Barnett-Cowan, Alyson, Faith, Worship and Ministry of Canada, Waterloo, 305, 312
Bede, 79-80
BEM, Baptism, Eucharist and Ministry, 241-42, 259-60, 315
Benedict XVI, 120, 324, 326. *See* Ratzinger
Berryville, Virginia, 166, 171, 173, 175
Bishop of Rome, 252-53; Anglicans and primacy, 256-57; before full communion, 258-59; collegiality and pope, 256; difficulties, 248, 250-51; ministry of, 246-47; sign and bond of Communion, 242-44
Bishops, ELCA, interchangeability of, 311-12
Blessed Trinity, in Augustine, 64, 150, 227, 229
Bloom, Metropolitan Anthony, 270
Book of Common Prayer, 3, 263, 266; laity and, 115-16; American version, 124
Brooks, J. Phillips, 144-45; allegory, 156; church as body of Christ, 158-59, 162; doctrine: formalism in, 150, interpretation of, 156; evangelical roots, 157; faith, demands of 160; ecclesiasticism, 158-59; homiletic skill, 148; Jesus Christ, 155, 157-59; *Lectures on Preaching,* 155; liberal stance, 149-50; life, emphasis on, 156; Orthodoxy: broad, 147-48, 159-60; limitations in,

145, 156-57; Rome, 120-21; sermons, 152-55, 157; theological reflection, 152; Trinity, 150; truth: aspects of, 158-60, nature of, 155, 159, provisionality of, 153

Called to Common Mission, Episcopal Church and ELCA, 224, 231-34, 236, 309
Calvin, John, 206
Campenhausen, Hans von, 18-19, 27
Catechesis, and confession, meaning of, 27
Chadwick, Henry, 232-35
Charry, Ellen, *aretegenic* role of theology, 155
Chaucer, 69
Christ, in Augustine: divinity of, 64-65; grace in, 58, 60; human soul, 64; resurrection of, 65; will, 60; Word of God, 51, 64; in John Paul II; action of, 188; church: function, political, 185, 190, revelatory, 184, relation to, 186-89; mission, 188-89; office: threefold, 185; redemption, 185-86; solidarity, anthropological, 186; teacher, 187-88
Christianity, and Hebrew scriptures, 69
Christians, gay and lesbian, 121-22, 126
Church, contemporary and nationalism, 205
Church of England, 121, 195-97, 199
Clement of Alexandria, 30, 35
Collegiality, bishops, 246; National Conference of Bishops, 330
Colonne, Guido della, *Historia Destructiones Troiae,* 79
Comestor, Peter, *Historia Scholastica,* 78-79, 82
Commedia, 71, 73; allegory in, 70, 81, 85-86
Confession in Dialogue, 243
Concordat of Agreement, adoption of, 298; Cold Ash and CCM (Called to Common Mission), 303, 307
Congregation for the Doctrine of the Faith, parity of persons, 332, 334-35; universal church, 329-30
Consensus Fidelium, 236

Constantinople, model for non-papal Catholicism, 263

Cord, 74-75, 78; *capestro,* 76: allegorical meanings, 94-96; Gregory the Great and, 94, 97; leviathan and, 91-92

Council, ecumenicity of, Dublin Report, 252; Ephesus, 56; Nicea, 236; councils, of churches, regional and national, 210

Creed, Apostles', 15; Calcedonian formulation, 227; declaratory, 26-28; evolution of, 18; instrument of catechesis, 14; Nicene, 227

Creedal: antecedents, 15-19; utterances, 20

Creeds: content of, 27; proof of faith, 14

Cullmann, Oscar, 17

Curia, Roman, procedures of, 321

Culture, church's adaption to, 68

Cyril, 56; second anathema, 61-62, 66

Dante, 69-73, 79, 84; and Geryon, 79; and Horace, 83-86; Virgil, dependency on, 81

Disciples, of Christ, 253

Divorce, Orthodox procedures, 277

Doctrine, differentiations in, 227; discipline and worship, 228; socio-cultural context, 227

Dominus Jesus, Asia, traditional religions of, 326-237; Canterbury and Rome, 325

Dublin Report, ecumenicity of a council, 252

Ecclesia Anglicana, 100, 102; Julian as representative member of, 103

Ecclesiology, Baptismal: ministry of all the baptized, 213; 259; structure of ministry, 253, and communion, 328

Ecumenical Concerns, ad extra: Faith and Order, 214; human sexuality, 214; *ad intra:* Baptism, centrality of, 215; liturgical observances, 217; Charismatic Movement, 215, 217; clergy, 216; consultation on Common Texts, 215; conversion and reform, individuals, and communions, 214-15; corporate discernment, 215; deaconesses, 216; diaconate, 215; lay leadership, 216;

peace and justice, 215-16; spirituality: spiritual direction and retreats, 215

Ecumenical Movement, 208; reception, 235

Ecumenism, *Ecumenism of the Possible,* 218, 221; Rome, committed to, 279-81

"Eclogue," 70-72; Truth and Falsehood, 82; Virgilian, 70, 84

Eliot, T. S., "Tradition and Individual Talent," 96

Elizabeth I, 101, 115, 118

Emerson, Ralph Waldo, "Quotation and Originality," 96

Episcopacy, Anglican-Lutheran International Continuation Committee, 297-99, 301

Episcopal Church, 116; Anglican Communion and, 222-23; authority: bishops, 126, *Concordat* and CMC, 314-15; and ELCA, 309; civil rights, 125; function of reason in, 125; identity, 268; ordination and full reciprocity, 231-33; origin, 123; structures, 124; succession: common participation, 314; Temporalities Act, 127

Episcopate, doctrine of, 273; historic, 223, 231, 315; synodal, 212

Episkope, Christian unity, 252

Evangelical Revival, 268

Ex Cathedra, 252

Faith, apostolic, 259, 235-36; barrier to, 238; Christian, 225-26, 236-37; criterion for unity of, 229; different, but not diverse, 228; infallibility and, 250; shared, 228, 230-31

Faith and Order Commission, Lima, 1982, 250, 259-61

Fellowship of SS Alban and Sergius, 273

Full Communion, 232-34; "Agros" Report, 303-4; Anglicans and Lutherans in Canada, 305-6; CMM, 211, 224, 234, 312; definition: of, 224-25, 297; Anglican-Lutheran, 305-6; differences 221; Episcopal Church and Anglican Communion, 222-23; Lutherans: Reformed Churches and 210; Niagara Report,

consecration of bishops, 302; theological implications of, 237-38, 240; *Waterloo Declaration*, 298
Franciscans, 75-76

Gassmann, Gunther, and *Porvoo*, 312
General Convention, and American Anglicanism, 122-26; authority, 124-26; scripture, 122-23
Germanos, Bishop of Thyateira, 282
Geryon, 73, 75, 80-81, 83-85, 88-89; Augustinian influence, 94; Embodiment of Fraud, 86, 87, 96; in Horace, 87
Gift of Authority, 117-18, 238, 258, 316; ARCIC: final report of, 317-1; Baycroft, Bp. John and, 320, 322; ordination of women, 320, 324
Gift of Authority III, 255, 258
"Glorious Revolution," 266
Grace, and free will, 66
Grace Church, 165; African and Europeans in, 163-64; contributions, 168-69; financial support, 168; organizations, in, 169; parish life in, 163; pew rent, 167-68; rector, 166; treasurer, 166-67; vestry, 166-67, 169, 178-80
Greek Fathers, 92
Gregory of Nyssa, 93, 95
Grillmeir, Aloys, 56, 60

Harnack, Adolf von, Apostles' Creed, 15
Hide, Kerrie, in Julian, soteriology, 103
Hippolytus, anthropology, triadic, 36
Hobart, John Henry, 129, 132, 134, 139; apostolic character of, 137-38; church and city, 139, Episcopal Church: distinctiveness of, 142-43; high church, 137
Holy See, and contemporary religious phenomena, 334
Holy Spirit, 11, 17, 210, 212; Irenaeus, 26; Origen, 46; scripture, 48, 237, 240, 246, 254-55
Hooker, Richard, 125, 130, 202, 205

Incarnation, 227, 229
Infallibility, Anglican-Orthodox, 243; doctrine: 117, reception of doctrine,
258; and jurisdiction, 248-49; papal: Roman understanding of, 254-58; pope and, 244-46; Reformed and, 244
Intercommunion, 223
Irenaeus, Christian identity, 37

John Paul II, 120, 182-84; Christology, 185, 189-90; Mariology, 187; *Ut Unum Sint*, 259
Johnson, Samuel, 131
Judeo-Christian, prophetic movement, validity of, 332
Julian of Norwich, faith, 102-3, 110-11, 113-14; incarnation, 105; justice-mercy paradox, 105-6, 111-13; conflict between, 108-9; reason, 113-14, 119; salvation, 105; scripture: reliance on, 108; interpretation of, 114; sin, 105, 109, 111-12; theology: 99, 103-4; Trinity, 105, 107-8; understanding, 113-14, 119
Justification, 285

Kasper, Cardinal Walter, 208-18, 323
Kattenbusch, Ferdinand, New Testament and creeds, 15
Kelly, J. N. D., early Christian creeds, 14, 17-18, 25

Lambeth Commission on Communion, *Windsor Report*, ordination of non-celibate gays and lesbians and blessing of same-sex unions, 230
Lambeth Conference (1878), 222; (1908), permanent committee for Orthodoxy; (1920), 274; (1948), 201; (1968), Anglican-Orthodox relations, 280; (1978), women and episcopate, 278; (1988), 202, 225; "Intercommunion," 281; (1998), 314
Lambeth, Chicago Quadrilateral (1866-1888), 213, 272
Leviathan, 90; and cord, 91-92, 96
Lietzmann, Hans, confessional patterns, 16-21
Loukaris, Patriarch Cyril, 264-65
Lumen Gentium, 253, 255, 257; authority and, 320, 324

Luther, Martin, 206, 287; Augustine of Hippo, 290, 292; Bernard of Clairvaux, 293; Church Fathers, 292-2 94; councils: appreciation of, 287-89, limits of, 289-90; St. Cyprian and rebaptism, 290

Lutheran, doctrine: consensus in, 287; Evangelicals, 212; Reformation, 288; Reformers and early church, 294-95; Lutheran–Roman Catholic Report, 245; Lutheran World Federation, 213, 329

Lutheranism, in America: American, Protestant character of, 285, 307; creeds and the Book of Concord, 293-94; and Orthodoxy, 285-86

Lutherans, church unity and gospel, 285, 294

Mary, 65; in John Paul II, 187

Messiah, eschatological, 10

Messianic Age, church called to embody, 12; movement, importance of, 8-9

Methodists, and teaching authority of church, 255; Methodist–Roman Catholic Report, 254

Metousiōsis, 274-75

Ministries, 306-7

Ministry, Bishop of Rome, 321; of oversight, 300-301; of seniority, Anglo-Orthodox, 251-52

Mission, *ad gentes,* nature of, 330-31

Moralia, Gregory, imagery, 91-92; exegesis, 93

National Council of Churches of Christ in the USA, 210-11, 214

Natural Law and ethics, 333-34

Neoplatonism, 60

Nestorius, 56, 61-63; Antiochene tradition, 66

Neufeld, V. H., subject of baptismal confession, 19

Newman, John Henry, 268-69

Niagara, and *Porvoo,* 297, 299-302, 315

"Nonjurors," 266-67

Oaths of Allegiance and Supremacy, 266

Ontology, Aristotelian-Thomistic, 60

Ordination, Anglican, Lutheran, Orthodox, Roman Catholic, 4, 117; Anglican-Orthodox Dialogue, 237; challenge of, 220-21; Eames Commission, 230, 237; gender and sexual orientation, 229-30, 238-39; theological and sacramental issues of, 219, 278-79; women, and John Paul II, 320

Origen, 43; Alexandrian school, 44; Christian identity, 39-41; *Contra Celsum,* 44; conversion, call to, 53-54; *Hexapla,* 45; pre-Origen authors: 33-34; scripture, 40-41, 50, 52; and call to conversion, 53-54

Orthodox, and Eastern Oriental Churches, *autocephalous* nature of, 213; Orthodox–Roman Catholic, Valamo Report, 252; theological positions and Church Fathers, 264

Ousia, 63

Ovid, *Metamorphoses,* 79

Oxford Movement, 4

Palmer, William, and Russian Orthodoxy, 269-70

Papacy, *Confessions in Dialogue,* 242-43

Paul VI, ecumenism, 242; unity with Anglican Communion, 317, 324

Pelagianism, 66-67; Pelagians, 56, 66; anti-Pelagians, 59

Pentecostal–Roman Catholic Report, 253

People of God, 250, 336

Petrine Ministry, 213, 223, 241, 252, 259; and Reformed Churches, 205, 245, 252

Plato, *Phaedrus,* 83-84

Pontifical Council for Promoting Christian Unity, 208-9

Porvoo Agreement, 3, 297; Anglican acceptance of, 314-15; criticism of, 309-10, 312-13

Priesthood, and women, 4-5, 12

Primacy, 253-55; collegiality and conciliarity, 258; jurisdiction, 245-46, 258; Lutherans and Methodists, 243; Malta Report, 244, 245; Methodists and, 247-48; ministry of, 260; Reformed and, 244; Roman Church, 253, 257; universal, 242, 249, 251, 253, 259

Prosopon, 63

Protestants, and episcopate, 212

Pulloch Report, Anglican-Lutheran International Conversation, 310

Purgatorio, 89; Siren and Virgil, 87

"Puritan," and Orthodox Church, 263

Ramsey, Archbp. Arthur Michael, 101; unity of Anglican Communion and Roman Catholic Church, 317

Ratzinger, Cardinal Joseph, 323

Reconciliation, of the churches, 225

Redemption, 227, 229

Reformation, 101; characteristics of post-Reformation Anglican life, 114, pre-Reformation, 103; and episcopal office, 313

Religion, popular: various forms of, 334; religions, great world: and common ground, 332-34; of the Book, 332

Roman Catholic Church, and synodal institutions, 320-21; law and culture, 322

Rule of Faith, 26-28

Scriptures, allegory, 48-51; and conversion of life, free from error, 47; inner meaning of, 48; inspiration of, 52; interpreted by scripture, 50; sacred and secular, 70-71; supreme norm of, 255; typology, 71

Segregation, 165; new forms of, 173; support of, 175

Sister Churches, Canterbury-York and Leo XIII, 330; catholicity: mark of, 328-29; in *Dominus Jesus,* 326-27; *Ecclesiam Suam, Nova Millennio Ineunte,* 328-29; restriction of, 327

Soderblom, Archbp. Nathan, "evangelical catholicity," 199

Spencer, Edmund, *Faerie Queene,* 87-88

Stanley, A. B., Dean of Westminster, 144

Stephenson, W. Taylor, worship and prayer, 102

Subsidiarity, principle of, 213, 249

Succession, agreement on, 314; break in, 307-11

Sunday school, 170; Alexandria and Richmond, 171. *See* African Americans

Synod of Bishops, role and ministry, 324

Syrian Orthodox–Roman Catholic Churches, 228

Tertullian, 31, 37-38

Theodore, 66-67

Theotokos, 65

Transubstantiation, 274-75

Truths, hierarchy of, 226, 239

Twelve, significance of the, 7, 9

Unashamed Anglicanism, authority: dispersed, 201; doctrinal positions: plurality of, 200; Anglican ecclesiology: need for, 203, 205

Unity, Anglican-Lutheran differences, 305; and comparative religion, 331; Declaration of Anglican Essentials, 230; of faith: criterion for, 229; theological consensus, 239

Vatican, and Protestant Christians, 213; Vatican I, 246, 248, 250, 251, 257; Vatican II, *Decree on Ecumenism,* 226

Virgil, *Aeneid,* 68; Carolingian period, 70; Christianity, 69; pseudo-Virgilian, 70

Ward, Benedicta, visions, Julian of Norwich, 103

Waterloo Declaration, 298-99; and CMM, 315; and full communion, 305-6, 308-9

White, William, architecture, 139-40; republicanism in, 136; sermons, 132-36; worship: functions of, 133-34; aesthetics in, defense of, 139; social utility of, 139-40

Windsor Report, 230

Wickliffe Parish, 165, 168, 171-72

Wood, Gordon S., *Radicalism of the American Revolution,* 136

Women, and ARCIC, leadership roles of, 8-9; ordained ministry of, 13; priesthood and, 4-5, 12. *See* Ordination

Index

World Methodist Conference, 213
Wright, J. Robert, 100, 182; Anglo-
Lutheran relations, 296; Anglo-papal
relations, 127-28; Brooks, Phillips, 162;
code of canon law, 119-21; ecumenical
movement, 127, 261; ecumenical texts,
317; ecumenism: agenda, 241-42, dialogues, 325, interests in, 248; Episcopal
church as eighteenth-century institution, 125-27; historian: medieval, 70,

Christianity in England prior to the
sixteenth century, 199; Faith and Order
Commission, 250; Lima meeting, 257;
man of the church, 324; parish life: interest in, 163; patristic tradition, commitment to, 295; teaching vocation,
316; thanks owed to, 315

Zizioulas, Metropolitan, and church
unity, 217